INTERNATIONAL STUDIES

of the
Committee on International Relations
University of Notre Dame

INTERNATIONAL STUDIES

DIPLOMACY IN A CHANGING WORLD

EDITED BY

Stephen D. Kertesz

AND

M. A. Fitzsimons

GREENWOOD PRESS, PUBLISHERS
WESTPORT, CONNECTICUT

Library of Congress Cataloging in Publication Data

Kertesz, Stephen Denis, 1904-   ed.
   Diplomacy in a changing world.

    Reprint of the ed. published by University of Notre
Dame Press in series: International studies of the
Committee on International Relations, University of
Notre Dame.
    1. Diplomacy--Addresses, essays, lectures.
2. International relations--Addresses, essays, lectures.
3. World politics--1955-1965--Addresses, essays, lec-
tures. I. Fitzsimons, Matthew A., 1912-   joint ed.
II. Title. III. Series: Notre Dame, Ind. University.
Committee on International Relations. International
studies.

[JX1662.K4 1974]   327'.2   74-2587
ISBN 0-8371-7408-2

Reprinted in 1974 by Greenwood Press,
a division of Williamhouse-Regency Inc.

Library of Congress Catalog Card Number 74-2587

ISBN 0-8371-7408-2

Printed in the United States of America

PREFACE

THIS is the first of two volumes surveying the problems and resources of diplomacy in a world characterized by a radical departure from the past, and at the same time, a radical interconnection and interdependence of one part of the world with another. In such a world a study of diplomacy's resources is a measure in the service of peace, for with sacrifice, perseverance, and imagination, diplomacy may be flexible enough to tame the furies of the contemporary international scene. This first volume attempts to deal with the new diplomacy on a world-wide and comparative basis. Next year the editors will publish a volume on American diplomacy which will complete the survey.

Versions of Chapters II, III, IV, VI, IX, XII, XIII, XIX, and XX were presented and discussed at conferences held at Notre Dame between 1956 and 1958. These discussions proved to be very helpful in the clarification of some of the basic aspects of contemporary diplomacy.

The editors are grateful to Bernard Browne for the preparation of the index.

CONTENTS

I. General Issues

II. *Some Major Powers*

III. *New Actors and Changing Roles*

IV. *The United Nations*

I

General Issues

Chapter 1

INTRODUCTION

M. A. Fitzsimons AND S. D. Kertesz

THE subject matter of diplomacy is the relations of one state to another state or to other states, and the relations among a number of states ranging from those in an alliance or regional organization to those in the United Nations, as well as the relations of states in such alliances to other powers or groups of powers. The classical simplicity of bilateral negotiations remains the core of diplomatic activity, but multilateral diplomacy including conference and parliamentary diplomacy now plays an important part in it. This change presents its many difficulties. The diplomat has ceased to be a solo virtuoso, a first violinist, or even a chamber musician. Now, his fate is to conduct or play in a highly discordant orchestra whose members are committed to no single scale or tempo.

The contemporary diplomat must deal with a staggering range of state interests and his work is influenced by the greatly extended range of state activities. He does so because diplomacy contends with the realities in conflicts of interest. Diplomacy would well deserve oblivion —which in turn would soon engulf mankind—if it did not deal with realities. For diplomacy today the realities are a world continually in flux, a Heraclitean world, in which states and even international organizations are major agents of change. Diplomacy inevitably and properly reflects this swirling transformation.

The older states of Europe, the classic actors in the diplomacy which elaborated the customs, traditions, and law that became the accepted, though not always honored, prescriptions for international intercourse, have declined in power. No major Western European state commands the share of the world's resources that it did in the nineteenth century. No major Western European state attempts to maintain a war establishment comparable to the number of men maintained before the First World War, although it is difficult to make a valid comparison because of the changed armaments, costs, and military organizations. Moreover, in the contemporary world of great powers most of the lesser powers are increasingly aware of the restrictions on their freedom of action and, therefore, reluctant to contribute more for military purposes than absolutely necessary. They believe that the great powers will maintain their arms establishments anyhow and, thus, become even more the decisive factors in the power struggle. This feeling is strengthened by changes in military technology. Membership in the contemporary great power club is restricted to those states which are able to produce nuclear weapons.

These European states, moreover, are committed to measures of social welfare which represent objectives that have been newly defined as permanent national interests. In the minds of many Europeans the new interests take precedence over the demands of power. In all of these states public opinion frequently sets stark limits to the commitments that political leaders may wish to make. This decline of European world power, which began in the late nineteenth century, acquired great momentum in the First World War, and approached a climax in the Second World War. The first decade of postwar peace marks the end of a political world order.

Two political facts characterize the new world situation. The first is that the giant lands to the east and west of the European world, Russia and the United States, have fulfilled the dread expectation of many nineteenth-century European prophets, and have developed power and resources to the point where they as superpowers dwarf the rest of the world. They have emerged in rivalry that engulfs the world. They are rivals in a world of change compoundedly accelerated by technology. With the pace of change so rapid, there is little rashness in the guess that if the bipolar world does not culminate in self-destruction, the superpowers will not be limited to two for long. The other fact is the conclusion of Western imperial rule overseas, a process essentially completed in the Americas, all but completed in Asia, and well under way in Africa. From the former Western colonies have developed nationalistic, though frequently multinational, states. Their existence signalizes the end of what the Indian historian and diplomat, K. M. Pannikar, has called "the Vasco da Gama epoch of Asian history." [1] In Pannikar's eyes this epoch was marked by the dominance of maritime power over the Asian land masses, and by the imposition of an international commercial economy upon people whose economic life had been centered on agriculture and internal trade, as well as by the domination of the European maritime powers over the people and affairs of Asia.

Not only has the subject matter of diplomacy, the interests of states, become numerous and complex, but the actors in the global diplomatic drama, that is, the number of states, have been greatly enlarged and the leading men of the past are relegated to supporting roles for new principals.

Under any circumstances these transformations would pose enough difficulties. But the changes appeared rapidly, following a devastating war fought on all the continents of the world. Moreover, the two great powers, the United States and the Soviet Union, are states of continental size and both in very different ways contributed to the world's unrest.

The leaders of the Soviet Union oscillate between concern, an obsessive concern in the Stalin era, with the security of the Soviet regime, and the fostering of new gains for Communist Russia, which, in its growing power, can with some grounds indulge in the *hybris* of the Marxist historical objective, the universal supersession of capitalism by communism. In sum, the Soviet leaders are calculating realists as tacticians of revolution and fairly clear appraisers of power. But their ideology imposes on them, as the witches imposed a royal ambition on Macbeth and his wife, the unlimited aspiration of world dominion. The leaders of the Soviet Union have therefore little interest in fostering political stability. The fact that the strongest territorial power is at the same time the center of world Communism, an essentially conspiratorial movement, influenced the Soviet Union's *modus operandi* in international relations.

Several features of Soviet diplomacy are worthy of mention. The amalgamation of Russian national and communist ideological objectives in Soviet foreign policy affects the nature and methods of Soviet

[1] K. M. Pannikar, *Asia and Western Dominance* (New York, n. d.), esp. p. 12.

diplomacy. On the one hand, the Soviet Union rigidly demands all the traditional freedoms and privileges for its diplomatic establishments but it does not reciprocate. Foreign diplomats in Communist countries are usually gravely restricted. On the other hand, the Soviet Union, in addition to the network of its regular diplomatic establishments abroad, uses as agents, informants, and tools of Soviet policy, the members of Communist Parties all over the globe. While communist activities are ubiquitous, and Soviet diplomacy displays uninhibited concern in many areas of the globe, the Soviet bloc is sealed off by an Iron Curtain. Events such as the Hungarian uprising are considered as internal family matters of the Communist bloc. Khrushchev at times speaks of coexistence in such a way as to appeal to the desire in the non-Soviet world for a settlement based on the *status quo*. But his view of the *status quo* considers communist expansion as a natural and historically necessary phenomenon. In the Soviet world, however, "natural" and "historical" necessities are maintained by the liquidation of all non-Communist political parties and potential sources of opposition to the Communist Party.

The political and territorial gains of the Soviet Union in the Second World War, the occupation and control of the East Central European satellite states, and Russia's obvious expansionist designs in other areas provoked the United States into a reluctant assumption of the leadership of opposition to further encroachments by Soviet power. Where the Soviet Union has the capacity for making quick and secret decisions as well as undebated reversals of decisions, the advantages of a totalitarian dictatorship, the United States arrives at decisions with ponderous delays of deliberation, and publicizes policy debate to such a degree that the words of American debate are sometimes heeded as intently as are the policy decisions and actions. In the course of the struggle with the Soviet Union, the citizens of the United States supported their government in making many commitments. But its citizens are primarily concerned with devoting themselves to domestic and private affairs, and the near primacy of domestic affairs over foreign affairs has limited the Government's capacity to act, and for effective leadership has made necessary persistent presidential explanation and persuasion, which have not always been forthcoming. The struggle in which the American people are engaged severely tests their optimistic activism. Their impatience with the continuing emergency and its burdens sometimes caused them and some of their political representatives to espouse unlimited courses of action that brought tremors of terror to the rest of the world.

Resistance to Soviet expansionism compelled the United States to calculate in terms of power politics. Appealing to the non-Soviet world, which Americans frequently call the free world, the United States entered into a series of alliance systems, all of which expanded the field of conference and consultative diplomacy. But here the United States ran into serious difficulties. Thirteen European states joined NATO but a large number of the new states of Asia and Africa do not consider Soviet expansionism as a danger to themselves and are reluctant to be associated with their former imperial masters as allies. They do not feel directly involved in the struggle between the Soviet and non-Soviet worlds. Neutrality in the global struggle is appealing to uncounted millions, as before 1939 neutrality appealed to Americans. The perversion of genuine "neutrality" of the Swiss type is often called "neutralism," which frequently is pseudo-neutrality and in reality may cover a great variety of shrewdly calculating policies.

Thus, in the years since 1945, the major factors in world politics have been the prominent position of the two superpowers as well as their rivalry, the continuing reduction of the power of European states, and the appearance of the new states of Asia and Africa, states in various stages of development but almost all of them aspiring to rapid industrialization and to the status of modern nations.

Communications, technology, trade, and the influence of Western ideas, the last contributing in part to the schism of the world, have welded the world into the proximity that would normally contribute to the formation of a community. But the world today is a community *manqué*—a community which can not come into being because of the lack of consensus.

This new world is well reflected in the heterogeneous nature of the United Nations, originally designed to continue the wartime cooperation of the anti-Axis powers. The UN has expanded to include most of the states of the world—with the major exceptions of Communist China and the divided states, such as Germany. It frequently expresses the high and hectic hopes of the bewildered and inexperienced leaders of the many new states of a divided world.

The UN enjoys privileges and immunities and has a legal personality.

But it has no more power than its individual members are willing to give it. The rivalry of the superpowers has restricted its scope from its first meetings in 1946. At times the UN has been completely impotent. But it provides a new and important stage on which diplomacy has to function. In many respects the sessions of the Security Council and the General Assembly create an atmosphere adverse to the reconciliation of conflicts and the mediation of interests. But they have fostered the development of a new method of diplomacy, they do provide a forum for the meetings and exchanges of a divided world, and they have facilitated the solution of some dangerous conflicts.

The UN is equipped with a multitude of specialized agencies to serve many of the various needs of the contemporary world. Among these is UNESCO, which has to face frontally the manifold ramifications of the world's aspirations, movements, and divisions in education, science, and culture. The concerns of UNESCO have ranged from projects to find and foster unity, behind or in the face of the world's divisions, and projects to formulate a historical consensus on the origins of the community *manqué,* to the assistance of new and underdeveloped states in matters of science and education. Thus, it has opened a new dimension in diplomacy, which governments also reflect in their cultural interchange programs.

The countries of the world have responded diversely to this world scene of transformation manifested in a community *manqué,* a community which—in the words of Charles de Visscher—is only "a potential order in the minds of men." Their diplomacy has been a major instrument of their response to the contemporary challenge. But within the various countries there, also, have been disagreements as to what their response and diplomacy should be.

Thus, the contributors to this volume do not speak in harmonic chords. With the exceptions of the Secretary General of the United Nations, Mr. Dag Hammarskjöld, and the Permanent Representative of the United Kingdom to the United Nations, Sir Pierson Dixon, the contributors are not official persons. But common to all the contributors is the recognition of the high importance of diplomacy as the flexible instrument for the conciliation and negotiation of the interests of the world's states. Diplomacy operates within the vast area between the play of imposed force and war, on the one side, and the security of law on the other. Where, as today, law is so fragile and war is so dangerous, the scope of diplomacy includes the whole range of Cold War.

Some of the essays deal not with institutions and countries but with general and functional problems: the influence of specialists, the significance of decision-making, of military people, of international law, and of moral considerations. One article on "The Permanent Values of the Old Diplomacy," echoed by most of the authors, concentrates on the relations and processes that remain inevitably the same in the midst of change.

Chapter 2

THE PERMANENT VALUES
IN THE OLD DIPLOMACY

Hans J. Morgenthau

I

THE traditional methods of diplomacy have been under continuous attack since the First World War and have to a considerable extent been discarded in practice since the end of the Second. Three main arguments have been directed against them. First, they have been held responsible for the political catastrophes which have befallen mankind in the last four decades or so; methods which appear to have been so unsuccessful must be replaced by better ones. Second, traditional diplomacy has been held to run counter to the principles of democracy, and from the assumption that democracy makes for peace and autocracy for war, it has been concluded that diplomacy must be "open," that is, exposed to public scrutiny in all its processes. Finally, the traditional diplomatic practices with their seemingly useless and wasteful formalities, horse-trading, and compromises have seemed to violate moral principles with which democratic nations have felt themselves identified; in other words, the age-old conflict between political realism and idealism has been transferred to the sphere of diplomacy.

These arguments against traditional diplomacy arise from the basic philosophic position, prevalent in our time, that political practices are the result of subjective preferences, to be changed at will. In truth, however, the traditional methods of diplomacy have not been invented by stupid and evil nor, for that matter, wise and good men—even though they have certainly been used and abused by such men—but have grown ineluctably from the objective nature of things political. In their essence, they are the reflections of that objective nature, to be disregarded only at the risk of political failure. Whenever two autonomous social entities, anxious to maintain their autonomy, engage in political relations with each other, they cannot but help resort to what we call the traditional methods of diplomacy. And it does not matter in this respect whether these diplomatic relations are carried on between two members of a family, two businessmen, two baseball clubs, two political parties, or two sovereign nations. On all levels of such relations, secrecy of negotiation—to mention only their most prominent and controversial aspect—is not an arbitrary procedural device to be used or dispensed with at will, but grows from the objective nature of negotiations. No negotiations of any kind—be they for the contraction of a marriage, the sale of a piece of property, a deal for baseball players, or an international treaty—can be carried out in public without defeating their very purpose: the transformation of conflicting or inchoate interests into a common purpose of the contracting parties.

The specific arguments against the traditional methods of diplomacy are as untenable as is the basic philosophic position from which they stem. If it be true that the traditional practices of diplomacy constitute the method by which the business of foreign policy must be transacted, the failure of a particular foreign policy or of a whole era to bring peace and order to the world cannot be attributed to these practices *per se* but, at worst, to their incorrect use. This logical deduction is borne out by the experiences of recent history. For the disorganization of international society since the First World War has indeed been concomitant with the neglect, misunderstanding, and abuse of the traditional practices of diplomacy. While it would be far-fetched to suggest that the decline of diplomacy is responsible for the catastrophes which have befallen the world in recent times, it cannot be doubted that that decline has contributed to international disorder, itself being an outgrowth of a deep-seated disorder in the intellectual sphere.

Both the arguments that democracy means peace and that diplomacy is immoral and, therefore, undemocratic have grown from an intellectual attitude which is hostile to the very idea of foreign policy as an independent sphere of thought and action. They assume that the kind of foreign policy which a nation pursues is determined by the kind of domestic institutions it possesses and the kind of political philosophy to which it adheres. All of recorded history militates against that assumption. The national interest of great powers and, in good measure, the methods by which it is to be secured are impervious to ideological or institutional changes. As far back as April 30, 1823, Canning warned that "the general acquisition of free institutions is not necessarily a security for general peace." Our experience of total wars, waged by democracies for democratic tenets, gives substance to that warning.

The argument that diplomacy is particularly immoral and, hence, incompatible with democratic government similarly assumes that one can escape from the moral dilemmas of foreign policy by forswearing foreign policy itself. At the bottom of this argument there is a dual illusion: the illusion of the moral superiority of domestic politics over foreign policy and the illusion of the possibility of escaping foreign policy altogether. Both philosophic analysis and historic experience show that the moral problems which foreign policy raises are but a peculiar—and particularly drastic—manifestation of the moral problem of politics as such. Taking a wider view, one can even say that the moral problem of politics is but a peculiar instance of the moral problem which man encounters whenever he acts with reference to his fellowmen. What distinguishes in this respect foreign policy from domestic politics and from the human situation in general is not the substance of the problem, which is identical on all levels of human interaction, but the social conditions under which the problem arises on the international plane.

There is, then, no road by which one could escape the moral problem of politics, domestic or international; we can only endeavor to smoothen its sharp edges and to mitigate its practical consequences by changing not its substance but the social environment within which it is bound to arise in one form or another. It is not by accident that those who have tried to do more have taken a negative attitude toward foreign policy; for in the traditional methods of diplomacy they could not help but see the outward manifestations of the political risks and moral liabilities of foreign policy itself. Opposition to the traditional methods of diplomacy is everywhere intimately connected with either an isolationist or universalistic attitude toward international relations. Both consider the traditional methods of diplomacy at best superfluous and at worst pernicious, for they so regard foreign policy itself. In the isolationist view, a country can afford to dispense with an active foreign policy and, hence, also with diplomacy. In the universalistic view, foreign policy, carried on through diplomatic methods by sovereign nations, belongs to a dying age and is a stumbling block to the establishment of a more peaceful and orderly organization of the world.

This thought reveals itself in the recent attempts to set up the procedures of the United Nations as an alternative to the traditional methods of diplomacy. Here again, we are in the presence of the assumption that nations have a choice between the traditional methods of diplomacy and some other way of dealing with each other, a way which somehow leads to freedom from the risks and liabilities of foreign policy. In truth, of course, the procedures of the United Nations, as they have emerged in the practice of the organization, do not differ in substance from the traditional practices of diplomacy. What distinguishes the former from the latter is nothing but the social setting and the legal requirements which influence the way in which the traditional business of diplomacy is carried on within the agencies of the United Nations. The United Nations and traditional diplomacy are not mutually exclusive alternatives between which nations must choose. Rather, they supplement each other, serving identical purposes and partaking of the same qualities and characteristics. The Secretary-General of the United Nations, in his *Annual Report on the Work of the Organization for July 1, 1954 through June 15, 1955,* has called attention to this relationship in these words:

We have only begun to make use of the real possibilities of the United Nations as the most representative instrument for the relaxation of tensions, for the lessening of distrust and misunderstanding, and for the discovery and delineation of new areas of common ground and interest. . . . Conference diplomacy may usefully be supplemented by more quiet diplomacy within the United Nations, whether directly between representatives of Member Governments or in contacts between the Secretary-General and Member Governments. The obligations of the Charter, the environment of institutions dedicated to seeking out the common ground among the national interests of Member States, the wide representation from all continents and cultures, the presence of the Secretariat established as a principal organ of the United Nations for the purpose of upholding and serving the international interest—all these can provide help not to be found elsewhere, if they are rightly applied and used.

Within the framework of the Charter there are many possibilities, as yet largely unexplored, for variation of practices. . . . It is my hope that solid progress can be made in the coming years in developing new forms of contact, new methods of deliberation and new techniques of reconciliation. With only slight adjustments, discussions of major issues of a kind that have occurred outside the United Nations could often be fitted into its framework, thus at the same time adding to the strength of the world organization and drawing strength from it.

II

With these considerations we are entering into the positive task of ascertaining what the functions of traditional diplomacy are and in what its permanent value consists. A nation, existing as it does as an equal among other nations, can deal with the outside world in one of three different ways. It can deny the importance of the other nations for itself and its own importance for them and retreat into the impotence of isolation. Or it can deny the equality of the other nations and try to impose its own will upon them by force of arms. In either case, at least in its pure, extreme realization, a nation can afford to dispense with diplomacy. Or a nation can want to pursue its interests in active contact and on the basis of equality with other nations, assuming universality of that desire. In that case it cannot do without the constant redefinition and adjustment of its interests for the purpose of accommodating the interests of other nations.

Conflict of interests—actual, seeming or potential—is the overriding fact of international society, as it is one of the overriding facts of all societies, even those most highly integrated and centralized. Diplomacy in all its diverse historic and social manifestations is the technique of accommodating such conflicting interests. That technique proceeds in two stages: the ascertainment of the facts of conflict and the formulation of the terms of settlement.

Nation A pursues certain interests and so does nation B, and the interests of A and B are on the face of them in conflict. Both nations want to settle this conflict peacefully. How can they go about it? They have to define their respective interests and ascertain the point of conflict. That investigation may lead them to one of three possible conclusions.

If what A wants, being vital to itself, B cannot cede without endangering its vital interests, if not its very existence, because of the intrinsic importance of the territory, frontier, port, or airbase at issue, diplomatic accommodation is impossible. When Francis I of France was asked why he always made war against the Holy Roman Emperor, Charles V, he is reported to have answered: "Because we both want the same thing: Italy." As long as both kings wanted Italy badly enough, they could either go to war over it or else leave the issue unsettled, hoping for future developments to deflect the energies of both sides toward less contentious objectives. Often in history nations have indeed avoided war over their vital interests by allowing time to take the sting out of their conflicts. Yet in such cases it is to the restraint of war-like passions and the renunciation of quick and radical solutions rather than to the practices of diplomacy that the credit for the preservation of peace must go.

Nation A may again pursue an objective vital to itself, which nation B could cede only at the price of a vital interest of its own. Yet in contrast to the type of conflict just discussed, the importance of the objective to both sides is here not intrinsic to the objective itself, but rather the result of a peculiar configuration of interests which are subject to manipulation. For instance, the Soviet Union has a vital interest in preventing a united Germany from joining the Western alliance, and the United States has a similarly vital interest in preventing such a Germany from being absorbed by the Soviet bloc. Taken by themselves, these positions are obviously incompatible and, as the history of East-West negotiations has thus far shown, not subject to diplomatic accommodation. Yet one can well imagine, without committing oneself to its practical feasibility in the immediate future, an overall European or world-wide settlement of which a German settlement would form an organic part, satisfactory to the interests of both sides which could not be reconciled to the unification of Germany considered in isolation. In situations such as this, it is the task of diplomacy to redefine the seemingly incompatible vital interests of the nations concerned in order to make them compatible.

This task of diplomacy is, as it were, strategic in nature and truly creative, not often attempted and rarely successful. It yields in practical importance to that function with which diplomacy is typically associated in the popular mind: the function of bargaining issuing in a compromise. In conflicts to which this function applies, nation A seeks an objective which nation B either is willing to grant only in part or refuses to grant at all without compensation. Conflicts of this kind concern non-vital interests of which nations are willing to dispose by way of negotiations. The technique of diplomacy consists here in ascertaining the interests of both sides and in allocating the objective at issue in view of these interests and of the power available for their support.

The same diplomatic technique serves not only the peaceful settlement of conflicts among nations, but also the delineation and codification of common interests. In this respect it performs its classic function for the negotiation of treaties serving a common purpose of the contracting parties. Called upon to settle a conflict between two nations, diplomacy must create out of the conflicting interests a community of interests, a compromise which cannot satisfy all parties completely, but with which no party will be completely dissatisfied. When the representatives of two nations meet to negotiate a treaty, say, of commerce or alliance, they must discover and make precise an already existing community of interests. This community of interests, before it is crsytallized in legal stipulations, is amorphous and inchoate, obscured and distorted by seeming and real conflicts. It is the task of diplomacy to define the area of that pre-existing community of interests and to express it in terms sufficiently precise to serve as a reliable foundation for future action. It need only be mentioned in passing that this function of diplomacy is identical with that of contractual negotiations on all levels of social interaction.

III

It must be obvious from what has been said thus far that the traditional methods of diplomacy are of vital importance to a nation which seeks to pursue its interests successfully and peaceably. A nation which is unwilling or unable to use diplomacy for that end is of necessity compelled either to forsake its interests or to pursue them by war. As pointed out before, nations have always had a choice among three alternatives: diplomacy, war, renunciation. Which one of these alternatives a nation would choose in a concrete situation was a matter of rational calculation; none of them was *a priori* excluded on rational grounds.

Modern technology, especially in the form of all-out nuclear war, has destroyed this rational equality among diplomacy, war, and renunciation, and has greatly enhanced the importance of diplomacy. In view of that technology, there is no longer safety in renunciation, nor victory in war. From the beginning of history to the Second World War, the risks inherent in these three choices were commensurate with the advantages to be expected. Nations would miscalculate and suffer unexpected losses; but it was never rationally foreordained that they could not win. War in particular was a rational means to a rational end; victory would justify the risks and losses incurred, and the consequences of defeat were not from the outset out of all proportion to the gains to be expected from victory.

The possibility of all-out nuclear war has destroyed these rational relationships. When universal destruction is the result of victory and defeat alike, war itself is no longer a matter of rational choice, but becomes an instrument of suicidal despair. The pursuit of a nation's interests short of all-out nuclear war, then, becomes a matter of self-preservation. Even on the assumption—at present a moot one—that limited wars can and will still be safely waged, the risk of such a limited war developing into an all-out nuclear one will always be present. Hence, the imperative of the avoidance of all-out nuclear war at the very least gives unprecedented urgency to the pursuit of a nation's interest by peaceful means. Such peaceful pursuit, as we know, spells diplomacy. Neither diplomacy nor all-out nuclear war is today one among several rational choices available to a nation. As all-out nuclear war is tantamount to suicide, so successful diplomacy provides the only certain chance for survival. A nation which under present conditions is either unwilling or unable to take full advantage of the traditional methods of diplomacy condemns itself either to the slow death of attrition or the sudden death of nuclear destruction.

IV

The vital importance which the traditional methods of diplomacy receive from the possibility of all-out nuclear war is underlined by the more specific political developments which may well mark the year 1955 as the beginning of a new era in international relations. The first decade following the Second World War was characterized on the international scene by three basic political phenomena: the bipolarity of international politics, the tendency of this bipolar political system to transform itself into a two-bloc system, and the policy of containment. These three basic facts combined in minimizing the traditional methods of diplomacy, both as a matter of fact and in terms of the objective opportunities available.

During that decade, effective power for purposes of foreign policy was concentrated in Washington and Moscow, and these two power poles tended to attract like magnets most of the other centers of power. Whatever they might have preferred had they been free to choose, Great Britain and France, Poland and China had to lean upon one or the other of the superpowers for political, military, and economic support. Such countries could not have remained neutral, let alone changed sides, in the East-West conflict, short of a domestic revolution of radical dimensions. In such a situation, rigid in its alignments and inflexible in either side's conception of the interests involved, the main task of both sides is not to make and receive concessions but, at the very least, to hold the line and, at the very best, to advance it unilaterally. Since the balance of power made the latter alternative unfeasible short of a general war, both sides were of necessity reduced to a policy of containment which for all practical purposes forsook advancement at the expense of the other side while at the same time preventing the other side from advancing.

Such a situation of cold war offered little opportunity for the use of diplomatic methods either within the two-power blocs or between them. The inner coherence of the two blocs resulted primarily from the ineluctable necessity which made their members seek shelter under the roof of one or the other of the superpowers. During that period, the discrepancy of strength between the two superpowers and their respective allies was so obviously extreme and the consequences for those who would dare step out of line so obviously dire, that there was very little need for diplomacy to crystallize so obvious a community of interests.

The relations between the two blocs were no less clearly defined by the objective situation. The essence of the policy of containment was military rather than political. It consisted in the main in the warning, supported by actual preparedness, that a step taken by the other side beyond the line of military demarcation of 1945 would of necessity lead to general war.

The services which diplomacy was able to perform for this policy of containment were hardly different from those diplomacy has traditionally performed for the conduct of real war. It could announce the conditions for the settlement of the cold war and use such and similar announcements for purposes of psychological warfare. The very modalities of the cold war, then, inevitably transformed diplomacy into a mere auxiliary of a war waged against the enemy not for the purpose of accommodating conflicting interests but for the triumph, however verbal, of one nation over the other. Thus it is not by accident that during the first decade following the Second World War the traditional methods of diplomacy virtually ceased to operate in the relations between East and West and that the moves which were carried on under the labels and with the personnel of diplomacy at the many East-West conferences and within the United Nations served purposes not only far removed from, but often diametrically opposed to, those of traditional diplomacy.

If indications do not deceive, this period of post-war history has come to a close. It is being replaced by an era which is marked by greater flexibility within the two power blocs, tending toward a loosening of their inner coherence and, consequently, by greater flexibility between the two power blocs as well. To meet the problems of this new era the methods of the cold war will prove to be inadequate. As the conditions of the cold war led necessarily to the disuse and misuse of the practices of diplomacy, so the new era of international relations with equal necessity calls for the restoration of these practices.

Four facts are in the main responsible for this fundamental change in international relations: the decrease in the dependence of the great powers of second rank upon the superpowers, the rise of Germany and Japan to great power status, the impending dispersion of atomic power among a multitude of nations, some of which will thus gain or regain the status of great powers; finally, the spread and sharpening of the colonial revolutions in Asia, Africa, and Latin America.

Viewed from the vantage point of the United States, each of these new facts requires the vigorous application of the traditional practices of diplomacy. Since neither the American atomic monopoly nor extreme dependence upon American support can any longer be relied upon to secure the coherence of the Western alliance, the United States must again resort to the time-honored diplomatic method of fashioning a legally and politically viable community of interests out of the one that objectively exists in an inchoate and ill-defined form. Germany and Japan, no longer being the object of the victors' dispositions, must be persuaded by the same methods to see in association with the West the best chance for pursuing their interests. It is hardly necessary to emphasize that a similar approach to the colonial revolutions has been long overdue.

Thus the contemporary situation poses the perennial problem of diplomacy with renewed urgency. The objections to its use are without merit. Its indispensability for a successful and peaceful foreign policy grows from the very nature of things political. The possibility of all-out nuclear war has made its successful use the condition of survival.

Chapter 3

MORALITY AND CONTEMPORARY

DIPLOMACY

Louis J. Halle

I ACCEPTED the invitation to prepare this paper the more readily because of the topic suggested to me: moral problems in contemporary diplomacy. No one can spend a dozen years in the State Department, concerning himself with the development of our foreign policy, and not face such problems. Though he has no interest in ethics and no regard for moral considerations, the question of morality in foreign policy will be constantly thrust upon his attention by the press and by the political orators. He will find, in fact, a marked tendency for public criticism of our foreign policy to express itself in moralistic terms. If our government makes a commercial loan to a Latin American dictatorship, the official in the State Department may expect that he and his colleagues will be exposed to the public as a group of morally callous cynics who hold democracy in contempt. If it makes a concession in diplomatic negotiation with a rival government, that is because he and his colleagues prefer appeasement to moral principle. If the State Department exhibits routine diplomatic politeness to a disreputable foreign official, or if it fails to insist on a full measure of righteousness in the foreign and domestic behavior of some other sovereign government, its action or inaction may be termed morally shocking.

I repeat—the official who is exposed to this, day-in day-out, does not have to be a Hamlet to consider the bearing of morality on action in the foreign field. Fortinbras, himself, would at last be brought to soliloquize on the subject.

21

Hence my alacrity in grasping the opportunity to soliloquize on it here.

When I came to think of what I should say here, however, I was given pause. It struck me that, while there would be no need for me to define foreign or diplomatic policy, since the common idea of what it is would serve, I could not avoid discussing the meaning of morality. In accepting this invitation I, who could claim some familiarity with foreign policy, had innocently undertaken to discourse on the subject of ethics at a great university, the seat of men who were learned in these matters as I was not.

I had no choice but to proceed, however, on the assumption that those who invited a student of foreign policy to speak here on moral problems knew what they were doing. Moreover, I did not doubt that Christian charity was to be found at such an institution as this.

*   *   *

Foreign policy has its expression in the realm of fact. Morality has its expression in the judgment of facts—the judgment that we exercise in discriminating among facts. As a matter of our foreign policy, let us say, we either do or do not maintain relations with governments that oppress the people under their sway. We either do or do not make a point of living up to our engagements. We either do or do not attempt to enlarge our national jurisdiction by conquest. Persons with the most disparate ethical views may readily agree on what the fact of our policy is. However, whether that fact represents morality, or immorality, or neither is quite another kind of question. The answer to it does not lie in the realm of observable physical events but in the inward conscience of the man who gives it. It depends on the moral criteria that you or I or the next man chooses to apply on the basis of his own personal philosophy or religious belief.

I could hardly address myself to this subject at all if I did not believe, however, that all of us in the western world are members of a single civilization or cultural community, which we call Christendom and which represents certain moral criteria fixed by its own history and tradition. Even an explicitly secular state like our own is based on a conception of man, of his innate dignity or spirituality, that owes everything to Christian tradition. The Declaration of Independence and the Constitution of the United States are Christian documents, part of the essential record of Christian thought. The ethical views of which they are an expression go back in direct line to the recorded teachings of Christ.

Anyone who reads the Gospels must be impressed by the clear distinction that Christ makes, repeatedly, between those who claim to represent righteousness and those who actually do represent it. If there are obscurities in the Gospels I venture to say that this is not among them. Can anything be clearer than the parable of the Pharisee and the publican in the eighteenth chapter of the Gospel according to St. Luke (verses 10–14)? "Two men went up into the temple to pray; the one a Pharisee, and the other a publican. The Pharisee standing, prayed thus with himself: O God, I give thee thanks that I am not as the rest of men, extortioners, unjust, adulterers, as also is this publican. . . . And the publican, standing afar off, would not so much as lift up his eyes towards heaven; but struck his breast, saying: O God, be merciful to me a sinner. I say to you, this man went down into his house justified rather than the other: because every one that exalteth himself, shall be humbled; and he that humbleth himself, shall be exalted."

The Kingdom of Heaven, Christ said, was not for the self-righteous, and He condemned self-righteousness in absolute terms. He enjoined against it. "And when ye pray, you shall not be as the hypocrites, that love to stand and pray in the synagogues and corners of the streets, that they may be seen of men. . . . But thou when thou shalt pray, enter into thy chamber, and having shut the door, pray to thy Father in secret. . . ." (Matt. 13:6). Morality, then, is not to be identified with the views of those who make a show of it in public, offering themselves as examples.

I do not limit myself to citing Christian authority for what seems to me a basic human truth. Men feel the need of privacy for their most profound beliefs and feelings. A man who genuinely loves his wife shrinks from talking about it, from exposing his love to the vulgar gaze. The man who does proclaim his love in public is properly suspected of being a hypocrite. That is why the first scene in Shakespeare's "King Lear" is a parable in itself. Lear's hypocritical daughters, Goneril and Regan, who compete with each other in extravagant public expressions of their love, stand for the Pharisees, whom Christ likened unto "whited sepulchres, which indeed appear beautiful outward, but are within full of dead men's bones, and of all uncleanness" (Matt. 23:28). Cordelia, the only sister who genuinely loves her father, remains silent. The tragedy is that the old man, in his vanity, lacks the wisdom to recognize that genuine feeling is incapable of making an exhibition of itself.

And the same principle surely applies to love of country. We share the blindness of Lear if we think that the orator who wraps himself in the flag and loudly proclaims his hundred–per cent Americanism is a better patriot than the man who shrinks from such public avowals.

If the appreciation of this principle is, as I think, an indication of maturity, then we in this country have suffered a retreat from maturity in the past decade. This national community of ours has for a moment of its history allowed itself to be persuaded that patriotism and morality are the property of those who make public avowal of them, of those who subscribe to loyalty oaths and stand on the street-corners inveighing against un-Americanism, of those who mouth the language of morality on radio and television. In the past ten years we, the American public, have generally failed to distinguish between the Pharisees and the representatives of that opposing righteousness for which Christ spoke. The Pharisees have usurped Moses' seat (Matt. 23:2), and we have taken their word for it that morality is conformity with the views, the standards, and the practices for which they speak. This is the same moral error, let me say bluntly, that two thousand years ago led to the crucifixion of Christ. It has led among us to the exaltation in our government of policemen who represent it, and who now monitor the morals of an important part of our population in terms of it, hunting out those who transgress against the tradition of the ancients as conceived by them (Matt. 15:2).

A morally bizarre event occurred in Washington half-a-dozen years ago. One of our high officials at a press conference was asked to express his attitude toward a man who had been his friend but who had fallen into evil ways. The official answered that each man's attitude in a case like this must be determined by his own standards and his own principles. For him, he said, those standards and principles had been stated on the Mount of Olives and set down in the twenty-fifth chapter of the Gospel according to St. Matthew, where Jesus enjoins compassion for sinners. Accordingly, he said, he would not turn his back on the man who had been his friend. You will recall the shock and the expressions of moral outrage that this statement aroused throughout our country. A substantial part of our public was persuaded that the man who thus honored the precepts of Christ, who applied the morality of the millennium in our own time, was unfit for public office. When he was finally compelled by public clamor to make a further statement, declaring his abhorrence of the evil itself into which his friend had fallen, he stated that he accepted the humiliation of doing so. His record should have spoken for itself. But in the eyes of the Pharisees what is of first importance is how a man declares himself. To a notable extent, the security agents and investigating Congressmen have relied on emphatic avowals of hatred for un-American doctrine, which any hypocrite can make better than an honest man, to separate the righteous from the reprobates.

Let me mention another and related paradox. At least some of the few who have publicly opposed, as irrelevant, the application of the common moral tests to foreign policy are manifestly men of conscience, responsive in their actions to moral scruples; while others who make a point of proclaiming their devotion to moral principles have seemed particularly callous when it came to meeting the morally ugly necessities which belong to the profession of politics as they have chosen to practice it.

* * *

It has seemed to me impossible to embark on a meaningful discussion of morality in foreign policy without first establishing this distinction between the claims of the Pharisees and that Christian morality which stands, at important points, in such sharp opposition to those claims. I apply this distinction to the plight of the official in the State Department, which I mentioned at the outset of these remarks. Orators and editorial pages repeatedly identify those of his fraternity as enemies of morality in foreign policy. But what morality and whose morality is it that these critics represent? From where the official sits, a preponderant part of the morality that is urged upon him and his associates appears simply as the morality of the Pharisees.

In some cases it takes the form of a narrow nationalism. Such a morality holds Americanism to be synonymous with perfection, it thanks God that we are not as the rest of nations, extortioners, unjust. . . . Such a morality is not content with love of country but

requires, as well, contempt of foreigners. It insists either that we reform foreign countries, making them over in our own moral image, or
if they persist in their barbarous ways that we have nothing to do
with them. This is the morality of the Pharisees who were shocked
when Jesus sat down to eat with publicans and sinners (Matt. 9:11).

Another form of this is the insistence on ideological conformity,
abroad as at home. If other countries want to associate with us, if they
want to be our friends or allies, then they must maintain political
systems that are morally worthy of such an association—which is to
say, they must maintain political systems as much like our own as
possible. The insistence on this kind of morality has especially be-
deviled our foreign policy in Latin America, where most of the governments that we have to deal with—and other countries do not ordinarily offer us a choice of governments—are rather primitive, reflecting their environment in that respect. It has also made a moral issue
of our relations with the present governments of Spain and of Yugoslavia.

This ideological morality is variable in degree. In its extremest form
it is, perhaps, indistinguishable from the xenophobic nationalism to
which I have referred. Most ideologists, however, are more moderate
or more discriminating. Some would collaborate with a Conservative
government in England but not with a Labor government. Some
would collaborate with a Fascist dictatorship but not with a Communist dictatorship, or with a Communist but not with a Fascist dictatorship. Many would merely have us preach more idealism and ideology
to foreign countries, informing them of our virtue.

For all these people foreign policy appears to be in considerable
part a matter of morality, and when the government in its external
dealings violates the particular precepts of any of them they are quick
to accuse it of cynicism and an affinity for evil.

But to the man in the State Department the daily tasks that confront him do not ordinarily present themselves as moral issues at all.
They present themselves as practical problems to which he has to find
practical answers. Perhaps an American airline needs our government's
support in negotiations which it is conducting with a foreign government, and our national interest, as he sees it from his point of special
vantage, lies in giving it that support. The question which comes
before him is not, in his eyes, one of the foreign government's worthi-

ness to be approached by us. It is simply part of the necessary daily business of an imperfect world, which can be conducted only in the context of that world's imperfections. He sees quite clearly that everything would go to pieces unless this daily business were continuously conducted.

Or perhaps a shortage of dollar-exchange needed for the importation of essential food-supplies threatens disorder in a country whose stability is important for our defense. The question is whether to comply with its government's request for a credit. Again, to the State Department official the issue is practical rather than moral. He does not ask whether his grocer has ever committed adultery before he buys his groceries, because that would seem irrelevant to him. In like manner, the question of how virtuous the foreign government's domestic rule may be seems largely irrelevant to the question of the credit.

I do not mean to be absolute in this. A case might arise in which a grocer had committed such an unspeakable moral outrage that any of us would prefer to buy elsewhere; and there may be similar cases in international affairs. I can imagine circumstances in which a police regime was torturing the rebelliously inclined population under its sway, and in which a loan from us might save that regime from overthrow. In that case I think there might be humanitarian, moral, and sound practical reasons for not making the loan, whatever the technical justification—reasons that were not pharisaical. But such cases would be exceptional. They are unknown to the bulk of international affairs. Ordinary tyranny or corruption, unfortunately, are too common to call for an attitude of outraged virtue on the part of any except the habitually self-righteous or the utterly innocent, those who are tasting the apple for the first time. We, ourselves, have not been without examples of corruption, even of tyranny, in our own past and current history, so that self-righteousness becomes us no better than it did the Pharisees.

When the official has done his job, however, he is likely to find that to the pharisaical part of the public there was a moral issue involved which quite transcended the practical question that had preoccupied him. This bewilders him and makes him most uncomfortable. He does not relish being identified in the press with the forces of cynical "expediency." He does not see how his service to the national interest makes him a moral monster. If he is an intelligent man who thinks for himself he may eventually come to the conclusion that morality, as his critics speak for it, is irrelevant to the problems of foreign policy, that the orators and editorial writers are simply misconceiving the real nature of foreign relations.

The fact that this self-righteous insistence on the moral question makes the State Department official uncomfortable is not of the first importance. More important is the fact that it distorts the logic, the rationale, of foreign policy, creating problems that should never have existed at all but that, once raised, tend to take on a life of their own. The problems become none-the-less real, with the lapse of time, because they were falsely conceived to begin with.

Let me give an example. Traditionally, although there have been many exceptions, the act of recognizing a foreign government has had no moral connotations at all. In recognizing the foreign government you simply recognized a fact, the fact that there it was, exercising the actual powers and responsibilities of government in Japan, in France, or wherever. Whether you approved or disapproved of its origin, its nature, or its existence was beside the point. You might even recognize it as an enemy government, as we recognized the Nazi government during World War II, but still you recognized it.

A generation or two ago, however, we in this country departed from this traditional basis of recognition, moved by a desire to impose our kind of morality on political processes in the Caribbean republics. We expressed our moral disapproval of the way certain governments had come into power by withholding our recognition. A few years later we practiced a like non-recognition policy toward the government of Soviet Russia. The notion thus took root in our minds that one did not recognize new governments of which one could not morally approve.

Now this notion has a corollary. If moral disapproval is a reason for non-recognition, then recognition suggests moral approval. It is no longer neutral. It becomes a sort of accolade in the public mind, a moral endorsement esteemed as such by the government on which it is conferred, by the rest of the international community, and by our own people. Moral considerations, which had been irrelevant, are so no longer.

The trouble with this introduction of moral criteria into the practice of recognition is that, in terms of international realities, it is unworkable. There is necessary business to be done with those who exercise the authority of government in foreign countries (and whom we did not choose for their posts), business that cannot be abandoned because we disapprove of their morals. For example, we could have no hemisphere solidarity or hemisphere defense-system if we practised such a morality literally in Latin America. We should have to cut off the exchange of goods and services with most Latin American countries, abandoning our access to commodities essential to our defense or to our economy. We should have to abandon the interests of our nationals and give up our influence in much of the hemisphere, thereby making way for rival or hostile influences which we do not consider more salutary than our own, on moral grounds or any other. And much the same thing would hold for our position in the rest of the world. If other governments are not good enough to be allowed to cooperate with us, then we must find ourselves deprived of their support, even if that means living alone with our unique virtue in a world of enemies.

The acceptance by our public of this moral criterion for recognition, however, has compelled our government to practice a transparent and undignified pretense in our foreign relations. For a while after the war, and still today in good measure, we could expect coals of fire to be heaped on the State Department whenever our government recognized the government of a Latin American dictator. Accordingly, our government gave way and, to take two examples, refused to recognize the governments that had established themselves in Argentina and in Nicaragua, respectively. But because we had essential business to transact in those two countries, because we could not drop that business without dire consequences, we refrained from closing down our embassies in their capitals, and those embassies continued to function unofficially. Our diplomats, figuratively and perhaps literally as well, went in at the back doors of the foreign offices and presidential palaces to deal more-or-less covertly with the officials whose authority they did not officially recognize. The process of having, on occasion, to ask consideration of governments which we would not recognize in public had its embarrassments and even its humiliations. Eventually we found means of ending the farce by a belated recognition in each case.

This single problem of recognition should suffice to show what I mean when I say that the introduction of a self-righteous morality into our foreign policy distorts its logic, makes it falsely pretentious, and compels the adoption of disingenuous stratagems. In the degree that it thus promotes moral hypocrisy it injures the cause of morality itself. Experienced and morally responsible men are compelled, then, by their own honesty to say that these moral questions are irrelevant to the conduct of foreign relations. Whereupon they draw down upon their heads fresh coals of fire from the righteously indignant, who depict them as unregenerate cynics, enemies of our American idealism.

* * *

To say that the pharisaical self-righteousness which calls itself morality is irrelevant to foreign relations is one thing. To say that morality itself is irrelevant would be quite another. If you eliminate the claims of the Pharisees to morality you eliminate with them, I think, the issues in which the putative moral test has been most vociferously applied. But you still have not answered the question of what relevance morality, validly conceived, has to foreign policy. Are there moral tests which ought to be applied, and if so what are they?

I have already stated my belief that our country was founded as the expression of a certain philosophy which was not devoid of ethical implications. This has traditionally constituted a justification in our own eyes for our national existence. It has made us self-respecting. It has also provided a basis on which we could feel entitled, without self-righteousness, to the respect of other nations.

Now I am cautious of attributing moral virtue to nation-states, my own included. If we are all sinners as individuals, how much more are we sinners as nations! The best nations generally represent a low common denominator among the individuals who compose them—at least in those times when some crisis does not bring out an otherwise latent heroism. Yet I would not be willing to say that the sinner was without a soul. If we sinful men are morally responsible, as I think we are, then that moral responsibility extends to our institutions as well.

For nation-states are human institutions. They belong to people and are at their command. Their actions are the actions of people. They are merely devices through which morally responsible human beings work together for the realization of common purposes that do not lie outside the area of their moral responsibility. If you accept this view —and it is a premise of our Constitution—then you cannot maintain that, while human beings are morally responsible for their acts, states are not. The moral responsibility of states is essentially indistinguishable from the responsibility of the human beings whom they represent. It is not just a similar responsibility, it is the same responsibility.

In practice, however, we find that the standards of behavior for nation-states are lower than what we regard as reasonable standards for individual behavior. The daily behavior of nations toward one another would be considered intolerably boorish, immature, egotistical, and threatening among individuals in any civilized society. By the standards of individuals in a civilized society our nations are all barbarians. We recognize and accept this when we refrain from judging national behavior by the standards that we apply to individual behavior. What would we think of an individual who went around saying: "Me first"? But some of us appear to find a certain nobility in proclaiming the principle of "America first." Senator Beveridge went so far as to say that he was not just for "America first," he was for "America only."

I suppose there are several reasons for this relatively low standard of state behavior. Accountability for the behavior of a state is more or less diffused through its domestic society. The education and maturity of the many, even in a democracy that emphasizes public education, is less than that of the ablest or most fortunate few, so that a relatively low common denominator may prevail. Finally, international sanctions against bad behavior are, for the most part, lacking. Despite the valiant efforts of international lawyers since Victoria and Grotius, nation-states still carry out their functions in a largely lawless, anarchic environment in which it is difficult for any state to rise by itself above the morality of the jungle and still survive.

States also have their own internal moral conflicts, corresponding to the inner conflicts that all conscientious and thoughtful men experience on occasion in making their decisions as individuals. No more notable example of this inner conflict exists in our own history, I think, than the debate which we carried on from 1898, when we found the Philippines on our hands, through the presidential election-campaign of 1900. The "anti-imperialists" said that we were morally precluded, by our established principles, from holding another people in subjection, from governing without the consent of the governed. The "expansionists," or many of them, argued that Destiny had summoned us to assume the moral responsibility of civilizing our fellow men across the seas. This was, I believe, a genuine moral issue on which conscientious men divided, and it could only arise because as a nation we recognized, for the most part, that we had a moral responsibility under God. The difficulty—the perennial difficulty for men and nations alike —was to know what that responsibility was in terms of the particular circumstances of the moment, how it should be applied in choosing among the alternatives open to us. Casuistry, it appears, is no easier for nations than it is for us individuals.

That pitiful figure whom I introduced at the outset of these remarks, the public official, is properly concerned with these problems of casuistry because the nation for which he acts has to resolve such problems in its policy and action. But his own personal morality has less to do with the matter than his critics would sometimes have us believe. As an agent—and in his official capacity he is only that—he is not free to resolve the nation's problems by reference only to his own conscience, his own ethics. Although he is, let us say, a pacifist, he is not free to use his official position to institute pacifist policies for a nation that is not pacifist. His position is, rather, like that of the corporate director who, however much he believes in charity, is not entitled to give away the stockholders' assets as if they were his own.

This confronts any highly conscientious official with a casuistical dilemma of his own when, as an agent of the public, he finds himself under constraint to act by standards of morality opposed to his own personal standards. You will perceive the bearing that this has on the official, to whom I referred earlier, who cited the precepts of Jesus at a time when those precepts were as unacceptable, politically, as they had been two thousand years before.

I shall not reveal the answer to this moral dilemma, since I am quite unsure of it myself. In fact, I don't know it. Perhaps, like the practical answers to most problems in casuistry, it lies in a compromise that sacrifices logic. I shall not pretend to say whether it was right of the official to be right, if he was right, when the nation was not right, if it was not right. It may be that he should simply have evaded or straddled the issue. Or perhaps he should, in his representative capacity, have been as wrong as the country was wrong, if it was wrong. But if representation imposes this latter requirement does it not follow that we must look elsewhere than to our political agents for moral leadership and the good example? I merely pose the question. If it is better to be right than to be president, is it ever right to be president? Let each of us look into his own conscience and give his own answer according to what he finds there.

My only point here is that a representative government can never conduct itself and the national policy according to essentially different standards of morality from those of the society it represents. In the generation of our founding fathers, before we became a democracy, our government effectively represented only that small element of our nation which was, by education, most disciplined and sophisticated in matters of ethics—in other words, most civilized. The moral standards by which it was guided then would give scant comfort to our pharisees today. How, for example, did old John Adams define "the spirit of patriotism"? He said that the spirit of patriotism comprehended: "Piety, or the love and fear of God; general benevolence to mankind; a particular attachment to our own country; a zeal to reform its happiness by reforming its morals, increasing its knowledge, promoting its agriculture, commerce and manufactures, improving its constitution and securing its liberties. . . ." Note that the order in which he listed these attributes of patriotism places God first, then mankind, then one's own country. And what, according to John Adams, is the patriot's proper attitude toward his own country? Does he look upon it as a paragon against which to measure the sinfulness of other countries? Not at all. He sees it as an imperfect society needing constant reform and improvement. The business of Americans, it seems, is to reform themselves and to be respectful of mankind at large.

The same modest and magnanimous note is struck in No. 63 of the Federalist papers, written by either Hamilton or Madison. "An attention to the judgment of other nations is important to every government for two reasons: the one is, that, independently of the merits of any particular plan or measure, it is desirable, on various accounts, that it should appear to other nations as the offspring of a wise and honorable policy; the second is, that in doubtful cases, particularly where the national councils may be warped by some strong passion or momentary interest, the presumed or known opinion of the impartial world may be the best guide that can be followed. What has not America lost by her want of character with foreign nations; and how many errors and follies would she not have avoided, if the justice and propriety of her measures had, in every instance, been previously tried by the light in which they would probably appear to the unbiased part of mankind?"

These words of our founding fathers may sound disturbing to our ears today. In them, however, I detect the historic soul of our nation. Who can read the record of our founding, by the men who thought in these terms, and say that a nation-state cannot be a manifestation of moral principles? But, though it may have a soul in this sense, I think that any nation-state stands always in danger of losing its soul, especially when it achieves bigness, material prosperity, and power. That appears to have happened to ancient Athens in the fifth century, and the consequence was her downfall. Can we be sure that this has not been happening to us, as well? I do not know, but the signs of corruption are many, and whether it has been happening or not, the danger is there. I, for one, believe that if we do lose our soul in this sense, if we do forget those ideals of our human dignity which have animated our national community, then we will go the way of Athens by the same course of consequences.

I conclude, therefore, that our national behavior does have to reflect a moral responsibility, which means that our whole policy, foreign and domestic, must represent the discharge of such a responsibility. We have to be true, in our policy, to the moral principles for which I hope and believe we still stand. The objectives of our policy must be— as I think they truly are today—such as are compatible with human dignity. In our dealings with others we must show our good faith, and this imposes real limits on foreign policy. Finally, and this seems hardest of all, we ought in our dealings with others to practice that magnanimity which expresses itself in modesty, in compassion, in a reluctance to concern ourselves with the mote in our neighbor's eye rather than with the beam in our own. Morality, more than charity, begins at home.

Chapter 4

DIPLOMATISTS AND MILITARY

PEOPLE

William T. R. Fox

THE task of diplomatists, it is often maintained, is to save the peace, and, when they lose it, to move off the stage of world politics until the military men win it back again.[1] The task of military men would then be to win the war and, when they win it, to retire from view until the diplomatists again lose it.

This is a popular, and it must be admitted from a British and American standpoint, a plausible view of the role of diplomacy and arms. It presupposes a night-and-day, black-and-white view of war and peace. It denies any role to force in being during peace and any scope to diplomacy during war. Of course, only the insular powers,[2] Britain and America, have in modern times through a combination of high power potential, favorable location and naval preparedness been able

[1] Cf. Cordell Hull, *Memoirs* (New York, 1948), II, pp. 1080, 1101–1102, 1109. Secretary Hull commented regarding the last stages of his conversations with the Japanese prior to Pearl Harbor: "I had to assume the responsibility of concluding that the diplomatic phase of the negotiations was finished and of stating that the task of safeguarding the nation had passed into the hands of the Army and the Navy."

[2] The United States, like Great Britain, is separated from the European continent and the continental great powers by water. Thus, set apart from the major arena in which the general wars of our modern state system have been fought and traditionally free from attack by a North American neighbor of comparable power, the United States may be thought of as an island power in relation to the international politics of the European continent.

to count on not being defeated in a short war and on having time to mobilize after the war crisis so as finally to be victorious in a protracted war. It was thus a special and past state of affairs which permitted diplomacy to be conducted relatively free of short-run military considerations.[3]

The soldier-diplomatist relationship described in the first paragraph is not even plausible and is certainly inaccurate when it is applied to the major Continental European countries in the nineteenth century. In the present century the benefits of insularity have steadily declined not only for Britain but also, though more slowly, for America. It is this loss of insularity which most readily accounts for the great transformation in the role which soldiers and civilians in the two countries play in making foreign policy and national security policy.

What is a relatively new experience for Britain and America is an old story on the Continent. Alfred Vagts's *Defense and Diplomacy: the Soldier and the Conduct of Foreign Relations* [4] draws the bulk of its evidence from the Continental experience prior to 1914. Particularly in the nineteenth-century heyday of the *Blitzkrieg* a gulf between foreign and military policy could have been disastrous. The constitutional and administrative arrangements of the major European countries admitted military experts to governmental deliberations at the highest level, and thus reflected their need most of the time for preparedness and for defensive alliances.

As Dr. Vagts's book demonstrates in detail, the soldier has had a role to play at many points, in foreign relations in peace as well as in war. Foreign Offices and general staffs have many problems to solve in collaboration as well as in competition. When the possibility of a very short war cannot be excluded, defensive alliances must be backed up by coalition military planning in detail and in advance of the actual war crisis in which the efficacy of the plans will be tested. The Anglo-French military staff conversations before World War I, like those of the NATO countries after 1950, are examples.

Soldiers have sometimes been used as their country's diplomatic representatives, but in such cases it is not as soldiers but as diplomats

---

[3] Cf. Arnold Wolfers and L. Martin, eds., *The Anglo-American Tradition in Foreign Affairs* (New Haven, 1956). See especially pp. xv–xxvii in Professor Wolfers' introductory essay.

[4] New York, 1956.

that they operate abroad. On the other hand, it is as soldiers that they go abroad as military attachés, as members of military missions, as negotiators of armistices, and as leaders of armed demonstrations or of armed forces stationed abroad for occupying or deterrent purposes. It is as soldiers that they set the military conditions for co-ordinating strategy and diplomacy and set the military requirements for industrial mobilization.

Whether by the test of the effective subordination of military policy to the aims of civilian government or by the more pragmatic test of success in the military policy adopted, the diplomatist-soldier relationship was not always satisfactory in those European countries which before World War I recognized the need for closely co-ordinated foreign, military, and industrial mobilization policies. The brash German naval policy after 1898 consolidated Anglo-French opposition to Germany's further expansion, and it can in large part be explained by Kaiser Wilhelm II's willingness to take advice directly from his naval chief, Admiral von Tirpitz. The famous Schlieffen Plan had a similar defect. The violation of Belgian neutrality multiplied and energized Germany's foes. Whether the political cost of German defense in a two-front war could have been lessened by an alternative military plan, civilian German chancellors apparently were never able to find out. Nor were they able to prevent the German campaign of unrestricted U-boat sinkings which paved the way for American participation in World War I.[5]

The difficulty was not always that the military man was believed to be more willing than the diplomatist to invoke his conception of the national interest at the expense of the conception of the civilian government. It has been alleged that sometimes the military man was more interested in preserving his position within the society than in preparing efficiently for a possible trial at arms.[6] Thus, the demands were sometimes made in the name of "honor," whatever their relation to the national interest. One example is that which restricted the career

---

[5] The German experience has been carefully examined in a number of recent books, including Gordon A. Craig, *The Politics of the Prussian Army* (Oxford, 1955); Walter Goerlitz, *The History of the German General Staff* (New York, 1953); John W. Wheeler-Bennett, *The Nemesis of Power* (London, 1953). See also Samuel P. Huntington, *The Soldier and the State* (Cambridge, Mass., 1957), Chap. V, for a discussion of "objective civilian control" in Germany.

[6] Cf. Alfred Vagts, *A History of Militarism* (New York, 1937).

of military officer to the sons of the right families.[7] Also, the warrior claimed the right to communicate directly with his supreme warlord, the king or emperor, a practice which made possible the intimacy between the Kaiser and Tirpitz ultimately so fatal to Germany.[8]

It is possible that military policy and foreign policy were, even in Britain before 1890 and America before 1940, more closely articulated than has commonly been assumed. The archives of the victorious insular, democratic powers have not been opened as wide as those of defeated Germany after both wars and Austria-Hungary after the first. Even had they been opened, one could hardly be sure. Governments of the major powers, as Professor Medlicott has pointed out, have rarely asserted that it is military weakness which is responsible for a relatively inactive policy; [9] and liberal historians in the first half of the twentieth century were not often inclined to offer an interpretation of their government's policy which would be powerful ammunition for those who favored a larger military budget. The cry for "scholarships, not battleships" so often heard on American campuses in the 1930's may have been of left-wing origin, but it evoked a sympathetic response from all those who believed that "welfare" expenditures by the state were productive and therefore good, and "war" expenditures were destructive and therefore bad.

Whatever may be the truth in this matter, three generalizations seem possible. The connection between foreign and military policy has until recent decades been much less direct in Britain and America than on the Continent. More recently, both countries have striven hard to integrate the two kinds of policy, although not on the pattern which once prevailed in the Continental autocracies. However imperfect and discordant the "concert of judgment" between the diplomatist and the soldier on the Continent, the connection between their efforts was explicitly recognized.[10]

---

[7] *Ibid.*, pp. 205, 220–221.

[8] On the vice of "immediacy" see Vagts, *Defense and Diplomacy*, pp. 80, 491–500.

[9] W. N. Medlicott, "The Scope and Study of International History," *International Affairs*, XXXI (1955), 420.

[10] The phrase "concert of judgment" is Arthur Macmahon's and was used to describe the triangular foreign affairs-defense-Bureau of the Budget relationship out of which key decisions relative to United States national security emerge. See his *Administration in Foreign Affairs* (Tuscaloosa, 1953), Chap. 1.

II

The diplomatist, using this term broadly to refer to anyone responsible for diplomatic activity, whether he is stationed at home or abroad, is likely to see himself charged with the promotion of a multiplicity of national objectives and having to take account of a whole complex of international relations only some of which are military. The soldier, he may sometimes think, is charged with a much more narrowly defined task and is expected to be expert only on military affairs.[11] The diplomatist is thus seen as broad and flexible, the soldier as narrow and rigid.

The soldier, when he asserts that he is speaking from a purely military point of view, may by implication be asserting that he has nothing to do with "politics" or with anything but "facts." He may find the diplomatist vacillating and imprecise and somehow lacking the power of decision.

The roles which diplomatists and military people are called upon to play in our Western state system may have been productive of friction and misunderstanding between them. The friction, though not the misunderstanding, may in political systems in which the pattern of consent is properly structured contribute to rational policy, that is, a policy logically and efficiently related to the national interest as it is understood by those in control of government.

It has already been suggested that whether the phrase "properly structured" has reference to the promotion and maintenance of the basic values of society or to narrower considerations of technical efficiency, the Continental pattern was found wanting. In Britain and America the case was a little different and was profoundly affected by a belief that a large standing army was more of an internal threat than it was a protection against external threat. Oliver Cromwell and his major-generals taught the English-speaking nations a lesson which their insular position made it possible for them never to forget, at least until the last half century.

[11] A recent analysis of American military education, John W. Masland and Laurence I. Radway, *Soldiers and Scholars* (Princeton, 1957), points to the tremendous effort of the American armed services to produce an adequate supply of career officers with the additional quasi-military and non-military skills useful in participating in politico-military policy-making. There is no evidence that the diplomatist has undertaken a comparable effort to acquire the soldier's expertise.

Geography, power potential, and naval power in being, the combination which gave assurance against "sudden death" in inter-Great Power war, provided the shield behind which liberal attitudes toward the armed forces could, with small risk to national survival, become quasi-pacifist.

Concern with "keeping the high brass from taking over" has, during much of English and American history since the time of Cromwell, seemed a more vital concern than any concern lest military strength fall short of that needed to repel a foreign foe.[12] The Constitution of the United States is studded with provisions reflecting a prevailing fear of unchecked military power and, specifically, a large standing army in peacetime.[13] The President of the United States is designated "commander-in-chief," and his powers are hedged about by a variety of Congressional powers, including the "power of the purse"[14] and the power to declare war. Finally, the provisions limiting army appropriations to a two-year period and recognizing the dependence of the United States for its security "on a well-regulated militia" reflect the determination of the Founding Fathers to prevent the emergence of an independent military power.

A curious confirmation of the hypothesis that fear of the army as a possible decisive force in the nation's internal political life persisted down into the nineteenth century in England comes from the Duke of Wellington. The Duke advised Queen Victoria in the 1850's "that the Army should be commanded by a member of the Royal Family, so as to ensure, in the event of a revolution, that the troops would be used in defense of the throne, and not in obedience to the Orders of Parliament!"[15] The Queen accordingly in 1856 appointed the Duke of Cambridge commanding general, a position which he held until 1895.

If there was fear of the military on the civilian side, there was contempt and suspicion of politics and politicians on the other. As late as

[12] Even in recent years, or perhaps especially in recent years, with the dramatic rise in importance, in prestige and in influence of military leaders, concern for subordinating the military power to the civilian has been evidenced in a continuing stream of publications. Cf. Louis Smith, *American Democracy and Military Power* (Chicago, 1951).

[13] Article I, section 8, clauses 1, 11, 12, 13; Article I, section 9, clause 7; Article I, section 10, clause 3; Article II, section 2; Amendments II and III.

[14] Cf. Elias Huzar, *The Purse and the Sword* (Ithaca, N. Y., 1950).

[15] Sir William Robertson, *Soldiers and Statesmen, 1914–18* (London, 1926), I, 3.

1910, Lord Kitchener was writing to L. S. Amery: "If there is a war and they want me, I'll take a house well away from the War Office and run the war from there." [16] And in the United States a commanding general, William Tecumseh Sherman, of "Marching through Georgia" fame, had in the 1870's even tried the experiment of insulating the Army from politics by moving its headquarters from Washington to St. Louis.

One additional circumstance which promoted the divorce between military men and military policy, on the one hand, and diplomatists and the high politics of inter-Great Power relations on the other was the extra-European orientation of British and American interests in the period between general wars which it is conventional to call "peace." Soldiers and marines found themselves "from the halls of Montezuma to the shores of Tripoli" dealing with what Kipling called "lesser breeds beyond the law." They were making travel, trade, and investment safe in ever new areas by extending the realm of law and order. American armed forces were doing it in the American West and in the Caribbean. British forces were doing it in various parts of Asia and especially in India. This *ad hoc* exhibition or application of armed force on a relatively small scale did not require any complex integration of military and foreign policy.

On the civilian side, it was even argued that it is dangerous to seek to define military policy at all or to have any agency of government specially charged with defining it. Sir Henry Campbell-Bannerman, a Liberal politician who was shortly to become Secretary of State for War and in 1905 Prime Minister, wrote in 1890 that Continental countries might need a general staff, for they were

concerned in watching the military condition of their neighbors, in detecting points of weakness and strength, and in planning possible operations against them. But in this country [Great Britain] there is in truth no room for "general military policy" in the larger and more ambitious sense of the phrase. We have no designs against our European neighbors. Indian "military policy" will be settled in India itself, not in Pall Mall. In any of the smaller troubles into which we may be drawn by the interests of our dependencies, the plan of the campaign must be governed by the particular circumstances, and would be left (I presume and hope) to be determined

[16] L. S. Amery, *My Political Life*, Vol. I, "England Before the Storm, 1896–1918" (London, 1953), 217.

by the Officer appointed to direct the operations. And as to the defense of these Islands, and of our depots and coaling-stations, although there may have been some slackness and delay in the past, we have reason to believe that now, if full provision has not yet been made, that complete schemes at least have been matured for protection against attacks which cannot vary greatly in character. I am therefore at a loss to know where, for this larger branch of their duties, the new department could find an adequate field in the circumstances of this country. There might indeed be a temptation to create such a field for itself, and I am therefore afraid that while there would be no use for the proposed office, there might be in it some danger to our best interests.[17]

This exceptionally interesting quotation is almost an epitome of what might be called "the civilian mind" as it conceived of military men and military policy in the liberal Britain and America of the last century. Some of the essential elements may be briefly recapitulated: A new Cromwell is more of a threat than a new Napoleon. The insular countries, with their sturdy militias, are so little vulnerable that there is more danger from having a military policy than from not having it. Expenditures on the armed services are unproductive and therefore, beyond the barest minimum essential, are bad. The greater safety lies in starving the military. No technological change can alter the relationship of the insular powers to Europe and its power politics. There are the resources and there will always be the time to organize defense in case of attack. To plan for a particular war contingency and to arm in anticipation of the possibility is somehow to bring it closer. It is also evidence of aggressive intent. This is particularly true of any plan or any rearmament which envisions the use of British (or American) armed forces on the Continent of Europe.[18]

III

The Boer War was for Britain and the Spanish-American War was for the United States a rude shock. The revelation of incompetence

[17] Quoted in Robertson, *op. cit.*, I, 7, and Amery, *op. cit.*, I, 197 from *Further Report of the Hartington Commission*, February 11, 1890, p., xxix.

[18] Robertson, *op. cit.*, I, 12, quotes Campbell-Bannerman's successor as War Minister: ". . . it will be distinctly understood that the probability of the employment of an army corps in the field in any European war is sufficiently improbable to make it the primary duty of the military authorities to organize our forces efficiently for the defense of this country." Memorandum of Mr. Stanhope, War Minister, June 1, 1898 *Official History of the War in South Africa, 1899–1902*, I, 5.

and rustiness and of the yawning gulf between public policy and military capabilities created a demand for reform. In the two countries, the war ministries were shortly to be headed by brilliant lawyers, Richard B. Haldane (later Lord Haldane) in England and Elihu Root in the United States, who were to bring about internal reform of Army organization, particularly by the creation of general staffs.[19] These reforms would make the two countries' armies much more responsive instruments of national policy.

There were other influences at work which have significantly affected the policy-making role of the military in the English-speaking countries. These include the political realignment of the great powers, developments in military technology, public administration and industrial mobilization, and differential rates of growth in the material power factors which determine a country's power potential. Germany's rapid industrial growth, her diplomatic successes under Bismarck, and her unsettling diplomacy and naval activity after the accession of Kaiser William II brought about a sharp redefinition of Britain's relations with the United States, Japan, Russia, and above all France in the years after 1895. The Entente Cordiale meant that Britain recognized she could no longer count on the Continental powers to be so evenly poised that she could incline the balance at her leisure. She had to have allies and to be an ally. France's relative decline in strength in relation to Germany meant that Anglo-French coalition military planning had to envision British troops fighting alongside their French comrades in a German war.

All this meant that army and navy policy could no longer be separately developed, nor could either be developed independently of foreign policy. In the old days, when the British Army's function was to fight the colonial and side-show wars while the Navy by distant blockade and grand fleet engagements was expected to keep the European peninsula of the Eurasian land-mass in its grip by interdicting Europe's main line of communication and trade around Europe from the North Sea through the English Channel, the Straits of Gibraltar, to the Eastern Mediterranean, the two services could go their separate ways. In the new day, when a European war would be settled

---

[19] Cf. Sir Frederick Maurice, *Haldane, The Life of Viscount Haldane of Cloan* (London, 1937), I, Chaps. VII–XII; Richard Burden Haldane, *An Autobiography*, Chap. VI, "The Liberal Government and the Army: 1905–1910" (Garden City, N. Y., 1929); Amery, *op. cit.*, I, Chap. VIII, "Army Reform and National Service"; Philip C. Jessup, *Elihu Root* (New York, 1938), I, Chaps. XII–XIII.

disadvantageously to Britain unless British power were applied on the Continent, when railroads, canals, and improved roads provided superior means of internal communication on the Continent beyond the reach of British sea power, and when the urbanization of England and the Continent made overseas supplies of critical importance, naval policy and military policy had to be co-ordinated. Leviathan could not simply plan to fight another Leviathan. It was Behemoth who was the prospective enemy.

Foreign policy, military policy, and naval policy had all to be brought together. A cabinet-level committee seemed to be called for. Because in the new day Britain felt she needed the voluntary help of her maturing and already self-governing overseas dominions as much as that of her new French ally, the cabinet-level committee was called the Committee of *Imperial* Defence (1904).[20] Thus, more than a third of a century before our National Security Council was created, the analogous cabinet-level committee was created in England. Its secretariat, small but efficient, worked so well under its prewar secretary, a Marine officer acceptable to both the Army and Navy, Captain Hankey, later Sir Maurice and now Lord Hankey, that he continued to function as secretary for the War Cabinet under Lloyd George and for peacetime cabinets which followed, as well as for the Committee of Imperial Defence.[21] It may be significant that today at one point where the necessity for inter-service, defense-foreign affairs and inter-ally co-operation coincide, in the North Atlantic Council in Paris, the first Secretary General of NATO and vice-chairman of the North Atlantic Council, Lord Ismay, and his senior assistant, Lord Coleridge, were both professional military men and alumni of Lord Hankey's school of inter-service, inter-department and empire-wide military planning, the secretariat of the Committee of Imperial Defence.

IV

The need for and the development of American policies which integrated considerations of foreign and military policy lagged behind the similar need in England by about a generation. So did the need

[20] "Imperial" referred to what would today be called "Commonwealth and Empire" and the C. I. D. in present-day terminology would have more properly been called the Committee of Commonwealth Defence.

[21] See Lord Hankey, *Government Control in War* (Cambridge, Eng., 1945).

for institutions within which integrated policy could be elaborated. The Spanish-American War, the Boxer Rebellion, and the Russo-Japanese War all brought American involvement in the politics of Eastern Asia, but the first decade of the twentieth century saw no similar American involvement in Western Europe nor any acceptance of such involvement as a contingency for which plans must be made. The heady wines of Admiral Mahan's writing had fired the imagination of the high priests of naval policy. Lacking clear policy guidance either from the Department of State or from any Cabinet-level committee on questions of what we now call national security policy, operating under a Secretary of the Navy who was traditionally supposed to be involved more with procurement than with policy and not much with that, they conjured up their own image of national policy and formulated their own force-level goals appropriate to that policy. It is perhaps not important that their primitive-Marxist, trade rivalry image of world politics and of inevitable wars with the other two great trading nations, Britain and Germany, was wrong. They had at any rate some image of the United States in world politics.[22]

With the enthusiastic support of President Theodore Roosevelt and the not wholly reluctant assent of Congress, the Navy set out on the path of expansion. Naval parity with Germany was an intermediate goal, and the challenge to British naval supremacy was seen as an ultimate objective.[23] In this period it was our Navy men who saw the world, who were the sophisticates of our armed services.

With the era of Indian-fighting brought to a close, Army officers did from time to time leave the Continental United States but only to go to the Caribbean, the Canal Zone, Hawaii, and the Philippines.[24] Two world wars have reversed the situation. Instead of the war the

---

[22] See Warner R. Schilling, "Civil-Naval Politics in World War I," *World Politics*, VII (1955), 572–591.

[23] See Harold and Margaret Sprout, *The Rise of American Naval Power, 1776–1918*, esp. Chapter XV, "Mahan Triumphant: The Policy of Theodore Roosevelt, 1901–1909" (Princeton, N. J., 1946); see also George T. Davis, *A Navy Second to None* (New York, 1940).

[24] Army officers had of course occasionally been sent on foreign missions. Among them was General Emory Upton, who has been described as "the Army's Mahan." Travel, research and reflection led him to write *The Armies of Asia and Europe* (New York, 1878) and *The Military Policy of the United States* (Washington, 1904). The latter was published twenty-three years after his death. See Richard C. Brown, "General Emory Upton—the Army's Mahan," *Military Affairs* (Fall, 1953), pp. 125–131.

admirals envisioned, a war of naval power against naval power, with the destiny of nations decided in grand fleet engagements in a single afternoon, a war which emphasis on the building of capital ships had seemed to imply, the Navy found its function in European war as being to conduct and protect a gigantic trans-oceanic ferry-boat service so that land-based forces in Europe could defeat Germany and its allies. Its great enemy was the U-boat, not the battleship. To change the metaphor, the Army leapfrogged over the Navy. And it was the Army leaders whose massed forces were decisive in World War I, who had to negotiate with their opposite numbers in the Allied armed forces, and who had to govern the occupied areas after the victory had been won.

All this is not to say that our Navy and Air Force did not have the broadening experience of intensive collaboration with allies. They did, and do, particularly with the forces of Britain.

As a matter of fact, none of the three services in World War II had the intimate experience of combined operations with their Soviet ally such as all three had with Britain in that war. Even if there had been no barriers of ideology and mutual mistrust, the physical separation of the two main theaters of land war relieved the Western allies of the necessity of co-ordinating their strategy and tactics except at top political levels. In American conduct of the war in the Pacific in World War II, there was not the necessity of as close co-ordination with Britain as in the European-Mediterranean theater. The legacy of two world wars then is a generation of American professional military leaders, particularly Army leaders, with quasi-diplomatic experience, particularly in Europe, and particularly with Britain on European questions.

For a brief moment in history, the United States could play vis-à-vis the powers of Europe a role similar to that which the other great power, Britain, had played before 1895. It turned out that Britain's entry into the two-bloc system of pre-World War I Europe was only sufficient to make World War I protracted, not quite enough to insure the defeat of the Central Powers. The untapped reservoir of American strength determined the issue.

Again in World War II, it was American power which seems to have finally tilted the balance against the German-led coalition. But the aftermath of that war revealed that America was no more free to stay out of post-World War II Europe than Britain had been free to remain aloof from pre-World War I Europe. Like Britain, the United States learned that it had to have allies and, therefore, it had, also, to be an ally. Like Britain, the United States was shown to have an interest in maintaining the independence of its European allies. Like the other insular power, the United States had to make its plans in peacetime to apply its power across the water and in the Rimland areas of Europe. Organs of inter-service collaboration, of foreign affairs-defense collaboration and of inter-allied collaboration had all to be developed. Under the stress of World War II, with the imperative need for co-ordinated Army and Navy effort in general and the specific need for a unified American point of view in the combined staff conversations with the British, the Joint Chiefs of Staff emerged. During the war its only legal basis was a Presidential directive, but at the end of the war Congress established it by law on what was meant to be a more permanent basis.

The National Security Council is an innovation of the post-war period, though the need for diplomatic-military co-ordination at levels below the White House was recognized in a variety of ways during World War II. The Secretaries of State, War, and Navy formed a "Committee of Three" to lunch together weekly and deal with matters of common interest. Problems of military government and civil affairs in occupied areas created the need for the State-War-Navy Co-ordinating Committee (SWNCC). Senior diplomatic advisers were assigned to theater commanders as, for example, Robert Murphy to General Eisenhower in North Africa. With the British experience of a cabinet-level Defence Committee available as a model, the National Security Council was created in 1947.

It was under the double impact of the first Soviet explosion of an atomic weapon (1949) and the attack on South Korea in 1950 that the final steps were taken in the United States to energize the war machinery for inter-service and diplomatic-military collaboration, and to do in peacetime three things that the insular powers had previously found it necessary and possible to do hitherto only in actual war: to bring peacetime mobilization to a high (thirty-five to forty-billion dollars) level and keep it there, to launch a massive, multi-billion dollar program of military and economic aid, and to establish the machinery in NATO for coalition military planning. The last two of these things are of special interest in any discussion of the role of the military in the diplomacy of this changing world.

V

In the era of total war, as well as in that of cold war or "total diplomacy" which followed, measures directed at expanding one's own mobilization base or contracting the opponent's have been of great importance. One brings, for example, indirect pressure on the enemy by economic warfare measures which deny him neutral sources of supply. This aspect of the conduct of war by the insular powers was prominent in both the first and second wars. It was a major task of diplomacy, as is shown by the importance of the men sent as ambassadors to such neutrals as Spain and Turkey. The United Kingdom, for example, sent its former Foreign Minister, Sir Samuel Hoare, to Madrid, and Hitler sent one of his predecessors in the office of *Reichskanzler*, von Papen, to Ankara.

In wars which are so protracted that industrial potential is the ultimate arbiter, the coalition with the greater potential naturally seeks to sever enemy supply lines essential to his continued fighting effort. It tries to dry up supplies going from or *via* neutrals to the enemy. This requires a close co-ordination of military pressure on the enemy and diplomatic and economic pressure on the neutrals.[25] An important British effort in the early years of the Second World War derived from a belief that the whole German war effort would falter if Swedish iron ore shipments to Germany were sharply reduced.

Of course, an even more effective way of severing the neutrals' supply lines to the enemy is to bring the neutral in on one's own side. One may also do this to broaden the coalition base of the war effort or to give strategic room for maneuver. The bloody stalemate of the machine-gun and trench warfare of World War I was such a ghastly memory that great ingenuity and effort were expended in getting at Germany *via* pressure on neutrals, particularly Scandinavian neutrals, in this indirect fashion. The Chamberlain and Daladier decision to intervene in the Russo-Finnish War and to ask Sweden for transit rights

[25] See W. N. Medlicott, *The Economic Blockade*, I (London, 1952). "Blockade," writes Professor Medlicott, ". . . adorned and transmogrified with a new name [economic warfare] . . . had become in 1939 Britain's secret weapon" (p. xi). For the American experience, see D. L. Gordon and R. Dangerfield, *The Hidden Weapon: The Story of Economic Warfare* (New York, 1947).

across Sweden can be understood more easily if one remembers that this West-to-East troop movement would cut off the North-to-South flow of rich Swedish ore. It also, of course, seemed to offer escape from stalemate in France by opening up a battlefield in the North where the lightning blow deftly struck would knock Hitler off balance. It was a left-hook strategy for World War II somewhat similar in conception to Churchill's shattered dream of World War I, the right-hook strategy which underlay the Gallipoli campaign.

In the upside-down world today, the competition for industrial potential, as well as the bidding for neutral support and the pressure on neutrals to cease giving the enemy all kinds of valuable things, may be more characteristic of cold than of hot war; for it is in cold war that staying power and indirect maneuver involving the co-ordination of foreign and military policies are decisive. A third world war may very well not last long enough for the skillful waging of economic warfare, or for any other slow-acting measures such as the bombing of industrial targets, to affect the outcome significantly. Neither can the capacity to provide massive economic and military aid to one's allies help very much if the war is short.

It follows that effective efforts to deprive the opponent of crucial items of supply and to make up for the deficiencies of one's friends and allies ought to precede the outbreak of war. Indeed, if the object is to deter a prospective aggressor, they must precede.

It has been an object of American legislation and American diplomacy to cut off the supply to the Soviet Union and to the Chinese People's Republic of goods which it is believed would aid in their rearmament effort, but it would hardly be argued that this effort has been as significant as that to strengthen America's non-Soviet friends and allies by economic and military aid. The aid program, which has now persisted for a decade, was at first primarily economic and primarily oriented towards Europe. The combination of the ending of the American atomic weapons monopoly and the Korean aggression tended to shift the emphasis to military aid and to include Asia as well as Europe.[26]

[26] William T. R. Fox and William W. Marvel, "Military Assistance and the Security of the United States, 1947–56," in *The Military Assistance Program of the United States* . . . prepared at the request of the Special Committee to Study the Foreign Aid Program, United States Senate (Washington, Government Printing Office, 1957).

As the foreign aid program has come to be seen not as a "one-shot" emergency program for Europe but as a continuing program for the whole non-Soviet world in a cold war of indefinite duration, the program has had to be brought into harmony, country by country and region by region, with the whole of the foreign and military policies of the United States.

So long as the American atomic arms monopoly persisted, the need for close co-ordination of foreign and military policy, and of aid policy with both, was perhaps not so urgent. Since 1950, the opponent knows that the ultimate sanction cannot be lightly invoked by the United States or by the Soviet Union. A multiple system of deterrents resting on coalition military planning and massive foreign aid, as well as on United States rearmament, drives the diplomatists and the military people into ever more inescapable peacetime collaboration with each other, and with their fellow diplomatists and soldiers abroad of states within the coalition.

VI

In the World War I period, Allied statesmen and soldiers had to work with each other and with their foreign opposite numbers in a degree of intimacy previously unknown. The preceding decade of Anglo-French military staff conversations had achieved more technical than policy co-ordination. The wartime experience was novel and at times bitter.[27] Lloyd George was not happy in his relations either with his senior military commanders or his gallant French ally. It is remarkable how much more smoothly Anglo-American relations appear to have been in the Second World War than had Anglo-French relations been in the First World War. It may have been the experience of the earlier war or it may have been the development of efficient instruments of inter-service, inter-departmental, and inter-ally collaboration. Of course, it may also have been a clearer recognition by the partner in the more immediate danger of its desperate need for help and of the consequent absolute necessity for having good relations.[28]

[27] There are many memoirs by civilian and military participant-observers of which Lord Beaverbrook, *Men and Power* (London, 1957) is only the most recent. See especially the books by General E. L. Spears concerning Anglo-French relations on working levels in both wars, including *Prelude to Victory* (London, 1941).

[28] W. H. McNeill, *America, Britain and Russia: Their Co-operation and Conflict, 1941-1946* (London, 1953), pp. 5-20, emphasizes a closely related point, that

Apparently, it was more than simply the accidental felicity of the personal relationship between Franklin D. Roosevelt and Winston Churchill or that between Roosevelt and General George C. Marshall.[29]

Even without the Hitlers and Stalins, Anglo-American soldiers and diplomatists would have had to work together more closely in the period since 1945 than in earlier days. The new necessity to make war plans on the assumption that the first days might be decisive in a new war means that it is preparedness before the war crisis rather than mobilization after it, on which security depends. The new recognition that in two-way atomic warfare the cost of victory would be hardly less than the cost of defeat—there is not much satisfaction in having one's major cities spared from destruction for ten or twelve hours longer than the enemy's—means that force is mobilized so as to emphasize deterrence. But deterrence requires that the force be available in time to deter, as for example the United States Sixth Fleet was in the Eastern Mediterranean during the years before NATO and the Mutual Defense Assistance Program had brought Western Europe back to the point at which there was some hope of defending that area against direct attack. Recognition of the unacceptability of two-way atomic war seems also to have given a new importance to means of pressuring the opponent less drastic than two-way nuclear war. If local aggression can be countered locally and neither side wants two-way nuclear war, then the aggressor can be held. He was so held in Berlin at the time of the air-lift and in Korea, though it has now become a partisan controversy as to just what kind of a victory was foregone there by one administration or what kind of peace was made by its successor.

The local aggressions as well as the general aggressions have to be deterred or defeated; for, as has been frequently said, being nibbled to death is as fatal as being devoured at one bite. This need to counter local aggressions as well as to deter a major aggression means an Amer-

---

the United States had far greater power potential than Great Britain. However, with beleaguered Britain fully mobilized and in need of further help, it could hardly have made much difference just what were the respective power potentials of the two countries if neither had been mobilized or committed.

[29] The recent publication of selections from Lord Alanbrooke's diary, in Arthur Bryant *The Turn of the Tide* (London, 1957) suggests that the *apparent* lack of friction was the result not only of the absolute necessity for Britain not to risk an open break but may be due in part to the fact that all the participants have not yet "told all."

ican concern with the military situation in Asia and in Europe. It gives a new importance not only to application of force in peace, but also to its use for demonstrative purposes. The Berlin air-lift was as notable as a logistic feat for American air power as it was for its success in checking local aggression locally.

Finally, the very long lead-time between decisions to arm and the delivery of end-items means that mobilization planning and coalition military planning must not only precede an actual war crisis, but that the critical planning choices have to be made several years ahead. Thus, the soldier has to be consulted at the highest levels of government in peace as well as in war. He has to work with the foreign affairs specialists in the field as well as in Washington.

There are, in fact, about as many United States military officers assigned abroad in some representative capacity as there are foreign service officers, somewhat more than two thousand in each case. There have long been service attachés and military training missions. The latter were common before the First World War, particularly in the Near East and in China.

What is novel today are the Military Assistance Advisory Groups which the United States sends to about thirty foreign countries. They go abroad to advise foreign governments in connection with applications to the United States for assistance under the Mutual Security Program, officially called the Mutual Defense Assistance Program (M-DAP). They also report on the use being made of military end-items already supplied. Members of MAAG groups are thus both inspectors and negotiators.[30]

A particularly interesting United States mission abroad is the mission in Paris headed by the United States special representative to NATO and certain other European international organizations (USRO).[31] In this mission is the Defense Annual Review Team (DART) which analyzes the military plans of all NATO members prior to the Annual Review at the December meeting of the NATO Council. As chief provider of military assistance to the Western Euro-

[30] W. T. R. Fox, "Military Representation Abroad" in *The Representation of the United States Abroad*. Final edition of background papers and final report of the Ninth American Assembly, Graduate School of Business, Columbia University (New York, 1956), pp. 120–154.

[31] Located in the Hotel Talleyrand, USRO is quite separate from the United States embassy in Paris.

pean defense establishments, the United States has a certain measure of influence with NATO members, though events in 1956 along the Suez Canal suggest that the United States has less influence on British and French policy outside Europe than American officials may have believed. But its influence, Suez or no Suez, is certainly very great on coalition military planning for Europe. The Defense Annual Review Team helps it to exercise that influence in a discriminating way.

Whether through DART or through the MAAG's, the flow of military information to Washington must be without parallel, for a request for military aid can hardly be justified without rather full disclosure of a country's strengths and weaknesses. It has even been said that the age of dollar diplomacy has been succeeded by the age of M-DAP diplomacy. Certainly, the supply of wanted military end-items—including more than 7,000 planes and 38,000 tanks and other combat vehicles prior to 1956—valued at more than eleven billion dollars, must have made easier the task of coalition military planning.[32]

VII

The tendency in the post-war period to use retired military men as ambassadors—such as Admiral Alan G. Kirk and General Walter Bedell Smith, both sent to Moscow—and as high officials in the State Department—General Marshall and General Smith have been Secretary and Under Secretary, respectively—is sometimes cited as evidence that the military's role in diplomacy has, at least in the United States, expanded "too far." Several comments are possible.

(1) This tendency was particularly marked in the Truman administration. When at the conclusion of the war the nation's industrial, financial, and intellectual leadership was rushing pell-mell back to civilian pursuits, all but military leaders seemed to be in short supply for ambassadorial appointments. Civilians of comparable quality may not always have been available, and if they were, may not have been known to President Truman, who was so suddenly elevated to the presidency. The tendency now appears to be declining.

(2) In the United States, and in England too, there is a barrier to civilian understanding of military problems even among talented and

---

[32] See "Report to Congress on the Mutual Security Program" by the President of the United States, semi-annual since 1951. Figures cited may be found in "Report—for the six months ended June 30, 1955," p. 1.

responsible students of public affairs. This barrier, which earlier in this paper was attributed to the Cromwellian heritage and to the quasi-pacifistic heritage of nineteenth-century liberalism, was called the "civilian mind." It has often led to a certain impatience with diversions of national energies into national defense and international politics. During many, indeed during most, years of American history, the military threat was remote. It is not remote in the 1950's, and attitudes have accordingly to be revised. The threat is by no means exclusively military, and diplomacy today requires a capacity to deal with a breadth of military and non-military considerations without parallel. The political training of the military leadership in war colleges and elsewhere, and the politico-military experience in military assistance programs, in coalition military planning, and in a variety of overseas and Pentagon assignments, has produced at least some military men who are broader in their outlook than many civilians who might be appointed in their stead, particularly those whose outstanding qualification for foreign appointment has been the size of their contribution to the victorious party's campaign in the previous presidential election.

(3) The three types of activity which formerly the United States was able to delay until after an actual war crisis—high-level mobilization, massive economic and military aid to its friends and allies, and coalition military planning—are all, as was observed earlier, driving civilian diplomatists and military diplomatists together and keeping them together. Whether military men are occasionally appointed to the highest posts in the Department of State or not, their participation in the formulating and implementing of national security policies and in the negotiations with foreign governments which are the logical consequence of these policies will continue to be very great.

Chapter 5

THE ROLE OF INTERNATIONAL LAW

IN CONTEMPORARY DIPLOMACY

Quincy Wright

THE writer has elsewhere defined diplomacy "in the popular sense" as "the employment of tact, shrewdness, and skill in any negotiation or transaction" and "in the more special sense used in international relations" as "the art of negotiation, in order to achieve the maximum of group objectives with a minimum of costs, within a system of politics in which war is a possibility." [1]

This definition indicates that the term diplomacy is used to describe both the methods used by the agents conducting the foreign affairs of a state and the objectives which such agents seek to achieve. In the first sense it is almost equivalent to the term "negotiation," implying methods of persuasion rather than coercion, and is, therefore, contrasted with war. Negotiation, however, under conditions where physical coercion is practically impossible, as in business or domestic government, is not usually called diplomacy. In the second sense, diplomacy is almost equivalent to foreign policy and implies devotion by its practitioners to the national interests of their respective states. It is, therefore, contrasted with international law which implies that respect for the international legal order is an end superior to the national interests of the state. Foreign policy, however, conducted without respect for such basic principles of international law as *pacta*

[1] Quincy Wright, *The Study of International Relations* (New York, 1955), p. 158. See also C. K. Webster, *The Art and Practice of Diplomacy* (London, 1952); Harold Nicolson, *Diplomacy* (2nd ed., New York, 1952), p. 13.

sunt servanda, cannot effectively utilize negotiation but becomes war, either hot or cold, and so is not diplomacy. Thus diplomacy, though contrasted with both war and law, implies the existence of the first as a possibility and of the second as a potentiality. Diplomacy does not exist either in a "state of nature," which Thomas Hobbes described as a *bellum omnium contra omnes,* or in a developed state of society, where law is effectively administered. It is characteristic of the society of nations where war is possible and law is imperfect.

The essence of diplomacy, therefore, is flexibility, adaptation to continually changing conditions.

It escapes the rigidities of military tactics on the one hand and of the application of law on the other. Although in both law and war, as in all the practical arts, the circumstances alter the means or even the ends of action and the applicability of generally accepted principles and rules, yet this is true in diplomacy to an exceptional degree. The art of war proceeds by deciding upon objectives and then seeking to achieve them even at great sacrifice. The will to achieve the objective is the essence of war. The art of law proceeds by establishing rules and principles to which behavior must conform and tends toward a system of *positive law* in which the opportunities of interpretation are reduced and rigidity increases. Negotiation, however, cannot be successful if it assumes the logical form either of a plan to be realized, of a principle to be applied, or of a rule to be observed. It must rather assume the logical form of a dialectic or conversation in which each event is in a degree creative of the next. Diplomacy, more than either war or law, proceeds by a process of action and reaction. Initial plans, general principles, and customary rules are adapted and modified until at the end those relied upon by both participants may have been radically altered. History is, therefore, the natural form for expounding the art of diplomacy. Its essence is in the process by which a result, unplanned, unforeseen, and undetermined at the beginning, emerges at the end. The possibility of such a result depends upon a certain vagueness and flexibility of expression, upon attitudes of opportunism and expediency, and particularly upon a refusal to close doors. Ultimata mark the end of negotiation. . . . Diplomacy always leaves every possible solution open. It closes only those which are impossible.[2]

Diplomacy is, therefore, closely related to both war and law. This chapter confines attention to the latter relationship, which has varied considerably in different historic periods.

[2] Wright, *op. cit.,* p. 164.

Modern international law, which began to develop in the practices of diplomacy, trade, and war during the late Middle Ages,[3] was formulated by theoretical writers in the sixteenth and seventeenth centuries, as the hierarchical structure of the Middle Ages, dominated by the papacy, gave way to a system of equal territorial states.[4] The invention of gunpowder and artillery capable of destroying feudal castles, and of the printing press capable of widely distributing vernacular literatures creative of a national consciousness; the Reformation destroying the unity of religion and the Renaissance informing of conditions in antiquity; the rise of science and geographical discovery altering the prevailing picture of the world; and the development of critical history, exhibiting the role of power in politics, all contributed to this transition. Human thinking, however, adjusted itself slowly, and the period was one of almost continuous war in which competitive religious ideologies and emerging national ambitions both played a part.[5] When these struggles had been in a measure settled by the Peace of Westphalia (1648), the dominant position of sovereign territorial states was recognized and a system of international politics began to emerge based upon the expediency of maintaining an equilibrium of power for the security of all. This system was formally accepted in the treaty of Utrecht (1713) as the basis of European order. Only after that did modern international law which had existed in sporadic practices and theoretical treatises for several centuries, exert much influence.[6]

In the eighteenth century, the impact of international law on diplomacy and also on war was important, especially through its definition of diplomatic privileges and immunities, of procedures and formalities of treaty making, of rules and principles of treaty interpretation, of rights of neutral commerce in time of war, of rules of land warfare, and of the limits of state territory on land and sea.[7]

The influence of international law on diplomacy decreased during

[3] Julius Goebel, *The Equality of States* (New York, 1923); Georg Schwarzenberger, *Power Politics* (New York, 1951), pp. 29ff.

[4] Edwin D. Dickinson, *The Equality of States in International Law* (Cambridge, [Mass], 1920).

[5] Quincy Wright, *A Study of War* (Chicago, 1942), pp. 166ff., 598ff.

[6] *Ibid.*, pp. 196ff., 332ff.

[7] *Ibid.*, pp. 335ff., Sir Geoffrey Butler and Simon Maccoby, *The Development of International Law* (New York, 1928), pp. 193ff.

the period of French Revolutionary and Napoleonic Wars, when ideas of nationalism, of human rights, and of mass warfare were developed with the emergence of the industrial and democratic revolutions. The contrast of this period with that which preceded it was noted by Dugald Stewart in 1816. He bracketed the works of Grotius with those of Locke, Montesquieu, and Adam Smith as "the works which have most directly influenced the general opinion of Europe during two centuries." "From the peace of Münster to the French Revolution," he wrote, "the law of nations was a principal part of the education of all politicians" and the treatises on the subject "were appealed to by all sovereigns and states in their controversies." Consequently, "it was scarcely any longer a metaphor to call Europe a commonwealth in which the energy arising from national distinction was reconciled with the order and safety of general laws." But, continued Stewart, writing soon after Waterloo, "In our times" international law "began to be openly renounced in the most wretched period of rage and fear; furious enthusiasm or uncontrollable despotism for the time seemed to have banished it from Christendom." [8]

The following century, from Waterloo (1815) to the Marne (1914), witnessed an increasing influence of international law. This was the most peaceful period of European history since the *Pax Romana* of the Antonine Caesars. Aside from the Crimean War and the wars of Italian, German, and Balkan nationalism, there was peace in Europe, though European armies were developing empires overseas and non-European states were fighting major civil and international wars in Asia and the Americas.[9] Great Britain, with the dominant navy, was able to maintain a balance of power among the great states of Europe and to give effective support to principles of international law, especially those defining the operation of the diplomatic and consular systems; the modes of acquisition and determination of the boundaries of territory; the freedom of the seas subject to belligerent rights of capture in times of war; the sanctity of treaties especially those establishing the European system; the responsibility of states for injuries to aliens; and the procedures of negotiation, mediation, and arbitration.

Within this framework of power equilibrium and legal principle,

---

[8] *Edinburgh Review*, XXVII (1816), 235; XXXVI (1821), 244.

[9] Quincy Wright, "The Historic Circumstances of Enduring Peace," *Annual Report of American Historical Association*, 1942, III, 363ff.

and utilizing the agencies and procedures established and regulated by international law, diplomacy functioned to settle international disputes, to adjust problems arising from overseas expansion; and to tidy up European states and boundaries, often through the "Concert of Europe" as in the Belgian and Balkan problems; and sometimes through the toleration of limited wars as those utilized by Cavour and Bismarck to unify the Italian and the German states. The extensive use of arbitration, reintroduced to international practice by the Jay Treaty of 1794; the movement for codification of international law initiated by the Declaration of Paris of 1856, and the development of international cooperation in matters of river navigation, postal and telegraphic communication, public health, the elimination of the slave trade, standards of weights and measures, and other matters through multilateral treaties (international legislation) and administrative organizations (public international unions) provided the community of nations with embryonic agencies of adjudication, legislation, and administration. At the same time, guarantees of independence and neutralization to critical states, such as Switzerland, Belgium, and Luxembourg, indicated a possible development of international executive agencies. These developments culminated in the Hague conventions of 1899 and 1907 designed to crystallize international law through codification, especially of the laws of war and neutrality, and the facilitation of arbitration and other means of pacific settlement; and to stabilize the power equilibrium through regulation of armament.

These objectives were only partly achieved. German dissatisfaction with the distribution of power in Europe and overseas, as its industrial potential and naval power began to rival those of Great Britain; new nationality movements in the Hapsburg Empire, the Balkans, and the Arab area; the entry into high politics of non-European powers, especially the United States and Japan; and the changes in military technique, especially the emerging possibilities of the submarine and the airplane increasing the vulnerability of the British Isles, all of these factors tended to impair the capacity of Great Britain to maintain the balance of power and contributed to the outbreak of World War I.[10]

As, at the time of the French Revolutionary Wars, the influence of international law was reduced. Established principles of the laws of

[10] *Ibid.*, p. 368.

war and neutrality were violated. Time-honored boundaries in Europe were modified. New states were born and old states disappeared. Diplomacy after the war functioned in a less clear framework of legal principle, yet the establishment of the League of Nations and the Permanent Court of International Justice, and the progress of disarmament in the Washington Conference (1921) and the League discussions gave a new confidence to international lawyers, in spite of the defection of the United States from the League of Nations and the anxiety about Russia and China, both in a state of revolution. The interwar period, especially after the adjustment of relations with Germany at Locarno, was one of juristic optimism.[11] The organization of the community of nations, developed in the system of the Hague Conferences, seemed strengthened and expanded by the League and related organizations, and the opportunities for multilateral or conference diplomacy, supplementing bilateral diplomacy, seemed adequate to provide the necessary flexibility under a general regime of law.[12]

Russia, it is true, riven by revolution and at first politically and militarily weak, indicated its contempt for traditional international law, but adjusted itself to diplomacy within international law as its leaders became convinced that this was necessary if the Soviet Union was to be recognized. When Hitler and Japan became threatening, Russia entered the League and sought to strengthen collective security and the legal conception of aggression. China, weakened by revolution, invoked the League and international law to defend itself from Japanese aggression.

The immediate threat to international law lay less in the countries upset by leftist revolution than in their neighbors. The confidence in international law and organization manifested by the great Western powers, though more in the expressions of jurists than the practice of statesmen, was not shared by important elements in Italy, Germany, and Japan. Italian fascism, seeking expansion and power, while accepting the League during the 1920's, was by nature hostile to the law which it supported. Germany, eager for revenge, fearful of bolshevism, and aware of the weakness of the successor states carved from the

---

[11] Quincy Wright, *Research in International Law Since the War* (Washington, 1930).

[12] Maurice Hankey, *Diplomacy by Conference* (New York, 1947); Nicolson, *op. cit.*, pp. 154ff.

Hapsburg and Romanoff Empires, was ready to heed Hitler's urgings for revolt from the legal system established by the Versailles Treaty. Japan, worried by the Chinese Revolution, beset by population problems, and resenting the discriminations in American immigration and tariff policies, though at first an exemplary League member, generated parties ready to embark upon ventures forbidden by the law. It may be that the very strengthening of international law through the new organizations contributed to the determination of the dissatisfied elements in these countries to make common cause in upsetting the whole system. In any case, after these countries had more or less outlawed themselves by their ventures in Manchuria, Ethiopia, and the Rhineland, they combined in the Axis alliance for that purpose.[13]

World War II was more devastating to international law than had been either the Napoleonic Wars or World War I. Little attention was paid to the laws of war and neutrality by either side as military strategists found advantages in uses of the submarine, airplane, high explosives, and atomic bombs which those laws did not sanction. Racial and ideological concepts destroyed respect for the laws concerning prisoners of war and reintroduced the concept and practice of genocide. Military occupations, ideas of national self-determination, and the propaganda of communism shattered empires. The relative power-position of Europe as a whole declined while that of America and Asia increased. After the war, the United Nations Charter, the renewed World Court statute, and the Nuremberg interpretation of the Kellogg-Briand Pact provided a more thoroughgoing system of international law to maintain collective security than had the League system. But the effectiveness of that law was seriously impaired by the ideological split between communism and democracy, by the new conditions of technology, and by the demands for self determination and influence of the new states of Asia and Africa voiced at the Bandung Conference (1955). Furthermore, the extreme instability of the power equilibrium, because of the bi-polarization of power with the establishment of the NATO and Warsaw Alliances and the creation of power *vacua* consequent upon the temporary disappearance of several great states, undermined the foundations upon which international law had rested.

Many statesmen were convinced that the traditional international

[13] Quincy Wright, *A Study of War*, pp. 342ff., 1319ff.

law of the Hague conventions was obsolete, but the new international law of the Charter was untried and uncertain.[14] Consequently politics dominated law.[15] Writers on international relations warned against "legalism and moralism" in foreign policy and suggested that diplomacy should be guided by national interest alone.[16] Orators in the United Nations seemed more intent on propaganda than on utilizing legal standards and peaceful procedures to settle differences. Resorts to the World Court, whether for decision or advisory opinion, were less frequent than during the League period, and the work of the United Nations International Law Commission aroused little interest among either governments or jurists.[17]

A change in the situation may be detected since the passing of Stalin and the development of a general conviction that war with hydrogen weapons would be devastating to all countries. The atomic stalemate has directed attention to the need to revive international law and to control armaments if peace is to be put on a more stable basis than mutual fear.[18] It is recognized that the task of achieving disarmament agreement, of solving major international controversies, of stabilizing the power equilibrium, and of reducing international tensions are problems for diplomacy; but it is coming to be recognized that diplomacy cannot function without law. References to the need for international law had been increasingly abundant among statesmen. Thus, Secretary of State John Foster Dulles said in addressing the American Society of International Law in 1956:

When we review the task of making peace a stable institution through processes of law and justice and enforcement thereof, it is easy to become

[14] Quincy Wright, *Contemporary International Law, A Balance Sheet* (Garden City, 1955); "International Law and the United Nations," *Academia Inter-Americana de derecho comparado e internacional, Cursos Monograficas,* V (1956), 319ff.; *The Study of International Relations,* pp. 228ff.

[15] Quincy Wright in *Law and Politics in the World Community,* George A. Lipsky, ed. (Berkeley, 1953), pp. 3ff.

[16] George Kennan, *American Diplomacy, 1900–1950* (Chicago, 1951, p. 95; Hans J. Morgenthau, *Scientific Man versus Power Politics* (Chicago, 1946).

[17] Shabtai Rosenne, "The International Court and the United Nations," *International Organization,* IX (1955), 244ff.; Hersh Lauterpacht, *American Journal of International Law,* XLIX (1955), 16ff.

[18] On November 3, 1953, Prime Minister Winston Churchill told the House of Commons, "When the advance of destructive weapons enables everyone to kill everybody else, nobody will want to kill anyone at all." *Parliamentary Debates,* Vol. 520, col. 30.

discouraged. We must not, however, admit of discouragement, because the task is much too important. The fact that the task is difficult, and that the road to the goal may be long, is a reason not for delay or for despair, but rather for greater urgency and for greater effort.[19]

What then should be the role of international law in diplomacy. I suggest that international law may serve (1) as an assumption, (2) as an instrument, (3) as a result, and (4) as a goal of diplomacy. Let us consider these four relations.

1. *International Law as an Assumption of Diplomacy.*

Diplomacy functions in a nebulous field but it must take something for granted. Governments cannot negotiate unless they can take for granted the immunity of the diplomat who represents them, the mutual observance of agreements arrived at, a common understanding of the situation under discussion, and a common acceptance of relevant facts. Each of these requirements may be considered in greater detail.

Governments must take it for granted that their diplomatic agents are not under physical duress or other pressures which would prevent them from fully employing their ability to carry out their instructions. It is true that the development of telephonic communication and aerial travel make it more possible for chiefs of state and foreign ministers to limit the discretion of intermediate representatives, but the services of the diplomat in personal contact with other diplomats remains indispensable, and so long as it is, common observance of the rules of international law defining diplomatic immunities must be assumed. Regular diplomatic intercourse is impossible except between states that have a high degree of mutual confidence that these rules are understood and will be observed. It is, therefore, not surprising that this branch of international law was the first to develop historically and that revolutionary groups, though sometimes inclined, in their enthusiastic desire to reconstruct the world on an entirely new model, to repudiate pre-existing international law, discover, as soon as expediency demands negotiation with other groups that they must accept at least this part of it.

Governments must also be able to take it for granted that if diplomatic negotiation results in agreement, this agreement will be observed; at least so long as the conditions which led to it continue.

[19] American Society of International Law, *Proceedings*, 1956, p. 23.

The principle *pacta sunt servanda* has been regarded by some jurists as the basic norm of international law, and philosophers like Thomas Hobbes have believed that men cannot emerge from the "state of nature" in which there is a condition of war of all against all without organizing in a society which maintains this principle.

The "cold war" has been to a considerable extent a consequence of the lack of confidence between the communist and democratic worlds. "Soviet promises," said Secretary of State Dulles in a broadcast on July 22, 1957, "have not proved dependable. We will not change our military posture merely in reliance on paper promises." Therefore disarmament agreements must provide such provisions for inspection that violations can be immediately detected.[20] To similar effect, the Soviet leader Nikita Khrushchev said on July 26, 1957 to a group of American tourists: "We have to live on the same planet in war or peace. The latter implies confidence. We did not ask you to empty your pockets before entering my office—we had confidence in you as nice people." [21]

The value of mutual confidence in good faith as a background for diplomacy is less obvious and less absolute than is the value of mutual confidence in respect for diplomatic immunities. Machiavelli thought good faith was less necessary than a reputation for good faith, perhaps insufficiently appreciating the close relation between the two. No state is without blemish in its history of treaty observance. All have occasionally been accused of violations and the issue of whether there has actually been a violation often becomes technical. Doubtless there are factors, other than past performance, such as common interest, common ideology, common fears which may give confidence that the results of a negotiation will be observed. However, diplomacy is greatly facilitated, if negotiating states can assume that each accepts the principles of international law which require good faith in the observance of treaties and which provide criteria for determining whether good faith has been observed in particular circumstances.

Another point which diplomacy should be able to take for granted is mutual understanding of the objects of negotiation. This implies not only that an agenda had been agreed upon and will be observed, but

[20] New York *Times,* July 23, 1957.
[21] *Ibid.,* July 27, 1957.

that the meaning of the items be understood and that there is a common comprehension of the situation. Negotiation between India and Pakistan on Kashmir bogged down in 1957 because there was a difference of opinion whether a plebiscite was intended to transfer Indian Territory to Pakistan or to determine the sovereignty of a territory to which neither had title. In 1956 negotiation between Great Britain and Egypt over the Suez Canal floundered because it was uncertain whether it was intended to assure Egyptian observance of the Constantinople Treaty of 1888 in administering the Canal or to deny the Egyptian right to administer the Canal. Discussion of the South African racial discriminations in the United Nations General Assembly has suffered because of uncertainty whether South Africa was being asked to observe an obligation of the Charter or to subject a domestic policy to the opinion of the Assembly. In all of these cases the parties differed as to the nature of the situation.

Doubtless, the formulation of a problem greatly affects the solution. Diplomats will seek to interpret the agenda and the situation to their advantage, but the more a mutually accepted framework of international law decides the *status quo* from which negotiation is to proceed and thus narrows the issues in controversy, the more likely is negotiation to succeed. Advisory opinions were often utilized for this purpose by the League of Nations, less frequently by the United Nations.[22]

It is true that legal determination of the framework of negotiation shackles the diplomat. Such determination tends to convert negotiation into adjudication, a government of men into a government of law, and as the writer has noted elsewhere: "This may not be either practical or desirable unless the field in which the decision is to function is homogeneous in respect to the attitudes, opinions, and values of the systems of action within it. In an extremely heterogeneous field, decision-making must operate through controversy, negotiation, and conciliation, rather than through legislation, administration and adjudication." [23] The field in which diplomacy functions is heterogeneous and lacking in common understanding of values. Consequently situations are by their nature flexible, and their definition must, in con-

---

[22] Above n. 17.
[23] Wright, *The Study of International Relations*, p. 580.

siderable measure, be left to the imagination of statesmen, free to build an atmosphere which may itself provide a definition.[24] In such circumstances, excessive rigidity may make for instability.

On the other hand, too much flexibility is also incompatible with stability. The more accepted rules of international law provide a definition of the situation with which diplomats deal, the more their efforts are likely to contribute to stability rather than to the aggravation of tensions.

Apart from the definition of the situation, diplomacy profits by common assumptions concerning the facts. Machiavelli paid no more respect to truthfulness than to good faith, and Sir Henry Wotton said that "an Ambassador is an honest man sent to *lie* abroad for the good of his country." [25] The expediency of these suggestions has been increasingly doubted.[26] International law favors both truthfulness and good faith by qualifying the rule *pacta sunt servanda* by the right to consider a treaty invalid if fraud is found to have occurred in its negotiation. It insists that negotiators have a right to believe factual statements made by their opposite numbers in the course of negotiations.[27] If there is mutual confidence in the observance of the rule of truthfulness, the course of negotiation may provide a common basis of factual information helpful in reaching agreement.

International fact-finding commissions of assured reliability can be of assistance. The corrupting influence of a lack of confidence has been exhibited in the difficulties of the United Nations in establishing such commissions acceptable to both the communist and the democratic nations.[28] The rules of international law facilitating the discovery of relevant facts and discouraging lying by negotiators provide a useful background for all negotiations.

[24] *Ibid.*, p. 575; C. K. Webster, *op. cit.*

[25] Izaak Walton, "Life of Sir Henry Wotton," in *Reliquiae Wottonianae*, (4th ed., London, 1685).

[26] Nicolson, *op. cit.*, pp. 107ff.

[27] Harvard Research in International Law, "Draft Convention on Treaties," Art. 31, *American Journal of International Law,* Supp., XXIX (1935), 1144ff.

[28] At a Conference at the Hague on July 12, 1922, M. Litvinoff expressed the opinion that it would be impossible to find an impartial arbitrator between the Soviet and Western worlds saying: "Only an angel could be unbiased in judging Russian affairs." Louis Sohn, *Cases and Other Materials in World Law* (Brooklyn, 1950), p. 1046.

2. *International Law as an Instrument of Diplomacy.*

Few would doubt the value of international law as an instrument of diplomacy. Its function in providing assumptions underlying negotiation may be more necessary, but its provision of means for the realization of diplomatic objectives is a more obvious utility. Diplomats need a common language, available procedures and forms for manifesting agreement, criteria for settling disputes about the substance of agreement, and arguments of persuasive value. International law can provide all of these.

The more diplomats, and the governments and nations behind them have in common, the easier is negotiation. The "group dynamists" emphasize the extreme difficulty of fruitful discussion among people with different preconceptions.[29] Representatives of nations with different cultures, conditions, interests, and languages maximize this difficulty. International law provides a common language. Its key terms are similar in all vernaculars and are defined in the literature of international law. Through sophistication in the meaning of these terms, diplomats can make themselves understood, even though the language and culture of their respective nations differ greatly.

The ambiguity often discovered in treaties may indicate failure of negotiators to achieve real agreement, but sometimes it indicates inadequate understanding of the language of international law by the negotiators. Problems of interpretation that so frequently arise over treaties emphasize the importance that diplomats be thoroughly grounded in that language.

The drafting of agreements requires more than a common language. It requires the observance of procedures and forms that will be subsequently accepted as making the instrument legally valid, and the inclusion of provisions that will maximize the probability of actual observance.

The accepted procedures of exchange of full powers, signature, ratification, and exchange of ratifications; the accepted forms concerning ratification, reservation, accession, coming into force; and customary provisions concerning arbitration of disputes over interpretation of the instrument, guarantees, and denunciation, should all be

[29] Wright, *The Study of International Relations,* p. 58.

observed if the results of displomacy are to have a maximum chance of enduring success. An important function of international law is to provide diplomats with precise knowledge of these forms and procedures.

Unfortunately international law remains uncertain on some aspects of treaty making. This is true of the effect of reservations to multilateral treaties. The International Court of Justice and the United Nations International Law Commission have expressed different opinions on this matter when raised in connection with the Genocide Convention. The International Law Commission has recognized the need for a clarification of international law on the general problem of the procedures and formalities of treaty making, especially because of the problems which have arisen with the increased use of multilateral and law making treaties, and of informal agreements. It has been preparing a draft convention on this subject.[30]

Even with the greatest care in drafting, subsequent disputes are likely to arise over the meaning of the treaty. It is a rule of international law as well as of common sense, too often forgotten by national politicians, that neither party can unilaterally and definitively interpret the meaning of an international instrument. Diplomacy must, therefore, be concerned with such disputes and must resort to international law for criteria with which to extract a meaning from the text, or to submit that task to arbitration or adjudication for solution under that law. The value of *travaux préparatoires* indicating the context of the negotiation (mischief and remedy), the relation of parts of the treaty to the whole (construction), and the presumptions arising from the expressed purpose of the negotiation (effective interpretation) and from the presumed reluctance of states to qualify sovereignty (restrictive interpretation)—these matters must be considered and on all of them international law can provide answers useful for interpretation.[31]

Finally, international law can provide the diplomat with arguments to support his cause. The diplomat's arsenal of weapons is extensive.

[30] Lauterpacht, *op. cit.* in n. 17.

[31] H. Lauterpacht, "Restrictive Interpretation and the Principle of Effectiveness in the Interpretation of Treaties," *British Year Book of International Law*, 1949, pp. 48ff.; Harvard Research in International Law, *op. cit.* in n. 27; Quincy Wright, *Problems of Stability and Progress in International Relations* (Berkeley, 1954), p. 27ff.

He can try to persuade his opponent by compromise, bargaining, or rewards, and, while direct threat or use of force registers his failure and is prohibited by United Nations law unless there is a necessity for defense or an authorization by the United Nations itself,[32] he can exert certain pressures economic and political. He may also try to create a favorable atmosphere by information or propaganda addressed to his adversary, to third parties, or to world public opinion. Such publicity may appeal to principles of morals, humanity, and civilization, as well as to national interests. Appeals to international law, however, are likely to be more effective to the broader audiences, because its principles are more generally accepted than those of any particular moral or cultural system. The diplomat, able to persuade world opinion that international law is on his side will have the advantage, and the diplomat not versed in international law is likely to let this advantage go to his opponent, whatever the actual legal merits of the case may be. So far as the parties in actual negotiation are concerned, the more equal is their power position, the more the negotiations are multilateral including some less interested states, and the more negotiations are public, the more useful is the appeal to international law likely to be.[33]

International law is especially valuable when diplomatic activity is concerned with the solution of a dispute. Diplomacy has many other objectives. It may seek to protect national agencies and national interests in the territory of another state; to protect the national territory and culture from invasion, propaganda, subversion, or other dangers; to influence the policy of another government on commercial or other matters within that government's domestic jurisdiction; to increase national or world prosperity by regulating or stimulating trade, investment, and economic development; to improve international cultural relations by exchange of persons and information; to reduce international tensions and prevent hostilities; to increase the relative power position of the state or to maintain the general balance of power; to strengthen and contribute to the functioning of alliances and international organizations; or to deal with "situations" not formulated

---

[32] Q. Wright, "The Prevention of Aggression," *American Journal of International Law*, L (1956), p. 526; "International Law and the United Nations," *op. cit.*, in n. 14, pp. 385ff.

[33] Webster, *op. cit.*

as "disputes." [34] Informational, educational, and propaganda activity; the establishment of contacts and the conduct of conversations; and the making of representations and protests may contribute to these ends without negotiation. While international law may not be directly involved in some of these activities, it is always indirectly involved because it sets limits to the methods which are appropriate by the distinction which it draws between international relations and the domestic jurisdiction of states. This distinction requires the diplomat to exercise great discretion in dealing with matters within the domestic jurisdiction of another state if he is to avoid defeating his object by developing local resentment. International law can, therefore, be of great value in indicating the reaction to be expected from any diplomatic *démarche*. Where an international obligation established by treaty or custom is under dispute, the diplomat has a *locus standi* which is lacking when this is not the case and the matter is, therefore, within the domestic jurisdiction of the other state. Very different reactions can be expected in these two situations. [35]

When an issue is sufficiently formulated to be designated a "dispute," the value of international law is more direct. Diplomacy is usually the first method attempted for settling disputes. If it fails, various alternatives are available: dictation, perhaps involving the use of force; utilization of an international procedure such as inquiry, mediation, conciliation, arbitration, or invocation of the jurisdiction of a regional arrangement, of the World Court or of the United Nations; or dropping the matter, with the hope that the issue will become obsolete or that changed circumstances may provide a better opportunity for settlement. International law cannot be neglected in any of these procedures whether they aim at a settlement or seek to select a method among available alternatives. Its rules will inevitably be appealed by one side or the other to determine the validity of the claims presented or the nature of the dispute. International law must be invoked to decide whether the dispute is *legal,* in the sense that rules of international law are available to decide the merits; *political,* in the sense that such rules are lacking; or *domestic,* in the sense that

---

[34] Situations and disputes are distinguished in the practice of the United Nations, see Charter, Arts. 33–38.

[35] Wright, "International Law and the United Nations," *op. cit.* in n. 14, pp. 362ff.

international law recognizes the competence of one party to decide the matter at discretion.[36] If it is agreed that the dispute is legal, international law is necessary to support the arguments urging a particular settlement. If diplomacy fails either to settle the dispute or to characterize it, international law may still prove useful in deciding what to do next, unless, indeed, there is mutual consent to let the matter drop for the time being. Is the use of force prohibited by a treaty, by the Charter, or by a customary rule? Are there obligations to submit to international inquiry, conciliation, arbitration, or judicial settlement? What are the respective competences in the matter of the United Nations and of relevant regional arrangements? These and similar questions can only be answered by appeal to international law and the task of finding correct answers has become exceedingly complex with the development of a network of bilateral, regional, and general treaties, including the Charter, and of divergent interpretations of their meanings and their relationships. If the issue is submitted to inquiry, arbitration, or the World Court, international law must appraise the evidence and provide the arguments; but the case will in such circumstances usually be out of the hands of diplomacy and in those of legal advocates. If the dispute goes before a conciliation commission, a regional agency, or the United Nations, diplomats will often have to present the case, but can only do so if they understand international law. This will be particularly true if a request for an advisory opinion of the Court is made in such agencies. The probable results of the Court's action upon such a request and consequently the expediency of submission cannot be appraised without extensive knowledge of international law.

It is clear from the preceding discussion that international law can be an extremely useful instrument for diplomacy especially if the objective of diplomacy is the achievement of agreement and solution of difficulties. If its object is the maintenance of tensions and preparation for war, international law may be less useful.

3. *International Law as a Result of Diplomacy.*

International law is a result of diplomacy partly because much of international law is conventional and it is the function of diplomacy

---

[36] H. Lauterpacht, *The Function of Law in the International Community* (New York, 1933), p. 159; Wright, *A Study of War*, p. 1425.

to produce international conventions or treaties. While bilateral conventions may contribute little to developing general international law, diplomacy has become increasingly multilateral. Conference diplomacy characteristically produces general conventions, sometimes called "international legislation," because they are intended to make international law among the parties. Such conventions constitute a growing *corpus* of conventional international law.[37]

States which engage in diplomacy desire their agreements to be legally binding. Consequently, they necessarily wish diplomacy, as a by-product of its activity, to develop international law. If they are opposed to international law in general or to its development in particular fields, they refrain from participating in the making of general treaties in that field. Undoubtedly the Bricker amendment movement in the United States, designed to restrict the treaty-making competence of the federal government, was motivated by opposition to the development of international standards in fields normally within the legislative power of the states of the union, and, particularly, to the development of international law for the protection of human rights and for the punishment of inhuman crimes such as genocide.[38]

Insofar as diplomacy resorts to legal arguments for the settlement of disputes or submits disputes to arbitration or judicial settlement, it contributes to the development of international law. That contribution is most important when disputes are submitted to the World Court composed of jurists versed in international law and bound by the statute of the court to apply it.

A great deal might be added concerning the way in which diplomacy has contributed to the development of international law, not only by treaties and submissions to adjudication, but also by the very process of diplomatic correspondence appealing to international law and asserting positions on the subject by formal declaration. *The Digests of International Law* prepared for the United States Government by John Bassett Moore and Green Hackworth consist largely of such fruits of diplomacy. They constitute a source of international law no less important than the opinions of courts and text writers.

---

[37] Manley O. Hudson, *International Legislation*, 9 vols. (Washington, 1932–48); Hankey, *op. cit.* in n. 12.

[38] Q. Wright, "Congress and the Treaty Making Power," *American Journal of International Law*, XLVI (1952), 48ff.

4. *International Law as a Goal of Diplomacy.*

To say that diplomacy results in the development of international law is not to say that such development is necessarily a goal or object of diplomacy. The extent to which diplomacy has or ought to have that goal is extremely controversial. Diplomats and foreign offices usually say that their objective is to serve the "national interest" and they usually define the national interest in terms of the political security and economic prosperity of the nation, sometimes adding maintenance of its independence and power position as supposedly contributing to both prosperity and security. More sophisticated diplomats often recognize maintenance of the balance of power as a national interest. Great Britain has long done so. If each state recognizes the maintenance of equilibrium as the essence of its own security, the beginning is made toward subordinating the sovereignty of the state to the stability of the world community. Policies of balance of power naturally lead to policies of collective security which become institutionalized through common organs, procedures, and rules of law to assure that aggression will always be confronted by overwhelming force. International organization to promote "collective security" is, therefore, only a planned development of the natural tendency of balance of power policies. It is the natural tendency of states, when faced by an emergency, to gang up against the aggressor, who, if successful against his first victim, is likely eventually to turn on the others one at a time. Collective security seeks to supplement this natural tendency by positive obligations, appropriate procedures, and convenient agencies to assure that common action will be enlisted when aggression begins. Whether the gain in certainty compensates for the loss in flexibility depends upon the presence or absence of general conditions favorable to cooperation among states.[39]

Public opinion and legislative bodies within a nation may define the national interest differently from the diplomats. Parties and other groups may identify the national interest with the policies in which they have a particular interest at the moment. "Economic self-sufficiency," "America for Americans," "Victory in cold war," and "Strengthening NATO," are slogans which appeal to some, while

[39] Wright, *The Study of International Relations*, pp. 140ff., 163; *A Study of War*, pp. 743ff., 749.

"making the world safe for democracy," "expansion of democratic Christian civilization," "promotion of world understanding," "Strengthening the United Nations," and "establishing an effective international legal order" appeal to others. Thus, the controversy concerning the proper goals of diplomacy may be defined in terms of what is the "national interest." Enlightened self-interest may approach the most comprehensive altruism.

States and federations have grown through a broadening of the conception of their self interest held by smaller groups. At first each considers maintenance of its autonomy and augmentation of its own power—known to the Greeks as *hubris*—as its major interest. With the extension of communication and contact with its neighbors, with increased opportunities for friction and increased vulnerabilities to attack, together with increased opportunities for fruitful cooperation, economic or political, neighboring groups become aware of the virtues of reciprocity, of the value of law, of what the Greeks called *themis*. Such developments may result in a merging of the self-interest of each with the interest of the larger group.[40]

As is well known, citizens of the states of the United States, after a century of discussion and civil war, decided that the interests of each state were, in considerable measure, merged with the interest of the United States. Citizens of western European states have been attempting, since World War II, to decide whether the national interest of each should be identified with the interests of Europe. Some have already expressed this identification by amending their constitutions to assure the national execution of the decisions of European organs.[41] Presidents of the United States have, on many occasions, said that the major foreign policy of the United States for security is to strengthen the United Nations.[42] Such changes in the concept of national interest

[40] Quincy Wright, "The Prospects of International Law," *Proceedings, American Society of International Law,* 156, p. 22f., "International Conflict and the United Nations," *World Politics* (Oct., 1957).

[41] *American Journal of International Law,* XLVII (1953), 537ff.

[42] In his State of the Union Message, January 14, 1946, President Truman said that "the security of the United States" required that the United Nations be more than a "process of consultation and compromise" but become "the representative of the world as one society," and that it was the continuing policy of the United States "to use all its influence to foster, support and develop" it in its purpose of "preventing international war." Department of State, *Bulletin,* XIV (January 14, 1946), 136–137. See also *Ibid.,* XIV (April 14, 1946), 622; XV (November 3,

can be expected to take place only gradually, often with local or general setbacks, but the conditions of the contemporary world suggest that each state can save its sovereignty only by losing it in some measure in an effective international legal order. As it is accepted in national legal orders, that the only liberty which the individual can enjoy is liberty under law, so it may be accepted that the only sovereignty states can enjoy is sovereignty under law.[43]

If this is true, international law may become a goal of diplomacy. Diplomacy may appreciate that the national interest in prosperity and security, hitherto served by developing national independence, national power, and a balance of power, may be better served by strengthening international law and the international agencies which maintain and develop it. By its success in such an endeavor, diplomacy, as the art of negotiation where war is a possibility, might become obsolete, because war as a duel between nations would cease to be a possibility even though its possibility as an international crime or as an international policing operation continued.[44]

Elsewhere, the writer has suggested such a process.

As diplomacy becomes institutionalized, it may make use of good offices and mediation; of commissions of inquiry and conciliation; and of arbitration and judicial settlement, thus approaching the methods of adjudication

---

1946), 812. In transmitting to Congress on February 20, 1948 the report of the work of the United Nations during 1947, he said "strengthening of the United Nations continues to be the cornerstone of the foreign policy of the United States." *Ibid.*, XVIII (February 2, 1948), 279. See also *Ibid.*, XVIII (March 28, 1948), 419–420. In his inaugural of January 20, 1949 he placed "continued unswerving support to the United Nations" as the first of four points which his administration would emphasize. *Ibid.*, XX (January 23, 1949), 124. President Eisenhower said in his first inaugural January 20, 1953, "we shall strive to make the United Nations, not merely an eloquent symbol, but an effective force." *Ibid.*, XXVIII (February 2, 1953), 169. On the 10th anniversary of the United Nations on June 20, 1955 he referred to the country's "unswerving loyalty to the United Nations" and "reaffirmed" the "support" of the government in "the purposes and aims of the United Nations and in the hopes that inspired its founders." *Ibid.*, XXXIII (July 4, 1955), 3.

[43] Wright, "Woodrow Wilson and the League of Nations," *Social Research*, XXIV (1957), 81ff.; "Public Opinion and Communication" in *Strengthening of United Nations*, Arthur Holcombe, editor, for the Commission to Study the Organization of Peace (New York, 1957), pp. 89ff.; "International Law and the United Nations," pp. 319ff.; "International Organization and Peace," *Western Political Quarterly*, VIII (1955), 149ff.

[44] Wright, *Study of International Relations*, pp. 151, 154, 164.

familiar within the state. It may also make use of consultation, conference, or periodic meetings of councils and assemblies as in the League of Nations and the United Nations, thus augmenting the role of common opinion and of disinterested parties, and approaching the legislative procedures familiar within the state. It may also make use of permanent alliances, guarantees, obligations of mutual assistance, and international procedures to determine and stop aggression as in the United Nations Charter, thus approaching the executive function familiar within the state. Finally, it may establish consultative and administrative agencies for performing common functions as in the international unions and the specialized agencies of the United Nations, thus approaching the administrative activity familiar within the state.[45]

With such a development, diplomacy would become merged in international organization and international law. Tendencies in this direction are to be observed, but the existence of high tensions, the differences between the western, the communist, and the Asian worlds, and the differentials in the local standards of culture, economy, and opportunity indicate that diplomacy will long retain its importance. It will continue to benefit by international law as an assumption and as an instrument. It will continue to create international law and gradually it may make the strengthening of international law its goal.

[45] *Ibid.*, p. 160.

Chapter 6

DECISION-MAKING

IN FOREIGN POLICY

Jacques de Bourbon-Busset

EVERYWHERE * in the world today, we see forces defying each other, preparing to invade other countries as well as organizing resistance to invasion. Is it possible that out of this turmoil of interests, emotions, opinions, impressions, a constructive and coherent international life can emerge? Are we simply at the mercy of events and of conditioned reflexes, or is it possible that a constructive foreign policy can be conceived by rational thought and pursued consistently in the light of reason?

Now that our planet has become a single political world, each nation has not only to face its relationships with its immediate neighbors but also to take account of the world program of foreign relations of every other nation. No longer can any state live on its own, in isolation. Nor can any continent. The interdependency of all nations is expressed by the United Nations, both in a concrete and a symbolic manner. It is reinforced by strategic necessities, and these bear a fatalistic character due to the absolute acceleration of history.

We live in a fluid world, where ideologies and political galaxies are being created, transformed, and undone at great speed. Hitlerism emerged, conquered part of Europe, and disappeared, all in fifteen years. Never before has the future been so hard to decipher. Any upset, any change is possible. It is practically impossible to draw a valid

* Translated by Professor John U. Nef, University of Chicago.

picture of the political world. The only configuration which appears to be permanent, is the existence of two colossi: the United States and Russia. But even this bipolarity could easily be upset by Mao's China, which is developing very fast in so many fields.

No state can disregard this frightful plasticity. Any day it may find itself pushed into an adventure that apparently is none of its concern: who could have said, in January, 1950, that during that very year, the world would be on the verge of a conflagration not because of Germany but because of an almost unknown country—Korea? Could a Turkish army officer have then imagined that he would be fighting the Soviet Power a few months later, not on the northern border of his own country, not even in Europe, but as part of an international army battling along the Yalu?

In short, anybody's business is the whole world's business. Since a long time ago, white spaces have disappeared from our maps. Paul Valéry foresaw in 1930 that "the time of the finished world had begun," that frontiers in the old sense could no longer exist. An explored, classified world is also the world of war and peace, indissolubly bound together. A very deep discontinuity separates our epoch from all previous ones, but never before has such an inexorable continuity bound the events which occur everywhere together with every political decision.

By whom are these decisions made? It is easy to answer: by the heads of governments and their ministers of foreign affairs. Sometimes these ministers, like the American Secretary of State, take decisions by themselves. But is that easy answer a true answer? Is it a human being who makes these decisions? Are they not explained by a kind of fate, imbroglio, which leaves to statesmen only a sort of formal liberty, which actually shrinks as the situation becomes more serious? An international crisis resembles an infernal machine, except that nobody understands its mechanism. Once set in motion nobody can stop it.

Yet do not certain decisions help sometimes to give an impulse to events? It is very difficult to answer. In the field of foreign affairs the tree is judged according to its fruits. Once the crisis is over, it is said that war has been prevented, but nothing can prove that it would have occurred. On the other hand, was it possible through appropriate decisions, to avoid the 1914 and 1939 conflicts? One can always say yes.

There is no doubt, however, that in any particular situation the adoption of a certain attitude can either slow down or speed up evolution, even if it cannot change its direction. For example, the sending of an ultimatum can be deferred, very often for accidental reasons, and this unplanned change of schedule will sometimes later on appear as a determinant, for one factor can press more or less heavily on events at one moment or the other.

The summer of 1914 provided examples both of precipitate action and of hesitation. For technical military motives the Russian government turned its partial mobilization into general mobilization as early as July thirtieth, in spite of a German warning and, by so doing, provoked the ultimatum of William II. The British government, on the other hand, had decided to intervene in the conflict as early as August third, but the effective decision to do so was deferred until the fourth, and taken only as a result of Germany's violation of Belgian neutrality. Thus it came about that two different causal series were brought into contact to light the spark of a general European war which was soon a world war.

If it is difficult to estimate the amount of liberty which the course of events allows, it is relatively easy to determine with whom the responsibility of exercising this freedom of choice lies. In economic affairs the powers of the state are almost always divided among several members of the government, but in foreign policy, these powers are concentrated in all countries in the hands of one minister—placed under the control of the head of the government. It is therefore up to the minister of foreign affairs, and him alone, to decide on a policy, for which he and the prime minister are solely responsible to parliament, or to the head of the state in those countries where parliament is only a shadow. He is the decision-making unit. Therefore, foreign policy is the sum of the decisions taken by the ministers of foreign affairs and the heads of governments. The relations between the ministers of foreign affairs and the heads of governments are the fundamental basis of foreign policy and one of the most difficult to appreciate. The relations of subordination that bind them together, the care taken by the minister of foreign affairs in order to keep his own autonomy, the fear of the prime minister that his collaborator may carry him too far towards a policy of which the parliament disapproves and that he will have to declare that he has been confronted with a *fait accompli,* the general tendency to hold numerous international meetings at the highest level, all this creates between these two men, even when they belong to the same political party, a fatal competition. (An entire book could be written concerning the relations between Churchill and Eden.) The initiative of the one will seem dangerous to the other. The caution of the one will be called cowardice by the other. The two personalities make still more difficult the delicate operation of reaching decisions which are those of two men, but which bind the entire country. And they must always reach a decision. Otherwise, the whole government has to be called in to arbitrate between them. A council of the ministers, or cabinet meeting, is usually of at least twenty persons. It cannot solve, in a few hours, problems of which such a number of men seldom know the real issues. They are more disposed arbitrarily to change the data than to propose a clear-cut solution.

There is no field where the collegial system is so dangerously inefficient (as was shown in France in June 1940) as in the field of foreign policy, where the gambler's attitude is essential, because risks have to be taken. How can one gamble when there are more than two partners involved? To vote is not to gamble, but to follow either one or the other of the gamblers, and therein lies a great difference. Some of the incoherence of the present Soviet policy may be explained by successive and contradictory votes of the Secretariat of the Party's Central Committee. Whatever the regime, the situation is alike: there is inside the government a small cohesive team chosen more for the personalities of a few men and their political weight than for the positions they occupy in the cabinet. If this restricted group has to take great decisions about foreign policy, the task of formulating the dilemma remains, nevertheless, with the minister of foreign affairs. In the end, he alone will be responsible for the execution of the policy, which therefore means that in foreign policy a decision is never taken once and for all, but is always adjusted according to events.

Decisions in foreign affairs have such serious consequences that through them the lives of all the citizens of a country can be upset in a few hours. It seems paradoxical, therefore, that these decisions should be in the hands of only one man. But it cannot be otherwise. Diplomacy can be said to be the art of arranging difficulties from day to day, and foreign policy is an adaptation to external necessities with long-term objectives. For both reasons foreign powers have to be met by a single partner. If there are more, it would be too easy to pay off one minister against another. The only example of duality in ministers of foreign affairs occurred recently in Holland. The experiment ended and is far from being encouraging.

How then does this single man, this solitary man, on whose shoulders are laid such heavy responsibilities, make his decisions? How does he assemble the data? How does he formulate the questions?

Let us not take a defeatist attitude and say that it is impossible to answer these questions. In a letter dated September, 1626, addressed to Princess Elizabeth of Bavaria, Descartes wrote: "The principal motives behind the actions of Princes are very often determined by such special circumstances that, if one is not a Prince himself or has not been for a long time closely associated with the secrets of a Prince, one cannot imagine what the motives are." It would certainly be an illusion to suppose one can describe somebody else's mental processes. Yet when one has lived "near the Prince," it is not impossible to reconstitute the atmosphere in which he works and acts. Let me attempt to do so. First, let us remember that the life of a foreign minister is spent in his office. There he is very seldom alone. His collaborators lurk about, seeking to detect his moments of solitude, and pounce on him in those moments in the hope that he will adopt the decisions they suggest.

It is a pretty common opinion that the foreign minister is only the spokesman of the administration of which he is the leader. The minister of foreign affairs is thought of as a politician, as contrasted with the civil servants around him, who have been trained for diplomacy and who are therefore thought of as competent by definition. Consequently it is assumed that the decisions of the minister have been determined by his subordinates and that he is only echoing carefully thought out views which have been whispered in his ears behind padded doors.

This summary picture contains a grain of truth. Actually this is the way things happen in the case of an inexperienced minister of foreign affairs. A sensible man, even if a little infatuated with himself, cannot risk a quarrel with a foreign government just for the sake of proving to his associates that he can get along without them. He cannot avoid the fact that when he takes office he is immediately surrounded by distrustful condescension on the part of his subordinates, who regard themselves, and are regarded by public opinion as his natural advisors, if not his teachers. Even when the minister is an older man he finds himself in the position of a young lieutenant just out of an officers' training camp faced with capable and seasoned regular army sergeants. He has to apologize for the authority he has been called on to exercise. Yet, if he does not get the upper hand from the start, he is bound to store up trouble.

His trump card is that the civil servants who surround him are all seeking their own advancement in the service. They cannot therefore neglect to court the foreign minister's favor if they wish to gain influence. This struggle for influence by his advisors is the normal climate in which the minister must operate. We must neither be astonished nor offended by this. Were it not so, the civil servants would just be nothing but rubber stamps.

The very fact that a battle is always going on, not as it is too often believed between ideological lobbies, but rather between small groups within the ministry, each following a different leader, either a high ranking civil servant or a politician, makes it easier for the minister to play his own hand. He can create a balance among these various influences fighting for his favor. The composition and cohesion of these various groups are unstable, and this widens the minister's range of choice. It is often said that a political leader is a man who binds together scattered will powers and projects them towards an objective of his own choosing. The minister of foreign affairs is rather like a man whose task is to produce an equilibrium between various competing influences and to discover his own way in spite of the contradictory guideposts which he finds at every crossroads.

In fact, he cannot escape that continual volley of veiled advice, suggestion, partial information. His is everyone's business: that of members of parliament, newspapermen, men of letters, businessmen, and of personalities in the widest and largest sense of the word. All ministers have to run the gauntlet of such a bombardment, but the minister of foreign affairs is exposed to another even more effective barrage from prominent foreigners, from his ministerial colleagues, from other countries' ambassadors, and from journalists of foreign countries. There, the sifting process which he must carry through in his mind is still more difficult. It is relatively easy for him to decipher the motives which have prompted his parliamentary colleagues and so to make the necessary adjustments in his decisions, but when he has to deal with foreigners whose sociological and psychological background is unknown to him, it is more difficult to decide what weight should be given their views. And then he has on top of this the constant parade of callers, whose remarks he would like very much to cut short—but this would subject him to an attack that he is inaccessible, that he cuts himself off from public opinion. So it sometimes comes to pass, that some chance intruder to whom he was about to show the door, rises and makes a remark of no apparent importance, which nevertheless starts in his ministerial mind a comparison, an association of ideas, which actually determines a decision that wise counsellors have been fighting against for weeks.

As a result these counsellors, whose advice has been all the more blatantly neglected because it has been so solemnly phrased, sometimes undergo emotional crises. They ask themselves whether they can go on participating in a policy they disapprove of. Their warnings become more and more frequent. For instance, many German diplomats believed that Hitler was leading their country to disaster. The case of the German Ambassador to Moscow, von Schulenburg, who in 1941 fought obstinately to prevent a break with Russia, is particularly striking. His warnings had the result that he was left in complete ignorance concerning the plans of his government. It was concerning him that Goebbels noted in his diary: "There is no doubt that a government is very wise not to inform its diplomats about changes in its policy."

Few men would dare to adopt openly this formula of Goebbels, but in their heart of hearts, many approve of it. As Richelieu emphasized in his *Political Testament,* anything diplomatic worthy of being called a grand design must be conceived in secrecy. Leaks can ruin any project whose attainment requires time and the most frequent leaks are involuntary. A foreign minister may, therefore, keep his collaborators in the dark concerning his inner thoughts out of prudence as well as of distrust.

Such distrust is almost inevitable. If the foreign secretary wants to make his own policy and not that of his office, and after all he is solely responsible for policy, he is bound to come into conflict with his service as a whole and particularly with the man who is their chief and their spokesman. In France, Italy, and Belgium, as in many other countries, this man is called the general secretary of the ministry, in Great Britain the permanent under secretary of state, in Russia the first vice-minister, in the United States the under secretary of state. The holder of this post is caught between the anvil and the hammer. If he wants to retain the confidence of his subordinates, he must not hesitate to displease the minister of foreign affairs by making known to him the reservations and fears which his chief's initiative has aroused in him. If he wants to retain any influence over the mind of his chief, he must play the part of a sort of personal technical advisor, independent of all the interests arising out of his administration and of all the prejudices which members of parliament ordinarily attribute to that closed body whose gates he would like to see more often opened to one or another of his direct collaborators, parliamentary colleagues, or former colleagues. Every administration automatically defends itself against anything alien, when it is confronted with the obligation of making appointments that the government has at its disposal and that are very often made under the influence of politics. In addition the foreign minister and other members of the cabinet who are no diplomats, fear in good faith from diplomats a routine attitude hostile to all new projects they themselves did not plan. Thence comes a desire to change the air by bringing into the administration external elements.

The life of the minister of foreign affairs is not, however, just a fight with his subordinates. With time, prejudices and reticences are smoothed away on both sides. The diplomats are the ordinary intermediaries belonging to the minister's cabinet or who are in charge of it, and who try to hasten this favorable evolution. Furthermore they all must face with the minister attacks from the press and from parliament. So, on the inside front solidarity grows through the need of meeting external opposition.

This solidarity is not without its flaws. A high official who does not agree with his foreign minister on one subject, will manage not to shoulder the argument for the government when the law is proposed to parliament. He may even indulge in a secret campaign against it in the lobbies, drawing the attention of former and future ministers to the dangers of the policy involved, begging them to prevent the government from taking this fatal step. If the minister in power and his cabinet learn of this maneuver, they proclaim it treason, and it will not be long before the culprit is promoted and assigned to the foreign service. Such are the ways in every democratic country. A balance between the government and the permanent administration is nowhere perfectly achieved.

The theoretical power of the foreign minister and his civil servants is so complete and total that there is a need for traditions and practices to hold it in check. But in any event discipline must prevail and the military principle holds in the end for every administration: they discuss matters with the chief but it is he who makes the decisions which are then executed without grumbling.

The minister is very well aware that he cannot discard technically the personnel who are already there and who know and take care of the documents which bear on every case. He is under pressure from the staff brought to bear upon him through the permanent under secretary, who is under the same pressure from his heads of departments. Policy is not determined on the level of assistant secretaries of state and heads of departments but it is on that level that the questions which have to be settled are formulated. A decision is always a choice between various opportunities, each of which is heavily loaded with inconveniences and even dangers. The way in which the alternative is presented is therefore an essential matter. If the problem is rendered too schematic, and the possible solutions are reduced to two, a third solution which may be better than either often escapes attention. By this I do not mean a compromise between two proposals, which is an inevitable result of a presentation of two possible procedures. I mean rather a quite different kind of attack on the issues. It is just here that the imagination has an important role to play, and it is by no means sure that minds accustomed to rely on administrative precedents and on examples derived from history are particularly suited to undertake such a creative effort.

But one must not exaggerate, however, the role of tradition in the shaping of foreign policy. No ministry of foreign affairs developed a body of doctrines to which the members are bound to conform. In every country there are traditions of public opinion which carry some weight and which are expressed by parliament and by the press: for example, a lack of taste felt by the Poles for their neighbors, the fear of Germany felt traditionally by the French, the jealousy felt by Spain for France. It goes without saying that such common prejudices will naturally influence the minds of diplomats who, by the necessities of their profession, are bound to read a lot of newspapers and magazines. But genuine diplomatic traditions are rare, if we except those based on strategic and geographical imperatives.

It follows that the minister of foreign affairs has a permanent problem of finding a balance in his own mental processes, between a desire to follow the line of conduct laid down by his predecessors and a desire to adjust his thinking to new circumstances whose evolution is now often so rapid that they brook no delay.

It is the problem of adjustment that confronts the foreign minister today. The ways of diplomacy have been changed so profoundly that traditional procedures often retain only a symbolic value: the ambassador is no longer that faraway character that he once was, entrusted with powers of interpreting for himself the directives he received before he was sent on his mission. In France the ambassador is always a civil servant and the only difference between him and his colleagues in the administration in Paris is that he does not use the internal tele-system of communications of the ministry, but only *telecommunications.*

On the other hand, the minister, on his trips, gets in touch with his ambassadors and sometimes oftener than with his own assistant secretaries and heads of departments. He sees more of them during international conferences where he takes them with him, than he sees of them in his own office in Paris.

It is not the minister's fault if, like a flying star, he goes from one place to the other, at full speed, followed by his satellites. His itinerant diplomacy is hardly based on discriminating choices. It is imposed upon him by the rhythm of contemporary life. He has often no more choice than a contemporary farmer when it comes to deciding between a tractor and a horse to plough his fields. It is certainly not the foreign minister's fault if the multiplication of bilateral, multilateral, and world conferences turns him and his colleagues into air-borne traveling salesmen.

This method was started by Napoleon Bonaparte, whose genius enabled him to take care completely of one problem without losing sight of the others. This method has been pushed farther by the circumstances of two world wars which made necessary frequent contacts between the allies at the highest level. So it came about, that the American and British heads of government—Roosevelt and Churchill with their foreign ministers—met ten times between December, 1941 and December, 1943.

Let me now call your attention to the number of meetings which a French or British foreign minister is bound to attend every year:

The General Assembly of the United Nations
The NATO Council
The Committee of the Ministers of the Council of Europe
The Committee of the Ministers of WEU (Western European Union)
The Council of OEEC (Organization of European Economic Cooperation)

It is to be noticed that some of these organizations hold several plenary sessions every year. And then we must add to this list the meetings between the three great, or the four great powers, meetings which are held irregularly and each one of which may last for quite a stretch of time.

Moreover the foreign ministers do not confine themselves to meetings between allies within the same bloc of states or to those of opposing blocs. They undertake journeys solely on behalf of their own governments or on behalf of their personal inclinations. And these trips are generally speaking ultrarapid trips. In 1953, the American secretary of state on a journey to the Far East visited seven countries in seven days. In each country he met and talked with the head of the state, the head of the government, and the foreign minister.

The acceleration of meetings and interviews has hardly always rendered the solution of conflicts easier. Actually their solution demands the ripening of what may be described as a certain dose of difficulties, clashes, compromises, false starts, and false returns. The various episodes in this dramatic evolution have been brought closer together for purposes of inspection by the frequency of the meetings, but their intensity has not been lessened, nor has their weight been lightened. And here is a supplementary source of those legendary shocks which ruffle the touchy vanity of ambassadors, luckily often only over matters of protocol. Now the susceptibilities of the foreign ministers are subjected to new tests. They learn to know one another better but they also bring back from these repeated meetings a rich harvest of suspicions, slights, misunderstandings, and resentments. New meetings solve some of these, but give birth to others. When the minister emerges, apparently relaxed and smiling, experts, who have got bored waiting behind doors, begin to get anxious. Has their chief been seduced, misled? Has he not made ill-considered commitments? They try to pin him down to precise declarations that he is all the less willing to make because he senses the suspicions, and they irritate him. The foreign ministers very often sin through weakness. One has to trick the other, experts always believe that it is their own minister who, being deprived of their advice, gave up too much. And in fact such meetings, which are held without any witnesses, tempt the participants to relax and to weigh their words much less carefully than around a meeting table. Words fly, they are caught by one of the participants and given a peculiar twist, then it becomes necessary for the minister to deny or withdraw what he said. A new meeting may clear up the misunderstandings but, it is almost sure, new misunderstandings will arise from it. Is it possible, out of such political impressionism, to follow a continuous line even when it is traced for a certain time by the same hand, and that is very seldom the case? A volume could be written about such celebrated meetings. And the list of them, from a certain point of view, creates a catastrophic impression: the inanity of the meetings between Laval and Mussolini in 1935 and between Hitler and Chamberlain in 1938 is sufficient to prove it.

Traditional diplomacy will not succeed in handling the new international problems whose dimensions, scale, and fluidity require great flexibility in their conception and speed in the decisions which can only come from those responsible persons: the foreign ministers.

The margin of influence of the ambassadors is very narrow in the formation of foreign policy. The reports they send home offer them almost the only opportunity they have to influence the foreign minister and his advisors in the directions that seem best. Even in the task of influencing the direction of foreign policy, the ambassador faces very great difficulties. It is not that he is likely to fall into the temptation of flattering the minister, by putting in the forefront the elements favorable to the minister's policy and hiding the impediments; though he is under a great temptation to do just this, because he knows how irritable an overworked man becomes, how allergic to pessimistic views and susceptible to subtle flattery. But the ambassador is subject to a graver danger. It is his duty not to lose sight of the general perspective of his country's foreign policy. In this context the place that has been given to the particular relations with the state to which he is assigned may seem to him insufficient and badly worked out. In the throes of such a moral conflict it is to the honor of many ambassadors that they tell their governments to forget all about the particular importance of the relations for which they are responsible.

The role of an ambassador is becoming more and more limited to maintaining and developing the relations with the state to which he is assigned, whether they are concerned with foreign trade or with cultural exchanges. In these spheres the presence of the ambassador is a stimulating force. He is first and foremost the non-specialized publicity agent for his country. Agriculture, medicine, ballet, naval affairs, archeology, aeronautics, sociology, nuclear physics, all concern him whenever his country's prestige seems to be at stake. This enumeration which I have made chaotic on purpose and which is far from complete, shows what a remarkable evolution has taken place in the notion of prestige. It is no longer a matter of face-saving but of acquiring and reinforcing the position one's own state occupies abroad. It is less the methods of diplomacy that have changed—for jet planes do not modify the way of starting, following through, and ending negotiations—than their very content. Diplomacy is no longer concerned with an abstract residue of subject matter, which is the veritable essence of generality, but with the sum of all the relations, in their most concrete form, which bind two countries together.

Thus diplomatic relations take on a total character which they never had before; they tend to melt into international life as a whole instead of being as they once were, practically the sole and special expression of this life. As the world has become a single political unit, diplomacy has ceased to be a special subject.

And it is at the ambassador's level much more than at the minister's that the necessary synthesis is achieved. Surrounded by his specialized attachés, military, commercial, cultural, social, always in contact with accredited experts, the ambassador tries to keep the map of the relations between his own country and the country in which he lives constantly up-to-date. It is his responsibility to understand the political meaning of an economic decision, to realize an industrial objective, to put the brakes on an expert who has mistaken himself for a diplomat, and to have his collaborators enlarge their contacts until they reach the most varied circles. His aim is to weave a network of relations, at once wide and firm, so that their range and complexity can, if need be, provide a shelter from the consequences of international misunderstandings, and even of a temporary rupture of diplomatic relations. What is most original about the contemporary ambassador is the role he is assigned, of acting as an animated and sometimes as a hidden conductor.

Before our times, diplomatic relations were not of course reduced to the making of diplomatic reports, but the number of nondiplomatic travelers was then relatively small. In those days it was mainly specialists in foreign trade and banking, and a few of the privileged rich people who could afford to undertake what were then always long and often difficult journeys. Today, students, engineers, workers, doctors, even peasants, participate in educational congresses held in foreign countries. A continual mixing is now going on between neighboring countries and even between continents, and this contributes to the formation, if not of a world opinion, at least of links which transcend and escape state control.

So a further complication presents itself to the score or so of foreign ministers, who are overworked and almost torn apart by the problems they face, torn also between the capital cities, and who bear the responsibility for world affairs. It would certainly be most unwise on their part to neglect the clandestine and diffused opinion which is born out of the frequent meetings at all levels between intellectuals, representatives of labor, and every kind of technician.

Such meetings provide training for international cooperation better than the meetings between diplomats and experts. The essential difference between these two types of meetings lies in the fact that representatives of private associations are seldom bound by instructions and never by governmental instructions. In contrast, in the meetings of civil servants, whatever the ministry to which they belong, the representatives are very closely tied by the instructions they are given in advance of their departure. Of course it sometimes happens that these instructions were of their own making or at least that the instructions were written by their colleagues. It makes little difference. Having received them they cannot change them at their own will even when they agree on the changes. They may be entitled to a certain margin of interpretation but when totalitarian countries are involved, this margin ceases to exist. Sometimes negotiations have to be almost abandoned simply because some delegates have to wait for an answer to their requests for more instructions. Stalin did not leave much initiative to his ministers, who were very much afraid of displeasing him. That is why the stiffness of Soviet policy, which has been often contrary to Soviet interests, led the Russian delegates to settle into positions utterly out-of-date when account was taken of current events, and this for no better reason than the absence of instructions bearing on the new situation that had developed.

This is naturally an extreme case.

Yet even among the democracies, delegates who are equipped with governmental instructions, bring to the conference table an atmosphere very different from that which facilitates diplomatic bargaining.

In other words, the intergovernmental conception of international relations puts the damper on the development of any kind of international, or to speak more accurately, any supranational spirit.

A supranational spirit is found in international private organizations whose members find a solidarity within both professional or ideological limits.

In fact ideas provide a basis for international solidarity which is seldom provided by professional interest. It is very rare that the industrialists' or the farmers' interests of different countries converge. They are more often in competition. On the other hand, in democratic countries, political parties have a tendency to develop more and more on the international plane. The three successive internationals set an example. It is not necessary to insist on the essential international role played by the third international or the cominform, or of whatever took its place. In that respect, the relations between the cominform and Tito are especially revealing. It would be too simple an explanation to say that it is only a question of personal antagonism between the heads of the Kremlin and the head of the Yugoslav state. There is no doubt that the cominform all by itself and as the leading international organization of the Communist parties played its part in this struggle.

Since the war, some of the parties in democratic countries have tried to organize, much more firmly than before, on an international basis. Thus the Committee of the Socialist Parties created the "COMISCO"—Committee of the International Socialist Conference, which was later on to become the Socialist International. This did not demand a very strict discipline from its members. In any case it was entitled to take, under certain circumstances, an attitude valuable to all Socialist parties. The Christian Democratic parties created, under the name of "New International Teams," an organization of the same kind. Even the Liberals, though this sounds paradoxical, created an International Liberalism.

These examples help us to appreciate the part played by political parties in creating an international political outlook. This part is played mainly within each country. Yet there is a field in which political parties are beginning to have an effective role which cuts across national frontiers. I am thinking of the European institutions. It is obvious that this role is most efficient in restricted areas of activity. In the Council of Europe, the tasks are relatively vague, political parties do not really manage to form cohesive blocks to deal with policy as a whole. What happens is this. Socialists join the Social Commission of the Council of Europe, while Liberals join its Economic Commission. Thus they devote themselves to the subjects which concern them most directly, but they do not take the trouble to achieve any general doctrinal cohesion. The Common Assembly of the European Community for Coal and Steel provides a better setting for the real political groupings. We find there a Christian Democratic group, a Socialist group, a Liberal group. The Assembly of this community even decided to grant these new groups funds necessary to develop their activities. At the beginning of 1957, out of seventy-eight members of Parliaments belonging to the Assembly, the Socialist group included twenty. They were led by a Belgian member of Parliament who succeded Guy Mollet and they took a position as a cohesive block on some questions that involved the whole group. They organized a meeting of the Socialist parties of the member countries of the European Community for Coal and Steel.

This solidarity is obviously in strong contrast with the general world situation where any such cohesion is lacking. Thus the conference of the Socialist International held in Copenhagen, condemned the Anglo-French intervention at Suez and this obliged the French delegation to leave the conference meeting room. Nor must one forget that the

Asiatic Socialist countries created an organization different from the Socialist International, called the Asiatic Socialist Conference. This conference includes the Burmese, Indian, Indonesian, Malayan, Pakistani, Israeli, Japanese, and Yugoslav parties. It is noteworthy, that the Israeli and Japanese parties belong, at the same time, to the Socialist International.

In short it cannot be claimed that, with the exception of the Communist party, international parties have had any continuous and cohesive influence in international affairs.

It can be claimed, however, that political leaders, not as members of their parties, but as members of parliaments, play an ever more important and ever greater part in foreign politics.

Here the decisive initiative was taken by President Wilson at the end of the First World War. The Supreme Council included four statesmen: Wilson, Lloyd George, Clemenceau, and Orlando. This Council prepared, almost by itself, the peace treaty with Germany. The League of Nations, which was conceived as a true international parliament, was intended to represent predominantly members of parliament as the heads of delegations rather than diplomats who were assigned the rank of mere experts.

From that time on international relations have taken over a certain number of characteristics from parliamentary methods. The first of these characteristics has been publicity.

Wilson held that secret diplomacy had been an important source of the first world conflict. He spoke in favor of "open covenants openly arrived at." By this he did not mean that negotiations must be public, but that the texts of treaties must be published and that there must be no secret clauses. So there arose the obligation of having treaties registered with the League of Nations and, later on, with the United Nations.

One cannot be certain that Wilson's objective has been reached, but it is certain that the insistence on open diplomacy has led to a kind of contamination of his original idea. It is now the negotiations which undergo public scrutiny. There are even cases where newspapers announce secret meetings held between diplomats! That is what happened, for instance, several years ago when representatives of the Soviet and the Western powers met in New York, to discuss privately the Berlin blockade. In considering this new publicity, it is well to remember some words of Richelieu in his *Political Testament;* "If you announce a plan when it is in the slow process of execution it is the same thing as to talk about a thing in order not to do it."

The procedure of voting in the new international organization is another example of borrowing from parliamentary method. Instead of solving questions that are pending by some kind of bargaining, according to the traditional methods of diplomacy, the questions are submitted to the various assemblies in the UN: the Security Council, the Political Commission, and the General Assembly, where the delegates debate them and then vote on them. So the final solution is not a compromise between carefully worded diplomatic resolutions, but between various texts submitted to the hazards of amendments, very often improvised during the session, and sometimes clothed in a strange dress according to the fancy of the representative of a country not actually concerned with the proposed legislation, whose vote nevertheless proves decisive.

Moreover the general atmosphere of the debates often brings about a cleavage between problems that are obviously interdependent. The United Nations takes hold of a particular problem: for instance, the borders of the state of Israel, when the whole question of the Middle East calls for a general solution. Diplomacy has always been the story of a series of more or less artificial crises, but the length and the complexity of UN parliamentary discussions end up by focusing attention on some artificial aspect and by crystallizing world opinion on particular situations which are not necessarily the critical issues calling for solution at the time. It is also obvious that international assemblies are particularly sensitive to problems that may have repercussions on the internal policy of the member states. The question of Israel is a case in point and it has been for a long time. So is the Spanish question.

That is not only because the delegations include a great number of members of parliaments, it is also because the ministers of foreign affairs are very sensitive to aspects of international relations which influence public opinion at home. They focus their attention on that monster that hinders their sleep: public opinion, and this means the opinions which are expressed through the newspapers, the radio, and television. These opinions are both the reflection and the nerve of internal policy. And the interactions between internal and external policy are one of the main features of the world, today.

What is more, the minister of foreign affairs is almost always, first and foremost, a man who is afraid to displease public opinion lest this bring him into conflict with the parliament and particularly with those much feared foreign affairs committees which in every country are the nests where the Pitt, Talleyrand, and Bismarck vocations hatch. And everyone knows that a foreign minister, instead of acting as if he were his own successor, is anxious about eliminating his possible successors.

Scarcely a ministers' conference is held, in which some of the ministers fail to say, "Alas I have to think of the internal difficulties of my own government," or "Public opinion would not understand it if I took any other position." And those ministers who do not say these things may be the ones who believe them most strongly.

It follows that the diplomatic compromises which are effected reflect more the current difficulties in the internal policy of the governments which foreign ministers represent than a real arbitration of the so-called national interests, which are always very difficult to define and which are nowadays very changeable.

The problem of German rearmament illustrates this truth: in the United States, public opinion wanted to see German youth share in the sacrifices and thus lighten the GI's burden. In France, memories of the German occupation were still fresh. In the Netherlands and some other countries fears of a peripheral strategy which might uncover their territory to invasion crowded the minds of many persons. All these reflexes played a very important part in negotiations over German rearmament and determined their course doubtless much more than technical military considerations.

Nothing is actually easier than to create an artificial bundle of opinions, expressed by recognized organizations, frequently enough to produce a spontaneous convergence of minds, which then becomes irresistible.

Very often the foreign minister has no alternative to making himself the mouthpiece of opinions which he perhaps himself formerly wished to arouse.

It is consequently impossible for the minister of foreign affairs not to attach intense importance to opinions other than his own. What is called opinion is nothing else than a synthesis of the opinions of incompetent persons as to what the minister's opinion should be concerning current events. Thus, the minister has to incorporate in the action that he takes the thought of others, which in this case is as risky as the events themselves. Every statesman worthy of the name is wounded by this servitude. And he seeks to find within himself a counterweight to this external pressure which brings him no convincing motive at the time when he has to take a decision. That is when certain dogmatic schemes impose themselves on his harried mind by their simplicity and also by their historical background.

It would be easy to demonstrate that bitter memories of the Munich conference of 1938 have exercised an influence of capital importance on European leaders.

Similarly the mere mention of Pearl Harbor arouses in every American statesman certain attitudes which are very close to being reflexes.

To evoke historical precedents, even when they are drawn from the recent past, is always of dubious value. The lessons of history should help us to distinguish the present from the past rather than to confuse the two. But there is a great temptation to extract from the past, prescriptions for action which, amid the chaos of information, advice and contradictory warnings, seem to provide a leading thread. So it is with maxims such as: "It is better to do something than to do nothing," "The worst risk is not to take a risk," or, on the contrary, "Don't be zealous, great problems solve themselves."

But one has to act. The minister is urged by his critics to assemble all the advantages and to avoid all the disadvantages of action. It is an impossible task. One must choose between disadvantages and the disadvantage one chooses is the counterpart of the advantage by which one is tempted. A long range evaluation of possible gains and losses is impossible. The ultimate consequences cannot be foreseen, and even some certain immediate and practical consequences are bound to escape one's attention when one is reduced to the most elementary choice: "To move or not to move."

Here another danger presents itself, that of confusing pressures with priorities. An urgent matter is not necessarily important, but the responsible civil servants, mindful of technical efficiency, press the foreign minister to settle it. At the same time, the really essential matter is allowed to lurk in the dark; it comes to a head in spite of the neglect by the policymakers, and when it breaks it is too late to deal with it rationally, for it is already settled.

The foreign minister, in trying to escape a contingency which hounds him on all sides, wants to create some necessity on his own account, and so he tries to "have a policy." This policy begins with his initiative, that is to say with what appears to be an independent act, not imposed on him by the course of events, and it follows a dialectic of its own, to the great regret sometimes of its author.

It is normal enough that the chief diplomatic officer—the foreign minister—should want to be the creator of his country's foreign policy. The difficulty is that there is hardly an isolated decision in this field. The minister cannot keep for himself a special area where he is the only master. He must take care of everything or of nothing. Unless he is to abdicate, he must have his own interpretation of the international situation, and, if possible, formulate this in a theory. Here, more than anywhere, words play the principal part. We recently found the world, as a whole, believing in the dogma of an easing of the world political drama, with the same fervor that it had previously believed in the cold war. The execrated author of that war, Joseph Stalin, actually made the first gesture of conciliation, a few months before he died, for which his successors for a time got so much credit. Hardly a statesman is free from this verbalism. They are usually responsible for it. It is in fact less risky to diagnose a situation than to engage oneself in an action that is always a gamble. Nowadays the gesture of one little finger can loosen immense unstable rocks and precipitate a cataclysm.

Like philosophers, statesmen launch ready-made formulas. To convince ourselves of this I need only enumerate a few: "Aid to Underdeveloped Countries," "European Integration," "Pacific Co-existence." Each of them is susceptible to several interpretations, some of which contradict others. They all reveal the embarrassment of today's leaders confronted as they are with a world that has never been more closely bound together, yet never more divided, where national states have never been so numerous—each year marks the birth of new ones— and never so devoid of real sovereignty as now, where historical fatalism is invoked in every situation, where every move is made to seem contingent and reversible, where the dense traffic made possible by new means of communication sweeps along not universal ideas, but the narrowest fanaticisms, where no one knows whether a defeat of today may not prove to be a victory tomorrow, and whether a collapse may not provide the occasion for reconstruction if one does not make the mistake of supporting that which now exists as new.

As a matter of fact today the policymaker who refuses to be a mere electronic machine, has less reason to be concerned with what has been or what is being done, than with what has never been done and with what might soon be done. We live in a century of anticipation. He who can anticipate is certain to win. This is not merely a matter of foreseeing. To foresee is to remain within existing frameworks, while to anticipate is to break down these frameworks and to conceive new ones. That is why the underdeveloped countries soon have the advantage in the diplomatic struggle. In contrast with older countries, cluttered up with traditions and memories, concerned with ridding themselves of ghosts, the newer countries are likely to have the advantage of an easy stride and of the availability characteristic of youth. They are free to make and break alliances and to do so to advantage because the least certain ally is likely to be the one to whom one grants the most. On the contrary, those countries which rely on a rich past, find it difficult to distinguish the permanent from the variable factors, the principles which should be maintained at all costs and those which could be modified. This choice is only possible within plans which are worked out in detail, whose very precision make it possible, under certain circumstances, to change the details. Otherwise there is a great risk that, in the absence of clear insight concerning the relative importance of the various factors, the accessory will be mistaken for the essential, the policy will *glue* itself to positions leading to a dead end and overlook the real possibilities of the future which statesmen actually hold in their hands.

The fatal danger of improvisation is this: chance will bring to light some fact and some attitude, which responsible men adopt and present as their own decisions when this fact and attitude have been determined by events, or even by the decisions of their antagonist. In chess such tactics would quickly lead to disaster. The victor is always he who sees clearly farthest ahead.

But in politics, the game is never finished. Victories and defeats are never definitive. The stakes are always obscure and fluid.

What precise ideas lie behind such words as national interest, prestige, power? None would stand a close analysis. Is national interest what is determined by statesmen at a certain time, or what political writers deduce from their study of national history? Talleyrand's policy at the Vienna congress was a masterpiece of tactical diplomacy but the result, so objectionable from the French point of view, was to have Prussia on the Rhine. In that case, Talleyrand did not consciously act against the national interest. He did not even, which sometimes happens, prefer a spectacular short-term success, to a long-range profit, for he could not see the future then as we do looking back on it.

The only thing that appears never to change is a community of ideals. All the other factors, even those resulting from geography which apparently get their solidity from the very earth, are subject to risks. They are at the mercy of technical evolution, of those historical eddies which exalt the humble and crush the powerful.

The maintenance of a common ideal is the only objective worthy of escaping the scorn of the future; it is the only true justification of any national policy.

The tragedy of certain countries lies in not knowing how to reconcile conflicting tendencies and so in ending that healthy combat between opposed ideas, so necessary when the moral unity of the community is at stake. This is also the tragedy of humanity itself, torn, split apart yet eager nevertheless for peace and harmony. Humanity hardly believes any more in the mythology, in which it has been made to live and that is periodically crushed down under the pressure of events. The events in Hungary in November 1956 awakened it from the slumber into which its leaders had plunged it with the help of its own obliging complicity.

In 1953, at the end of his book *Man and the State,* Jacques Maritain recommended the constitution of a supranational council of wise men that would express the people's conscience. A phrase of John Nef in his article "Renewal" shows how this suggestion meets the crucial problems of our period. "Science and machinery," Nef writes, "have enabled humanity to command the material resources of the planet in ways that have made world government indispensable. At the same time science and machinery are depriving individuals and societies of the vision and of the control over themselves, which alone might make world government human and worth having."

Maritain's suggestion for a council of wise men may seem utopian. In fact it is much more realistic than Machiavellian politics. What the world needs today is much less a formal unity, based on the uniformity produced by scientific and technological progress, than deep and clear agreement among free men on some fundamental Christian principles, such as the dignity of man.

Chapter 7

HISTORY AND DIPLOMACY

AS VIEWED BY A DIPLOMATIST

George F. Kennan

WHILE our subject is the very broad one of "History and Diplomacy," I thought I would narrow it somewhat and attempt merely to describe something of the aspect in which diplomatic history presents itself to a diplomatist who has turned late in life to the study and writing of history. In doing so, I hope that I have not taken too great a liberty with the subject our hosts had in mind.

I must first offer the usual disclaimer about generalizations—in this instance, of course, with regard to that race of beings which goes by the name of diplomatist. There are all shapes and sizes of people, today, within the increasingly generous and hazy delimitations of this profession. I naturally cannot pretend to speak for all of them. But I believe that what I am about to say would meet with understanding on the part of most of those who have had their noses rubbed for long in the classic and central diplomatic function, which is the wearisome duty of negotiating and mediating between governments with conflicting interests—and that this would be true not only of those who are our contemporaries but also of a long succession of diplomatic representatives stretching back into history at least as far as the Venetians. Prior to that, I gather, very few people were ever saddled with the necessity of practicing this thankless, disillusioning, and physically exhausting profession as a permanent and regular livelihood.

Diplomatic history is, of course, only one phase of political history generally. It is a part of the study of man in his behavior as a political animal; and it concerns itself with what occurs at that particular point of friction where the activity of one sovereign political authority rubs and grates on that of another. It is, of course, the element of *sovereignty* on both sides that gives to the contact at this point that peculiar delicacy, that charged, explosive quality, that final unpredictability by which it is distinguished. All other human contacts, it seems, take place within the limits of some recognized framework of obligation, supported by some sort of physical sanction. There is always, at least in theory, some rule or some higher authority to which appeal may be taken. But the sovereign national state, this child of the modern age, notwithstanding the mantle of nebulous moral obligation in which it likes to wrap itself, still recognizes in the crucial moments of its own destiny no law but that of its own egoism—no higher focus of obligation, no overriding ethical code. I am often accused of approving this state of affairs because I insist on the recognition of its reality. Actually, I think, no one could be more sadly conscious than is the professional diplomatist of the primitiveness, the anarchism, the intrinsic absurdity of the modern concept of sovereignty. Could anything be more absurd than a world divided into several dozens of large secular societies, each devoted to the cultivation of the myth of its own overriding importance and virtue, of the sacrosanctity of its own unlimited independence? A thousand times right are the enthusiasts of world government in their protest against the philosophic childishness of this concept, however many times wrong they may be in their ideas as to how it might be corrected. But the diplomatist, as people frequently forget, is the servant of this system of national states; it is precisely to the working of this imperfect mechanism that his efforts are dedicated. He is professionally condemned to tinker with its ill-designed parts like a mechanic with a badly built and decrepit car, aware that his function is not to question the design or to grumble over the decrepitude, but to keep the confounded contraption running, some way or other.

When, therefore, the diplomatist thinks about diplomatic history, his thoughts turn in the first instance to the nature and personality of the sovereign state. He knows this in part, of course, from the example of those governments with which he has been obliged to deal as a foreign representative. But he knows it better still from his intimacy with his own government. The personality of his own government presses itself upon him over the course of the years with a great vividness, with a sort of inexorable and commanding finality. It is the primary, overriding, inalterable reality of his professional world. And he is often moved to reflect on the extraordinary nature of this governmental personality: on its imperious authoritarianism toward its servants; its indomitable self-righteousness; its smugness and self-centeredness; its infuriating air of optimism and unconcern; its preposterous claim to infallibility; its frequent impoliteness; its stubborn and impudent silences; its insistence on the right not to answer letters; its bland assumption that because *it* has not made up its mind, reality should be expected to stand still until it does. And when the diplomatist, saturated as he is with the consciousness of this personality, then chances to pick up a book about diplomatic history, or to thumb through old dispatches in some dusty Foreign Office archives, he soon observes, not without a touch of exquisite intellectual pleasure, that it is not only his own government and not only governments in his own age that are this way; but that governments have been this way for a long time in the past, throughout, in fact, the entire range of history of the national state.

Realizing this, the diplomatist is moved, first, to marvel that a number of institutional personalities so difficult, so impossible by every normal criterion of social behavior, so outrageous in all respects, should have been able to live side by side in the same world and to deal with each other as long as they have, without even a larger number of conflicts and catastrophes. But secondly, he would have to be very uncurious indeed if he failed to inquire what it is, in the experience of being sovereign, that makes governments behave the way they do. And in this way he soon finds himself led unerringly to the classical problems of political science: to the inquiry as to how men tend to behave in the exercise of governmental power, and why they behave just this way.

Now I cannot attempt to generalize about the political philosophy of the devotees of my former profession. There is probably not much more agreement among them than there is among the rest of us on these questions that have divided the contemplative portion of mankind since the days of Plato and Aristotle.

But the diplomatic representative is made aware at every point of one curious feature of the sovereign government: and that is the duality of its motivation as between national interest and party interest. I have often found in my friends among the enthusiasts for universal international organization what seems to be a somewhat naive view of the nature of the governmental voice in world affairs. These people assume that when a government speaks its word or casts its vote in an international forum, what one hears is the genuine expression of the aspirations of the people for whom it speaks. Now that may conceivably be the case and sometimes is; but it is not necessarily so; and it is rarely entirely so—for the following reason. It is clear that every government represents only the momentary product of the never-ending competition for political power within the respective national framework. In the most direct sense, therefore, it speaks only for a portion of the nation: for one political faction or coalition of factions. There is always another portion of the nation that is in opposition to it and either challenges its right to speak for the nation as a whole or accepts it only grudgingly and unhappily. This is true, in one version or another, whether the country's political life operates on the principle of parliamentary representation or whether it is based on some form of authoritarianism.

Yet it would be wrong to jump to the other extreme and to assume that the voices of governments, as heard on the international forums, reflect exclusively domestic-partisan interests. The interests of every political regime will be found to be bound up with, and in a certain area identical with, the interests and fortunes of the nation as a whole.

What emerges, therefore, from the hopper of the political process in each country and proceeds to speak for the country in international affairs is always to some degree a corrupted voice—in part the expression of national interests or aspirations, as seen by those momentarily entrusted with their definition and manifestation, but also partly the expression of the desire of one group of men to retain the power they already enjoy and to defend their position against their competitors within the national framework. And the diplomatist sees that there is very often a conflict between these two elements of motivation, and that the men who write his instructions and define the governmental position he must represent are torn, in conscience and interest, between the one and the other. He sees that in the great dramatic moments of history—especially when danger presents itself in the purely physical and external form, as when war threatens or already exists—the domestic political competition is, by common consent, thrust somewhat into the background, and statesmen even find it possible to think almost exclusively, for a time, in terms of the interests of the nation as a whole. But he also sees that in the long dull intervals between these dramatic moments, in those prosaic reaches of everyday life where the element of danger is more remote and more subtle and often not entirely external—in these times the primacy of domestic policy comes into its own and the voices that resound on the forums of international intercourse are more apt to be the voices of internal factions, intent on their competition with other factions within the given country, saying and doing on the international plane those things which, in their judgment, are most likely to promote their political prospects at home.

And this is a great pity; because it is precisely in these long, dull periods of peace that the most decisive things really happen. It is in these times that the predicaments and dilemmas are created, from which the wars and catastrophes then flow. Yet people are rarely aware of this at the moment. And by the time circumstances have developed to a point of drama and danger and simplification at which people realize that solemn issues, overriding the interests of this generation alone and beshaming the ambitions of any single political faction, are at stake, it is usually far too late for any remedy. And then all the idealism, all the capacity for sacrifice, all the comradeship and nobility of spirit are poured out—alas—into the negative undertaking of war—an undertaking which people like to picture to themselves at the moment as conducive to some glorious end; and one which may indeed, in certain circumstances, be preferable to its immediate alternatives; but one which represents in reality a physical and emotional debauch from which every people emerges in some respects poorer and unhappier, its strength and substance in some degree wasted, its youth brutalized, its social fabric weakened, its future mortgaged by the wastage of so much young blood, the exhaustion of so many hopes and energies, and the inevitable abuse practiced on the habits of its life. Into this sad and depressing exercise—the product of man's failures rather than his successes—are invariably poured his highest capacities, the ultimate of what he can muster in the way of unselfishness, heroism, and devotion. But in the long period between wars, when there is opportunity not only to avoid further debauches of this nature but also to do things that might promote the beauty and health of human existence and bring men closer to a situation where they could contemplate the future of the race with feelings other than horror and dismay—during these times, selfishness and shortsightedness again ride supreme; the primacy of foreign policy is forgotten; and the microphone for international discussion is returned to those who are interested in it only incidentally as a means of improving their competitive fortunes at home. In this way international affairs become once more a fumbling encounter among the distracted and the semi-blind—an absent-minded Donnybrook among participants each of whom is preoccupied with his own parochial problems and has something less than half an eye for this ulterior involvement.

I must confess that the professional diplomatist is often possessed by a congenital aversion to the phenomenon of domestic-political competition. He sees it, everywhere, as a seething cauldron in which there rises to the surface, by the law of averages, a certain mutation of the human species. And while this mutation differs somewhat in every country, depending on the nature and tradition of government, the diplomatist takes a dim view of it everywhere. Too often, it appears to him as the distillation of all that in human nature which is most extroverted, most thick-skinned, most pushing, most preoccupied with the present, least given to a sense of historical proportion, least inclined to be animated by any deeper and more subtle philosophy of human affairs, and—by that same token—least inclined to look deeply into the realities of international life, to comprehend the relativity of all national virtues, and to grasp the need for tolerance, forbearance, dignity, generosity, and integrity in the dealings between states. There are, of course, always the great and wonderful exceptions; we have them today—we have had them in the past. Without their efforts, God knows where we should now be. But by and large the diplomatist, sensitive as he is to the immense demands that modern scientific advance has placed on man's ability to adjust international differences, looks with misgiving to the domestic-political personality in its confrontation with the problems of international life. He has little confidence in its vision or disinterestedness, little tolerance for its egotism, its ambition, its thirst for popularity, its taste for the phrase and the cliché. The diplomatist inclines, I fear, to the view that only those men are truly adequate to the responsibilities of statesmanship who do not seek them but come to them reluctantly, from a sense of duty, and with great distaste.

Let me be quite plain. It is not the humdrum ranges of the domestic-political process to which these feelings relate. Most diplomatists understand very well, I think, the legitimacy and indispensability of the political profession—the inalterable necessity of reconciling a thousand stubborn and conflicting interests at the grass roots. They recognize the immense qualities of common sense, patience, and insight that go into this process. It is not the modest workhorses of politics to whom the diplomatic skepticism relates; on the contrary, the diplomatist feels a certain affinity to them; for their task resembles, in its thanklessness and strenuousness, his own. His suspicion and dislike are reserved for the more pompous and ruthless and successful of the political fraternity: for the bombast, the demagogue, the jingo, the poseur, the man touched with the intoxication of power, the man for whom the issues at stake in his country's relations with the outside world are means to a personal end. And too often it seems, to one looking at it from an embassy in a foreign capital, that such are the natures bound by the law of averages to be propelled most often to the surface in the uninhibited workings of political competition.

Out of such reflections is born, I think, the weary skepticism that characterizes the more experienced ranges of the diplomatic profession in their approach to diplomatic history. The professional sees the relations between governments as largely the product of the follies and ambitions and brutalities of that minority of the human race which is always attracted by the possibility of exercising power over the remainder of it in whatever political framework the age provides. He sees the task of diplomacy as essentially a menial one, consisting of hovering around the fringes of a process one is powerless to control, tidying up the messes other people have made, attempting to keep small disasters from turning into big ones, moderating the passions of governments and of opinionated individuals, and attempting to transmit to one's own government the unwelcome image of the outside world—but always, mark you, only in discreet, moderate doses, bearing in mind the lowliness of the diplomatic estate in the general governmental order—bearing in mind that the truth about external reality will never be wholly compatible with those internal ideological fictions which the national state engenders and by which it lives.

The diplomatist believes deeply in the importance and necessity of his menial function. He harbors the desperate, instinctive conviction that if he were not there to perform it, things would be much worse. And he cherishes this conviction with double intensity, because he is so lonely in it. He knows that he has little possibility of ever making his usefulness widely comprehensible to the people he serves. He knows that he could win much greater approval and popularity, at any given moment, by a liberal measure of charlatanism: by abusing the responsibilities he bears, by exploiting the ignorance and prejudice of others, by inflaming rather than assuaging the passions of men and then making himself the mouthpiece of those passions. But this, happily, is rarely—almost never—his nature. It goes against the grain of the inner discipline that his profession exerts.

As one who is no longer a member of the diplomatic fraternity, I may perhaps be permitted to say that in its obscure and tireless activity and in the modest, almost despairing view that most of its devotees take of their efforts and achievements, there is a surprising measure of real idealism, and sometimes even of nobility. But do not look to the diplomatist for any verbal acknowledgement of this idealism, for any belief in human perfectibility, for any optimistic philosophy of public affairs. The professional diplomatist is, after all, only a species of physician. He has, like all physicians, a shabby and irritating group of patients: violent, headstrong, frivolous, unreasonable. He will go on treating them as long as he is permitted to, saving them from such of their follies as he can, patching up the damages done by those follies from which he could not save them. He will do this because it is his professional nature to do it, and because he probably loves these shabby patients in his heart even while he despairs of them. But do not ask him to enthuse about them, to idealize them, or to expect them to change. Whether he approaches them from the vantage point of a diplomatic chancery abroad or from the standpoint of a late and poorly baptized historian, the difficulty is the same. He has seen them too much. He knows them too well.

Chapter 8

HISTORY AND DIPLOMACY

AS VIEWED BY A HISTORIAN

Raymond J. Sontag

DIPLOMACY has changed so greatly since the beginning of the twentieth century that the diplomatic historian is driven to wonder whether his subject has any relevance to the contemporary world. Then and now—let us set them against each other. Then Europe was the center of diplomatic action; now the diplomat's mind must compass the globe. Then he need take account of a few powers, all with settled traditions of policy. Now he must try to estimate the direction of policy in states with no settled traditions, like Indonesia, while even in older states like Italy and Germany tradition is not a safe guide. Then the diplomat was, for the most part, concerned with narrowly political subjects; now he must study and report on many and diverse subjects. Then information was easy to come by; now, over much of the earth's surface, heroic efforts are made to conceal essential facts and figures. Then there was intimacy and confidence within the group concerned with diplomacy in any country; now discussion is carefully kept within the scope of the lowest security clearance in the room. Then diplomacy was a leisurely business—Bismarck buried in the country for months on end, Salisbury deep in chemical experiments at Hatfield House, Grey feeding his beloved ducks. Today incessant activity is the mark of the statesman. "I spent 350 of my 562 days as Secretary of State at international conferences," boasts Governor Byrnes. Secretary Dulles' air mileage surely exceeded that of any traveling salesman.

Move a little farther below the surface. For all their defects, the volumes of *Die Grosse Politik* give a fairly accurate picture of German foreign policy and action. Not so the volumes of *Documents on German Foreign Policy* dealing with the Nazi years. The volume on "Germany and the Spanish Civil War" is bulky, but it does not record with any firmness the course of German policy and action; control over both had moved outside the Foreign Ministry. A comparable process has taken place in democratic countries. Year after year scholars have sat in the Department of State working through the files of the Department, selecting materials for publication in the volumes entitled *Papers Relating to the Foreign Relations of the United States*. When, however, these scholars set out to collect the papers on the Yalta conference they found "it was necessary to obtain much documentation that was never in the files of the Department of State, notably Presidential and military papers." Here is a shift, the full import of which is not yet clear. The historian is familiar with past efforts of the military to dominate the foreign policy of this or that country; he is familiar also with the impact of treasury decisions on foreign policy. But by 1945 it was becoming difficult to know how American policy was formed. All one could say with confidence was that, as the Yalta papers show, the files of the Department of State did not tell the story and that it was necessary to take into account other names like Treasury, Defense, White House. But what those names meant was not clear, and was not clear to Mr. Truman when he suddenly found himself responsible for policy. His efforts to bring order out of the confusion by the creation of the National Security Council, and the efforts of President Eisenhower to perfect the machinery of the Council are familiar to all.

These efforts are bound to awaken the admiration of the historian familiar with the more informal practices of a simpler day. Essentially what the Council machinery does, at every stage from the gathering of information up to the formulation of policy alternatives, is to coordinate the views of experts, each representing an interested agency of our government. Almost without exception the agencies have an important stake in the outcome of the deliberations. Yet the discussions proceed, usually amicably, and usually to agreed positions. The process is endlessly time-consuming, and energy-consuming, but it does work —when it is used.

Policies do not, however, implement themselves; they are implemented by the many agencies now concerned with foreign affairs. And the agencies all too often interpret the broad language of the policy statements in very different ways. To prevent confusion, the execution of foreign policy is also coordinated. This task is performed by officials with the modest title of assistants to the President, but men of cabinet stature and power.

The President has, of course, always been solely responsible for foreign policy, but traditionally the formulation of policy, and the execution of policy, were functions of the Department of State. Over the last two decades, however, responsibility both for the formulation of policy and for the execution of policy has shifted from the Department of State to the White House, that is, to the President himself.

This shift reflects the rise of our foreign relations from relatively minor to transcendent importance in our national life. The historian, watching this never-ending process of coordination cannot but wonder what the end will be. One thing is evident: the process imposes a killing pace on all who aspire to more than a routine performance of their task, a pace which kills first the ability to reflect, to stand apart from partial problems and see the problem of American security as a whole.

All those concerned with the coordinating process are aware of this result, and repeated efforts have been made to keep some few, at least, outside the pressure of day to day decision. George Kennan initiated one such experiment, the Policy Planning Staff, which was intended to be a small, carefully selected group with no fixed duties and no responsibility except to reflect on long range policy. How has it worked out? Today, when the airplane lands at Geneva, or the helicopter at Camp David, out steps the chief of the Policy Planning Staff. Some remarkably perceptive studies of American foreign policy have been written by members of the planning staff—but the studies were written after the planners had left the staff and had time to think. The history of Mr. Kennan's idea could be repeated in other agencies. By now there must be hundreds who came to Washington with the promise that they would have no duties and no responsibility except just to sit and think, and who soon found that what they had least time to do was think. It was worth bringing them to Washington, of course: it takes time for mental focus to shift from policy to the details of policy, and that time can be put to profitable use, not just once but repeatedly, if there is time for mental focus to widen again. There is at least one distinguished mediaevalist who is always certain of a warm welcome in Washington when, with mind refreshed by contemplation of things mediaeval, he is willing to look at the contemporary scene.

As the historian studies the machinery of the National Security Council, the conviction grows that this never-ending process of coordination is being asked to produce something it cannot, in the nature of things, produce, and that is precise knowledge of the future. The Council machinery—if it is not overloaded—is an effective instrument for collecting, evaluating, and presenting information. But when the last fact is in, and in its proper place, there still remains the necessity for decision on policy, and no one can estimate with precision the consequences of any decision.

That has always been true, but seldom has it been so difficult to estimate consequences, and never has the penalty for error seemed so great. Here is where the contrast between then and now is most violent and terrifying.

Consider the really decisive changes of the last half century. Then no part of the world had a Communist government; now one third of mankind is under Communist rule. The rise of Communist power has been recent and swift. Our knowledge both of conditions within the Communist world and of the men directing the destinies of that world is incomplete and uncertain. Inevitably, therefore, even experts differ widely in their estimates of probable Communist courses of action, and few are so rash as to be certain that their estimates furnish a firm basis for action.

It is even more difficult to estimate the consequences of a second decisive shift. A half century ago the revolt of subject peoples against their European masters was just beginning. Today the revolt of subject peoples against their masters, and the resentment of recently emancipated peoples against their former masters, have attained a passionate intensity which may lead to acts of suicidal recklessness. Certainly, in their efforts to cope with this revolt which convulses the non-Communist world, the diplomatists of the Western democracies must try many expedients and expect many failures, and here the diplomatist is confronted with a third change which has taken place since the beginning of this century.

While it was certainly true, even then, that the freedom of action of the diplomatist was sometimes limited by popular or parliamentary feeling and prejudice, that freedom is now much more narrowly circumscribed. At times the search for a simple popular explanation of failure has obviously disastrous results, like the recent search for scapegoats within our Foreign Service. Less obvious, but even more disastrous, is the paralysis of policy which is likely to be induced by fear of abuse or repudiation. Even in the relatively stable nineteenth century a statesman like Lord Salisbury thought it axiomatic that no one could accurately estimate the balance of advantage between alternative policies. Today, what diplomatist would predict certain success for any course of action in the Middle East or Southeast Asia? And as the policy maker listens to complicated and conflicting expert disquisitions on possible Soviet courses of action he must sometimes wonder if greater confidence could not be placed in auguries drawn from the entrails of a chicken.

Chastened by his knowledge of history, and of the contemporary world, the diplomatist of the early twentieth century could report and recommend courses of action, tentatively to be sure, but with tranquillity of spirit. In an atmosphere of recrimination and suspicion, tranquillity undoubtedly disappears, but the more courageous will continue their task unafraid. But courage may well fail in face of the last of the changes of the recent past, the changes in the nature of warfare.

When this century opened, war was thought a dangerous but controllable instrument of policy. Now war is thought an instrument lethal to friend and foe alike. Paradoxically, consciousness of this shift has had a reassuring effect on many. If, the argument runs, war has become an instrument deadly no less to him who wields it than to him attacked, then no one will dare pick up that instrument, certainly not unless his preponderance of power is clearly overwhelming. If, then, we preserve our retaliatory capability, there will not be war. By and large American opinion has lost its fear of war as conviction of the deadly nature of war has won acceptance.

History, as the diplomatist knows full well, offers no support for such optimism. While it is possible to survey man's recorded history without concluding, with Hegel, that history is a "slaughter-bench," it is hard to believe that fear alone will end war. Moreover, the diplomatist knows from experience that the decision for war is unlikely to come out of a clear sky; it is far more likely to be the last of a series of decisions, none of which is intended to precipitate war, each of which makes war more difficult to avoid, until at the end there remains no alternative except war. And negative as well as positive decisions can be links in the series. The decision to abandon an exposed position or to acquiesce in the subversion of a friendly government may make war more, not less, difficult to avoid. Moreover, while antagonists may agree on the necessity of avoiding war, in seeking to achieve their objectives they may be willing to accept varying degrees of risk of precipitating war. That, after all, was the essence of Hitler's "artichoke" policy; the Nazis were confident that in the war of nerves their nerves would prove to be the stronger. Finally, history can show many examples of wars precipitated by the weak but reckless despite the wish for peace among the strong and prudent.

The moral burden carried by those who rule men today is undoubtedly heavier than in any earlier epoch of history. The impulse to escape that burden by evading decision, or by the delusion that the change in the nature of war has ended the danger of war, must be almost irresistible. The diplomatist, who must furnish the information and the advice upon which the decision is based, shares both the burden and the temptation to escape the burden. History is not a comforting counsellor to the sore-beset men and women responsible for the fate, not alone of our country, but of mankind today. But the long and turbulent history of man, the story of the rise and fall in war of so many great civilizations, can at least nerve the statesman and diplomatist alike against taking refuge in the fatal hope that men will now, very suddenly, cease to act as they have acted through thousands of years. Beyond that, from history the diplomatist can draw courage as he sees how, in the past, man has won through to success when he has been willing to forego pleasure and to defend with calm resolution those values which far transcend the comforts of daily living.

II

Some Major Powers

Chapter 9

THE NEW CHALLENGE

OF THE KREMLIN

Philip E. Mosely

UNDER Khrushchev's leadership, Soviet diplomacy is making bolder use of a wider and more varied arsenal of weapons than in Stalin's last years. At its "peace-loving" extreme the spectrum of diplomatic tools now includes the granting of economic development credits on favorable terms and the lavishing of political support for any form of anti-Western nationalism, no matter how reactionary it may be at home, provided it can serve to weaken the influence of the West. At the other extreme of the spectrum Khrushchev has been making increasingly frequent threats of nuclear and missile destruction against "any point on the globe." The mixture of weapons and tactics has become variegated and kaleidoscopic. What does this portend for the peace of the world? Is this change of tactics due in part to the new dictator's personal ebullience, or does it reflect an extremely serious and long-term shift in the world balance of power?

Before we turn to these most difficult questions, we must first consider briefly whether the Soviet regime is changing its character at home, and if so whether these changes are likely to modify its purposes in world politics over the next few years.

KHRUSHCHEV'S RUSSIA

The Soviet Union and the United States are now the only powers sufficiently large and powerful, and sufficiently self-contained, to generate their own foreign policies primarily from within. In greater or lesser degree all other governments today tend to adapt their policies to those of one or the other of the two strongest powers, or to the fact of their rivalry. Hence it is essential to consider whether the inner drives of the Soviet leadership are now undergoing any significant changes.

In the past many observers have argued that the psychologically belligerent posture of Soviet policy was due to a feeling of inferior power. Once it had achieved "security," whatever that is, the Soviet leadership would, the argument ran, relax its hostility toward outside powers and would gradually become a more tolerant member of the family of states. As it became more assured of its own permanence, it would also accept the permanence of its own coexistence in a world of differing social and political systems. It would relax its pressure to reshape the entire world in its own image. Today the Soviet Union is one of the two strongest military powers in the world; in some respects, difficult for the layman to measure, it has surpassed the military technology of the West and it also maintains far larger conventional forces. Yet the Soviet leadership, now that it feels vastly secure in its power, appears to be stepping up the frequency and the intensity of the crises that it provokes directly or encourages indirectly in widely separated regions of the world.

The Soviet Union is also one of the two major industrial powers of the world. Its rate of industrial growth, while slackening somewhat, promises to be sustained at a pace more rapid than that of most other countries. So far from feeling inferior in this area of achievement, since 1955 it has been offering large-scale technical assistance and development credits to a wide range of countries. The seven-year plan of 1959–1965, like the five-year plans of Stalin's era, places its major emphasis upon the development of heavy industry—power, steel, machine-tools, chemicals—and promises only modest improvements for the consumer. Since 1953, it is true, the average standard of living has improved substantially, with special attention to foodstuffs, clothing, and housing, but the economy remains firmly oriented to the industrial and military demands of the state. Khrushchev has committed his regime to overtaking the United States in the basic fields of heavy industry, and this ambition has both symbolic and practical implications in world politics.

So far from pressing their rulers for new concessions and new comforts, the long-enduring Soviet people appear to accept gratefully the modest and gradual improvements in their way of life. They now believe for the first time that the regime seriously intends to carry out its promises of a better life for the people. It can be argued that the improving standard of living, far from arousing new discontents and new demands, has given the people more confidence in the benevolent intentions of their rulers than at any time since the beginning of the five-year plans, in 1928. Formerly, when the Soviet leaders claimed to be promoting the highest standards of living in the world, many Soviet people, on the evidence of their own eyes and memories, could not believe this claim, and this skepticism and hostility sometimes extended to Soviet propaganda claims to be the most "peaceloving" regime in the world. The gap between propaganda and reality was one of the factors which led Stalin's regime to apply massive measures of control and repression.

Since 1953, Stalin's successors have turned to a milder policy. They have relaxed labor controls substantially, granted more adequate pensions, and undertaken a major effort to overcome the great gap in urban housing. They have shortened the work week from 48 to 46 hours and promise further curtailments. They appear to have largely abandoned the prison camp system of forced labor and there is now no evidence of large-scale and arbitrary repression. To all these new advantages soviet people naturally respond favorably. Rather than demanding further changes, they work hard to please the regime and avoid a return to Stalinist methods. By increasing the size of the carrot and cutting down the weight of the stick, the post-Stalin Soviet leadership has actually, as I see it, gained a much wider freedom of action, politically and psychologically, in pursuing its aims both at home and abroad.

The spread of education, it is argued, is bound sooner or later to lead to a questioning of Soviet doctrine and Soviet propaganda, and this will eventually weaken the government's ability to enforce its highly doctrinaire view of the world, making it more wary of risking its stability and even its survival in foreign adventures. Not all is tranquil, it is true, in the intellectual sphere, as shown by Khrushchev's repeated and forceful interventions against even mild forms of dissent or indifference. The problem of how to develop vigorous thinking and intellectual initiative in order to meet the need of the regime for intelligent and responsible administrators and experts in all fields, while simultaneously maintaining full control over all aspects of thought and expression, has always worried the Soviet leadership and will continue to do so. Stalin's successors have demonstrated repeatedly their uncertainty as to whether to loosen the reins of intellectual control a little, in order to overcome the heritage of fear and apathy, or whether to hold them tight, in order to forestall the growth of diversity and heresy. They have, however, endeavored to carry out this somewhat erratic shift back and forth between "hard" and "soft" lines of thought-control without resorting to outright terrorism.

The problem of where to hold the line in the intellectual and ideological field is a difficult one, probably an insoluble one, for a totalitarian regime. But are we justified in leaping from the evidence of these confusions and perplexities to the hopeful conclusion that the spread of independent thinking among influential segments of the apparatus of rule will inevitably lead to basic changes in the system of control and in the purposes of the regime? This is a very long leap, indeed. In order to present a more relaxed and confident posture to the outside world, the Soviet leadership has permitted freer access by foreign visitors, but it keeps a firm grip over all information which reaches its people and over the expression of ideas. If a continuing poverty of economic thought, philosophy, and artistic creation is a part of the price the regime must pay in order to protect its monolithic psychological structure, it seems as willing to pay that price under Khrushchev as it was under Stalin.

Today Soviet feeling and action leave a strong impression of national pride, even national arrogance. A powerful though intellectually barren type of Soviet chauvinism permeates both the leadership and its active instruments of rule. This emotion, which is fed by industrial achievements and growing military might, by pride in the expansion of the Communist system to Eastern Europe and China, and by Khrushchev's bold strokes and threats, is much more widely felt and shared than the earlier Bolshevik commitment to a messianic worldwide mission, but, like it, it recognizes no moral or political barriers to its eventual domination of the world. Khrushchev is in deadly earnest when he boasts that Communism will triumph everywhere by the end of the twentieth century, and many Soviet hearts beat faster when they hear this boast.

Meanwhile, on the whole, the claim of the Soviet Communist party to be the sole correct interpreter of history seems much more widely accepted at home than ever before. The chafing of the hard-working, efficient, and curious soviet youth against taboos on knowledge and thought may worry the leadership; it is not likely to endanger the survival of the Soviet system or lessen the ability of its leadership to pursue its self-appointed course in world affairs.

THE TOOLS OF SOVIET DIPLOMACY

Under Stalin it could be said with confidence that, although he was willing to exert pressure where it could be exerted without serious risk, and was eager to bring under his control any international real estate which was not adequately protected by countervailing strength, he did not intend to involve his regime in a major war. Indeed, even on those occasions when Stalin raised the risks of war to a high pitch by his miscalculations, as in his imposing of the Berlin blockade, in 1948–1949, and in unleashing communist aggression in Korea, he generally tried to calculate carefully the margin of risks which he could afford to take. Today, the margin of risks open to Khrushchev has been greatly enlarged, and the outside world cannot be sure just where in Soviet calculations that margin of risk lies. Crucial developments in Soviet military technology have contributed to this change. The development of a major nuclear capability was one of Stalin's dominant aims after 1945. Even while he was both denying the decisive importance of nuclear power and making every effort to mobilize the fear of a new war against the only possessor of that new weapon, he was bending every effort to match the West in nuclear power.

The outside world was surprised at the speed with which the Soviet Union achieved an atomic and then a hydrogen capability. Apparently, the non-Soviet world has been even more astounded at the Soviet Union's great technological advances in the field of guided and ballistic missiles. The launching of Soviet sputniks since September 1957 has marked the beginning of a new appraisal of the nature and location of advanced military power. Soviet space achievements demonstrated that Soviet technology had, at least temporarily, outstripped the West in its ability to launch large and heavy space-vehicles and in mastering the intricacies of missile guidance systems. Khrushchev was quick to turn this new weapon to political advantage. Even before he announced the launching of a Soviet intercontinental ballistic missile, he had added a new note of menace to the arsenal of Soviet policy. During the Suez crisis of 1956 he sent notes to many Western capitals, informing them that he was now able to destroy their cities, their industries, and their power of resistance. A year later Khrushchev had expanded his threats to North America and, indeed, "any point on the globe."

Whatever the unauthorized and over-enthusiastic boasts of private individuals may have been, no similar threats were ever made by the United States government or its official spokesmen, during its period of monopoly over nuclear power, except as a form of deterrence against clear and direct aggression. Are Khrushchev's threats an over-reaction to the postwar years, when the Soviet leadership felt that its advantages in conventional manpower and weapons were being nullified by the nuclear capability of the West? Or do they mark a deliberate heightening of tension, designed to hasten the achievement of definite aims through exploiting the changing shift of power?

Even in its published discussions, Soviet military thinking has undergone a remarkable change in the past four years. It no longer holds to the traditional concept of a defensive war on land begun by an attack on Soviet-controlled territory and to be ended by a victorious counter-offensive by massive conventional forces. Soviet discussions now speak openly of a "pre-emptive blow," designed to defeat a presumed aggressor *before* he can get in the first attack.[1] The new Soviet analyses of strategy emphasize for the first time that a war can be won or lost through the element of surprise. Apparently, the only difference between a "pre-emptive blow" and a "preventive war" is that a pre-emptive blow would be struck only after there was clear evidence that an aggressor was about to attack the Soviet Union, whereas a preventive war would be launched in the absence of such evidence. The difference may loom large in the subtleties of the dialectic, but in a delicately poised situation of strategic balance it might not have much practical significance.

As missiles increase in size and destructiveness, in accuracy and concealment, the question of how each side can evaluate the imminence of an attack becomes almost insoluble. In the age of full-scale missile

[1] Herbert S. Dinerstein, "The Revolution in Soviet Strategic Thinking," *Foreign Affairs*, January 1958, pp. 241–252.

power,—the main reliance for both offense and retaliation,—an error of judgment, one way or the other, may result in unleashing an unintended but overwhelmingly destructive war or in suffering the irretrievable elimination of a nation's power. It would surely be no consolation to know that a war of this new type had been let loose only after highly skilled technicians had examined radarscopes and decided that an enemy attack was already on its way.

The most novel and alarming aspect of Khrushchev's apparent view of nuclear strategy is his conviction that the Soviet leadership is now in a stronger position than the democratic West to force a new crisis close to the brink of war and to compel the other side to flinch from this fateful decision. Instead of bringing to the Soviet leadership a greater sense of power and security, the achievement of nuclear parity, combined with some slight and uncertain margin of missile superiority, has raised the level of risks, stepped up the frequency of crises, and increased the danger of war.

In the past it has been assumed that the Soviet leadership wished to avoid an all-out war because it would place in question the survival of its regime. But what if the Soviet leadership now believes, as it appears to, that a nuclear-missile confrontation places in question, not its own survival, but that of its strongest adversary, or, at the very least, the survival of the far-flung Western alliance system? It would be comforting to say that no military expert can assure his political chiefs of a one hundred per cent certainty of success, and that, in the face of this continuing margin of uncertainty, the Soviet leadership will therefore always pull back at the next-to-the-last minute from the final showdown. With so little known in the outside world about this type of Soviet strategic calculus, it would be rash to build a strategy, military and political, on this assumption. The frequency with which the Soviet leadership has in the past misjudged the political and psychological situation in other countries today offers no guarantee that its mathematical and technical calculations of the new balance of power will be less efficient than those on which its post-1945 scientific advances have been based.

Undoubtedly, the Soviet leadership would prefer to utilize its military advantages for political purposes without incurring the risk of resorting to the direct use of force, and it asserts with vehement conviction that no war will henceforth remain a limited one. The Kremlin would surely prefer to see Communist or at least pro-Soviet regimes come into power in areas presently beyond its control. It would then hope, through nuclear threats, to deter any outside intervention into these newly attached areas, without utilizing its conventional forces in a direct invasion. Khrushchev, no doubt, calculates that, if he should succeed through combined political and military means in detaching a number of strategic areas from the opposing bloc, this would destroy the self-confidence and mutual confidence of the opposing alliances, thus greatly increasing the opportunities for the non-military expansion of Soviet influence and control.

With the spread of the new military technology, only two major powers are equipped to carry on an all-out war, and both of them are now vulnerable to attack in their heartlands. Under these new circumstances, a truly farsighted Soviet leadership might be well advised to adopt the recipe of that arch-imperialist, Theodore Roosevelt, who favored "walking softly and carrying a big stick." As the two major powers continue to outstrip more and more astronomically all other powers, it might be to Soviet advantage to promote a prolonged period of international relaxation, to increase the sense of strategic hopelessness among most nations of the world, and to diminish the fears which Soviet policy has periodically revived through its actions and its words.

Viewed from this point of view, for example, the survival of NATO is a great advantage to Soviet policy. NATO sets its armament goals as ceilings, not as floors; it lays down its goals of strength for several years in advance; it is not engaged in building more than a minimum of defensive force, perhaps not even a minimum. If the Soviet leadership under Khrushchev, as under Stalin, pursues wholeheartedly its aim of breaking up NATO, this can only be, not because it fears NATO, but because it believes that NATO can be destroyed by threats, and that this event, accompanied by the withdrawal of British, Canadian and American forces from the continent, would greatly improve the Soviet Union's relative position in pursuing its local and intermediate goals of expansion. A Soviet leadership which sincerely wanted to achieve a continuing relaxation would welcome NATO because it brings former European rivals together in what can be only a defensive coalition. Khrushchev's increasingly vehement efforts to undermine NATO are motivated, not by fear, but by ambition.

COMMUNIST CHINA AND THE EUROPEAN SATELLITES

Since the consolidation of his power at home, Khrushchev's major miscalculations have occurred within the Soviet bloc. The search for a more flexible and more profitable way of managing the European satellites brought with it several costly setbacks. The Hungarian national uprising of October, 1956, and its bloody suppression by Soviet tanks, the achievement of a substantial measure of internal autonomy by the Polish satellite regime, the economic concessions which had to be made to the more obedient satellites, were costly to Soviet prestige and to Soviet economic interests. Khrushchev's efforts to bring Communist Yugoslavia into a renewed obedience to Moscow failed. In controlling the captive countries of East Central Europe it again came to seem psychologically more economical of effort, as it had under Stalin, to blame all resistance on "Titoism," rather than examine objectively the incompatibilities between Soviet demands and the basic feelings of the conquered peoples.

The new break with the Yugoslav Communists coincided with the celebration, in November, 1957, of forty years of the Soviet regime and the massive obeisance of other Communist regimes and parties before the shrine of Moscow's primacy. When Tito refused to sign the Declaration of Communist Parties and insisted, despite lavish Soviet promises of economic aid, on maintaining his independent position between the two blocs, on apportioning the blame for the cold war between the two blocs, rather than heaping it all on the West, Khrushchev turned upon the Yugoslav Communist leaders with the anger of a worthy suitor spurned. Did this return to overt hostility to the Yugoslav practice of independent communism reflect a basic shift in Soviet strategy, a shift provoked by the achievement of great missile power? Or was it primarily an after-reaction to the alarming outburst of national anti-Soviet emotions which had so recently shaken the Soviet domination over East Central Europe?

Western policy has too long assumed that the unrest, actual or potential, in the East European satellites has been due to the refusal of the West to recognize the legitimacy of the Soviet-imposed governments. As a matter of fact, any hopes among the people of this area that the West's symbolic intransigence would have any effect upon their own helpless predicament had faded by 1950. Neither a Western embracing of the satellite regimes, nor a breaking off of relations with them, would have any real effect upon the degree to which each satellite nation adapts or avoids adapting itself to its situation. It is equally an illusion today to assume that the Soviet leadership attaches any value to receiving from the West a "legitimization" of its domination over East Central Europe. The time has gone by when the Soviet leadership would have found any such symbolic act to be of material value to it.

The band of East European satellite regimes has far less immediate strategic value to the Soviet Union today than it had before the emergence of its nuclear-missile capability. The Soviet Union does not foresee any time when the NATO forces would pose an aggressive threat on land to its own very large conventional forces, even if it completely discounts the satellite armies in its calculations. The exercise of Soviet menace and deterrence is now carried out primarily by missile threats. This new type of threat can play on single states, at a great distance, promising immunity to those intervening countries which disassociate themselves from resistance to Soviet demands. Whether or not Soviet forces can be reduced in the satellite areas or even withdrawn from them has become a factor, not of over-all military strategy, but a part of the calculus of political strategy. If a mutual withdrawal led to the isolation of each of the West European states from each other and from North America, while the East European regimes, buttressed by strong Soviet-trained police forces and intimidated by nearby Soviet power, remained in political obedience, the Soviet leadership could accept a considerable range of risks and hope to gain substantially from an exchange of concessions of this character.

Communist China presents a quite different range of opportunities and risks to Soviet policy. Can there develop between Moscow and Peking a range of frictions and suspicions which would render their alliance ineffectual? Or is most of the speculation in the West about these frictions simply another form of political Micawberism? It is easy to assume that the Sino-Soviet honeymoon has long since been over. In the past several years Soviet credits have been offered and executed in substantial amounts to the benefit of many uncommitted countries, but not to that of Communist China. Embarked on an unprecedented effort of imposed sacrifice and rigid control, Communist China, in its "leap forward," must have special reasons for emphasizing that it is not only paying its own way but is rapidly repaying the earlier Soviet credits. When the Chinese Communist leaders read of Khrushchev's claims to possess an overpowering range of force, they must wonder why it is not exerted directly for the benefit of their own ambitions. Rather than Khrushchev prodding Peking in August 1958 to bombard the offshore islands, it seems more probable that he found it necessary, in person, to coordinate the degree of threat and risk which the Soviet leadership was prepared to back. Nor can it be assumed that Moscow and Peking always have the same evaluation of the level of risk which it is desirable for them to run in achieving a particular objective. When all these and other sources of possible friction have been measured, the overweening fact remains that the Soviet Union and Communist China have everything to lose by splitting apart and everything to gain by working together. The differences between them are presumably of degree and timing, not of basic purpose. Without Soviet backing, and even more so in the face of Soviet hostility, Communist China would be a power of medium weight, even in the Far East. Overt dissension between the two major centers of Communist triumph would destroy the psychological gains which they have made together in many parts of Asia.

If Khrushchev believes his own prognostications of the relative power curves, he must believe that the time is fast approaching when, under the cover of the Soviet nuclear-missile deterrent, Communist China may be able to exert its very great conventional strength to expand its power. Its strength, even if it remains without nuclear armaments, is growing much faster than that of all other countries of Asia combined. As this imbalance grows, the only available make-weight for the protection of non-Communist Asia against the might of Communist China is the power and determination of the United States. But if, as Khrushchev asserts, the central, nuclear, factor of that power can be neutralized, the United States and its allies would then lack the conventional forces, in adequate numbers and location, to offset the conventional strength of the Chinese Communists.

In the past Stalin moved slowly and cautiously from one area of crisis to another. The political disputes with the Western allies over the fate of East Central Europe and over the future of Germany were pitched to a nonmilitary key. When his attempt to prevent the integration of West Germany into the Western bloc failed, contrary to many predictions, over the Berlin blockade of 1948–49, Stalin sought a return to the previous *status quo* in Germany and made minor concessions in Austria. Slowly and massively Soviet interest then turned to the Far

East and after what must have seemed more than adequate preparations the attempt was launched, in Korea, to drive American influence (there were no American forces there) from the Asian mainland. When, three years later, Stalin's successors decided to liquidate an unprofitable stalemate in Korea, they renounced counter-productive claims against Turkey, Iran, and Yugoslavia and actually withdrew from a militarily useless base in Finland and from an unstrategic eastern Austria, in order to re-establish their good faith as negotiators. Each of these shifts was carried out by many small steps, from each of which withdrawal would have been easy.

Since mid-1958 Khrushchev has turned the "rolling crisis" with dizzying speed from the Arab East to the Chinese offshore islands, and then to Berlin. He has laid the groundwork for other crises against Finland, through severe economic pressure, against Iran, through his protests against the U.S.-Iranian military assistance agreement. Are we approaching a time when, instead of probing cautiously for one weak spot at a time and simultaneously making conciliatory gestures about other disputed questions, the Soviet leadership will feel free to provoke several crises at the same time? In the past Stalin must have feared that to provoke several simultaneous crises might bring on a military showdown, in which his conventional forces were offset by a disparity in nuclear power. Khrushchev may come to feel, at some stage, that it is to his advantage to try to burst apart the American defensive system at several points at once, by raising more challenges than the West can cope with at any one time. Whatever these calculations may be—and we must not presume too far in this murky chamber of Soviet inner thought—the strategic partnership between Communist China and the Soviet Union, greatly revivified since June 1958, is a continuing fact. It is a stubborn fact which cannot be brushed aside by wishful speculation on allegedly fatal frictions between the two powers, united by common ideology, by joint, if not entirely common, ambitions, and by a shared hostility toward those who resist those ambitions.

The Uncommitted Nations

The most striking innovation in Soviet policy since Stalin has been the new wooing of the uncommitted countries, particularly in Asia, but also persistently in Africa and Latin America. The new development was codified in Khrushchev's statement at the Twentieth Party

Congress, in February 1956, that the world was now divided into three blocs; in addition to the Soviet camp of "peace and democracy" and the bloc of "imperialists," there was now a "peace bloc," typified by India. Through state visits, cultural propaganda, technical aid and credits the new leadership undertook to win the sympathies and, it hoped, the political cooperation of a wide arc of countries, ranging from Egypt to Indonesia. Here Soviet propaganda, pursuing its traditional "anti-imperialist" line, met with a strong response, for the resentment against Western colonial rule or domination, withdrawn only recently, provided the strongest political motivation of the new nations. The burning issue of destroying colonialism, wherever it still existed, served further to bring many of these countries closer to accepting the Soviet insistence that this issue rather than the conflict between democracy and totalitarianism, is the only important question of our time. The granting of Soviet aid through trade, through an expressed willingness to purchase any surplus commodities in payment for Soviet industrial equipment, and the extension of credit without careful study and without conditions, further impressed many Asian political leaders with the advantages of cooperating part-way with Soviet policy.

Were the Soviet leaders running the risk of strengthening non-Communist regimes in the newly independent countries? After all, before Stalin, Lenin had argued for the need of pre-industrial countries to pass through a minimal stage of economic development, to develop national states, before they could become "ripe" for Communist revolution. Looking at the vast economic and social problems of most of these countries, at the pressure of population on resources, at the difficulty of acquiring adequate capital either through savings at home or through investment from abroad, the Soviet leadership must feel that the political risk of strengthening non-Communist governments, even those which suppress Communist movements at home, is not a great one. In many of the countries, as in India and Indonesia, the Soviet *rapprochement* with the nationalist leaderships was followed by greater freedom of action for local Communist propaganda and organizers, as well as for Soviet propaganda. In addition, the local Communist parties could profit politically both by the prestige of Soviet friendship for their countries and through the rapidly spreading awareness of the growing industrial and military might of the Soviet Union. Now, underdeveloped countries could, in effect, choose between the Western democratic model of economic modernization and the totalitarian communist model. It was in line with the Soviet assumption that only communism can solve basic economic problems for Khrushchev to assert, as he has often since 1956, that in some countries, weakly organized and administered, Communist parties may come to power through parliamentary means; and then, the changing strategic balance will prevent the "imperialists" from intervening to overthrow the new Communist rule.

Several factors have perhaps diminished Khrushchev's enthusiasm for the "peace bloc" and the "parliamentary path" to Communist rule since 1956. In some Asian countries the Soviet reconquest of Hungary left a strong impression, unlike Stalin's more creeping conquest of 1945–47. The Chinese Communist suppression of Tibetan autonomy was a direct shock to many Asians. There have been strong indications that the union of Syria and Egypt was prompted by fear of the growing influence of the Syrian Communist party, and the marked Soviet favoritism for the post-1958 regime in Iraq has led to bitter exchanges between President Nasser and Premier Khrushchev. Even the widespread enthusiasm in Asia for persuading the United States to recognize Communist China, presumably as a step toward the pacification of Asia, has given way, in some circles, to the feeling that it may even be desirable from their point of view, giving them a greater freedom of political action, to have American-backed Chinese Nationalist forces in direct contact with those of Communist China. Whether those Asian countries, such as Pakistan, Burma, and Thailand, and, less directly, Indonesia, which have placed more authority in the hands of the organized military forces have thereby raised enduring barriers to Communist pressures from within and without remains doubtful, but Moscow and Peking have left no doubt of their dislike of this presumed check to the expansion of Communist parties in South and Southeast Asia. The "peace bloc" and "united front" tactics have not brought the political successes which Khrushchev perhaps anticipated in 1955 and 1956. Indeed, his long speech to the Twenty-first Party Congress, in 1959, was remarkably taciturn on this subject.

The Prospects

Behind the kaleidoscope of greater variety and flexibility of tactics, Khrushchev's regime shows a basic continuity with that of his mentor, Stalin. Unlike Stalin, however, Khrushchev shows a less inhibited curiosity about the outside world, a willingness to expose himself to frequent and long conversations with prominent representatives of "imperialism." Perhaps having inherited his ideology ready-made, he has even greater confidence in his dialectical ability to impress on his listeners those arguments which fit the Leninist book. Basically, however, Khrushchev thinks in the same grooves. He believes that the Soviet system has alone resolved the fundamental problems of economic development and social welfare, brushing aside the far greater gains registered by other countries over the same decades. Like Stalin, he finds no contradiction between the ultimate goals of communism and the ambitions of the Russian state.

Khrushchev's Russia, like Stalin's, rests upon a psychological armature of life-long indoctrination "from the cradle to the grave," upon rapid decision at the top and immediate obedience below, upon a monopoly of information which presses Soviet views outward while admitting as little as possible of outside information and opinion. If the Soviet leadership once lost confidence in the superiority of its ideology, it is doubtful whether Soviet nationalism, even Soviet arrogance, would be an adequate cement. "Relaxation of international tension," which Stalin and his successors demanded constantly from 1952, proved fraught with great dangers abroad and even with minor worries at home. On the other hand, to assure their own peoples and the world that the danger of war had greatly receded required only minor adjustments for democratic leaders, for the essence of democracy is to believe in and act on an assumption of good faith, and this assumption is readily extended from one's own people and their friends to an adversary. For a democracy it is natural to believe that hostility must derive from an unfortunate misunderstanding. For a totalitarian ruler, on the contrary, the vanishing, whether sincere or not, of the dread of war presents great risks. While their precise form could not have been predicted, the events of 1956 in Eastern Europe followed logically from the summit conference of 1955, even though the meeting had no concrete achievements to its credit. Under the new strategic balance, however, it is far from clear that Khrushchev has been seeking a second summit meeting in order to bring about a genuine relaxation of tension. Perhaps now, in order to explore certain relative advantages in military power, he would like to confront Western political leaders with the alternatives which they would prefer to ignore.

The past three years, since 1956, have given Soviet policy a wider range of goals, a far greater variety of instruments. The adaptation to the new environment has not been without risks and costs to Soviet policy. All of these, in Khrushchev's eyes, appear to have been compensated by the rapid progress of Soviet strategic power. By 1948 Stalin could write to Tito that the Yugoslav Communists had no right to claim any credit for establishing a Communist regime in their own country, since it was the over-all strategic situation which had made this possible; similarly, the French and Italian Communists, who had been attacked by the Yugoslavs for their passivity, had been unable, so Stalin said, to establish "people's democracies" because "unfortunately," the Soviet armies were unable to help them in this. After a period of experimentation with the wider range of political, economic, and psychological instruments, Khrushchev seems again to be concentrating his main hopes on the deployment of Soviet military power, now arrayed in a new and even more ominous form. He seems determined, in one part of the world after another, or perhaps in several regions at once, to raise a major strategic challenge to the strength and cohesion of the free world.

Chapter 10

AMERICAN AND SOVIET

NEGOTIATING BEHAVIOR

Stephen D. Kertesz

NEGOTIATION, the essential activity of diplomats, is an important phase in the process of shaping and executing foreign policy.* *Il faut négocier, négocier et toujours négocier,"* suggested Talleyrand. Sir Harold Nicolson has even expressed the wish that the word "negotiation" be substituted for the word "diplomacy" because of the disagreeable flavor of the latter to many people. Success or failure of foreign policy is greatly influencd by the skill of negotiators, whose behavior can be more important for the course of history than is generally recognized. The skill of a negotiator, however, is determined not only by personal ability, but, more importantly, by the total political context, domestic and foreign, within which he operates.

In diplomatic negotiations much depends on the presence or absence of similar expectations and approaches of the parties. Images of past successes and failures are carried over in the minds of negotiators and generally form tactics, strategies, and eventually clichés for negotiating. Clear knowledge on the part of the negotiators of their own objectives and realistic assumptions concerning the aspirations and aims of others form a solid basis for negotiation and settlement.

* An earlier version of this essay was delivered at a meeting of the American Political Science Association in Washington, D. C., on September 9, 1956. Personal experiences of the author are based mainly on the years 1945–1947. During this period he was head of the peace preparatory division of the Hungarian Foreign Ministry, Secretary General of the Hungarian Peace Delegation at the Paris Conference, 1946, and Hungarian Minister to Italy, 1947.

133

The individual approach of negotiators is influenced by numerous factors, such as their social and educational background, power position on the domestic political scene, political philosophy and ethics, as well as national traditions, government system, particular views of the nature of world politics and the role of diplomacy, the presence or absence of permanent aims in foreign policy, and the nature of specific foreign policy objectives and issues. The negotiating potentialities of heads of government greatly differ from those of professional diplomatic representatives. In distinction from the latter group, political leaders may make decisions on the spot even without consultation of government agencies or of specialists.

In view of these general factors, it is important to know who is negotiating with whom, under what conditions, for what reasons, what the aspirations and expectations of the negotiating parties are and what their *Weltanschauung* is—their general view of the world and their specific views of each other. In the field of our inquiry it may be relevant to consider the position of the negotiators in their domestic political system and particularly the power and freedom of action enjoyed by American and Russian representatives below the category of leading statesmen; that is, what could they say and do occasionally without instructions? Who eventually makes the decisions? Moreover, what reactions could the American and Russian negotiators expect at home in terms of support, approval, or disapproval? Answers to these questions may throw some light on factors which influence actual negotiating behavior.

In the framework of these general considerations I shall examine a few aspects of Soviet and American negotiating attitudes. Although I do not intend to be dogmatic, within the limitations of a short essay I am bound to make generalizations which would usually require more practical illustrations and a series of qualifications.

I intend to take my examples mainly from the period 1933 to 1953—that is, from the establishment of diplomatic relations between the United States and the Soviet Union to the death of Stalin—and particularly from the greatly differing climates of the second World War and the Cold War. Although these two eventful decades did not elapse without changes on the world scene and were rich in surprising political developments, American and Soviet negotiating behavior underwent relatively few significant transformations. Virtues, vices, and institutional practices of nations do not change easily, and this has been manifest in American and Soviet negotiating patterns.

In all diplomatic negotiations a major stumbling block is failure to understand the different mentality and value systems of foreign nations. It is a remarkable phenomenon that both American and Soviet negotiators often have made false assumptions concerning others. Their assumptions not infrequently have been false in different ways and to a large extent for different reasons, but they have been false all the same, especially on the highest level of policy. Specialists and the field agencies usually have a clearer understanding of foreign ways, but their evaluations may not influence, or even reach, the makers of decisions.

The general difficulty of understanding foreign nations has, in the case of the United States and Russia, been increased by the dimensions of the two lands. Both are countries of continental size, worlds in themselves. Most of the individuals educated in such huge societies are almost inclined to equate foreign ways of thinking with those they observe in the vastness of their own country. It is hard for Americans and Russians to think themselves into the position of other nations and to understand aspirations and courses of action which have no appeal to them.

Another common characteristic of Russian and American foreign policy derives from the fact that both countries entered the world scene as superpowers almost simultaneously. In the period between the world wars neither the United States nor the U.S.S.R. was a leading star in international politics. Both nations remained outside the historical mainstream. The United States lived in self-imposed isolation, and the Soviet Union's ambitions for a leading position in world affairs were defeated. After Hitler's seizure of power the Soviet defeat resulted from the attempt to neutralize two different and mutually contradictory concepts, or sets of assumptions. The Kremlin was forced to assume for purposes of negotiation that the defensive Western democracies were genuinely interested in combining forces in order to restrain or, if necessary, defeat Hitler; at the same time, Soviet revolutionary dogmatism forced them to assume that somehow the capitalists were conspiring together against the Soviet Union.

When American and Soviet negotiators met at Potsdam in July, 1945 a new chapter of history began. Their meeting in the heart of

Europe confirmed the fact that the Old Continent had finally ceased to be the dominant force in international affairs. Europe had become only one of the arenas for the struggle of two giant powers, Russia and the United States. Unfortunately, however, the United States and the Soviet Union entered upon this new era of history with greatly differing traditions and expectations, and from these differences in world goals, basic human values, and diplomatic methods have come the many serious and extraordinarily baffling complications which beset present day international relations and make diplomatic negotiations simply episodes in a continuing struggle. The difference in goals affects not only the atmosphere of confidence in which negotiations are carried on but the basic purpose of carrying on negotiations at all.

At the outset I would like to call attention to the fact that the available sources for Soviet and American negotiating behavior are of different nature. For both we have the observations of persons who negotiated with them. For the American category we have dozens of memoirs, official documents, and a score of other comparable publications. These sources are not of equal value, and the validity of some is debated, a fact which makes even more difficult the evaluation of attitudes and actions. At the same time, the multitude of sources, available to whoever undertakes to evaluate American foreign policy and negotiating conduct makes almost every generalization in these areas subject to challenge and exception. In this way the evaluation of the Americans may, by contrast with the appraisal of the Soviets, seem less precise and definite.

Such difficulty does not exist in Soviet relations. Unlike the United States, the Soviet Government published few official documents, and Soviet leaders did not publish memoirs—only "holy books" in which we find doctrines explaining the past and present and revealing the course of the future. These writings, mainly by Marx, Lenin, and Stalin, determined all aspects of human life, including negotiating behavior. Thus, outwardly it is relatively easy to describe the Soviet negotiating attitude, because we know through experience that it has been in basic harmony with officially recognized doctrines.

However, I would like to add a note of caution. What we observe is only the outward manifestation of a monolithic state. We know little of the inner struggle on the highest level for establishment of the official party line which interprets doctrines, defines foreign policy, and determines negotiating behavior. There is substantial evidence that, during critical periods in the Soviet Union, conflicts raged in high party circles over divergent policies and on occasion a decidedly non-monolithic confusion prevailed. But once a policy was decided, only the official party line could bring salvation, and those who deviated were considered beyond redemption and were dealt with accordingly.

In discussing and comparing the operational codes of Soviet and American negotiators, let us examine first the less complicated and more readily understood Soviet attitude. Since the Soviet group has displayed considerable uniformity of behavior, it lends itself more easily to generalizations.[1]

I

Although the oscillations of Soviet foreign policy between 1933 and 1953 were truly remarkable, aims and methods of negotiating manifested a significant consistency. One of the reasons for this stability was the existence of precise Soviet objectives in world affairs. These objectives were based on the combination of two different political ideologies; the historical expansionistic traditions of Holy Russia and the recipe of Communist global conquest. Stalin kept these goals clearly in mind when he shaped the foreign policy of the Soviet Union during the 1930's, the second World War, and the immediate postwar years.

Stability in aims and methods was facilitated by the fact that decisions were made only on the top level. Numerous examples illustrate the fact that since 1939 Stalin was the only man who could change positions and could make concessions during negotiations. Although his chief negotiator, Molotov, was a leading member of the Politburo, we have several indications that he was reluctant to change positions without instructions during negotiations even in relatively minor matters. After Stalin's death Molotov's changed negotiating behavior was conspicuous. He acted with greater ease and freedom. His behavior became more like that of a Western foreign minister.

[1] Nathan Leites, *The Operational Code of the Politburo* (New York, 1951); Nathan Leites, *A Study of Bolshevism* (Glencoe, Ill., 1953).

Top Soviet negotiators were generally realists and occasionally even resorted to bluff frankness.[2] When in November, 1940, Molotov negotiated with Hitler and Ribbentrop, he made no secret about the direction of Russian territorial expansion.[3] One year later, in the most perilous period of the war, Stalin in a matter-of-fact way informed Eden about Russia's European territorial objectives and tried to obtain British approval for them.[4] Later even Churchill accepted the Russian aspirations.[5] Eventually, because of an energetic American protest, Molotov consented to leave the territorial clauses out of the Russo-British Treaty of Alliance in May, 1942.[6] In reluctantly accepting this omission the Russian leaders probably preferred an accelerated Lend-Lease which made possible the effective conquest of territories desired by the Soviet Union. But after Stalin's frankness only wishful thinkers could have had illusions about the reality and direction of Russia's territorial aims. Throughout the war the attitude of Soviet representatives was not promising for the freedom of Poland and the Baltic States. In that respect, Western wishful thinkers rather than Soviet deceit were the source of many later disappointments.

The ready, if not ostentatious, acceptance of such declarations of principle as the Atlantic Charter, various declarations issued in Moscow in November, 1943, or the Yalta Declaration on Liberated Europe was another expression of Russian realism. Stalin probably thought that theoretical statements of purpose could not do much harm so long as their interpretation and application in regard to the coveted occupied territories was in his own hands. Western opinion considered the acceptance of such principles a sign of conciliatory Soviet attitude and *rapprochement* toward democratic ideas. In reality, Stalin's "broad-mindedness" was made possible by his opportunistic and unscrupulous approach and his almost limitless power. He could reverse policies

[2] General John R. Deane, head of the U. S. Military Mission in Moscow, noted that the Teheran Conference "was characterized by the bluntness of Soviet diplomacy. Stalin made no attempt at oratory nor did he search for words that would satisfy diplomatic niceties. His comments were terse and to the point." *The Strange Alliance* (New York, 1947), p. 44.

[3] *Nazi-Soviet Relations 1939–1941* (Washington, 1948), pp. 244–246, 251–253.

[4] Winston S. Churchill, *The Grand Alliance* (Boston, 1950), pp. 628–629. Cf. *The Memoirs of Cordell Hull* (New York, 1948), II, pp. 1165–1177.

[5] Churchill, *The Hinge of Fate* (Boston, 1950), p. 327; Sumner Welles, *Seven Decisions That Shaped History* (New York, 1951), pp. 126–127.

[6] Hull, *op. cit.*, pp. 1171–1173.

overnight, and all changes were greeted enthusiastically by a directed public opinion. In the absence of moral principles or political ethics, solemn statements or promises did not influence his policies. These were directed by concrete power-political situations. From the very beginning Stalin had in mind well defined political objectives and specific territorial aims. He did not object to declarations of principle and signed everything. But at the same time he was thinking of specific issues and goals and shaped his policies accordingly.

On the lower level, negotiations with the Russians proved to be a frustrating experience. The famous "nyet" was the usual answer of Soviet negotiators to Western proposals. As long as leading statesmen negotiated and agreed on the top level on matters of general principle, a misapprehension existed that agreements were being reached. The real truth of the matter became evident in negotiating with the Russians on the lower level when the practical application of these principles was involved. Dependence on final authority even in minor matters and basic Communist doctrines and views on the nature of world politics and on the use of diplomacy were the chief causes of the rigidity and negativeness of Soviet representatives.[7]

The feeling of personal insecurity in Russia and the general Communist philosophy concerning the non-Communist world had a cumulative effect and enveloped the minds of Soviet negotiators in distrust. Repeated purges in the Commisariat of Foreign Affairs, particularly the great purge of 1938–1939, were not without effect on Soviet representatives. The resulting atmosphere of intimidation and fear made normal human contacts with them almost impossible. Communist doctrines and practices were strengthened by the traditionally suspicious Russian attitude toward foreigners, whether friends or foes. This almost pathologically mistrustful behavior became a familiar pattern blurring the judgment of Soviet negotiators on all levels. Their unresponsive attitude was all the more incomprehensible and frustrating to Western negotiators because it sometimes involved the rejection

---

[7] For a detailed treatment of this subject see Philip E. Mosely, "Some Soviet Techniques of Negotiation" in *Negotiating With the Russians,* edited by Raymond Dennett and Joseph E. Johnson (Boston, 1951), pp. 271–303. Lord Strang suggested that "The Soviet Government have imposed their pattern of diplomatic negotiation upon those who have dealings with them, and have constrained the rest of the world to acquire their negotiating technique." *Home and Abroad* (London, 1956), p. 206.

of proposals favorable to the Soviet Union. The Baruch Plan and particularly the Marshall Plan are cases in point. In many instances Soviet negotiators were apparently instructed simply to oppose all Western moves. The lack of instructions automatically brought about the same results.

Behind this behavior of Soviet representatives lie certain generally stable doctrinal positions which define the context of all Soviet intercourse with the non-Soviet world. And this all-important background makes necessary a few comments on the nature of Soviet diplomacy and its role in the international community. Although the professional element was eliminated from the Soviet foreign service in the early 1920's, Soviet diplomats outwardly follow the procedures and concepts of traditional diplomacy. While candidates for the foreign service must first of all be reliable Communists well schooled in party doctrines, they usually receive a careful training in the formalities and techniques of diplomacy, and not infrequently are more orthodox in observing forms and rules of procedure than are their Western opposite numbers. This is one of the reasons why Western representatives have often been surprised and shocked in the face of the "unreasonable" attitude of Soviet negotiators. The explanation is simple. The Soviet representatives have only a formal diplomatic status; they can hardly be considered diplomats in the customary sense. Soviet diplomacy is but one branch of Communist world organization. As defined by Soviet authorities:

Soviet Diplomacy in its general purpose as well as in its methods differs categorically from the diplomacy of the feudal epoch and the epoch of bourgeois domination. The principal aim of Soviet Diplomacy was and will be concentrated on the study of factors of social importance. For this purpose, Soviet Diplomacy has at its disposal unsurpassed Marxist-Leninist methods of perception of world conditions and to a certain degree also of conditions—in the full meaning of that word—connected with the economical, political, historical, class and other problems of the countries with which it deals. It is necessary always to remember I. V. Stalin's words: ". . . in order to avoid mistakes in politics and not to fall into the circle of idle dreamers, the Party of the Proletariat must proceed in its activity not from the abstract 'principles of human intelligence' but from the concrete conditions of material life of the society as the decisive power of the social developments." Marxist-Leninist theory "gives the Party the possibility of orienting itself in the situation, to understand the internal connections of the surrounding occurrences, to foresee the course of events and to recognize not only how and where the events will develop at the present time but also how and where they should develop in the future." Here in this foresight and recognition of present and future events, and not in deceit and intrigues, consists the strength of Soviet Diplomacy, which so brilliantly justified itself during the whole history of its activity.[8]

Acceptance of Marxist-Leninist doctrines and methods of diplomacy means that Soviet diplomats are, in practice, Communist agents who use diplomatic privileges and immunities for realization of Communist aims—that is, ultimately for undermining the state to which they are accredited. They are not disposed by education and professional training to work out compromise solutions with bourgeois representatives. They consider diplomatic contacts as skirmishes in the great fight against a corrupt and doomed system of society. In view of basic Communist doctrine, what Soviet "diplomats" really understand and practice is international revolution and not international cooperation and peace. Even if some Soviet diplomats are inclined to work for real understanding with non-Communist countries, they must carefully hide such ideas. Otherwise they could easily provoke their own recall, which may indeed have unpleasant consequences for them.

For Soviet representatives the hostile intentions of the foreign world have been axiomatic. Hence their isolation, their strange attitude. Objective reporting and interpretation of foreign nations cannot be expected from Soviet diplomats. In the central Soviet agencies there is available a vast amount of information from a variety of sources through Communist Party channels and diplomatic posts, but reporting and evaluation are made in the light of dominant party doctrines. Soviet representatives will not make an effort to be objective about non-Communist countries and do not dare give an impartial analysis of foreign ways. They are not channels of communication for their government in the ordinary sense. The two way flow of information is not one of the functions of Soviet diplomacy. A Soviet representative executes instructions in the strictest sense and then ceases to function as a diplomat. He is aware of the weak power position of a diplomat

[8] A. J. Vyshinsky and S. A. Lozovsky, *Diplomaticheskii Slovar*, Vol. I (Moscow, 1948), "Diplomacy," pp. 591–592.

in the Soviet state organization and accepts with grim determination the set of ideas, values, and methods imposed by ruling-party circles. He knows that the important foreign political decisions are not made in the foreign ministry, which has only formal authority and does not wield effective power. The forces which control Soviet diplomats are elsewhere. Nothing remains for him but to be a submissive conformist.

Although Soviet representatives are usually well informed about facts, formalities, and procedures in the Western world, this body of knowledge is filed away in an indoctrinated and/or intimidated mind which cannot or does not dare to evaluate and interpret freely. The old generation of Soviet negotiators, such as Chicherin, Krassin, Litvinov, or even Vyshinsky, understood the complexity of free societies better than the new representatives, who have been educated in the vast Soviet empire and have not been exposed to foreign ways. Societies whose ideal is individual freedom and not the omnipotent state are alien to them.[9] They live in an ambivalent atmosphere of superiority and inferiority feelings, such as contempt for and fear of Western ideas. They do not know and care even less about ideas and values which have made possible the miracle of world history; the rise of Western civilization based on Greek philosophical ideas, Roman law and organizational skill, Judaeo-Christian teaching, the Reformation and Catholic Reform, the French and American Revolutions. While these values and ideas have little meaning to Soviet representatives, they know only too well the shortcomings of a Western civilization which failed to respond adequately to the challenge of the contemporary world. Their policies and attitudes are influenced by these shortcomings and weaknesses without understanding the deeper values and potentialities of free systems of government. Stettinius noted that "the inaccurate information that the Russians had about the United

---

[9] Arthur Koestler's Ivanov defined well the basic difference between the two societies: "There are only two conceptions of human ethics, and they are at opposite poles. One of them is Christian and humane, declares the individual to be sacrosanct, and asserts that the rules of arithmetic are not to be applied to human units. The other starts from the basic principle that a collective aim justifies all means, and not only allows, but demands, that the individual should in every way be subordinated and sacrificed to the community—which may dispose of it as an experimentation rabbit or a sacrificial lamb." *Darkness at Noon* (Signet book edition, 1955), pp. 113–114.

States was a source of continual amazement" to the American delegation at Yalta.[10]

The inability of Soviet representatives to understand the non-Communist world results in a confusion of form and essence which often causes harm to the interest of the Soviet Union itself, not to speak of the larger interests of the world community. Fundamental Communist doctrines make Soviet negotiators believe that the Soviet Union is threatened by an encirclement of decadent and corrupt capitalist states, hence their constant suspicion about the outer world, no matter how other representatives behave.[11] Friendly gestures, concessions, and especially the policy of appeasement are considered as traps or signs of weakness. The suspicious Soviet mind finds an unselfish way of thinking and an independent political attitude incomprehensible, whether found in private individuals or in the representative of a "bourgeois democratic" government.[12]

[10] He further commented: "They had their embassy and consular staffs to report to them, as well as, presumably, the American Communist party. Possibly, of course, their representatives in the United States sent home only what they thought the Kremlin wanted to hear." Edward R. Stettinius, Jr., *Roosevelt and the Russians: The Yalta Conference* (Garden City, N. Y., 1949), p. 113.

[11] "Initiative (in diplomacy) . . . is an important factor. This is all the more necessary for the diplomacy of this country, which finds itself in conditions of *capitalist encirclement*, because the Soviet Union has continuously experienced hostile international actions. In such conditions it is not sufficient to guess at the schemes of the enemies, frustrate their plans and confine oneself to defense against hostile diplomatic activities. The conditions of capitalist encirclement require the application of extensive counter plans which would not only foil the enemy but would systematically improve the international position of the Soviet state and strengthen the economic and cultural contacts between the USSR and foreign countries." (*Bolshevik*, Vol. III, No. 10 (1946), p. 77).

[12] Secretary Byrnes summed up his experiences concerning the Paris Conference of 1946 in the following words: "Mr. Molotov assumed that we and the British had organized a bloc against him. The fact is I never attended a meeting that would even suggest such an effort. Later in the conference he even charged that we instigated amendments offered by the smaller powers. Many of these amendments supported objectives that had been included in our original proposals for the treaties. But we had been obliged to drop them because of the Soviet veto in the Council. Because Molotov exercised a tight control over the votes and the actions of his supporters, he assumed that we did the same. It was inconceivable to him that Belgium, the Netherlands, South Africa, Australia or New Zealand, for example, could have ideas of their own, and that we would hesitate to try to influence their views. So he charged us with the formation of 'blocs' aimed at destroying the work of the Council." James F. Byrnes, *Speaking Frankly* (New York, 1947), p. 140. Cf. below footnote 27, pp. 154–155.

Informal face-to-face exchange of views and the usual give and take, patterns generally accepted in cultures of Western European derivation, are not characteristic of negotiations with the Soviet representative. He will repeat his arguments endlessly, may emphatically deny facts or connect unrelated issues, and then may reverse his position without regard to what he had said in previous meetings. His behavior occasionally seems fantastic and entirely irrelevant to the questions on the agenda. Postwar negotiations in the Council of Foreign Ministers, in the Paris Conference of 1946, for the Austrian Treaty, and for the German peace treaty offer scores of examples of this apparently irrational behavior. The Communist attitude has, of course, its inner logic. But the objectives and operational code of negotiations differ greatly in the Soviet and non-Soviet worlds. Postwar conferences with the Soviet Union demonstrated that in international negotiations among great powers, the most reluctant government determines the maximum rate of progress and limits the potentialities of negotiations. In the bewildering atmosphere created by Soviet representatives even minor concessions brought general relief. Under these conditions the fundamental problems were avoided, and participants limited the issues and the range of discussions as much as possible. Procedural and other abuses in diplomatic negotiations clearly showed that Soviet representatives did not recognize the rules of the game developed by the society of states in the last three centuries.

The attitude of Communist representatives in the course of negotiations with non-Communist countries constitutes an outward manifestation of the fact that on the deepest level of thought and life Soviet diplomacy has broken with the traditions of the Western diplomatic profession and rejected the assumption of solidarity that lies behind those traditions. True, diplomats in the pre-1914 world were also working primarily for national interests; but the means and objectives of diplomacy were limited by well known and generally accepted moral and intellectual concepts. The Western states considered themselves members of the same society. Diplomats had an open mind and were actually able to work for international peace and for the good of mankind. Such an attitude is beyond the comprehension of Communist representatives. To the Soviet diplomat the most valuable traditions of the diplomatic profession are meaningless. Marxist-Leninist principles do not advocate progress through peaceful evolution but through revolution and upheaval. All means which promote Communist objectives are regarded as good and legitimate. Everything, with the exception of the final goal, is reduced to expediency. Hence Communist representatives are uninhibited in their tactics and procedures.[13] For them negotiations are part of the permanent struggle between the Communist and capitalist countries and thus cannot aim at real conciliation, understanding, and agreement.

The acceptance of Lenin's principles for the basis of Soviet diplomacy involves contempt for objective truth and morality. Communist negotiators thus are advised not to be influenced by "formalistic" objectivity but to keep constantly in mind the real aims of Communist philosophy. Lenin repudiated all morality independent of the class struggle.[14] Since Lenin's teaching is still the gospel of the Communist world, the lack of a common set of ethical values is an overwhelming stumbling-block to any genuine understanding between Soviet and

[13] Lenin's teachings contain a number of characteristic passages to this effect, such as the following:

"We Communists must use one country against another. Are we not committing a crime against Communism? No, because we are doing so as a socialist state which is carrying on Communist propaganda and is obliged to take advantage of every hour granted it by circumstances in order to gain strength as rapidly as possible." V. I. Lenin, "Speech to Moscow Nuclei Secretaries," *Selected Works* (New York, 1943), VIII, p. 284.

"The more powerful enemy can be conquered only by exerting the utmost effort and by necessarily, thoroughly, carefully, attentively and skillfully taking advantage of every, even the smallest, 'rift' among the enemies, of every antagonism of interest among the bourgeoisie of various countries, and among various countries, and among various groups or types of bourgeoisie within the various countries, by taking advantage of every, even the smallest opportunity of gaining a mass ally, even though this ally be only temporary, vacillating, unstable, unreliable and conditional. Those who do not understand this do not understand a particle of Marxism, or of scientific modern socialism in general." V. I. Lenin, "Left-Wing Communism, an Infantile Disorder," *Selected Works* (New York, 1943), X, p. 112.

[14] "We say that our morality is wholly subordinated to the interests of the class struggle of the proletariat. We deduce our morality from the facts and needs of the class struggle of the proletariat. . . . For us morality is subordinated to the interests of the proletarian class struggle." V. I. Lenin, *Religion* (New York, 1935).

"Morals or ethics is the body of norms and rules on the conduct of Soviet peoples. At the root of Communist morality, said Lenin, lies the struggle for the consolidation and the completion of Communism. Therefore, from the point of view of Communist morality, only those acts are moral which contribute to the building up of a new Communist society" (Radio Moscow, August 20, 1950).

non-Soviet negotiators and has made of dubious value the agreements reached between them.[15] This has been true in major and minor matters.[16] One of the most experienced American diplomats, Joseph C. Grew noted in May 1945:

> The most fatal thing we can do is to place any confidence whatever in Russia's sincerity, knowing without question that she will take every opportunity to profit by our clinging to our own ethical international standards. She regards and will continue to regard our ethical behavior as a weakness to us and an asset to her.[17]

Since Leninism means the negation of a common ethical basis with the non-Communist states, believers in Lenin's philosophy feel free to sign with good grace any declaration of principle provided it does not affect their actual power position. For example, at Yalta Stalin signed almost without discussion the Declaration on Liberated Europe. For him acceptance of principles such as "the establishment through free elections of governments responsive to the will of the people" was an empty gesture as long as Russia occupied East Central Europe and could organize the "elections" in the Soviet pattern.

Leninist philosophy established a dual psychology for negotiations: one set of rules within the Communist world, another in negotiating with bourgeois states. This necessarily leads to a double standard, and is the reason why Soviet representatives are past-masters in double talk; that is, they use words to conceal their thoughts rather than to convey them. According to the Communist way of thinking, negotiations with capitalist countries can lead only to temporary agreements which give the Soviet Union a respite for increasing Soviet power and for preparing the road to world revolution. Soviet representatives have

[15] For the meaning of agreements in Communist doctrine see Nathan Leites in *A Study of Bolshevism*, pp. 527–533.

[16] It is particularly instructive to read how the Soviet government violated the most elementary rules of diplomatic confidence in 1948 during the course of negotiations with the United States. Walter Bedell Smith thought that the incident was important because "it taught all of us, the hard way, that the men in the Kremlin had carried over into peace the tactics of breaking confidence, of indulging in practices of deception, falsification and evasion which we had always hitherto associated only with relations between enemy states in time of shooting war." *My Three Years in Moscow* (Philadelphia, 1950), p. 157. For a detailed description of the incident see pp. 157–167.

[17] Joseph C. Grew, *Turbulent Era* (Boston, 1952), Vol. II, 1446.

also been greatly influenced by the basic Marxist-Leninist doctrine on the inevitability of "imperialist wars" among the capitalist states themselves because of economic conflicts [18] and the inevitability of a final showdown between the bourgeois states and the Soviet Union.[19] It is true that Khrushchev in his speech to the Twentieth Party Congress blurred the line between these two categories of inevitable wars and de-emphasized this doctrine because of changed world conditions.[20]

[18] "Politically we must take advantage of the differences between our opponents which are due to profound economic causes. If we try to take advantage of small and fortuitous differences, we shall be playing the part of petty politicians and cheap diplomats. But we shall gain nothing worth while by it." Lenin, *Selected Works* (New York, 1923), VIII, p. 283.

[19] "We are living not merely in a state but in a system of states and the existence of the Soviet Republic side by side with imperialist states for a long time is unthinkable. One or the other must triumph in the end. And before that end supervenes, a series of frightful collisions between the Soviet Republic and the bourgeois states will be inevitable. That means that if the ruling class, the proletariat, wants to hold sway, it must prove its capacity to do so by its military organization" (Lenin, "Report of Central Committee at 8th Party Congress," 1919).

On the basis of this idea Stalin characterized communism's role in international affairs in the following way: "The tasks of the Party in foreign policy are: 1) to utilize each and every contradiction and conflict among the surrounding capitalist groups and governments for the purpose of disintegrating imperialism; 2) to spare no pains or means to render assistance to the proletarian revolutions in the West; 3) to take all necessary measures to strengthen the national liberation movement in the East; 4) to strengthen the Red Army" (Stalin, "Party After Seizure of Power," *Pravda*, August 28, 1921).

According to this line of thought, peaceful co-existence between the Communist and capitalist countries is necessary in order to delay the inevitable war until the proper moment: "We cannot forget the saying of Lenin to the effect that a great deal in the matter of our construction depends on whether we succeed in delaying war with the capitalist countries, which is inevitable but which may be delayed either until proletarian revolution ripens in Europe or until colonial revolutions come to a head, or, finally, until the capitalists fight among themselves over the division of the colonies. Therefore, the maintenance of peaceful relations with capitalist countries is an obligatory task for us. The basis of our relations with capitalist countries consist in admitting the co-existence of two opposed systems" (Stalin, "Speech to the 15th Congress of the Soviet Union, December 3, 1927" [Moscow] 1949).

[20] Khrushchev first described how world conditions had changed since the promulgation of the "Marxist-Leninist precept that wars are inevitable as long as imperialism exists." Then he concluded:

"In these circumstances certainly, the Leninist precept that so long as imperialism exists the economic basis giving rise to wars will also be preserved, remains in force. That is why we must display the greatest vigilance. As long as

The effect of this new interpretation on the methods of Soviet diplomacy, however, remains to be seen.

So far Soviet negotiators have proved to be either indoctrinated Communist agents and thus firm believers in Lenin's principles or intimidated human beings fearful for their own and their family's safety. In either case they were not reluctant to use negotiating methods such as deceit, false statements, and procedural abuses for the promotion of Communist objectives. "We have replaced decency by reason," states Koestler's Rubashov.[21]

Since Soviet philosophy rejects the concept of immanent moral principles, Soviet representatives do not have any built-in moral restraint in their system and can easily out-promise negotiators of democratic countries. It is not difficult for totalitarian governments to make promises when they do not intend to carry them out.

The "open diplomacy" of the United Nations is a particularly useful sounding board for such an opportunistic and irresponsible diplomacy. Reckless promises and unfounded statements cannot be matched by negotiators whose actions are scrutinized by a democratic public opinion and press and who are responsible to the organs of a democratic state. Because of such abuses by Soviet representatives many important present-day social and political problems have not found a solution through multilateral negotiations and the action of international agencies. Soviet sabotage, in the United Nations is only a manifestation of the basic contradiction between declared Communist revolutionary methods and objectives and the solution of "international problems of an economic, social, cultural or humanitarian character" through international negotiations—one of the main purposes of the United Nations.

We should note, however, that the bullying attitude of Soviet representatives in the United Nations occasionally revealed their inability to understand free societies and in consequence boomeranged against

---

capitalism survives in the world, the reactionary forces representing the interests of the capitalist monopolies will continue their drive toward military gambles and aggression and may try to unleash war.

"But war is not fatalistically inevitable. Today there are mighty social and political forces possessing formidable means to prevent the imperialists from unleashing war, and, if they actually try to start it, to give a smashing rebuff to the aggressor and frustrate their adventurist plans."

[21] Koestler, *op. cit.*, p. 126.

their aims. It exposed with some clarity the realities behind the professed principles and informed the democratic countries of real Soviet intents, methods, and manners. Some of Vyshinsky's speeches had a sobering effect particularly upon the American public. He substantially contributed to the development of a political climate in the United States which made possible the Marshall Plan, NATO, and the Point Four Program.

As a result of the factors mentioned, informal exchanges of views seldom if ever took place in the course of diplomatic negotiations with Russians. A Soviet negotiator follows his instructions to the letter and would not dare to express his opinion *à titre privé*. They can hardly believe that such freedom exists for any official representatives.[22] This means that professional private contacts and confidential exchanges of views on a personal basis, practices which have led to many fruitful negotiations in the past, even between states in disagreement with each other, seldom operate in relations between the Soviet and non-Soviet worlds. Apparently the Russians have great difficulties in handling the informal side of international contacts. Soviet representatives often give the impression that they are automata rather than real human beings. This situation has improved since Stalin's death but the measure of liberalization of social contacts of Soviet diplomats is

---

[22] As an illustration of the Soviet way of thinking I may mention a conversation between myself and the Soviet Ambassador to Italy, Mikhail Kostylev, in July 1947, while I was Hungarian Minister to Italy. When the Hungarian Government, because of a Soviet veto, declined the Anglo-French invitation to the Marshall Plan Conference in Paris, I invited Kostylev to lunch. During our conversation I explained to him the economic plight of Hungary and Hungary's need for industrial equipment and capital from the United States. I mentioned to him the fact that the U.S.S.R. was in no position to give us these things. In his lengthy reply he explained to me that I was wrong. Real planning and economic integration cannot take place in capitalistic countries. The Marshall Plan would be a good thing for a few American capitalists, but it could not and would not effectively help the people in European countries. Real planning takes place only in Soviet Russia and in the countries which are her neighbors, and eventually this will help the people much more effectively than the intervention of American capitalists, who intend to find an outlet in Europe for their products and to create industrial colonies there. He added emphatically that no matter what our personal opinion might be, we were government officials, and thus we must obey the orders of our governments. This settled the matter as far as our conversation was concerned.

This was the only occasion when I heard a Soviet diplomat hint that he might have a private opinion. Although Kostylev himself had an excellent economic background, he only repeated the official Soviet slogans to me.

carefully restricted to specific countries and belongs clearly to the sphere of tactics.

During the Paris Conference of 1946, I was able to establish direct personal relations with Western diplomats, usually at my first meeting. In some cases such contacts resulted in lasting friendships. Although I was technically a representative of an "enemy" state, we could discuss privately even the most delicate questions. Confidences were mutually exchanged and never abused. Anything similar to such relations proved to be entirely impossible with Soviet representatives. All my meetings in Paris with Soviet diplomats such as A. E. Bogomolov, F. T. Gusev and A. A. Lavrischev, took place in the same room of the Soviet Embassy, and the conversations were obviously recorded. Social occasions created a more relaxed atmosphere and even made it possible to crack a few jokes with each other, but all these occurred before witnesses and private informal contacts did not develop. When I complained of this peculiar Russian behavior to a French diplomat, he told me that a Soviet delegation arrived recently in Paris and the Quai d'Orsay attached a secretary from the protocol division to them as a matter of routine. The secretary in a few introductory words offered to show them the city and organize a few pleasant evening excursions. The Russians conferred among themselves for a while, and then their senior official replied in a stern voice that they refused to accept the offer. When the French secretary tried desperately to explain to them that he only wanted to make their stay in Paris pleasant, they again whispered among themselves and the senior official announced that the offer should be made through the proper channel, the Soviet Embassy.

I note at this point that probably little bilateral informal communication exists between Communist chiefs in the satellite countries and political leaders in the Soviet Union. Apparently from this point of view it does not make much difference whether Stalin, Malenkov, or Khrushchev is ruling in Moscow. The Communist satraps in the satellites are told at the last moment what to do and how to behave, and they have to follow, often with tongue in cheek, frequently-changing Russian instructions. I mention parenthetically that Nazi Germany held a similar attitude toward Italy and the lesser satellites. In early 1948 Mátyás Rákosi, a Communist leader of Hungary, gave a lengthy explanation to Chester Bowles concerning an East Central

European federation to be established in the near future under Tito's leadership.[23] It appeared that Moscow had not given him any forewarning about its imminent rejection of this concept or of the steps which it was preparing against Tito's position of relative independence.

After Stalin's death Imre Nagy replaced Rákosi as prime minister following the suggestion of the leaders of the Soviet Union at a meeting in Moscow in June, 1953. Imre Nagy himself described this scene in his *Defense of the New Course:* "It must be stated that it was not Mátyás Rákosi but the Soviet comrades, Malenkov, Molotov, and Khrushchev, who recommended what Rákosi and all members of the Hungarian delegation accepted with approbation. Thus, Rákosi . . . bears no responsibility at all for my nomination."

In the early postwar period Soviet diplomats, in the course of negotiations and other contacts with non-Communist representatives of satellite countries, usually displayed strict adherence to diplomatic courtesy. Sometimes they could even afford frankness, void of all diplomatic trimming.[24] They liked to argue in their advantageous position

[23] Chester Bowles traveled in Europe as Chairman of the United Nations Appeal for Children and as a consultant to Trygve Lie, Secretary General of the United Nations. In this dual capacity he was in Hungary for five or six days in late January of 1948. While in Budapest he received an invitation to call on Rákosi who launched into a long discussion of the Cold War and suggested that a major development of a constructive nature lay just ahead. He said that within a few weeks we would see the development of what he called the "United States of Southeastern Europe." He added that this new organization would include Yugoslavia, Albania, Bulgaria, Rumania, Hungary, Poland, and "possibly Czechoslovakia." He emphasized again and again that it would be under the leadership of Tito. This new Tito-led federation should be welcomed by the countries of Western Europe because it would increase the likelihood that a bridge could be built across Europe to prevent war and to exert a moderating influence.

In case of war, Rákosi was frank to say that the new federation would support the Soviet Union, as Western Europe would be pledged to support the United States. However, he emphasized that the states of the new federation, with their greater understanding of Western Europe, would inevitably exercise a moderating influence on the Soviet Union, as the states of Western Europe might be expected to exercise a similar moderating influence on the United States. In this way he hoped that a blow-up between the Soviet Union and America might eventually be avoided.—The source of this information is a letter to the author from Chester Bowles (October 9, 1956).

[24] Before I left Hungary in March 1947 to occupy my post as Hungarian Minister to Italy, I had a long conversation with the Soviet Minister to Hungary, Georgii Pushkin who later became Ambassador to Eastern Germany. He warned me that I should not follow the pro-Italian line of my predecessors. I told him that we fully understood the changed power situation in Europe but that it was next to

and tried to show in their own way the righteousness of their cause even in cases when they could and eventually did use force through the variety of channels at their disposal. Well applied bluntness and directness apparently impressed them in negotiations but did not change the course of their policy. A ranking Soviet diplomat pointed out to me in connection with a concrete incident that they appreciate openness and courage in other quarters even if this means opposition to Soviet policy. This statement was a manifestation of the ambivalent Soviet attitude which often expects reliability and fairness from the other side without feeling any obligation to reciprocate.

In satellite relations Soviet negotiators almost as a routine procedure exploited the numerous national claims and conflicts. For example, in

---

impossible to find in Hungary popular support for a pro-Russian foreign policy because of many unpleasant things and political mistakes which occurred after the Red Army occupied the country. Pushkin replied that undoubtedly mistakes were committed but that these were immaterial; not the present but the future counts. One should educate the new generation properly and this generation will co-operate.

On the same occasion I clarified the Russian view concerning Hungary's relations with the Vatican, about which contradictory opinions were circulating in governmental and ecclesiastical circles. The Smallholder Prime Minister and the Foreign Minister suggested to me that while in Rome I should explore the possibilities of the renewal of diplomatic relations with the Vatican and the conclusion of a concordat. They advised me, however, to discuss the problems involved with President Tildy. The President gave me ambiguous, noncommittal instructions. One of the Catholic bishops assured me that the Communists and Russians supported the plan. Cardinal Mindszenty remained skeptical about the sincerity of the Communist attitude. Since the Russian-dominated Allied Control Commission's consent was still necessary to the planned diplomatic move, I decided to clarify the Russian and Communist standpoint by a direct approach. In my interview with Pushkin I brought up the problem of exchanging envoys with the Vatican. I argued that Hungary had a large Catholic population and that it would be advisable for the new regime to settle all pending Church-State problems by the intervention of an experienced papal diplomat. The Russian Minister replied: "The Vatican is just an agent of American interests in Europe, financed by American capitalists. The new Hungarian democracy does not need the representative of such reactionary forces."

During one of my meetings with Ambassador Bogomolov in Paris, prior to the conference of 1946, I reminded him of Lenin's severe criticisms of the Versailles Treaty and argued that a genuine Danubian settlement should be made on the basis of self-determination of all nations. Bogomolov introduced his lengthy, philosophical but entirely negative answer with the statement that principles have only a relative meaning. Conditions change. What seemed just and true after the first World War may no longer be true, he said.

the course of the postwar conflict between Czechoslovakia and Hungary concerning the expulsion of the Hungarians from Czechoslovakia, both Voroshilov and Envoy Pushkin officially supported the Czechoslovakia thesis and in informal communications used the argument that Hungary could receive compensation from Transylvania if she accepted the Czechoslovak plan. At the same time Molotov resolutely opposed an American proposal in the Council of Foreign Ministers favoring a slight modification in the Transylvanian boundary line in favor of Hungary. During a conversation Pushkin explained casually to the Hungarian Foreign Minister that the Czechoslovak politicians committed a political mistake in not expelling the bulk of the Hungarians from Slovakia at the close of hostilities. The situation thus created would have facilitated negotiations for a settlement between the two countries, he added.

In connection with expulsion of the Germans from Hungary, the Russians first used a great variety of arguments and pressure in order to induce the Hungarian Government to accept an all-out, indiscriminate expulsion of the Germans. When, however, the Hungarian Government refused to accept the principle of collective responsibility and decided to remove only those Germans who had become servants of Hitlerism and traitors to Hungary, the Soviet delegation at the Potsdam Conference, in a sudden move, proposed that a provision for the expulsion of the Germans from Hungary should be inserted into Article XIII, which dealt with the expulsion of the Germans from Poland and Czechoslovakia. Since this Soviet proposal had obtained Western endorsement at Potsdam, Hungarian opposition against an indiscriminate expulsion of the Germans was greatly weakened.[25] Thus the machinery of an international conference was used to carry out Soviet policy which Moscow had not succeeded in achieving through bilateral negotiations in an, as yet, not entirely satellized country.

In summing up observations concerning Soviet negotiating attitudes one may say that, because of the permanent factors in Russian foreign political objectives, principles, and methods, there was relatively little change in Soviet negotiating behavior, especially on the level below the top, in the changing periods of Russo-American relations. The

[25] Cf. Stephen Kertesz, "The Expulsion of the Germans from Hungary: A Study in Postwar Diplomacy," *Review of Politics*, XV (1953), 179–205.

uncooperative Soviet attitude did not begin with the cold war. During the height of Russo-American friendship, when Russia most needed American help, General Deane experienced in Moscow suspicious, unresponsive, unreliable, and frequently offensive behavior.[26] The episodes he relates about Russian suspicions are not unlike those the Germans experienced in the era of Russo-German friendship in the course of the establishment and operation of the German secret military training grounds in Russia.[27]

[26] See for example Deane, *op. cit.*, pp. 34, 48, 50, 53, 84–85, 129–130, 133–35, 139–141, 160–161, 200–201, 254. We should note, however, that the Russians were greatly encouraged by the unprecedented American attitude. The anomalous practice developed that the Russians received military information through the American Lend-Lease representative in Moscow, while the American Ambassador and Military attaché were deliberately left out from this channel of communication. Cf. William H. Standley and Arthur A. Ageton, *Admiral Ambassador to Russia* (Chicago, 1955), pp. 236–239, 245–246.

[27] Helm Speidel, "Reichswehr und Rote Armee," *Vierteljahrshefte für Zeitgeschichte, I* (January 1953), pp. 9–45.

The negotiating behavior of Soviet officials was extremely well characterized by Laurence Steinhardt, American Ambassador in Moscow in 1941. He pointed out in his report of June 17: "My observation of the psychology of the individuals who are conducting Soviet foreign policy has long since convinced me that they do not and cannot be induced to respond to the customary amenities, that it is not possible to create 'international good will' with them, that they will always sacrifice the future in favor of an immediate gain, and that they are not affected by ethical or moral considerations, nor guided by the relationships which are customary between individuals of culture and breeding. Their psychology recognizes only firmness, power and force, and reflects primitive instincts and reactions entirely devoid of the restraints of civilization. It is [I am] of the opinion that they must be dealt with on this basis and on this basis alone. I feel fortified in these views, which I arrived at independently, by conversations with Count von [der] Schulenburg, who has on several occasions told me quite frankly that more considerate treatment was accorded German interests and the German Government by the Soviet authorities during the period when the violence of the German campaign against the Soviet Union was at its height than at any time prior or subsequent to that period. It has been my own experience that on every occasion that either the Department or the embassy has made concessions to the Soviet Government, or has approached it in a spirit of friendly cooperation or good will, these gestures have been received by the Soviet authorities with marked suspicion and a disposition to regard them as evidence of weakness, whereas on each occasion that our attitude has stiffened the Soviet authorities have regarded our demeanor as evidence of self-confidence and strength and have promptly reacted by a more conciliatory attitude which has noticeably increased our prestige. Nor have I found any evidence of resentment or bitterness at the reciprocal application of unpleasant measures." *Foreign Relations of the United States: Diplomatic Papers 1941.* Volume I, *The Soviet Union* (Washington, 1958), p. 765.

Sir Stafford Cripps, Britain's Socialist Ambassador's experiences were similar as it appears from Steinhardt's report of February 8, 1941. Cripps told Steinhardt

The explanation of this peculiar Soviet attitude is simple. The nature of world politics and basic foreign political objectives have changed only for the non-Communist states. From the Soviet point of view these objectives have not changed, and the Soviet operational code for negotiators has remained essentially the same during the ups and downs of world politics. The changing tactics have revolved around the same unchanging goals.

The greatest danger brought about by Soviet negotiating behavior has been the increase of uncertainty in international relations because of the minimizing, if not the eliminating, of such values as respect for honesty and mutual trust. As a result all reasonable bases for long-term negotiations disappear, and diplomats are restricted to momentary solutions dictated by current power politics and cannot consider larger horizons. Diplomacy as practiced by Communist negotiators destroys confidence instead of creating it. If the big lie is accepted as a routine means in diplomacy, as it frequently is by Soviet Russian representatives, then international negotiations necessarily have a limited value. This is why good faith in negotiating with Communists has so often proved ineffective.

II

Whereas Soviet negotiators have largely exhibited an inflexible purpose and uniform behavior, the American scene presents a less monotonous picture. As was mentioned earlier, one of the general

---

that "as London realizes more and more clearly that a policy of conciliation and appeasement with respect to the Soviet Government produces results diametrically opposite to those expected and that the Soviet Government responds more readily to an aggresive policy than to a policy of concessions the British attitude towards the Soviet Union is becoming stiffer." *Ibid.*, p. 160. Steinhardt characterized the transformation of Sir Stafford Cripps' strongly pro-Soviet attitude in the following way: "I judge from the Ambassador's recent attitude and general remarks that he has not yet lost all of his illusions about the virtues of the Soviet Government, but that he has now reached the stage of obstinately clinging to some of his earlier beliefs while being forced to recognize that the natural intentions and conduct of the Soviet Government are very much at variance with those beliefs which he has long championed. He is now realistic and at times even bitter, but will suddenly defend indefensible acts of the Soviet Government. His present state of mind is characteristic of that of virtually every Chief of Mission whose initial approach to the Soviet Government has been one of belief in its sincerity, integrity, or honesty of purpose and has invariably eventually resulted in a deep-seated bitterness and hatred as distinguished from those individuals who have never had any illusions about the character of the Soviet Government." *Ibid.*, p. 161.

characteristics of American representatives is their difficulty in perceiving how the world appears to others, in understanding the psychology of foreign nations. Americans are inclined to disregard the fact that their Constitution, the continental size of the United States, resources, and industrial potential together with other favorable factors in the dynamic American society, make feasible a pace of progress which can hardly be duplicated in smaller, less developed, and less fortunate countries. The assumptions of American negotiators, whether leading statesmen or subaltern officials, often reflect the subconscious idea that "what is good for the United States is good for the world; what is good for the individual in the United States is or should be good for less fortunate foreigners as well." Although this instinctive approach is an almost unavoidable consequence of the amazing achievements and high living-standard of the American people, it has been the cause of many irritations and failures in diplomacy, because foreign nations with different political institutions, social backgrounds, and economic conditions are unable or unwilling to take for granted the "American way of life," in particular, the American system of democratic government, and have little understanding of American "reform capitalism." This difficulty naturally affects the politician-negotiators more than professional diplomats, although there are remarkable exceptions in both categories.

The chief characteristic of top-level American negotiators has been that all of them were deeply rooted in domestic American life and had little experience, if any, in negotiating outside the English-speaking world. Although much depended on personality, all of them quite naturally were influenced by past negotiating experiences.

Besides these general factors, the paramount fact was that the American nation had suddenly been catapulted into a position of world leadership. In the past great powers had usually acquired their strength and skill in international affairs over generations. No such gradual development took place in the United States. The power position of the American nation changed relatively overnight, and at the same time the nature and meaning of international affairs underwent a revolutionary transformation. In contrast to the Soviet pseudo-diplomatic attitude, American diplomacy inherited, cherished, and took seriously the intrinsic values of Western European diplomacy, to which were added some specific American virtues and shortcomings.

But the techniques and methods of European diplomacy, developed in a homogeneous society of states, have not proven effective in the relations of the democracies with totalitarian dictatorships.

The primary source of American political philosophy is, of course, the American Constitution—a product of the eighteenth century. This philosophy and political pattern further developed in the favorable atmosphere of the nineteenth century, an exceptionally happy period of diplomatic history when the major participants in world politics recognized certain fundamental rules of the game, the United States lived outside the mainstream of world events, and few of its people were really interested in foreign affairs. It is one of the consequences of this heritage that American negotiators are disposed to argue in the spirit of fairness and humanitarian liberalism, principles permeating American education and political thinking. Since they are influenced by principles of justice and objective truth, they are inclined to cling to abstract ideas and to disregard the actually existing power-political situation. Hence the habit of promulgating and emphasizing general principles and the temptation to oversimplify complex foreign-affairs issues into moral problems or legalistic formulas.

We may note at this point that American negotiators and policy-makers are often inclined to disregard unpleasant facts and unwelcome possibilities in their operational thinking. They are disposed to believe that a thing is feasible because it seems just and desirable for the majority of men. This generally optimistic American outlook—a source of progress and many constructive achievements—may be a cause of self-deception. While the self-confidence which it engenders can be important, even though sometimes built on illusion, more often than not it boomerangs in the cruel atmosphere of international politics. The ineffectiveness of this approach in international affairs was demonstrated in the first World War and even more so during and after the second World War. With the collapse of the isolationist policy under the pressure of Hitler's aggression, and specifically as a consequence of the Japanese attack on Pearl Harbor, the United States suddenly found itself the partner of a totalitarian dictatorship which had expansionist and subversive objectives in world affairs. During the war years and, even, afterwards the chief American negotiators were blinded by their refusal to believe that the leader of the great Russian nation was a bad fellow, and thought that his acceptance of certain general principles would eventually spread the blessings of American democratic ideas and practices on a global scale.

Probably this was one of the reasons, besides practical military and political considerations, why during the second World War a major American goal was to leave the territorial and other important political decisions for the Peace Conference. This attitude changed only in the last phase of the war, when the Red Army already occupied key areas and it was necessary to face unpleasant *de facto* situations.[28]

There were numerous factors which constituted almost permanent handicaps for American negotiators in relations with totalitarian dictatorships. Although American negotiators may sometimes have a fair amount of leeway, their freedom in negotiation is limited by a great many factors such as political institutions, principles, and practices, wishes of the American people, and sensitivity of the Allies. They have to deliver results to the electorate and meet such political deadlines as elections. In changing situations it is necessary to persuade public opinion at home and abroad of the necessity of a different policy. This is sometimes a slow and arduous process, especially if sacrifices are involved.

Another handicap for the United States in negotiating with Soviet Russia has been the Anglo-Saxon spirit which, by tradition, is inclined to regard the making of compromises as the normal lubricant of the decision-making process. This virtue has more often than not been harmful in negotiating with Soviet delegates, for it was interpreted by them as a lack of firmness; instead of facilitating mutual accommodations, it failed to impress people educated in the inexorable atmosphere of a monolithic society, and thus opened the door for further Soviet demands.

Then, too, it is a particularly difficult task to organize and maintain an alliance system including countries with unrelated if not contradictory objectives. During the second World War there was the common foe, and in the period of the cold war the most important common tie was the fear of the Soviet Union. This common danger had different aspects in the various parts of the globe. Strains and conflicts exist within the non-Soviet world, and the United States can-

---

[28] Cf. Philip E. Mosely, "Hopes and Failures: American Policy Toward East Central Europe," *The Fate of East Central Europe*, Stephen D. Kertesz, ed. (Notre Dame, 1956), pp. 52–54.

not keep free countries together with methods contrary to Western principles. The situation is further complicated by the fact that in the United States it is almost impossible to coordinate all the major foreign policy-making factors. Contradictory statements emanating from them have world-wide repercussions and may create confusion among the Western allies and the uncommitted nations.

In the crucial years between 1941 and 1947, simultaneously with the unplanned expansion of American responsibilities in world affairs, there was no adequate organization for making foreign policy in the United States. Important differences existed among various military leaders and between officials even within the Department of State concerning American war and peace aims and methods of achieving them. The preparation of negotiations and of the negotiators themselves did not always follow well-established patterns, and the chief negotiators often behaved in a rather unorthodox way and acted on the impulse of the moment. For example, announcement of the unconditional surrender principle at Casablanca and acceptance of the Morgenthau Plan at Quebec occurred without preparation through regular governmental channels. Much depended on whims of the chief negotiators, whose experience in American politics were not the proper preparation for negotiating with Soviet leaders. Whether it was President Roosevelt at Teheran and Yalta, Harry Hopkins in Moscow, President Truman at Potsdam, or Secretary Byrnes in London, Paris, and Moscow, did not make much difference from this point of view. A common characteristic of these negotiations was that American specialists on Soviet affairs did not have a decisive influence, if they were consulted at all, and leading American negotiators approached the Soviet leaders with unwarranted good faith and fairness. Since they wanted to produce prompt results in the form of mutual agreements, they were too impatient to listen to the sobering comments of experienced advisors.

Negotiations on the lower level were conducted by diplomats and State Department specialists. Although this core of professional people could interpret foreign nations with fair accuracy, their views and suggestions many times were not taken into consideration, mainly because of the nature of the policy-making machinery in Washington and the relatively low prestige of American diplomatic representatives on the domestic political scene. Evaluations and recommendations emanating from military authorities were usually given more serious consideration by policy-makers, but there is no evidence that the realistic appraisals of Soviet conduct and the recommendations of General John R. Deane, head of the American Military Mission in Moscow in 1943–1945, had the slightest influence on decisions made in Washington, particularly in the administration of the all-important Lend-Lease program.

The practice of neglecting the State Department's advice in Russian affairs began even before the renewal of diplomatic relations in 1933. The State Department recommended to the President that the Russian debt should be settled before recognition, because recognition was the only effective weapon held by Washington. This procedure was abandoned in the course of the negotiations and only a carelessly worded "gentlemen's agreement" was signed by President Roosevelt and Litvinov in November, 1933. Subsequent events fully justified the State Department's apprehensions, and the Russian debts were never settled.[29]

Later the reports of American diplomats from Moscow proved that the nature, objectives and methods of the Soviet Union were no secret to people with sufficient background and experience.[30] During the war years diplomats and other State Department specialists on Russian affairs were keenly aware of the "menace of Soviet domination over East Central Europe" and desired "to ward off this menace." [31] When in the autumn of 1944 Cordell Hull began to realize that the Soviet Union was not carrying out the policy of cooperation agreed upon at the Moscow and Teheran conferences, he asked the American Ambassador in Moscow the reason for the manifestly changed Russian attitude. In reply, Averell Harriman cited examples of Russia's unilateral actions and her unwillingness to cooperate with the West, and in a later telegram suggested that "when the Russians saw victory in sight they began to put into practice the policies they intended to

[29] *Foreign Relations of the United States* (Washington, 1933), II, pp. 785, 789–790, 793–794.

[30] See especially the reports and memoranda of Loy W. Henderson and George Kennan published in *Foreign Relations of the United States: The Soviet Union 1933–1939* (Washington, 1952)

[31] Such realistic views were expressed in studies prepared by the Country and Area Committee within the Department of State during 1943 and 1944. See Mosely, "Hopes and Failures," *op. cit.*, p. 57.

follow in peace." [32] The briefing papers for the Yalta Conference were sober and realistic, but we do not have evidence that these were read, let alone appreciated, by the chief negotiators.

With the possible exception of the dictators, no man has greater power in foreign affairs than the President of the United States, and this is particularly true in wartime when he may often conduct foreign policy largely on a personal basis. This was the case with President Roosevelt. Although he understood certain aspects of foreign affairs extremely well, and in the period of the Hitler-Stalin collaboration strongly condemned Soviet policies, under the stress of the war he developed an unwarranted faith in Stalin's willingness to cooperate with the West. His negotiations were influenced by optimistic hopes that the Soviet Union could be brought into a democratic world community if treated with patience and magnanimity. His great mistake was to assume that scrupulous adherence to agreements or generosity would induce Stalin to reciprocate.

Cooperation with the Soviet Union was undoubtedly a necessity while the war was being fought in Europe, and Russian military intervention was thought necessary in the Far East. But Roosevelt's ideas went far beyond military considerations. He intended to develop an intimate friendship with the Russians and then to solve all postwar problems in close cooperation with the Soviet Union and within the framework of a general security organization. In Roosevelt's mind the ideological, political, and social differences between Communism and the Western state system were overshadowed by immediate military goals and by a rosy future based on the fraternal cooperation of the Four Policemen.

Although this "Grand Design" of four-power cooperation in keeping world order had a large element of wishful thinking in it, Roosevelt was not in complete ignorance about what Stalin might do after the war if left alone in Europe. He probably wanted to make a friend of a potentially dangerous enemy. His hopes for future peace were based on a new security organization, and the Soviet Union was considered one of the potential pillars of the forthcoming democratic world order. While Stalin appeared to him as an untamed and somewhat dangerous but not malevolent partner in a great human enterprise, he regarded the leader of the tottering British Empire as the representative of

[32] Hull, *op. cit.*, pp. 1459–1460.

nineteenth-century colonial imperialism. On the other side Stalin thought that both Churchill and Roosevelt were exponents of a doomed capitalist world order.

Churchill occasionally tried a more realistic approach, but he was the weakest partner and had to accommodate himself to political realities. Moreover, President Roosevelt was inclined to side with Stalin demonstratively in order to dispel Soviet mistrust. Meetings of the three political leaders showed the difficulty of negotiations by people having greatly differing backgrounds, different views on the nature of world politics, and mutually exclusive aims and expectations.

President Roosevelt's special negotiator in Russian affairs, Harry Hopkins, was a man of great ability and engaging manners, but—as appears from his papers—hardly a specialist on the U.S.S.R. or Communism.[33] Those who understood Russia and Communism were not given responsible positions which would have permitted them to advise and negotiate in Soviet matters. They were not in charge of decisive negotiations in American-Soviet relations and usually were not consulted by high policy-makers as the nature of Russian and American relations would have required.

Indeed one of the characteristics of the Roosevelt era was the President's dislike of specialists in general and of foreign service officers in particular. This attitude created difficulties in the conduct of foreign affairs and became the source of special difficulties at summit conferences, when he could negotiate and make agreements according to hunches, regardless of facts and realities. Sumner Welles has pointed out that the President was unwilling to dictate any memoranda of his own conversations with foreign statesmen and diplomats for the information of those who were running the Department of State, and that he harbored a "deep-rooted prejudice against the members of the American Foreign Service and against the permanent officials of the Department of State." He very rarely "could be persuaded to bring into White House conferences on foreign policy any of those State Department specialists who had devoted a lifetime to the study of some particular country or region."[34] On several occasions the Presi-

---

[33] See, for example, the document headed "Russia's Position," which Hopkins had with him at the first Quebec Conference. Robert E. Sherwood, *Roosevelt and Hopkins* (New York, 1948), pp. 748–749.

[34] Welles, *op. cit.*, p. 216.

dent acted alone or in cooperation with amiable amateurs, without looking into the briefs of the specialists and without consulting experts. Sumner Welles mentioned that neither during the Cairo Conference with Chiang Kai-shek nor later at Yalta did Roosevelt have at his side a political advisor on Far Eastern affairs.

An insight into Roosevelt's state of mind before Teheran is provided by Secretary Hull, to whom the President said concerning Poland and the Baltic States that, "when he should meet with Stalin, he intended to appeal to him on grounds of high morality. He would say to him that neither Britain nor we would fight Russia over the Baltic States, but that in Russia's own interest, from the viewpoint of her position in the world, it would be a good thing for her to say that she would be willing, two years or so after the war, to hold a second plebiscite in the Baltic countries." [35]

Nothing shows the difference between Soviet and American evaluations of negotiations more than the fact that American political leaders considered the Declaration on Liberated Europe and other agreements concluded at Yalta as diplomatic victories simply because the Russians made significant concessions on paper despite their effective possession of most of East Central Europe.[36] For example, the Russians agreed to free elections and the establishment of coalition governments in territories under their control. Actually, however, they accepted all kinds of declarations of principle only because they controlled the areas and thus could interpret and apply the principles. It is somewhat difficult to understand the good faith which American leaders attributed to Soviet Russia at Yalta, because in February 1945 there was ample evidence of Russia's attitude and intentions concerning Poland, Yugoslavia, and the rest of East Central Europe.

Soviet purposes had begun to emerge clearly after the victory at Stalingrad in 1943. Under the perils of the war and the influence of optimistic speculations, the Anglo-American leaders put forward no concrete plans for the reorganization of Europe. Apparently it was supposed that the European state system would somehow reestablish

---

[35] Hull, *op. cit.*, p. 1266. Roosevelt "thought that the same idea might be applied to Eastern Poland, . . . and that a plebiscite should be held after the shell shock of the war had subsided" *loc. cit.*

[36] Cf. Stettinius, *op. cit.*, pp. 306–307.

and assert itself. Without concrete political objectives, military goals remained for them the decisive factor even in that period of the war when the molding of the postwar world had begun.[37]

Whatever happened during wartime negotiations, the major mistake could have been corrected at the close of hostilities when the Anglo-American military might was superior to that of the Soviet Union. Stalin would have understood the only argument appealing to him, force, and a reasonable European settlement could have been worked out.

One of the great tragedies of the West was the untimely death of President Roosevelt, who in his last days had become sharply aware of Soviet duplicity. He might have changed Western policies toward Russia radically at a time when the United States was the strongest world power. But this was much more difficult for his successor. Vice-President Truman was not regularly briefed in foreign political questions. Since President Roosevelt in many ways was his own Secretary of State, no single individual could give President Truman a coherent picture of the world issues at stake and the major foreign policy motivations of President Roosevelt. President Truman was in no way able to draw upon the foreign political experiences of his predecessor. After having assumed the highest office, he was informed of the existence and advanced stage of atomic research and received other pieces of interesting information from half a dozen individuals, otherwise he had to learn the hard way, and this took time—perhaps the two most decisive years in American history.

Since President Truman was not sufficiently prepared in foreign political matters, he faithfully followed for some time the line of policy he had inherited from President Roosevelt. This attitude was conspicuous in his negotiations and in negotiations directed by him in 1945. Although he used strong words when Molotov visited him in Washington just prior to the San Francisco Conference [38] and energetically raised issues at Potsdam, the fact was that neither he nor

[37] According to John C. Campbell, wartime American mistakes of omission and commission fall into three general categories: failure to assess Soviet policies correctly; failure to define our objectives clearly and pursue them consistently; and failure to relate military power and military decisions to political objectives. "Negotiations with the Soviets," *Foreign Affairs*, XXXIV (1956), 307.

[38] *Memoirs* by Harry S. Truman, Vol. I: Year of Decisions (Garden City, 1955), pp. 79–82.

Secretary Byrnes had sufficient experience and insight into the world problems they faced.

At Potsdam, President Truman still "hoped that Stalin was a man who would keep his agreements." [39] Although his Secretary of State, James F. Byrnes had already had numerous dismal experiences with Soviet negotiators, he still hoped in Moscow in December 1945, that the United States and the Soviet Union had a "common purpose." [40] This optimism influenced American negotiators in the fluid situation of the immediate postwar period when well-planned negotiations could have improved the position of the Western powers in Europe. Tough language around conference tables did not impress the Russians because the gradually hardening Western attitude was accompanied by prompt demobilization of the American Army as a result of almost unanimous Congressional and popular demands. Moreover, while the Western Powers took a stand on many individual issues, they never formulated a comprehensive plan for the reorganization of Europe in the early postwar period. Thus there was no nucleus around which Western diplomatic positions could have been solidified and negotiations channelled into a constructive direction. The general lack of Western assertiveness gave the green light to further Soviet actions in East Central Europe and in the Far East. Diplomats who diligently drafted notes of protest could hardly change the course of events.

The eyes of American policymakers opened in early 1946 when Russia refused to evacuate northern Iran and Stalin advocated further development of heavy industry and armaments.[41] It took another year before the Truman Doctrine was promulgated, marking the beginning of a positive American policy directed against further Soviet expansion. This new American attitude in world affairs revitalized the economic power of Europe; it built up through difficult negotiations a network of defensive regional organizations and defeated the Soviet blockade in Berlin and aggression in Korea. But it could not liberate the countries already under Soviet domination.

Active American participation in world affairs made necessary a series of international negotiations during which an emerging situation

---

[39] *Ibid.*, p. 350. Truman adds, "We had much to learn on this subject."
[40] Cf. Byrnes, *op. cit.*, p. 255.
[41] Byrnes, *ibid.*

of strength gave American negotiators a wider range of action. For example, the effective use of conference technique and especially Dean Acheson's forceful attitude defeated Soviet maneuvers at the conclusion of the Peace Treaty with Japan in San Francisco.[42] Blaise Pascal's advice that we should "combine justice and might, and for this end make what is just, strong, and what is strong, just" was finally accepted.

The cold war, nonetheless, was also full of diplomatic "ups and downs," in the field of negotiations with Communist delegates. Even the few successful negotiations were preceded by frustrating experiences. Secretary Dulles pointed out recently that the negotiations which ended the Korean fighting took two years and involved 575 meetings, the negotiations for the Austrian State Treaty took eight years and involved some 400 meetings, the negotiations for the International Atomic Energy Agency took almost three years, and the negotiations between the United States and the Soviet Union for "cultural contacts" took two and a half years.[43] It should be noted at this point that the time factor has a different meaning for Soviet negotiators than for Americans. Once the Soviet leaders decided to make an agreement, the concluding negotiations developed with efficiency and surprising rapidity. Only a few meetings were required to end the Berlin Blockade and to resolve the Austrian Treaty, and the Korean Armistice was negotiated in less than three weeks.

The sorry chain of events in the past two decades has taught a lesson to American negotiators. Surely it has demonstrated that principles alone, without application of adequate military strength and political determination, cannot operate effectively. It has also indicated that lack of deeply rooted diplomatic traditions among practitioners of American diplomacy, a point often criticized, has in reality been almost an asset under quickly shifting world conditions. It may be true that the United States was not prepared politically for world leadership, but it is equally true, in view of the radically changed world condi-

---

[42] Cf. J. Lewe van Aduard, *Japan From Surrender to Peace* (The Hague, 1953), pp. 222–228.

[43] John Foster Dulles, "The Role of Negotiation," *Bulletin*, XXXVIII (1958), 159–163. Cf. C. Turner Joy, *How Communists Negotiate* (New York, 1955). William S. B. Lacy, "Exchange Agreement with the U.S.S.R.," *Bulletin*, XXXVIII (1958), 323–329. Foy D. Kohler, "Negotiation as an Effective Instrument of American Foreign Policy," *Bulletin*, XXXVIII (1958), 901–910.

tions and the suddenly unbalanced power relationships, that no country was prepared. In our time a fresh approach in policies and negotiating methods may open new avenues for solutions in world affairs, as has been the case since the enunciation of the Truman Doctrine.

III

I have dealt in this paper primarily with some aspects of American and Soviet negotiating attitudes in the period ending with Stalin's death. It would perhaps be a more timely task to evaluate recent changes in the negotiating methods of Soviet representatives and raise the question as to the proper American response to the attitude of the new Soviet leaders. Unlike the cautious and reserved Stalin, they are outwardly gregarious and most eager to negotiate.

First of all it should be noted that the friendlier behavior of Soviet representatives is not entirely new. There were periods under Stalin's rule when the Soviet attitude was cooperative. Let us recall the era of the popular fronts. Litvinov was the apostle of collective security at Geneva and behaved like an Oxford-educated foreign minister. The chief chronicler of the League commented: "From September 18th, 1934, until a few months before the outbreak of the second World War, Russia continued to be a convinced supporter of the League. Her record in the Council and the Assembly, and her conduct toward the aggressive powers, were more consistent with the Covenant than those of any other great power." [44]

Stalin himself used Russian patriotic slogans during the second World War, occasionally displayed friendly attitudes toward the West, and made such gestures as the dissolution of the Comintern and establishment of cooperation with the Orthodox Church. At times he could be extremely benign. Ambassador Davies suggested that Stalin's brown eye was "exceedingly kindly and gentle. A child would like to sit in his lap and a dog would sidle up to him." [45] General John R. Deane evaluated him more objectively: "I have seen him fawn over children before the multitude with the same political acumen that prompts similar public displays by American politicians." [46] Cordell

---

[44] F. P. Walters, *A History of the League of Nations,* 2 vols. (Oxford University Press, 1952), p. 585.

[45] Joseph E. Davies, *Mission to Moscow* (New York, 1941), p. 357.

[46] Deane, *op. cit.,* p. 291.

Hull thought that "any American having Stalin's personality and approach might well reach high public office" in the United States.[47]

While Soviet diplomacy was characterized by rigidity in Stalin's last years, his successors displayed great flexibility. The new Soviet leaders concentrated on diplomacy by propaganda almost as though they were applying Dale Carnegie's methods to international relations. Molotov's whistle-stopping tour across the United States, Bulganin's and Khrushchev's many visits abroad, the summit meeting at Geneva, and smiling Menshikov's friendly attitude in Washington are cases in point. But the men from the Kremlin paid only lip service to the settlement of serious issues between the Soviet and non-Soviet worlds. The withdrawal of Soviet forces and control from Eastern Austria was an encouraging sign after the record sabotage of Soviet negotiators, but this was not followed by similar actions. The many public proposals for a new summit meeting and the concomitant refusal to prepare them seriously through diplomatic channels, illustrate that Soviet diplomacy does not aim at serious negotiations but uses the general desire for peace and in connection with it, the popularity of summit meetings as a sounding board for communist propaganda. While Soviet diplomacy conducts crusades for peace and campaigns against the "imperialists," and supports popular nationalistic movements in the Middle-East, Southern Asia, and Africa, the Soviet Government inexorably applies brutal oppression and introduces atrocious methods of a new brand of colonialism in East Central Europe.

More recently the Chinese People's Republic violated with military action the agreement concluded in 1951 on Tibet's autonomy. The crushing of Tibet's limited freedom and the dramatic flight of the Dalai Lama to India brought home to many Asians the meaning of Communist pledges and morals more directly and urgently than did the experiences of the Hungarian Revolution. The Chinese Communist Government demonstrated the practical application of the principles of peaceful co-existence so eloquently advocated by Chou En-lai at the Bandung Conference in 1955.

Despite these obvious facts, one must concede that the baby-kissing methods of globetrotting Soviet representatives, wider participation in social life by Soviet diplomats and "diplomacy by reception" in Moscow did create a better atmosphere for international negotiations. The dis-

⁴⁷ Hull, *op. cit.*, p. 1311.

appearance of Molotov's frozen face and the more relaxed nature of contacts and negotiations between the Soviet Union and the United States were in themselves welcome developments. Invective, provocations, and other harsh methods exclude the possibility of serene and constructive diplomatic intercourse. However, any optimistic speculation about a changed Soviet negotiating behavior should be grounded in experience with Soviet Communist tactics over a period of four decades. We had to learn the hard way that Soviet diplomacy has often equated diplomatic negotiations with deceit and treachery.

Although in the past peaceful declarations preceded most of the Russian aggressions, Soviet propaganda almost convinced the world by early 1956 that Stalin's evil spirit had disappeared from the Soviet scene. Then, developments went out of control in Poland and Hungary. Dramatic events connected with the Hungarian revolution became new writings on the wall for the West. Debates in the UN exposed Soviet duplicity and armed aggression in Hungary. Many Soviet statements in the Security Council and in the General Assembly were contradictory and unrelated to facts. The heroic fight of the Hungarian students and workers convinced the world of the truly popular nature of the Hungarian revolution. The General Assembly condemned the use of Soviet military forces to suppress the efforts of the Hungarian people to reassert their right to independent statehood, and called repeatedly on the Soviet Government to withdraw its forces from Hungary. Even thirteen Afro-Asian nations voted for the condemnation of the Soviet Union. More recently the execution of Imre Nagy, former Prime Minister of Hungary and General Maleter, his Defense Minister, constituted an almost unprecedented breach of faith in the history of civilized nations. Imre Nagy was granted asylum by the Yugoslav Embassy in Budapest and the Soviet-installed Hungarian regime, after negotiating with Belgrade, gave a written safe-conduct pledge to the Yugoslav Government.[48] Maleter was arrested while

---

[48] Kadar, in his capacity as Chairman of the Hungarian Council of Ministers, stated in a letter addressed to the Yugoslav Government on November 21, 1956: "In the interest of terminating the matter, the Hungarian Government, . . . hereby confirms in writing its verbal declaration that it does not desire to apply sanctions against Imre Nagy and the members of his group for their past activities. We take note that the asylum extended to the group will hereby come to an end and that they themselves will leave the Yugoslav Embassy and proceed freely to their homes." The text is in the *United Nations Review*, August 1958, p. 30.

negotiating in good faith in the name of the Hungarian Government for the withdrawal of Soviet forces from Hungary. These executions are grim reminders that in negotiating with the Soviet Union good faith cannot be taken for granted but has to be proved by deeds.

Khrushchev apparently expressed his warmly held conviction in telling Adlai Stevenson that whatever went on in the Communist world—meaning Hungary and Yugoslavia—was their internal family affair and did not concern other powers; but events in the non-Communist world were the proper concern of the Soviet Government.[49] This double standard, openly advocated and practised by the Soviet regime, illustrates the basic difficulty inherent in all negotiations between American and Soviet representatives. This conflict is probably the necessary consequence of two different systems of human organization in political, social, economic, and cultural fields. The basic conflict cannot be solved until and unless one of the systems changes significantly its approaches and nature. Although the meeting of minds between the Soviet and non-Soviet worlds is very difficult at present, it is not a reason for shunning temporary arrangements.

There are mutually interesting topics for negotiations. Turning the cold war into a nuclear holocaust cannot be a policy objective for American or Russian policy makers. Thus the avoidance of mutual annihilation is a realistic common interest of the United States and the Soviet Union. Another common interest is the restriction of the spread of atomic weapons. The likelihood that within a few years at least a dozen nations will possess fissionable material and will be able to produce atomic weapons and, possibly, missiles, portends a disquieting future for the superpowers and constitutes an important motive for negotiations. The proliferation of atomic weapons and a general atomic free-for-all, must be no less frightening to the Russians than to the Americans.

A feeling of despair is unwarranted. Since the Communist aggression in Korea the United States and the Free World have become wiser and stronger economically, militarily, and perhaps even politically. This development has not been without effect on the Soviet Union, which has been corroded by the inner weaknesses of a totalitarian dictatorship. The condemnation of certain aspects of Stalin's rule and the increase of informed citizenry in the Soviet orbit may generate new

[49] *New York Times*, August 27 and 28, 1958.

forces which in the long run may change the character of the Soviet system.

Although the new policy reflects primarily the more flexible approach of Stalin's successors, the Soviet leaders may be yielding partly to overwhelming pressure. Internal concessions by Moscow may release forces of great significance, and changes made for tactical reasons may escape from the control of the Communist operators. Changes have not yet reached the point of no return, but important factors inherent in human nature are working against putting an early end to the liberalizing tendencies in the Soviet Union. The road ahead is probably long and arduous. Although it would be a mistake to exclude the possibility of important transformations within the Soviet orbit, we must be prepared for possible reverses, as long as we face in Russia a totalitarian dictatorship which may change its course overnight. Statements and tactical concessions are not enough without decisive deeds. A smoother negotiating technique in itself is not indicative of serious changes. Although the change of form may betoken for the distant future a real change in content, the time when Russia will fit itself into the truly cooperative state system as a reliable partner seems far away indeed. The assumption that friendly statements and refined negotiating methods would indicate a change in doctrine cannot be justified by Soviet history over the past four decades.

In conclusion I would like to refer again to Talleyrand, whose advice was to negotiate, negotiate, and always negotiate. One of the important things in negotiations with the Russians is to recognize the U.S.S.R. and Soviet representatives for what they are according to their own doctrines and practices and handle them on this basis. Then, within a limited framework, negotiations may bring realistic results. Well-planned negotiations may call the Soviet bluff and expose Communist duplicity, may promote liberalizing tendencies in the Soviet orbit, and may prepare for the day when the Kremlin will demonstrate its cooperative intentions with deeds. For the present, in the field of intellectual struggle, it would be a sign of weakness not to accept the Soviet challenge, so long as we keep our powder dry and are determined to defend our freedom and give all necessary support to the commonwealth of free nations.

Chapter 11

BRITISH DIPLOMACY

Sir David Kelly

IN all countries, irrespective of creed or color, there has existed a traditional assumption that British foreign policy and its diplomatic agents have been distinguished above all others by farsighted objectives and Machiavellian cunning in execution. Though I have always been familiar with this, I was surprised to find the French journalist Alexandre Metaxas writing on December 9, 1956, that "the Russians consider that the British—or more exactly, their politicians and senior officials—are the most cunning and subtle of all those with whom they have to deal"; that "British patriotism has a profound effect on the Soviet imagination" and that "for this reason they set an ever greater value on an agreement, however distant, with Britain." A belief of this kind can have great influence irrespective of its truth or falsehood, and in Anglo-American relations this fixed idea has been, and is, a permanent source of friction and of disappointment to the British. An American colleague once told me that even the most sophisticated and experienced American officers had an ingrained feeling like a superstition, that in dealing with their British opposite numbers they were likely to be "outsmarted." To the extent that the following brief survey can throw light on British foreign policy, it must help to clarify the causes which have led to this belief.

A substantial share in responsibility for the present state of the world must be attributed to the vulgar confusion at the end of the First World War between foreign policy, which should be the business of governments, and diplomacy, which should mean the actual carrying out of policy by trained officials through negotiations between governments. At this stage I only refer to this by way of preliminary definition of terms. In the Middle Ages England (Scotland was an independent kingdom) had no stable national foreign policy. Her kings were also great feudal lords in France. Without a standing army or navy, they were engaged periodically in dynastic wars in France (occasionally Spain or Portugal), civil wars at home; when there was no one else to fight, there was always Scotland! The dynastic wars made a close link with Europe, and a stronger tie arose from membership of the Catholic Church, involving the use of Latin as an international language and a constant exchange of teachers, students, artists, and ecclesiastics.

In the sixteenth century a new phase which lasted until 1688, began with the sale of monastic and ecclesiastical property by Henry VIII and Edward VI and the gradual divergence from the continental way of life. Throughout this period the English monarchy was engaged in a losing fight with the new forces largely created by the sale or gift of the church property, forces which controlled parliament and through parliament refused the monarchy the increased funds which inflation made indispensable for defense; without adequate military and naval resources no independent foreign policy is possible. Elizabeth I played between France and Spain. Oliver Cromwell through a religious dictatorship created a strong army and fleet, but his policy was directed against the decaying power of Spain to the advantage of the rising star of France. Charles II by becoming a paid satellite of Louis XIV (as did some of his Whig opponents), nearly restored the ancient power of the crown, but his successor's bungling and lack of judgment gave the game finally to the Whig oligarchy.

With the establishment of Parliamentary supremacy under William of Orange in 1688, finally ratified by the Hanoverian succession in 1715, mediaeval England ended and a British foreign policy was gradually built up which lasted till the second quarter of the nineteenth century; and whatever one may feel about the eighteenth-century British oligarchy on moral, religious, or democratic grounds, it is a fact that they took over in 1688 a relatively weak and poor country on the periphery of Europe, and in 1832 handed over to the middle classes and industrialists the government of the acknowledged greatest power in the world. When Victoria became queen (1837),

Britain was the undisputed mistress of all the seas, the industrial work-shop of the world, ruler of India, ready or about to cover the world with railways, telegraphs, gas, tramways; to provide the capital to develop North and South America, Africa, Asia, Australia, and New Zealand. She had saved Europe from Napoleon, and her free institutions made her the Mecca of "Liberals" all over the world.

The policy which had guided the oligarchy had not been an immediate creation of the men of 1688. For about twenty years the Whigs had favored continuous land warfare with Louis XIV; it was only after the Hanoverian settlement in 1715 that Whigs and Tories became basically agreed on the main lines of British policy. This foreign—or more accurately, national, policy—was not thought out as a coherent doctrine like Leninism-Stalinism, nor laid down confidentially in long state papers for the guidance of ambassadors, of the kind in which the French archives are so rich. It consisted in a few underlying assumptions, of which the application in practice was left open, to be decided in accordance with the particular circumstances. The attitude was—unusually—defined by a Head of Department who in 1930, in reply to a request from my chief for advice in case a certain situation should arise, wrote that "in the Office we don't like dealing with hypothetical situations!"

The guiding principles from 1715 until after the Napoleonic Wars and the political arrival of the new industrialists, was that the national destiny was to develop overseas trade, but that this must be combined with a balanced economy at home, meaning that agriculture and the basic raw materials must be safeguarded, if necessary at the expense of foreign trade. This expansion overseas was not held to involve the acquisition of overseas territories for the sake of acquisition; there were numerous examples during two centuries of the voluntary relinquishment of territories acquired during war, and of the refusal of opportunities to acquire territories, even when requested by the inhabitants. The object of the conquest and retention of Canada was primarily to safeguard the American colonies. The motives for driving the French out of India and then for the very gradual expansion of authority over the whole sub-continent were entirely commercial, for a century under the aegis of a commercial company. There was a constant fear that foreign possessions might involve expense, especially of maintaining garrisons, which would defeat the commercial object. Trading-stations and ports of call were a different matter, for these facilities were necessary for the navy and merchant marine. Naval operations directly promoted trade by protecting the merchant marine and breaking down foreign monopolies; land operations were a costly expedient only to be used as and when necessary for the defense of the home base and overseas trade. These considerations underlay the major assumption in the traditional British foreign policy, the necessity of the permanent maintenance of a balance of power in Europe, and the corollary that this should be maintained with the minimum amount of military intervention in Europe.

British policy and diplomacy, therefore, concentrated on building up alliances against whatever country constituted at any time a danger to the balance of power, and in the event of war, on supporting the Allies with subsidies and the minimum of land forces, while the main effort of Britain herself was devoted to attacking the seaborne trade and colonies of the main enemy and its allies. France, the main enemy for a century, was much richer and more populous than Britain, but the French monarchy was tempted to maintain simultaneously its dynastic supremacy in Europe and its overseas Empire. The dual effort proved too great; the overseas Empire was lost because reinforcements could not be sent at the critical time, and the financial strain led to its own destruction in the Revolution; while the same wars, because conducted by Britain on a mainly maritime basis, in the end more than paid their own way. An essential element in the balance of power was to keep Antwerp from passing under the control of a great power; this meant "a pistol pointed at the heart of England," and was one of the few circumstances justifying military intervention in Europe, whether the threat came from the French monarchy or later, from Revolutionary France, or from Kaiser Wilhelm II. To the neutrality of Antwerp (and the defense of Portugal) was added, in due course, the protection of the route to India as a vital national interest.

When we study in detail the working of this policy the paradox emerges that a policy based frankly not only on national interest but on commercial interest, a basis no twentieth century British government would admit, was in practice far more moderate and more tolerant of the interests of other governments than policies continually affected by shifting cross-currents of opinion expressed by pressure groups, policies which mix national interest with ideological conflicts and vague formulas of international action. It was more favorable to other countries and more conducive to a peaceful atmosphere because it was essentially a policy of *limited objectives*. The moderation and self-restraint of British governments were evident in all the great Peace Treaties from Utrecht in 1713 to Vienna a century later, in striking contrast, as will be stressed later, to the annihilation and damn-the-consequences crusades pursued against Germany in both World Wars. The British Government had been—after the deception of the Peace of Amiens—the most tenacious enemy of Napoleon; but the moment he was eliminated, the weight of British support was thrown at Vienna on the side of Talleyrand, the representative of the defeated French, and this was in accordance with the principle of the balance of power.

Minds confused by wishful thinking about "collective security," whether through the League of Nations or the UN, are apt to identify national self-interest with aggression and narrow selfishness, but these were not the characteristics of the British policy, which in asserting the balance of power was also defending the interests of all the lesser powers, and which, though it kept trade considerations steadily in view when involved in war, never deliberately engaged in war for purely commercial motives. It is true that Walpole in 1739 was forced by public excitement over Jenkins' ear into what was in fact a trade war with Spain; but five years earlier he had boasted to Queen Caroline that "there are fifty thousand men slain this year in Europe, and not one Englishman." The very fact that when involved in war British governments kept trade interests steadily in view meant that once the main objective—national security—seemed sufficiently safe-guarded, they were anxious to end the war as soon as possible and with the minimum of humiliation and injury to the other side. Those fox-hunting, port-drinking gentlemen did not indulge in verbal fire-works about making the world fit for heroes or fit for democracy, but neither were they willing to destroy the nation's accumulated wealth and worse still, the flower of its youth, for the empty satisfaction of totally smashing the enemy country and reducing it, and most of Europe as well, to anarchy or slavery. The whole spirit of the system was expressed in two statements of Lord Castlereagh: "It is not our business to collect trophies but to bring back the world to peaceful habits"; and "the more I reflect upon it, the more I deprecate this system of scratching such a Power" (that is, France).

Earlier in this introductory survey I suggested that there was a dividing line between the century preceding the end of the Napoleonic War and the century which ended in 1914. The change, however, was not in foreign policy but in that part of the national policy which had aimed at a balanced economy at home, and it was therefore a change which slowly and imperceptibly affected the basis of the foreign policy; but this did not become apparent until the period in which Sir Eyre Crowe wrote his memorandum of January, 1907. Canning, Palmerston, Gladstone, Disraeli, Salisbury, were great personalities who naturally played variations on the main theme; but they were in broad agreement on that theme. They accepted the principle of the balance of power and the preservation at all costs of the independence of The Netherlands and the route to India. To these they added— taking the century as a whole and ignoring periodic ups and downs— co-operation with the old enemy France; support of the weaker countries—Spain, Greece, the House of Savoy in Italy; and the maintenance of the Ottoman Empire.

The support of the Ottoman Empire, a policy which during the first quarter of the present century looked as if it had been a case of "backing the wrong horse," is now beginning to appear in a very different perspective. The primary reason was the function of Turkey as a barrier against Russian expansion to the shores of the Mediterranean and the Indian Ocean; the secondary one was the feeling of responsibility to the Moslems in India. Some weakening of political instinct allowed Turkey of the "young Turks" to fall under German influence and Britain became almost by accident involved in the lamentable war with Turkey of which the consequences, only now becoming fully apparent, belong to the third part of this survey.

All these principles, especially that of non-intervention in Europe (except in its Southeastern area), would have required no explaining to Walpole, Chatham, Pitt, Canning, or Castlereagh, but the change in national economic policy to which I have referred had gradually introduced an entirely new element. Briefly, the new industrialist and middle class society which from 1832 onwards steadily consolidated its political control, in the space of about twenty years changed the whole economic structure of Britain. The change being part of a comprehensive philosophy (Utilitarianism) also transformed the social and legal structure, but what concerns us here is that the mercantile system was swept away, with its principles of priority for national security through protection of strategic industries especially agriculture and shipping, and of using trade to promote and work in with national power. I am only concerned with this reversal of traditional policy from one angle—that it made British interests *vulnerable* all over the world and made the home base increasingly dependent on circumstances over which it had no final control—as Disraeli had predicted. The ultimate, unrealized, effect on the foreign policy which had been linked with the mercantile policy was clearly stated in Sir Eyre Crowe's memorandum of January 1907.

That a Foreign Office official—Sir E. Crowe was later Permanent Under-Secretary—should set down on paper a general exposition of motives was a rare event, and due probably to his domestic German connections. His primary object was to show that Germany was trying to dictate and to estrange France and Britain, and must be met by firm defense of British interests, with no more piecemeal unreciprocal concessions, as the only hope of a general settlement such as had been obtained with France; but he also explained that British wealth had become dependent on maritime preponderance and that to maintain this maritime preponderance it must be used with the minimum of provocation and be made identical with the trade and independence of other nations, which must be regarded as customers rather than rivals. Britain was no longer free to dispense with their goodwill. His underlying theory was given a new significance during the First World War, when four years' full-scale continental warfare led inevitably to gigantic losses of foreign investments, foreign markets, and the development of rival industries by the primary producers, cutting through the established pattern of the export of goods and services in exchange for food and raw materials. Free trade and the gold standard could not survive prolonged totalitarian war.

This potential weakness was not however the surface picture at the beginning of this century. When I was at Oxford (1911–1914) British prestige throughout the whole world resembled that of France in Europe in the days of Louis XIV and Louis XV in his first period, and looked unshakeable. British investors owned most of the public utility services of Latin America and Asia, and a substantial stake in the United States; British communities in Latin America and the Far East were allowed in practice an almost independent status and freedom from interference, and British travellers found the pound sterling the most acceptable of all currencies. The army had not had to fight an organized army for a century except in the relatively minor campaign in the Crimea; the navy had policed all the seas for one hundred years, suppressing piracy and the slave trade, and as Walter Lippmann has noted, had provided the real guarantee for the Monroe Doctrine. While class-friction was less evident than in most countries, and the Labour Party members of Parliament were a mere handful, the rich lived on a scale and with a solid luxury which dazzled the foreign or British overseas visitor, enhanced by a whole apparatus of appropriate institutions, notably the public schools, Oxford and Cambridge, the "officer and gentleman" in the army and navy, and jobs for the boys "on which the sun never set." Hence it was "chic" to talk English and cover the tables with English magazines and the corridors with English sporting pictures, in royal or aristocratic households from Tsarskoe Selo in Russia to Mafra in Portugal. Foreigners, however envious, could not but be impressed by the incomparable administrative work over a large part of Africa and in the glittering Indian Empire, and the material progress of the "Colonies" whose only complaint was that they were denied Imperial Preference. Mark Twain saw in British success the fulfilment of the Gospel: "Blessed are the meek, for they shall inherit the earth."

Such a record of achievement, with a minimum loss of manpower, was enough in itself to suggest some persistent Machiavellian inspiration in British foreign policy and British diplomacy, and the general belief was fortified by the actual mechanism of British diplomacy. It was not a costly mechanism for the taxpayer, for including even the Foreign Office doorkeepers and charwomen, there were in 1914 176 people at home and 446 abroad under the control of the Secretary of State, where there are now over 12,000, and the hundred and fifty diplomatists were officially required to have private means and even to pay for the transport of their furniture. The normal mission abroad was a legation, with a minister, one or two secretaries, an archivist, probably a locally engaged translator, one chancery servant who spent most of his time doing errands for the minister's wife, and sometimes a military or naval attaché. The legation, like its chief, was usually an unostentatious but dignified detached house in a quiet street, and the staff worked in two or three small rooms off the hall. The minister lived much as he would have lived at home—like a country gentleman "in town" for the season. The service was not a closed corporation full of titles as for instance were those of Germany, Austria, Russia, and Spain, but it was—the British equivalent—mainly recruited from a very few schools and was in practice a family party, rather like a smart regimental mess. Such men in their intercourse with foreign governments and societies maintained precisely the standard of decorum, detachment, and slightly Olympian reserve in which they had been brought up, and by these standards, intrigue and doublecrossing were undignified and "not the form." It was not unnatural that they should therefore be credited with extraordinary talent for adroit concealment of their secret maneuvers.

I have stressed that the traditional British foreign policy had been largely an unwritten convention. In its year-to-year application to circumstances it depended on an instinctive feeling, like that of a born master in any craft from surgery to gardening. Long after the transfer of political power to the middle classes, especially the bankers and industrialists, the men of leisure or landowners continued to exercise a special influence in the domain of foreign policy, and the landowner like the farmer tended to have a much stronger instinctive sense—linked with the slow rhythm of nature—than the businessman accustomed to be guided by actuarial considerations and market fluctuations. The landowners had unconsciously regarded their country as their private estate, and were basically guided by their sense of the past and thought for the future.

The closing years of the century coincided with the permeation of the Tory Party of Disraeli and Salisbury by "big business," which had been traditionally Liberal but was influenced by Chamberlain of Birmingham to see the commercial possibilities of all-out imperialism and to oppose Home Rule for Ireland. The Nonconformist left wing of the Liberal Party lost all sense of international reality in a nebulous atmosphere of pacifist slogans; the eventual disintegration of the Liberal Party was only temporarily postponed by the Tory adoption of protectionism and the anti-imperialist reaction following the Boer War. The influence of big business on foreign policy was already noticeable long before 1914—after which it became supreme. Bismarck may have had it in mind when he commented with some *Schaden-freude* on the "losing of the ancestral wisdom." In business, "principles" in the political sense do not count; the keynotes are caution, opportunism, compromise, acceptance of accomplished facts, and Sir Charles Petrie has shrewdly traced the influence of this training on the general character and attitude of the Tory Party leadership in the present century; and the influence has been not least in foreign and imperial policy.

I have deliberately devoted a quarter of this sketch to events before 1914 because I do not think British foreign policy in the last forty years can be understood without this background. For the great dividing line was the First World War (1914–1918), which within a generation ripened to full stature tendencies which might otherwise have taken a century during which the national organism might have adapted itself to slowly changing conditions; the Second War, and its still developing consequences, was inherent in the conduct and results of its predecessor. First, as to its conduct and aftermath. We have seen that despite the adoption of free trade and the gradual taking over of foreign policy by urban leaders with an industrial, commercial, or legal background, the basic tradition of the balance of power, overseas expansion (with its corollary of priority for the navy) and avoidance of large-scale military entanglement, had persisted: that indeed the increased vulnerability due to free trade had underlined the importance of export trade and investment, of keeping markets and minimizing disturbance of the *status quo,* for disturbance, wherever in the world it occurred, was bound to prejudice British interests. That First World War was not inevitable. It was especially due to the personal weakness of the then chief European monarchs and the excessive and wholly unfortunate influence obtained by their chiefs of staff and a few intriguing ministers; and we shall never know whether a firm and timely declaration of intention by the British Government might not have arrested the Gadarene rush, as Lloyd George himself later admitted. When, however, the die was cast, it does seem that the British intervention, and the despatch of the expeditionary force, was entirely in the tradition of the balance of power and the defense of Belgium. It must also be admitted that the creation, and use in France, of a much larger land army was rendered inevitable by the great numerical inferiority of France and the inefficiency of Russia.

Where, however, the British Government—especially after the fall of Asquith—broke with the national tradition was in the principles on which the war was conducted. These were, one, that the war must at all costs be continued until Germany was not only defeated but totally ruined and forced to become a republic: two, that because we had drifted ineptly into war with the Young Turks, therefore the Ottoman Empire which we had protected as the only bulwark against Russian infiltration into the Near and Middle East, must be not only defeated but totally dismembered: three, that to achieve these results, it was worth while that the whole delicate structure of cheap production, world trade, overseas investment, and (politically) of authority based on prestige in India and the many direct-ruled colonies should be thrown into the balance. For the first time the people who controlled Britain were obsessed for several years with a collective hysteria, which was maintained with the help of the new demagogic press, and ignored the future as completely as the lessons of the past, in a blind confidence that they had only to ruin Germany, and disrupt Austria-Hungary and Turkey, for everything to be as it was before, only better. Clémenceau of course shared their attitude. Millions of young men were slaughtered in the bull-headed frontal offensives on the ground that they were "killing more Huns," though anyone engaged in them could see, and the documents later proved, that this was a lie. The production of munitions grew to such a fantastic scale that even apart from the submarine warfare a substantial part of the export markets was lost permanently, as was much of the overseas investment, especially in the United States.

The sane and practical peace proposals of Pope Benedict XV, and of Prince Sixte of Bourbon-Parma, in 1917 which offered the Western Allies all the substantial results of the Versailles Treaty with reciprocal renunciation of war costs, would have averted not only the gigantic losses in men and material of the last twelve months of the war, but also the rise and success of Hitler and the Nazis, the Anglo-French estrangement—in short, the Second World War, with the emergence of Communist Russia as one of the two great world powers. A compromise peace in 1917 could have averted the atomization of

Central Europe and of the Middle East. Such considerations would have been present automatically to the minds of most British statesmen in the eighteenth and nineteenth centuries; in 1917 the only public figure who dared suggest a negotiated peace was a survivor from an earlier more rational age, the Marquess of Lansdowne, ex-Viceroy of India, ex-Secretary of State for Foreign Affairs, architect of the Anglo-Japanese Alliance and the Anglo-French Entente conventions. *The Times*, in the power of the new-style press demagogue, the Earl of Northcliffe, refused even to publish his letter, in which, as published in the *Daily Telegraph*, he said "we are not going to lose this war, but its prolongation will spell ruin for the civilized world and an infinite addition to the load of human suffering." This echo from a more liberal and balanced age was drowned in a storm of abuse and the three leading Western countries unanimously insisted on prolonging for many months a war of which such a responsible historian as H. A. L. Fisher (at one time Minister of Education) could write that it was fought "on an issue which a few levelheaded men could easily have composed and with respect to which 99% of the population were wholly indifferent."

After the collapse of the German army and of the institution of monarchy, the victorious powers dictated a treaty conceived in a spirit completely contrary to that of the Congress of Vienna or indeed of any of the great peace treaties of previous centuries: for it was dishonest (in the disarmament provisions), indefinite, unworkable: and far from making any effort to secure the eventual co-operation of the losing side, seemed deliberately intended to provide permanent pretexts for military pressure and intervention, with the absurd reparations assessment of 6,600 million £ sterling and the inclusion of war pensions and separation allowances in damage to civilians. President Wilson, in pushing the treaty through by what Sir Harold Nicolson, an eyewitness, called "an unparallelled exercise of secret diplomacy," had insisted that the League Covenant must be written into the treaties, and the desertion of the League by the United States has always been considered one of the major results of the repudiation of the President himself.

I think, however, a more important and certainly more immediate result was the repudiation in 1920 by the British Government—because the United States did so—of the Anglo-American guarantee offered to France in 1919 of military support "in the event of any unprovoked movement of aggression against her being made by Germany." This psychologically disastrous breach of promise by the United States and Britain was the main source of the stupid quarrelling between Britain and France, and between France and Germany, which formed the background of the Second World War. Of course the obsessing French fear (using the word obsession in a literal not pejorative, sense) of a renewed invasion by Germany was *prima facie* justified in the end (Foch had actually predicted a 20-year limit), but the actions into which French governments were goaded by their betrayal by their Allies contributed to the results they were trying to avoid. From their sense of anxiety and resentment the French sought relief in a "tough" line of treaty enforcement against Germany with rapidly growing criticism and disapproval from British opinion. This French pressure led inevitably to the German default, the French occupation of the Ruhr, and the collapse of the Mark, which broke the power and influence of the German middle classes and left the German stage at the mercy of a great revolutionary surge of the masses with the results already foreseen by C. G. Jung in 1918 ("the blond beast stirring in its subterranean prison and threatening us with an outbreak that will have devastating consequences"). Hitler ("an irresponsible, ranting psychopath, cursed with a keen intuition of a rat," to quote Jung again) appealed to all the unstable by his propaganda against financiers and unemployment which he abolished by mobilizing the whole industrial machine for the preparation of war, but also appealed to many who genuinely longed for a restoration of social order and morals and misunderstood Hitler as completely as the Western Labour and Socialist Parties who persistently identified him with "capitalist reaction." The elimination inside Germany of the old barriers to revolution—Monarchy, Aristocracy, the Middle Classes, the Officer Corps, had its parallel in the elimination outside Germany of the historical barrier to Prussian aggression—the dual monarchy of Austria-Hungary and the atomization of Central-Eastern Europe; and French governments always searching for the "Blue Bird" security made a cobweb of alliances with the Succession States, Poland, Czechoslovakia, Roumania, and Yugoslavia.

With the end of the First World War and the creation of the League of Nations, British foreign policy becomes something different from what it had been for two centuries. The first difference was that what had been a steady course with certain traditional objectives, became associated—I would say confused—with an entirely different conception, that of world conferences. The second difference was that as a result of the war, mass popular opinion became interested (in a very broad simple way) in foreign affairs and easily worked on by comforting formulas; and the new city board-room type of Prime Ministers and Secretaries of State found it increasingly difficult and inconvenient from an electoral point of view, to "put across" all the doubts and qualifications which they themselves felt about the slogans of the day. Hitherto the final criterion by which British Governments had justified their foreign policies had been that of national interest. Not in a narrow or aggressive sense, as I have already stressed: Disraeli had emphasized the importance of Europe, Salisbury had preached good neighborliness in the spirit of the good landlord, careful of the rights of his heirs but anxious to be respected and esteemed by his neighbors. Gladstone had said no one nation should be treated as a pariah, Palmerston said we had no eternal allies and no perpetual enemies, only "our interests are eternal, these it is our duty to follow"—we can easily judge how they would have reacted to the short-sighted treatment of Germany in 1919.

Now it had been shewn in 1914 that the conflict was precipitated by the absence of any standing international machinery for the discussion and attempted settlement of international disputes; had this been available it might conceivably have averted the catastrophe. If this were so, the provisions of the League of Nations Covenant which set up machinery for peaceful settlement of disputes could fairly be considered a British interest. Unfortunately, however, articles fifteen and sixteen went on to provide for automatic economic sanctions against any state which should resort to war in disregard of its covenants, while the League Council could "recommend" military sanctions to members. These threatening articles were safe in the background when it was a question of exchanging Turks and Greeks (after 1922) or arranging frontier disputes between Greece and Bulgaria (1925) or Turkey and Iraq (1926) or the Saar plebiscite (1935). President Wilson's tragic mistake lay in failing to realize that the settlement machinery depended on the goodwill of the great powers; that if one of these should be ready to defy the League, the others must either give way or engage in full-scale war; and that in practice no government would dare involve its people in a major war for any issue which was not clearly and immediately vital to its own security. So the minor settlements mentioned above were easy to impose as no major power felt vitally concerned as against another. When, however, Japan attacked China, or when Germany tore up the Versailles settlement which had been rashly tied up with the Covenant, there was no serious question of sanctions; while the amateurish attempt to use sanctions when Mussolini attacked Abyssinia, which practically brought the League to an end, was perhaps the worst of the blunders committed by British governments when they broke away from their national traditions. In the majority of countries this central flaw in the Covenant—that a great power would always "get away with it" unless its actions touched really vital interests of a stronger power or combination of powers—was fully recognized. There was no real feeling for the League except perhaps in Scandinavia and Holland; and for a special reason, in France, where the League was regarded as an ingenious device for collecting guarantees of military aid for France against Germany. The British ruling group, who still recognized at least in principle their duty to national interests, seem also to have understood these distinctions. In 1919 an official commentary on the Covenant warned that if the nations of the future were in the main selfish, grasping, and warlike, no instrument or machinery would restrain them. Sir Austen Chamberlain in a memorandum to the League Council insisted that the League's fundamental task was to diminish the *causes* of war, and stressed the gulf between the ordinary misunderstandings inseparable from international life and the deep-lying causes of hostility which divide great and powerful states. Balfour similarly warned lest "impossible tasks will be forced on it." British Governments therefore opposed the French conception of the League as a protection against Germany and hoped to build up gradually a habit of peaceful settlement. They wanted to build on the pacific features of the Covenant and distrusted the Sanction articles; they therefore objected to the 1923 Draft Treaty of Mutual Assistance and the Geneva Protocol of 1924. How then did it come about that in 1935 it was the British Government which, backing the crusade of its League Minister, Anthony Eden, forced what Neville Chamberlain described later as the "midsummer madness of sanctions" (without oil sanctions) against Italy through a reluctant League Assembly—though they were not applied by Germany, Austria, Hungary, Switzerland, Albania, China, Japan, Morocco, or by any American country except Canada, Mexico, and Colombia—while the British Embassy in Paris had to be guarded by 200 armed police? This dramatic *volte face* by a British government is at first sight inexplicable; it was bound to swing Mussolini into line with Germany and make him withdraw his protection from Austria, to consolidate Italian opinion behind the dictator and his Abyssinian enterprise, as King Fuad of Egypt used to point out to me with an air of despair. Incidentally, the British Government in 1923 had thought it very unwise to admit Abyssinia into the League, but had yielded in the face of French and Italian pressure!

The main reason lay in those changes in the conditions affecting British foreign policy which I suggested above; the new interest of the mass electorate in foreign affairs, not a genuine or informed interest, but an elementary obsession about war and peace; and the increasing fear of ministers to risk votes by unpopular warnings and explanations.

Successive governments allowed the growth and mass acceptance of a dogmatic belief (of a religious character) that the League plus sanctions would make major war impossible and that individual members of the League behind the shelter of "collective security" did not need to prepare for a major war. This childish dogma was a twofold obstacle to any rational foreign policy; it replaced clear-thinking about national interests by magical formulas about the League and collective security, and it allowed the national defences to run down (as happened also in France) to the point that Mussolini had no hesitation in calling the bluff. The League of Nations Union's propaganda in Britain had mobilized the latent focus of evangelical liberalism, together with the blind undiscriminating reaction against "war" of any kind; so its strength lay precisely in its purely emotional appeal and Messianic optimism which stopped all discussion. Part of the dogma was that as there was a general will to peace, the mere threat of sanctions would always in itself deter an aggressor; in fact the adoption of bluff as a national policy. The time came when the League of Nations Union was able to terrify the politicians with a "Peace Ballot," (a sort of house to house Gallup Poll "Do you want peace or war, Mum? Then sign here!") and Lord Cecil threatened to keep his Peace Ballot organization in existence until the next general election. The politicians were paralyzed by their own long record of lip service to the popular dogma, and felt they must drift with the tide or lose an election. It can be granted that the dangers inherent in blind confidence in the League did not become actual until the world economic crisis set in at the end of 1929, so that the dangers were not so obvious in the twenties. During the previous decade British governments had taken a principal share in a series of conferences and treaties which really looked rather hopeful and did not suggest that the invocation of the League's sanctions would ever be seriously in question. The Washington Conference (1921–22) produced, among others, the treaties whereby nine powers including Japan pledged themselves not to claim "special rights and privileges" in China and not to make new naval bases and fortifications in the Pacific; at the same time Britain under Canadian and U. S. pressure abandoned the Anglo-Japanese Treaty of 1902. This latter event weakened the prestige of the Japanese government and its last contacts with the West, thus facilitating the assumption of control by the Japanese army when the economic crisis halved Japanese foreign trade; while the Nine Power Treaty had the unintended effect of encouraging the new military regime in Japan to attack China in 1931 because the other powers had undertaken to make no new naval bases or fortifications in the Pacific. The next attempt at stabilization, this time in Europe, was accomplished on December 1, 1925, with the signature of the Locarno Treaties which their main author, Sir Austen Chamberlain claimed to be "the real dividing line between the years of war and the years of peace." His general idea was a sound one, in line with British tradition—to replace general guarantees by the settlement of specific problems, in this case by placing the existing Franco-German and Belgo-German frontiers under the guarantee of Britain and Italy. It had the obvious weakness of ignoring the eastern frontiers which Germany had never recognized, but the major weakness was that paper guarantees were by themselves of no more use against the spiritual—and imminent economic—crises which were generating Nazism and the growing military weakness of Britain and France, than King Canute's challenge to the tide. The classic illustration of the "let's pretend" atmosphere of that decade was the Briand-Kellogg Pact (1928). Mr. Hamilton Fish Armstrong has recently described how when the pact was signed Mr. Kellogg said to him at the Quai d'Orsay "with tears in his eyes," "Now there will be no more war!" A day or two later Mr. Hugh Gibson, a wellknown American career Ambassador, asked me (quoting a song of the period) what I thought of the "it ain't gonna rain no more pact"!

The dismal events of the nine years between the economic collapse and the Second World War should be still fresh in readers' memories, and they have already been partly anticipated in the preceding pages. The few permanent officials with inside knowledge of international affairs, unless they had no imagination and no historical sense, felt with an ever-increasing sense of fatality that they were living through a Greek tragedy, made sadder by the lack of distinction among the public figures, whose antics seemed to be part rather than causes of the slow stumbling drift to catastrophe. Here are in brief some main dates in the drift. (1) In September, 1931, the Japanese occupied Mukden and then the whole of Manchuria. The League of Nations Assembly, after investigation by a commission, solemnly approved a charge of unjustified aggression. The Japanese were ready to fight, and therefore in no danger of having to do so; on the contrary, having consolidated Manchuria, they embarked on a slow war of infiltration (with occasional truces) into China, which culminated in their large-scale invasion in July 1937. (2) On March 16, 1935, Germany, already for over two years completely under Nazi control, restored compulsory military service in direct breach of the Versailles Treaty. On April 11–14, Britain, France, and Italy met in conference at Stresa to consider the situation and "agreed to oppose by all practicable means any unilateral repudiation of treaties which may endanger the peace of Europe." It was a conclusion after the heart of Prime Minister Ramsay MacDonald, who seemed incapable of any meaningful statement and whose universal panacea in foreign policy was "let's get around a table and work it out." He was so anxious to gain time by a quick conference ending in a fine formula that he avoided mentioning Abyssinia— though the Italian intentions were quite well known in the Foreign Office—such an indiscreet discussion might have spoilt the conference. Yet by October 7, all the members of the League Council had recorded their opinion that Italy had resorted to war against Abyssinia in disregard of its covenants, and the League Assembly appointed a co-ordinating committee for sanctions which excluded petroleum, iron, steel, coal, and coke. While most members nominally accepted this program many, as already mentioned, did not apply even these farcical measures and formal withdrawals began in April, 1936. Abyssinia was conquered and annexed by May 9, 1936, and the last sanctions were withdrawn in July, 1936.

The basic facts were that neither Britain nor France was willing to fight; and that neither Britain nor France was *capable* of it. The British fleet which crowded into Alexandria Harbour when I was acting High Commissioner—15 admirals and 20,000 ratings—had ammunition for about twenty minutes: the G.O.C. Army in Egypt, "Rosie" Weir returned from leave relating that the C.I.G.S. had said to him with underlying seriousness, "It's no use, Rosie—the army can't play!"; the R.A.F. aircraft which were to win the Battle of Britain did not yet exist; the French aircraft industry had practically ceased production. Yet these elementary facts, naturally well known to Mussolini, were still so successfully concealed from the British public that the leakage, in Paris in December, 1935, of the commonsense Hoare-Laval compromise project to stop the invasion and total conquest of Abyssinia, was greeted in England by a storm of abuse—led by *The Times,* which forced Sir Samuel Hoare to resign. The ridiculous fiasco which brought Italy into the German orbit, and left Austria (hitherto protected by Italy) to await the *Anschluss* on March 12, 1938, was the climax of fourteen years of emotional propaganda and ministerial cowardice; and though it deflated the League, it did not restore moral courage to the politicians. These still did not dare to explain to the voters that the long decline in British (and French) military efficiency was the real reason for the growing boldness and success of the new dictatorship and the futility of the League; things had to get much worse before they began to hint at the truth with mysterious allusions to their "sealed lips" and "years which the locusts had eaten."

(3) The Treaty of Versailles had given the left bank of the Rhine and a strip on the right bank into allied occupation for fifteen years, to be followed by permanent demilitarization. In fact the French (who had remained the solitary occupying force) pulled out by June 30, 1930, to reward Germany's entry to the League. In March, 1936—eleven months after the Stresa declaration mentioned above—German troops without warning occupied the whole district.

This was the real end of the fifteen years "Between Wars" period of sham and pretence and the last opportunity offered to the free world to stop the drift. For the last time, Hitler was bluffing; weak though

Britain and France were, they could still have thrown him out of the Rhineland, which would have brought him down. The tremendous arms-drive with which Hitler had absorbed Germany's five million unemployed was just coming into operation and by the time he attacked Czechoslovakia it had made him more than equal to Britain and Europe combined. It was the last military opportunity, and politically a better title for intervention than the later one of the protection of Poland. The chance was lost because the British and French governments had long lost the habit of co-operation—perhaps since the repudiation of the Anglo-American guarantee; because both governments had drugged themselves for many years with soporific catchwords about collective security and sanctions and had acquired the fatal habit of conferences. In fact, they had lost contact with realities and were practically incapable of decision and action. In the foregoing pages I have only referred to such conferences as were relevant to the theme—but it is necessary to say a word about the "conference habit" in general, for it was one of the distinguishing marks of the new English foreign policy since 1918 and at least till very recently, still is. In the nineteenth century conferences were only occasional, and held only when success was considered assured, because it was already known through diplomatic channels that all the parties wanted a real permanent honest settlement and had reached a basic preliminary agreement.

It was equally understood that during a conference the whole proceedings must be confidential; and that the final terms of agreement must be precise and unambiguous. For example, the Congress of Berlin in 1878 did not begin till the British and Russian Governments had agreed on their minimum compromise terms. Since the period of almost incessant conferences began in 1919, all these conditions have been normally disregarded—notable exceptions were the London Conference of 1925 when MacDonald and Herriot had agreed beforehand on the Dawes Reparation Plan, and the Locarno Pact which followed on long secret negotiations between Stresemann, Briand, and Lord D'Abernon. To the absence of preliminary basic agreement was added the damning handicap of publicity; as Sir Austen Chamberlain had predicted, Ministers could not withdraw their published declarations and compromise without loss of face became almost impossible.

The situation, bad enough between the Wars, became farcical after the Second War when Soviet Russia moved into the centre of the stage; for the Soviet system is basically opposed to the Conference idea. The revolutionary philosophy of the Communist Party excludes genuine cooperation; the Party regards conferences not as meetings for negotiation but as opportunities for propaganda. While the Western delegations try to convince the Soviet delegation by old-style diplomatic arguments which assume the framework of the old International Order, their opponents treat these as moves in the game and concentrate on broad simple appeals from the conference table to the "toiling masses" and "uncommitted" nations. The opposed delegations are at cross-purposes; the Western are interested in specific limited objectives, the Soviets are interested in unlimited revolutionary objectives. (At the Geneva conferences in 1954 the situation was further complicated because the United States and British Governments had not even reached agreement with each other before plunging into conference with the Russians.) The basic fact which Western opinion is unwilling to realize is that whereas purely commercial or territorial disputes can be settled for a long time by negotiation (especially when there is a rough balance of power between the interested parties), "ideological" conflicts of a fundamental kind can only be settled by compromise as a result of mutual exhaustion. The religious wars in Europe during the century after the Reformation are an illustration. Both German race-mysticism and (even more) Russian and Chinese Communist "Demonology" are essentially *religious* in character, and twentieth-century history is a grim confirmation of the Duke of Wellington's wisdom when he said that "if we are to have a war, let it be a war of ambition, not a war of opinion."

The Second World War, though much less costly in lives for Britain than the First, involved an unparalleled economic and physical strain. It cost £10,700 millions in foreign capital and resources, without counting home capital and production; of which £5,000 millions in lend-lease, £3,300 millions in new sterling debt, £1,300 millions by the realization of foreign investments and gold and dollar reserves. By the time the United States entered the war, the disproportion between the strength and resources of Britain and the United States had become so great that the former was bound to take the secondary role, but for mainly psychological reasons the subservience to President Roosevelt's policies was carried to unnecessary lengths which contributed to turning the temporary destruction of Germany into the most "Pyrrhic victory" in history. As in 1916 to 1918, the British government were wholly obsessed with the immediate objective of winning a total war without regard for the consequences and it was wrongly imagined that this one supreme objective would be imperiled by any attempt anywhere to maintain British interests when to do so involved any United States objection. This was very marked for example throughout Latin America, especially in Argentina, with disastrous economic results; but the major effects were seen in the general conduct of the war. Through sentimental wishful thinking and the war-obsession there was a complete failure to appreciate that the driving force in Roosevelt's mind lay in his statement that "of one thing I am certain, Stalin is not an Imperialist," and in General Eisenhower's linking of the United States and Russia as being both of them "free from the stigma of Colonial Empire-building by force." This unrealistic assessment of the respective roles of Britain and Russia led Roosevelt to override the British plans for advancing from Italy and the Balkans into Central Europe, and to waste an army in the south of France; and it inspired him throughout the Yalta Conference (February, 1945). On these issues the British government was probably unable to resist, but it was not obliged to agree (as it instantly and uncritically did at Casablanca) to the "unconditional surrender" declaration which paralyzed the incipient revolt against Hitler and prolonged the war (as Ernest Bevin said when Foreign Secretary) until the total collapse of all authority in Germany.

The "victory" left a situation more unbalanced and dangerous than any known to Europe since the Dark Ages. The Soviet Empire with its army of five millions was deep in civilized Europe, occupying not only the Balkan and Baltic States but also Poland and Hungary, East Germany, part of Austria and soon to add Czechoslovakia—thereby dominating the Euro-Asiatic plain, which Mackinder had called the "Heartland" of the world, from the Elbe to the Pacific. The British and American armies were in full demobilization, France and Italy were on the verge of having communist governments. A further danger, largely unrealized at the time and still little known, was the planned communist advance through Greece into Italy using the communist-dominated E.A.M. (National Liberation Front) and its "Popular Liberation" Army, the "E.L.A.S." The preparations for this in Russia are described by Colonel Tokaev, who was well placed to know, and they were defeated by one of the last independent actions of a British government. This was the backing of the forces of order in Greece by a British force maintained there by Sir Winston Churchill in face of a storm of criticism not only by the American press but by a powerful section of the British press which was backing co-operation with the communist parties in Europe as the "turbulent new forces."

The danger of a complete subversion of the whole of Europe during the period when the British Labour Party came to power in 1945 still believing that the Soviet system was merely an "advanced" form of Labour Government, was averted by the misjudgment and over-confidence of Stalin and his advisers.

Soviet foreign policy is an integral part of the whole Soviet system and is unintelligible without some understanding of the system, of which the essence can be stated in a few main propositions. The Soviet Empire is governed in theory by the Communist Party (normally about four per cent of the population) which is nominally represented by the Supreme Soviet (about 1,600 members) and the Central Committee (255 members) but is in fact controlled by the group at the top—whether Stalin's Politburo of nine or the present Presidium of eleven (with its nine candidates or alternate members). The Council of Ministers—which in other countries would be the directing Cabinet —are the second line who carry out the decisions of the Presidium, to which only a few ministers—often not the most important, belong. This top group are always agreed on one point—that all their policies must be strictly within the framework of the Party doctrine as elaborated from a Marxist basis by Lenin and Stalin. (This is still so; the charge against Stalin is that he acted autocratically, without adequate consultation of his collective team.) The doctrine is held to be the permanent reality, the "strategy" of the World Revolution, but its application over short periods can and should be adapted to meet particular circumstances as a matter of "tactics."

In the period of Hitler's ascendancy, and throughout the war, tactics were prominent. Stalin's error at the end of the war was to believe that tactical appeasement and compromise were no longer necessary and to embark on a tough line, associated with Zhdanov. This involved thrusting into prominence an essential feature of the dogma, namely that reforming and Parliamentary Socialist and Labour Parties play the game of the "Imperialists" and Capitalists, hoodwinking the proletariat; this led him to flout and discredit the British Labour Government and so to open their eyes to the real character of the Soviet Empire. It led to mistaken advice to the French Communists and it culminated in the seizure of Czechoslovakia and the quarrel with the Western Powers over German reparations and currency. By forcing the pace he had already in 1946 disillusioned both President Truman and the British Labour Government, and the following five years are marked by one of the most remarkable "come-backs" in history, made possible by the deterrent effect of the atom bomb, the wise use of American economic power, and the full and energetic co-operation of the British government. The stages in the reaction must be briefly recapitulated. It had begun with the British military intervention in Greece. It continued with the American diplomatic intervention which made the Russians leave Azerbaijan, and the Truman aid to Greece and Turkey when Britain could no longer afford it. The Marshall Plan and the O.E.E.C. (Organization for European Economic Co-operation) in 1947, the Brussels Treaty and Western European Union in 1948, the Berlin Airlift in 1948/49, were the chief landmarks in the reaction and return to reality of the free world which culminated in the North Atlantic Treaty signed in Washington on April 4, 1949.

These events form together the most encouraging period in British foreign relations since 1914. After thirty years of divided aims, groping for firm ground among the shifting sands of conferences and world assemblies, and reluctance to admit her decline in national strength or the emergence of new powers (Nazi Germany and Soviet Russia) which had no intention of playing according to the old civilized rules, Britain had returned to the old principles of working for the balance of power in regional alliance with those countries which shared a common outlook and basic common interests. The North Atlantic Alliance embraced four fundamental needs of British policy; co-operation with Canada and the United States, economic security (because Britain could no longer afford to fight singlehanded) and the unity and recovery of Western Europe. It did not try to start at the top with pretentious claims to settle disputes among members, but set out to strengthen all the elements making for unity and to develop in practice into a co-ordinating unifying instrument—which as we have seen was the original British conception of the League of Nations.

NATO did in fact within a few years build an international executive body worked by fifteen nations, all of which agreed to communicate their defense estimates to an international staff and the North Atlantic Council and to the joint financing of local bases with an international budget. Its immediate results were a great reassurance to the Western countries and the complete cessation of Soviet aggression in Europe and towards Turkey and Greece.

Its formation was an implied condemnation of the United Nations Organization. Like the League of Nations, the UN presupposed a basic identity of aims among the members of the Security Council, but with far less reason—for the whole essence of the Soviet doctrine was the *duty* to achieve world revolution by fomenting the contradictions among all the countries outside and especially the chief powers. It was therefore inevitable that between February, 1946, and March, 1958, the Soviet veto was used 82 times to annul resolutions which had received seven votes. Apart from the paralyzing effect of the veto, the League of Nations had already demonstrated that in really important issues the resolutions of a world organization are only effective when one power of overwhelming strength is willing to take the initiative and the risk in enforcing them, and is also able to influence a large number of members by the "lively expectation of favors to come." These conditions were not present when Japan or Italy defied the League; they were present when South Korea was invaded, though Korea was a special case as there was no Soviet delegation to use a veto. The conditions were absent when the military dictatorship in Hungary would not even allow the entry of UN observers, or during the years in which Egypt has refused passage through the Canal to Israeli shipping—the Arab-Israeli disputes have produced over 200 resolutions. Mr. Dulles was quoted as saying on February 19, 1957, that in future there would be greater efforts to comply with the resolutions of the United Nations *except* on the part of the nations dominated by international communism—a frank admission that the United Nations do not count where the real dangers are in question.

The UN presents a special problem for Britain and her European allies as compared with the League of Nations. The League was essentially a European body; it met at Geneva and the leading personalities among the fifty-five delegations were European. In the UN with its 81 delegations the European countries with only seventeen votes are swamped in a network of pressure groups including the "Afro-Asian block" with twenty-nine votes. Even when these are not actually hostile, they are always ready to trade their votes in issues which do not concern them; as Lord Strang writes in his book on the Foreign Office, "A's vote in the quarrel between Y and Z is therefore likely to be cast in favour of Y for reasons unconnected with the intrinsic merits of the case." Incidentally, Britain contributes to UNESCO sums which would make all the difference to her own starved Information Services.

This survey has now reached the contemporary phase, which though among the most lamentable in British history, is far from finished and seems likely to lead to a rediscovery of a realistic national policy. I have tried to show that since the world of 1914 was shattered, British policy has been seeking a new basis in a world which was not only transformed, but has been in continual flux to a degree unknown for several centuries; and that the task of reorientation has been complicated by the much greater interest taken by a new mass public opinion. Sometimes the chief weakness of British governments during these forty years has lain not so much in lack of judgment as in fear, due to electoral considerations, of urging unpalatable truths; in some cases the governing circles themselves have been slow in appreciating the effects of changed conditions and reluctant to face unpleasant realities. The most serious failure in "public relations" was in regard to the League of Nations. Its early British sponsors realized its limitations and wanted to build it up gradually as an instrument for conciliation and negotiation, but their successors dared not fight the hallucination that "collective security" could by itself avert the necessity of serious effort by any one member, and therefore would make preparation for real war unnecessary. When an aggressor who means business is menaced with economic sanctions by weaker powers, most of which are anyhow not prepared to fight except for issues they think vital to themselves, it is sufficient for the aggressor to call the bluff. The result in 1935 was not merely the conquest of Abyssinia, but far more serious, the passing of Italy into the German axis and the absorption of Austria which made Czechoslovakia helpless. Most of the British ministers realized this, but they were prisoners of their own lip-service to the League and "collective security."

The chief failures of the governments themselves to appreciate the new conditions between 1918 and 1939 were in regard to (1) the permanent shift of the center of economic power from Britain to America, (2) the inevitability and real nature of the Nazi revolution in Germany, (3) the decline in British military strength, (4) the inevitability (in view of the changed state of British public opinion) of the triumph of nationalism and the consequences of this, particularly in the case of India, and (5) the habit of holding unprepared conferences that made it impossible to pursue a steady unspectacular rebuilding of confidence among the European states. Point three above was the most serious; after the failure to stop Hitler in March, 1936, there was really nothing which British diplomacy could do to avert the final catastrophe. The alternatives were neutrality or immediate total armament regardless of expense.

During and after the Second World War the Nazi danger was replaced by the enormously increased power of Russia and the full emergence of the Soviet doctrine of world revolution as a major factor in international relations. The United States was not only the leading military and economic power facing Russia; it had also become apparently indispensable to Britain in terms of economic and military support. The independence of India and Pakistan, involving the loss of the Indian Army for use in the Middle East, affected all the old assumptions about Mediterranean and Middle Eastern policy. This had occurred just when the Arab States which since 1918 had replaced the old Ottoman Empire were suddenly acquiring a new and great importance by the development of their petroleum resources, estimated at over two-thirds of the world's known potential supply.

Britain with her shrunken resources and crippling taxation had therefore to cope from 1944 with three main problems: her economic dependence on the United States, the serious menace of the Soviet Empire, and the protection of her interests in the Arab States and Arabic-speaking Egypt. The third problem should be considered first, as developments there are already reacting on the British attitude to the other two. Over the whole period down to 1954 British policy in the Near and Middle East had on balance enjoyed considerable success. Relations with Iraq, the best managed and most promising of the Arab States, were excellent: the quarrel with Iran over Iran's nationalization of the Iranian oil industry had been settled without serious loss, and all three countries had joined with our powerful, solid, and sincere ally, Turkey, in the Baghdad Pact. Egypt under the former political regime had no imperialist or expansionist designs apart from one issue, without which Britain would have had no serious difficulty in maintaining good relations throughout the whole area.

This issue was of course the Israeli question which has been the real source of all the recent developments and has opened the door to Soviet Russia. The assumption by Britain of the Mandate in Palestine in 1922 following the Balfour Declaration of 1917 was one of the greatest specific mistakes in British policy since 1914. In the original sentimental conception of Balfour under the magnetic influence of Chaim Weizman (though desire to please the United States was a subsidiary motive), it only involved the establishment of a National Home for the Jewish People, "it being clearly understood that nothing shall be done which may prejudice the civil and religious rights of existing non-Jewish communities in Palestine." The mistake lay in believing that successive British governments would possess the power and the will to maintain this proviso and prevent Palestine being eventually absorbed by Jewish immigrants (of whom hardly any came from within the British Empire). The attempts to restrict immigration were made more difficult by pressure from the United States, and even when Arab fear and hostility were reaching a peak after the Second World War President Truman pressed for admission of another 100,000 refugees—the Republicans were insisting on 300,000. Attacked by both Jews and Arabs and criticized (a mild word) in Washington, the British government withdrew in 1948, releasing at once the Arab-Israeli War which has never ceased, accompanied always by the "noises off-stage" of the UN but with the responsibility fastened to Britain throughout the whole Arab world. Even in 1937 and 1938 (when our post-treaty relations with Egypt were ideal) I found that all conversations with Egyptian Prime Ministers had to begin with a long monologue by the latter about Jewish immigration into Palestine; but after the great 1949 exodus of Arab refugees (700,000 into Jordan alone, outnumbering the original population) the subject became a major obsession. The defeat of the Egyptian army by the Israelis in 1948 was a leading factor in the military revolt in July, 1952, against the unpopular King Farouk. The revolt ended in the dictatorship of Colonel Nasser, whose ideal of Egyptian hegemony in the Near East and Africa created a new situation.

The essential importance of the emergence of the State of Israel is that the common hatred of it provided an issue—and the only issue— which unites the Arab States among themselves, and the Arab States with Egypt. The Arabs have always been centrifugal and tending to disunity and in the modern period dynastic feuds and national jealousies and fear (especially of Iraq and Jordan against Egypt) have only been offset by the common hatred of Israel which has sterilized the well known Arabic sympathies of successive British governments which had themselves originally encouraged the formation of the Arab League. From intimate personal knowledge of the area—which I visited again in the spring of 1956—I am convinced that but for the Israeli question the British influence could have been maintained indefinitely despite the loss of India and several mistakes (of which the last-minute forgiving of King Farouk in February, 1942, was the worst) and the way would not have been left open for the intervention of Soviet Russia in 1955. The previous abstention of Russia was partly due to the doctrinal belief that poor and primitive agricultural peoples were not ripe for revolution which was supposed to require an urban proletariat. The error of this had been proved by the success of Mao Tse-tung, who had won through with the Chinese peasants despite Stalin's advice; but the chief motive for intervention was the failure of Soviet diplomacy at the Berlin and Geneva Conferences (1954) to break the Western Alliance and disrupt NATO. Lenin had advocated looking for the most likely spark wherever there was inflammable material, and in 1955 the Soviet government, seeking compensation on the southern flank for its rebuff in Europe, did exactly this by its offer of £150 million of military equipment to Colonel Nasser. From this transaction—with its implication of full diplomatic support—flowed inevitably the seizure of the Canal (though the immediate motive was to save face when America suddenly turned down the aid for the Aswan Dam), and the Israeli counterattack against persistent Egyptian aggression in October, 1956. The reaction of President Eisenhower and a majority of the United Nations completely ignored the basic fact that Egypt had declared the destruction of Israel to be a fundamental objective of its foreign policy, and had consistently claimed to be in a state of war with Israel; that on this ground Egypt had continuously closed the Canal to Israeli shipping, forcibly prevented the use of the Israeli port of Elat, and had used the Gaza Strip as the base for constant raids into Israel. Finally Egypt had accumulated reserves of Russian equipment far greater than her army and air force could use for the moment. To call the Israeli sortie an unprovoked act of aggression, to demand total withdrawal without any conditions or guarantees, was an absurd legalistic and one-sided oversimplification which illuminates the mortal danger to peace inherent in the character of the United Nations.

The Anglo-French intervention in November was a classic instance of the failure to adjust policy to effective strength which I stressed as a recurring weakness of British foreign policy since 1914. A rapid seizure of the Canal would have been the end of Colonel Nasser and would have been hailed with relief by his Arab rivals; to launch such an enterprise without adequate means either in personnel or transport and then to stop halfway, was an unparalleled blunder. The miscalculation of resources was accompanied by an even more dangerous psychological failure to foresee the violence of President Eisenhower's reaction. In the first place, anger is always a bad counsellor, and the British Prime Minister had been profoundly shocked by Colonel Nasser's seizure of the Canal. The engagement in 1954 to evacuate the Canal was prudent, for the plain reason that the Canal cannot be held with a hostile government in Cairo, which raises insoluble problems, especially of labor supply. The Prime Minister, however, had believed the assurances that the occupation was the only obstacle to good relations with Colonel Nasser, an optimism which was not shared by anyone with intimate knowledge of Egypt.

The failure to anticipate President Eisenhower's reaction has a more complicated background. The fact that Britain and the United States have certain main interests in common—of which co-operation in NATO is the supreme example—has been the base for a superstructure of wishful thinking resulting in a most dangerous misunderstanding of the American attitude to British interests in areas where the danger of Soviet penetration has not been obvious. The depth and sincerity of American dislike of British "colonialism," and of the American ideal of obtaining moral supremacy throughout Asia, have been virtually ignored, and this lack of appreciation has been fostered and maintained by a conspiracy of silence which has been regarded (mistakenly as events have proved) as necessary for the preservation of harmonious relations. The greatest shock to British opinion has been the attitude of President Eisenhower *after* the ceasefire and the total capitulation of the British and French governments. The shock was followed by alarm at the indications of the President's policy in the Middle East. This has seemed to consist of condonation of Colonel Nasser's obstinacy and vindictive persecutions; of treating Israel as the "villain of the piece"; of undertaking to double and equip the Saudi army; and an undertaking to resist an overt aggression by Soviet Russia, which would be in fact quite contrary to Russia's interests. The present danger is not the open absorption of Middle East states by Soviet Russia, but of their pursuing policies inspired from Moscow; and the belief that gratitude and moral support can be permanently bought by lavish economic and military aid is likely to prove disastrous. One hopes there is no analogy with the optimism which during the war poured gifts on Chiang-Kai-shek and treated him at San Francisco as one of the four Great Powers, and which regarded Mao Tse-tung as a "harmless agrarian reformer."

However this may be, the Eastern debacle has had a psychological result which may lead to the re-establishment of British policy and of British-American friendship on a firm basis. While Britain has co-operated fully and effectively in NATO because of the part played in it by the United States, this has not been the case in regard to the sustained efforts of the Western European powers to work towards economic and military integration. British governments have stressed the technical difficulties of integration with Europe, but the underlying motive for hanging back has been psychological—a reluctance to admit the changes in Britain's relative strength and position in the world. Compensation for wounded pride was sought in emphasizing that Britain was primarily the equal ally of the United States and the head of a great oceanic commonwealth, with a chain of allies and bases extending from the Mediterranean to Singapore, and therefore must be careful not to compromise these wider interests or offend the Commonwealth by too intimate a connexion with the Old World. This attitude survived the experience of Hitler's bombs and rockets—which should have dispelled all illusions about isolation from Europe—and survived the loss of India in 1947, but there is good reason to hope it cannot survive the humiliations of Suez. Intimate co-operation—even without agricultural integration—with the Western European block, which has made such an impressive recovery, combined with membership of the North Atlantic Union in full co-operation with the United States, and with the utmost attention to the traditional solidarity with Australia, and New Zealand, will provide British foreign policy once more with a firm basis of principle, and a more solid basis for alliance with the United States on the main issues.

British influence in the Middle East is bound to recover, though in a different form. The very costly machinery of garrisons and subsidies has been a hangover from the "Route to India" days, and was in any case outdated since the Mediterranean itself will no longer be "viable" with modern aircraft and submarines and the Suez Canal can never again be relied on as a main artery for oil supplies. The situation of the Middle East is no longer a purely British interest since the danger is that of infiltration by Soviet Russia. In the European, especially the French, press there have been suggestions that the United States may do a deal with Moscow, which would *inter alia* safeguard the oil supplies. I do not for a moment believe that this would be practicable even if it were psychologically possible; it is a superficial hypothesis inspired by resentment. What does seem inevitable is that the East will be in constant flux and that the United States government which has taken the responsibility of directing events there, will encounter disagreeable surprises, and will have to make some rapid reappraisals. If Britain is freed from the excessive burden of the main reponsibility in the Middle East, takes her full share in Western European Union and NATO, and takes realistic action about the exaggerated pretensions of the United Nations, the end of forty years drift and confusion may be in sight.

Chapter 12

FRENCH DIPLOMACY IN THE

POSTWAR WORLD*

J. B. Duroselle

FRANCE, like all other countries in the world, has felt the impact of the new hierarchy of power established in the world at the end of World War II. If a great power is one which is capable of preserving its own independence against any other single power, it is obvious that only two countries, the Soviet Union and the United States, can satisfy this definition in the world of today; France cannot although it appeared to do so at least between the two world wars. Now she shares the fate of other countries like Great Britain, Germany, Italy, and Japan which have also fallen from high rank to secondary positions. This loss of standing as a great power is in itself of fundamental importance and explains in large part the evolution of French diplomacy since 1945.

But besides this general situation France has had to face a whole series of special problems of her own since 1945. These need to be described because diplomacy is not an end in itself. It is the principal, if not the only tool, of the foreign policy of a country. We cannot study the organization of the French diplomatic system without first

* I am very much indebted in the preparation of this article to Mlle. Nicole Deney, research assistant at the *Fondation Nationale des Sciences politiques,* who contributed very much to getting information, and to M. Raymond Laporte, Plenipotentiary Minister, who read my manuscript carefully and made invaluable suggestions to improve the picture I gave of the Quai d'Orsay. This chapter was translated by Professor James A. Corbett, University of Notre Dame.

trying to fit diplomacy into the general framework which is essentially political.

I. THE POLITICAL FACTORS DETERMINING THE EVOLUTION OF FRENCH DIPLOMACY

The first fact peculiar to France is that she was conquered in 1940 and occupied for four years, yet found herself in 1945 more clearly on the side of the victors than, for example, Italy. The Vichy government, which had never totally opposed the allies, collapsed in August, 1944. France never had the equivalent of the Republican Fascist government, or the Quisling government of Norway.

Several important consequences followed from this curious situation so different from that of November, 1918, when the French, though exhausted, considered themselves the great victors of the war.

1. In 1945 France still had, in theory at least, the whole of its enormous colonial empire while Germany, Italy, and Japan had lost theirs in 1919, 1947–1948, and 1945 respectively.

Now this quasi-miraculous maintenance of an old formula of sovereignty which had greatly contributed to the fortune of Western Europe seems to have indicated to French leaders the political line they should follow: the French flag must fly over all the territories it flew over in 1939 and be re-established where it had been struck as in Indo-China. As this policy coincided with the formidable emancipation movements first in Southeast Asia and then in Africa, France found herself engaged in a long series of costly, cruel, and inevitably disillusioning adventures. These have been signs that it is easier to be deprived of one's colonies by victors than to abandon them oneself. They also suggest that a conquered country, as France was, could less easily make the necessary adaptations than victorious Great Britain— if only for psychological reasons.

2. The apparent victory was one without profound joy for the French. Once the light-heartedness of the Liberation had been dissipated they rehashed over and over their four years of humiliation; this, too, had profound repercussions.

With some simplification we can say that the discontent expressed itself in four different ways. There were, first of all—a phenomenon more strange than important—the followers of a philosophy of despair: small groups of young intellectuals, or pseudo-intellectuals who pompously described themselves as "existentialists,"—without even knowing Husserl or Heidegger. They proclaimed the absolute vanity of existence by the strangeness of their clothes and hair dress.

There was also the strength of the Communist Party which reached its peak in 1947, but always succeeded in keeping 25 per cent of the French electorate in spite of a considerable loss of influence on daily political life.

The third course was that of isolationism linked, as it always is, with an emotional and intransigent nationalism: although all our allies abandon us and we face the world alone, we shall stand alone and proud in our haughty solitude.

Finally, the European spirit in its most exalted and mystical tendencies, is also a consequence of the discontent. It is certainly more constructive than others, but very characteristic; we are no longer anything by ourselves. Let us join other Europeans and become citizens of a great power able to talk again as equals with the two greatest powers of the world.

"Neutralism" has been deliberately excluded from the four attitudes which were born of a victory without glory, for the word covers too many contradictory realities. There is a communist or para-communist neutralism which consists of fighting against the alliance with the United States, one in which the neutralization of France would be only a step in the direction of an oriental alliance. There is a neutralism of intellectuals who, liking symmetry, would place on the same level the potential misdeeds of the two great powers. There is an ultra-nationalist neutralism which views the Atlantic Alliance only as an expression of general diplomatic solidarity and prefers solitude to an anti-Soviet alliance. There is, finally, a European neutralism which sees a united Europe only as a means of escaping the pervasive tutelage of the United States.

3. The end of World War II coincided in France with an extraordinary demographic revolution which is perhaps the most important phenomenon of the period. It was already felt in 1940 but the five year absence of the million and a half prisoners concealed its effects. France, with a low birth rate during the 1930's, and at times even a slightly higher number of deaths than births, has suddenly become since 1945 a country with a high birth rate, one almost equal to that of the United States and definitely higher than those of Germany,

Italy, and Great Britain. It has a population increase of 300,000 per year and, despite the predictions of certain specialists, there are no signs of abatement. The first half of 1957 has shown an increase in the birth rate and the number of marriages. All this can be explained by the almost unique system of family allowances, but even more, we believe, by a collective psychological phenomenon, namely, the re-birth of confidence in the future. It is not surprising that the upsurge began about 1940. This date coincides with the coming of age of those who never knew the horrible blood bath of 1914–1918 in which France lost 1,400,000 young men. The losses in World War II, estimated at 625,000 lives, were more evenly divided between men and women and did not engender the disequilibrium from which France suffered so much from 1918 to 1940.

THE EVOLUTION OF FRENCH FOREIGN POLICY SINCE 1945

This is not the place to write the history of French foreign policy, but rather to point out its principal stages.

1. At the time of the Liberation, France was part of the victorious coalition without really being one of the victors, whereas in 1918 she had played the essential role in the land warfare. Despite the heroism of those in the Resistance and the ten divisions which finished the war in Germany, France had been liberated by the efforts of the three great allies. Amidst the ruins there developed an atmosphere of discouragement and scepticism. Yet this was the period when General de Gaulle and his Foreign Minister Georges Bidault were trying to formulate a *"politique de grandeur."* Based on historical precedents— the present significance of which is debatable—this policy may be summarized as follows: France is potentially a great power and will become one again in fact. She must therefore be treated as one and be admitted into the meetings of the Big Three, and into the organization of the German occupation. France does not have to choose between the East and the Anglo-Saxons. She should play the role of mediator: hence the alliance she made with the Soviet Union in December, 1944, which was the prelude to a similar treaty she would sign with the United Kingdom. France should assure her security by dismembering Western Germany, and her reconstruction through reparation payments and the internationalization of the Ruhr.

2. This *"politique de grandeur"* came to an end in 1947 and was

replaced by a Western and European policy.[1] After the spectacular
resignation of General de Gaulle (January 19, 1946), circumstances
obliged Bidault, who had stayed on at the Quai d'Orsay, to reappraise
the situation in the light of the hardening policy of the Soviets. The
alliance, as General Catroux [2] pointed out, was not satisfactory since
Russia was always opposing French positions. The outbreak of the war
in Indo-China (December, 1946) and the renewal of social unrest
prompted Ramadier, the President of the Council, to dismiss the Communists from the government in May, 1947. This was a year of serious
social conflicts during which the Communists tried to foment political
strikes. After the quasi-insurrectional attempt of November-December,
1947, they were defeated. Bidault was obliged to abandon the idea of
France the mediator in favor of a France, ally of the West (Moscow
Conference in April, acceptance of the Marshall Plan in July, signing
of the Brussels treaty and of the Atlantic Pact, then acceptance of the
non-dismemberment of Germany, and the signing of the Treaty of
London regarding Germany, June 2, 1948, which assured the reunification of the three Western zones).

The time had come to take positive steps of leadership. In May,
1948, Bidault embraced the policy of European integration. The
guiding idea of the initiatives of Bidault, Schuman (Foreign Minister
from July, 1948, to December, 1952) and Pleven was complex. It was
based on the thesis that Western European countries could more easily
solve their political, military, economic, and social problems if they
built up a supranational federal authority over themselves. It was
linked to the desire to make Western Europe independent of the
United States and was, therefore, inspired by "neutralist" ideas. It
offered a solution to the aspirations for prestige: the *"politique de
grandeur,"* unthinkable on the national scale, was conceivable on the
level of Western Europe. It would, moreover, encourage idealism,
give people a cause to defend, especially that of rediscovered friendship between France and Germany.

Three spectacular initiatives were taken: 1) that of August, 1948,
aiming at the creation of an elected European Assembly—but because
of the complete opposition of England to things supranational this led

---

[1] Cf. J. B. Duroselle, "The Turning Point in French Politics: 1947." *The
Review of Politics*, XIII (1951), 302–328.

[2] *J'ai vu tomber le rideau de fer* (Paris, 1952).

only to the creation of a powerless Council of Europe; 2) the Schuman Plan of May, 1950, which led to the formation of the European Coal and Steel Community by the treaty of April, 1951; 3) the Pleven Plan of October, 1950, which proposed the creation of the European Defence Community. By advocating a policy of European integration France seems to have regained the dominant influence in Europe. Europe and the United States had their eyes fixed on France. Public opinion, which did not understand very much about integration, was vaguely flattered. The Treaty of Paris which created the European Defence Community was signed with optimism in May, 1952, by the six countries which were already members of the European Coal and Steel Community.

It was at this point that the about-face took place. An irritated world watched, without understanding, the long quarrel over the European Defence Community.[3]

The French people did not support their government. After two years of painful hesitation, the National Assembly refused on a procedural technicality to ratify the EDC on August 30, 1954, and thus seemed to have ruined the whole European reconstruction program. Already in June, 1954, the National Assembly had invested a President of the Council suspected of having lacked enthusiam for the idea of European unity. The vote on August 30 isolated France and brought down upon her an avalanche of criticism. What is the explanation for this historic about-face? We must stop to consider this for a moment if we would understand the succeeding phase.

The underlying reason was the rebirth of a certain French nationalism combined with an incapacity of the pro-European governments to give up the vestiges of the *"politique de grandeur."* Several survivals of this subsist: France managed to detach the Saar politically from Germany and to unite it to its own economy and to bring it within its own tariff walls. There was here a slowing down of the old traditions of annexation and the resurrection of a German State in 1949 quite naturally led to a current favorable to the reannexation of the Saar to Germany. The people of the Saar, who had profited from their French connection economically between 1946 and 1950, began to

[3] This is the French title of an interesting book edited by Aron and Lerner (Paris, 1956). The American edition is entitled *France Defeats EDC* (New York, 1957).

doubt the future advantages of such an arrangement when they compared the prodigious economic revival of Germany with the difficulties France was having, and especially when they saw the powerful ultramodern industry of Lorraine emerging at their very doorstep. With interest waning, sentiment gradually gained the upper hand, and this was quite naturally and legitimately a nationalistic German sentiment. In order not to lose the Saar, French governments from January, 1953, on made the ratification of the EDC contingent upon the prior acceptance of a Franco-German treaty recognizing the Europeanization of the Saar: the Saar would become the center of a united Europe and the seat of its capital. It appeared to be one more step toward a united Europe. In fact, it confused the issue, for a reawakened German nationalism could not understand why, under the circumstances, a piece of French territory like Lorraine, for example, would not also be Europeanized. The whole integration effort was accompanied by a bitter nationalistic Franco-German quarrel over territory.

The *"politique de grandeur"* also implied the maintenance of French sovereignty over the whole of the old empire, now called the French Union. This explained the outbreak in December, 1946, of the long and costly Indo-China War which kept the elite troops of the French army over 7,000 miles from home. Military victory in Indo-China seemed to be out of the question from the moment, in 1949, when the Chinese Communists took up positions along the 600-mile frontier of Northern Tonkin and began to give all-out aid to the Vietminh Communists. In time the war changed its character and became, like the Korean War, an episode in the East-West struggle without, however, losing completely its colonial aspects. Nevertheless, the United States without wishing to take part in it, became more and more interested and gave increasing amounts of military aid to the Franco-Vietnam forces. The war, thus, became less and less a French war and more one in which the French appeared to be mercenaries. Public opinion, for a long time indifferent, reacted violently when the siege of Dien Bien Phu ended in a serious defeat on May 8, 1954. It then seemed more important to liquidate this hopeless struggle than to solve the less preoccupying problem of European integration. The troubles in Tunisia and Morocco, which also sought their independence, helped to relegate the unification of Europe into second place. This explains why Schuman, accused of being able to think only about

Franco-German relations, was replaced by Bidault who returned to the Quai d'Orsay from January, 1953, to June, 1954. It also explains the quarrel over the EDC.

The Pleven Plan of October, 1950, was different from the Schuman Plan in two aspects. On the one hand, it was more a compromise than an initiative. It sought to prevent by a subterfuge the entrance of Germany into the Atlantic Pact which America had been calling for since August, 1950, as a consequence of the Korean War. The creation of a national German army could be avoided by integrating German soldiers into a European army from the six countries. It was a new step toward integration. On the other hand, public opinion would no longer have to wrestle with incomprehensible technical problems but with a sentimental one in which memories of the Occupation played an essential role. The army is the very symbol of the nation. Very divergent nationalistic currents crystallized in opposition to the EDC. Some opposed every form of German rearmament; others like General de Gaulle thought that the creation of a "denationalized" German army would not be worth the "denationalization" of the French army. Still others saw in the Six Power Europe the danger of a Franco-German dialogue in which the other partners, especially those of the Benelux group would, for obvious economic reasons, always be on the German side. Then there were those who preferred the effective integration of the French Union to any European integration and thought that the incorporation of almost the whole army into the European army would prevent France from solving her colonial problems. Others, seeing the weakening of the army in Europe as a result of the Indo-China War, thought a new German hegemony would emerge within the framework of the European army in spite of treaty stipulations. In the light of these perspectives, the election of Mendès-France and the vote of August 30 are easily understandable. France wanted its government to adopt a new foreign policy.

3. This new policy, inaugurated by Mendès-France, might be called, to use his own expression for it, a "policy of choice." He had defined it clearly in the declaration he had made on June 3, 1953, the day he could not obtain a constitutional majority:

The fundamental cause of the evils which crush the country is the multiplicity and weight of the tasks it is trying to solve all at once: reconstruction, modernization and equipment, development of overseas countries, raising

living standards and social reform, exports, the Indo-China war, a large
and powerful army in Europe, etc. Events have confirmed what reflection
made possible to foresee: one cannot do everything at once. To govern is
to choose, however difficult the choices may be.

The choice Mendès-France proposed to make was extremely clear:
he gave priority to economic reform and prosperity. This presupposed
peace in Indo-China, acceptance of the trends in Tunisia and Morocco,
and above all, postponing the efforts to integrate Europe. France would
only profit from such integration if, instead of entering the community
as a weak partner, she could eventually join it as a competitive and
prosperous member.

There followed a series of spectacular initiatives: peace in Indo-
China (July 20, 1954), the promise of internal autonomy for Tunisia
(July 31), the vote against the EDC (August 30), the substitution for
it of the Western European Union with Great Britain and the six states,
which involved the admission of Germany into the Atlantic Pact
(October 23), the signing of a Franco-German treaty on the Europeanization of the Saar and its submission in a referendum to the
people of the Saar (October 23). These steps recognized that in the
modern world true power was not linked with the amount of territory
under the same flag but with economic power. This revolutionary
concept was not always understood and led to the fall of its author in
February, 1955. Yet it was such an impressive one that his successors
at the Quai d'Orsay—Pinay (February, 1955–January, 1956) and
Pineau since then—have had to accept it in large part.

Some initiatives of Pineau show that this "policy of choice" was
linked to a reviving nationalism. France had the impression that she
was more and more being abandoned by her allies. The idea that the
United States was leaving her in the lurch in the Suez Canal crisis
prompted Pineau to unleash the hazardous military operation at Suez
which ended in a complete failure. But, curiously, this undertaking
rather strengthened the position of its author as public opinion saw in
it a legitimate expression of the pride of a misunderstood people and
in no way understood the problem which the uncommitted nations
raise for the United States. The tragic war in Algeria, the belief that
France was being unjustly tried in the United Nations by governments
incapable of relieving the misery of their own citizens, and that the
United States was no more than weakly backing her up on this oc-

casion, the suspicion nourished concerning American oil companies accused of supporting the Algerian guerillas in order to grab the latest riches of the Sahara—"the opportunity and the hope of France"—all these things contributed to the creation of a sort of haughty isolationism which prompted certain patriotic extremists to say: "We have only one ally left in the world: Israel."

At present, the "policy of choice" comes down essentially to this: should we grant independence to Algeria at the price of endless sufferings for the 1,200,000 Europeans living there and the loss of the Sahara, or should we continue a ruinous war against an ever-elusive adversary which means maintaining there a half million soldiers for years at a cost of 500 billion francs per year. This is a new kind of problem. Nowhere does there exist such a high percentage of colonists, some there for over fifty years, in relation to the number of natives. Moreover, the role of the Communists in the revolt is evident. Is there not a danger of seeing a new People's Democracy set up on the southern coast of the Mediterranean against which neither Bourguiba nor the King of Morocco could long stand? But before de Gaulle's accession to power in 1958 the Parliamentary majority was also pro-European; Pineau and Maurice Faure both want the Common Market. The question is whether France can have both the Algerian War and the Common Market.

French foreign policy has taken three different courses: the "policy of grandeur," the pro-European policy, and the "policy of choice"; there have been reasons for each one. To carry them out would require strong governments, but the constitution and the divisions of public opinion have made the governments weak. The pessimists foresee a gradual deterioration of French positions. The optimists pin their hopes on the profound transformation stemming from the dynamism of the nation, its high birth rate, the expansion of production which, during 1957, was greater even than that of Germany, the rise in living standards, which during the past four years have increased faster than anywhere in the world and are the highest on the continent after Switzerland and Sweden. French foreign policy is in its most dramatic phase since it must make the back payments on two world wars at a time when the country is becoming young and enterprising. This explains its hesitations and its failures, and also its immense possibilities.

French diplomats have to carry out this policy which they do not make. Have the reversals which this policy has undergone involved a transformation of methods? This question cannot be answered without first making a detailed and technical study of the French diplomatic service and its organization.

II. FRENCH DIPLOMATIC PERSONNEL

Although this study is primarily concerned with those who may properly be called the diplomats, it is also necessary to speak of the specialists and especially of the various attachés at the embassies.

The recruitment of the diplomatic and consular personnel before the war was done through two competitive examinations and several specialized examinations. The embassy attachés were selected through the "Major Examination" (*grand concours*), the consular attachés through the "Minor Examination" (*petit concours*). These were the starting points for two almost completely separate careers. One out of about ten of those who passed the "Minor Examination" ended his career as plenipotentiary minister. The two competitive examinations involved five parts: 1) a language examination where failure eliminated the candidate; 2) oral interviews (le "stage"); 3) an essay on diplomatic history; 4) an essay on international law; 5) an essay on economic geography. Then there were several supplementary written and oral examinations. The oral interviews lasted for a period of a few weeks during which the candidates were examined by a commission presided over by an ambassador. High officials of the foreign office could thus judge not only their intelligence and quick-wittedness, but also their personal appearance and distinction. Given the traditions of the diplomatic corps, the interviews unquestionably favored the relatives of diplomats, and the offspring of affluent noble and bourgeois families having connections and a certain standing. It often enough eliminated candidates of humble origins. It tended to make the career a caste affair as it was in most countries. Through other examinations the Secretaries of the Far East and the officers of the central administration were recruited. Finally, the Foreign Minister had the right to name as plenipotentiary ministers a varying number of personalities not belonging to the profession. In 1939 the proportion was as follows: 58% of the plenipotentiary ministers came from the Major Examinations, and 17% from the Minor Examinations and from among the Far Eastern officers; 27% were named by the Foreign Minister.[4]

The war brought about three profound changes. First, the decree of April 26, 1944, from Algiers set up a "supplementary group" (*cadre complémentaire*) designed to incorporate those who had served in the metropolitan Resistance or Free French forces. Included in this group were those who had certain diplomas or had performed diplomatic or consular duties for two years in a Free French legation, graduates of a military school of the French Committee of National Liberation (Algiers), or those who had "qualified by previous experience to fulfill diplomatic or consular functions even though they had none of the required diplomas." Then, every distinction between the diplomatic and consular careers was suppressed. Finally, the Major and Minor Competitive Examinations were dropped and replaced by a new system of recruitment through the National School of Administration, created by the Ordonnance of October 9, 1945.

In principle the National School of Administration trains all the high officials. There are two separate entrance examinations. One is open to students having diplomas equivalent to the "Licentiate"; the other to officials, graduates or not, having five years seniority. An equal number of positions (about sixty) are available to the candidates who succeed in the two examinations. Once accepted, the students go through a three-year course at the school, including a probationary period in different positions. The final examinations are the basis for assigning the graduates to the available positions. At the entrance examinations one may elect the much sought after "external affairs branch." Those with the highest grades who have elected this branch form part of the "external affairs section" of the National School of Administration. After the final examination they are assigned as embassy secretaries or commercial attachés, the former positions being preferred by the top students.

This system of recruitment has two advantages: 1) it suppresses the barrier which had eliminated candidates of modest fortune;[5] 2) since

---

[4] J. D. Jurgensen, "Notes sur les raisons du malaise règnant parmi le corps des conseillers et des secrétaires des affaires étrangères" in *Bulletin d'information du syndicat du ministère des Affaires étrangères* (F. O.) April, 1954.

[5] Thus a police inspector without a baccalaureate degree but having eminent intellectual qualities became an embassy secretary.

the entrance examinations are more general in character, more related to the general culture of the students, who are in contact with a substantial number of friends not working primarily for foreign affairs, their outlook is broadened. It also facilitates the admission of women. The entrance tests are very difficult. For example, in September, 1952, there were 681 who took the student examinations and only 62 passed, 609 who took the examinations for officials and only 67 passed. Only six from each group were admitted to the External Affairs Section.[6] These figures remain fairly stable though there is a noticeable increase in the number who take the examinations. In 1952, 52% of the plenipotentiary ministers came from the former Major Examinations, 16% from the Minor Examinations and from the Far East officers, 7% by nomination of the Foreign Minister and 25% from the Supplementary Group mentioned above. It is still too early for any of the graduates of the National School of Administration to have reached the rank of minister.[7]

In 1945 a certain number of officers, accused of collaboration with the enemy, were purged and a host of new officers entered the Quai d'Orsay. It was the last year of the Major and Minor Examinations. But there were two sections to it, one the normal group, the other a special one for prisoners, soldiers, deportees, members of the resistance, etc. Six agents were admitted through the normal Major Examinations, 17 through the special Major Examinations, 19 through the normal Minor Examinations, and 39 through the special Minor Examinations, 5 through the Examinations for the Secretaries of the Far East, giving a total of 81 new officers. On the other hand, the first class of the National School of Administration produced 10 officers; the Supplementary Group alone gave 250. Thus, in 1945 there was a total of 341 persons. The purge of collaborationists eliminated less than 150. It was a veritable inundation.

Various measures were taken to handle this load: 1) the graduates of the National School of Administration at present furnish very few diplomats (2-10 per year); 2) the laws called the "dégagement des cadres" (especially those of September 14, 1948, and of November 11, 1949), which applied to the whole French administration, permitted a 10% reduction of personnel. A law of June 7, 1951, however, restored

---

[6] National School of Administration (Paris, 1954), p. 69.
[7] Jurgensen, *op. cit.*

some of these because of their record in the war or in the Resistance. Moreover, some of those "purged" in 1945 won their cases and were restored. There is therefore a continuing plethora of personnel which makes promotion slow, especially at the level of secretaries and counsellors.

On the other hand, the problem of mixing together diplomats of various backgrounds has been well handled. Although the Quai d'Orsay has preferred to recruit directly without going through the National School of Administration, this preference has begun to disappear. The officers who had come from the exceptional group and had been assigned to less important positions had to take examinations between 1949–1951. The latest date for recruiting them was the first semester of 1946; since then only normal recruiting has been used. Today about 160 of these remain. It is important to note that some of them hold positions of the first importance, such as, for example, the position of Secretary General, the highest official of the Ministry. This position was created in 1918 and its first holder was Jules Cambon. Between the two world wars Maurice Paléologue, Philippe Berthelot, Alexis Léger and François Charles-Roux have held it. Since January 16, 1945, there have been four: Chauvel, a regular career officer; Parodi, who succeeded him on February 23, 1949, was not, but came from the Council of State and was a minister in the provisional government of 1944–1945; Massigli, agrégé of History and Geography, who had entered the Council of State and became Plenipotentiary minister in 1928 by appointment of the Foreign Minister and was named Secretary General on January 5, 1955. The present Secretary General, Louis Joxe, is also an agrégé of History and Geography who came to the Quai d'Orsay through the Supplementary Group in 1946. He was Secretary General in the Algiers government, then at Paris in 1944–1945. He has been in turn General Director of Cultural Relations, ambassador at Moscow and, later, at Bonn. Ten of the 79 heads of diplomatic missions are not regular career men.

If there were initially at least some rather understandable psychological reactions, there are no indications of them today. The Supplementary Group never formed a "party." Its representatives, like the normal career men, were deeply divided at the time of the fight over the EDC. Now, the absorption of the Supplementary Group into the careerists seems to be complete.

The problem of a dualism between departmental officers and foreign service officers, which was such a burning one in the United States a few years ago, has not arisen in France. Throughout all the central administrations of the state in France there are two levels of officials: "civil administrators" (*Administrateurs civils*) recruited through the National School of Administration who quickly rise to high positions, and the "administrative secretaries" confined to the middle positions. The Foreign Ministry does not recruit any "civil administrator." All the high positions are held by diplomats. Numerous secondary positions are held by diplomatic officers, especially chancellors. On the other hand, the central administration of the Quai d'Orsay needs administrative secretaries. These were recruited through an interministerial examination which is not an annual one. Since 1957 the Quai d'Orsay, no longer resorting to the interministerial examinations, has adopted a new method of recruitment of its own, furnishing men for the position of Assistant Administrative Secretary (*secrétaires adjoints des affaires étrangères*). In 1958 a group of Chancery Secretaries is to be formed by promoting former helpers and clerks.

There remains, however, one anomaly. A certain number of officers who came via the Minor Examinations before the war have not been integrated in the diplomatic service as unified in 1946. These are the *agents supérieurs* whose number, however, is declining. They often hold positions as vice-consuls or consuls and sometimes even direct General Consulates. They are being gradually integrated into the normal career service as are certain former officers of the High Commissioner in Germany or the diplomatic mission in the Saar.

As to statistics on personnel,[8] in 1957 there were slightly more than 4,000 persons ranging from the Secretary General and ambassadors down to the simplest clerk who were paid out of the Foreign Affairs budget. For the United States the figure is 20,250 of which 5,737 are in the United States and 14,513 abroad (of the latter number 9,125 are not American citizens).[9] In proportion to the population of the two countries the United States has one officer for 8,000 inhabitants and France one for 10,700 inhabitants. While this figure does not seem

---

[8] The last edition of the *Annuaire diplomatique et consulaire de la République française* (1954), 801 pp. The next edition is to appear in 1959. Exact figures for the years since 1954 are not available. They have not changed very much.

[9] "Toward a stronger Foreign Service" (June, 1954).

out of line, in fact the differences are considerable, for among France's 4,000 the Quai d'Orsay counts professors and teachers abroad. If these are excluded the number of persons employed in diplomacy comes to fewer than 3,000, or one for each 14,000 inhabitants.

On the other hand, if one considers only diplomats properly so-called, equivalent to the Foreign Service Officers before the Wriston Report of June, 1954, France has the modest figure of 666 while the United States has 1,318 (including heads of missions). But one must add to the American figures 207 Foreign Service Reserve Officers and a good number of the 5,373 departmental officers and employees. If we now consider the figures for the United States after the reform of 1954, the number of Foreign Service Officers is increased to 3,900 by the inclusion as career men of numerous departmental officers and certain Foreign Service Reserve Officers and numerous Foreign Service Staff Officers. It seems legitimate to compare Foreign Service Staff Officers to the *agents supérieurs,* decoders, chancellors, archivists, etc., of the French system. The figures, then, are 3,900 officers in the United States and 1,017 in France (this 1954 figure has since remained stable). Thus, in relation to the population the United States has one diplomatic or consular officer for every 41,000 inhabitants and France has one of the same category for every 43,000 inhabitants.

It may be concluded then that in the United States the personnel in the lower ranks is much larger than in France, but that the diplomatic personnel is roughly equivalent. The Personnel Office of the Quai d'Orsay has informed the author that the present tendency is to increase the number in the lower ranks while keeping stable the number of those in the higher positions.

The table below calls for certain observations. First, there were only nineteen ambassadors on duty in 1954. The last to be named was Daniel Levi, ambassador to Tokyo in 1951. In 1952 it was decided not to name any more ambassadors.[10] However, the present tendency in the world, stemming from a concern for equality among states in matters of protocol, is to suppress the distinction between embassies and legations. The new Asiatic states, for example, do not always recognize this distinction. In 1914 France had only ten ambassadors of which eight were in Europe. In 1939 she had sixteen, in 1952 fifty-four embassies and twenty legations: four behind the Iron Curtain—

[10] With the exception of the Secretary General of the *Quai d'Orsay.*

French Diplomatic and Consular Personnel in 1954 [11]

French Ambassadors [12]			19	19
Plenipotentiary Ministers,	special class		36	
"	"	first class	44	
"	"	second class	28	108
Foreign Affairs Counsellors,	first class		53	
"	"	" second class	76	129
Foreign Affairs Secretaries,	first class		120	
"	"	" second class	120	
"	"	" third class	100	340
Eastern, Far Eastern, and East European				
Counsellors,		first class	10	
"	"	" " second class	12	22
Eastern, Far Eastern, and East European				
Secretaries		first class	11	
"	"	" " second class	19	
"	"	" " third class	18	48
				666

Agents supérieurs	14	
Chancellors and Assistant Chancellors	277	
Decoders	52	
Librarians, Archivist-paleographers, geographers	17	
Translators	7	
	367	367
		1033

Rumania, Hungary, Bulgaria and Albania; and three in Asia—Burma, South Korea and Ceylon. As a result Plenipotentiary Ministers fulfill the functions of ambassadors, and they have the right to be called, as a courtesy, Mr. Ambassador, for life.

In the large embassies there are, besides the ambassadors, other ministers plenipotentiary called minister-counsellors. Of these Germany has two, Austria one, Belgium one, the United States three, Great Britain one, and the Vatican one. Even very important consulates general, though more rarely, are directed by ministers plenipoten-

[11] The figures are taken from the *Annuaire diplomatique et consulaire, de la République française* (1954).

[12] The dignity of ambassador has been suppressed since 1951. Of the eighteen ambassadors "dignitaires" of 1954, two have died, five have retired, six are diplomatic counsellors, five head the big embassies. MM. Chauvel at London, Dejean at Moscow, Payart at Saigon, Couve de Murville at Bonn, Alphand at Washington.

tiary. This was the case in 1954 for Munich, Montreal, Barcelona, New York, Genoa, Tangiers, and Monaco. As a rule, however, the consuls general are counsellors and the consuls are secretaries or chancellors in the foreign service.

Promotions are slow because of the relatively large numbers in the minister rank. Seniority does not play as great a role as selection. Those who are named ministers are usually between 45–55 years old, but in 1957 a man aged 38 was named minister. He had, however, been in the cabinet of General de Gaulle at London and at Paris. Counsellors are usually between 35 and 45 years of age.

There are very few women among the Foreign Affairs officials. The first and only one chosen via the Major Examinations was Mlle. Borel in 1930. She is now Madame Georges Bidault and the only woman today to be a plenipotentiary minister. She has never been an ambassador. France, unlike the United States, the Soviet Union, India, and Sweden has never entrusted a diplomatic mission to a woman. One other woman was received in 1945 at the last Minor Examination. The National School of Administration supplied one (before 1954); the Eastern, Far Eastern, and East European examinations have produced three. A few have been named by the Foreign Minister or come up through the Supplementary Group. But the total in 1954 was twelve (plus two available) out of 666 or the small percentage of 1.8%. The proportion is higher for chancellors, decoders, and archivists: 56 (besides twelve available) or 15.2% in this category. The Foreign Service remains overwhelmingly masculine.

The following table,[13] valid for 1957, shows the distribution of the officers in the department.

From this table it may be seen that 319 officers out of slightly more than 1,000 are in Paris. There are 191 diplomats out of about 650 and 128 other officers out of about 370. Each of the two categories retains a proportion of roughly one-third. Departmental regulations require that all secretaries and counsellors spend three years of their career in the Central Administration. Few diplomats in France, as elsewhere, like the requirement. As against the small number who prefer to be in Paris most prefer posts abroad. Here vocation and self-interest go together for in Paris they have only their salaries. In setting up the salary scales of public officials in 1946 diplomats were not favored

[13] Ministère des Affaires étrangères, *Administration centrale* (Paris, 1957).

	Ministers, counsellors, secretaries	Agents supérieurs chancellors, decoders, translators, archivists
Cabinet of the Foreign Minister	8	2
General secretariat	22	2
General Office of Political and Economics Affairs	1	
Policy Office	57	17
Office of Economic and Financial Affairs	29	4
General Office of Personnel and of General Administration	29	62
General Office of Cultural and Technical Relations	10	9
Office of Social and Administrative Affairs	22	16
General Office of Moroccan and Tunisian Affairs	6	2
Office of Protocol	4	2
Archives	1	11
Juridical Service	2	1
	191	128

because they enjoy substantial perquisites. But they have these only when abroad. Life in Paris is therefore expensive for them since their profession requires a certain amount of social life. Hence, they try to shorten their stays in Paris. Young third-class secretaries are generally held two years in Paris before receiving their first foreign assignment.

On the other hand, it is to be noticed that the General Secretariat, the Office of Political Affairs, and the Office of Economic Affairs absorb the largest number of those diplomats properly so-called, who live in Paris. This is due to a very important and characteristic feature of the French diplomatic system. Since 1954 France has recognized the independence of Vietnam, Cambodia, Laos, Morocco, and Tunisia. While some of the French officials who administered these countries more or less directly have remained in them as technical advisers to the new native officials, the rest have had to be absorbed in some capacity.

This is especially true of numerous *Administrateurs de la France d'Outre-Mer* (in former colonies) and numerous *contrôleurs civils* of Morocco and Tunisia (former protectorates). The Quai d'Orsay absorbed a substantial number, and in 1957 some of them held positions of great importance in those fields in which they are unquestionably competent. Thus, there are two *contrôleurs civils* in the sub-office of Levant, one in the sub-office of Africa, one in the sub-office of Latin America, one in the Office of Information and Press, one in the Africa-Near East section of the Office of Economic Affairs, one in the East European section of the same office, one in the Transportation section, one in the International Technical Cooperation Service of the United Nations Office, one in the Bureau of Technical Cooperation with Morocco and Tunisia. Above all, as is normal, the General Office of Moroccan and Tunisian affairs has fourteen *contrôleurs civils*. The administrators of Overseas France are found especially in the diverse services of the department concerned with Vietnam, Cambodia, and Laos. All told, seventy high officials are being integrated into the structure of the diplomatic service.

The total personnel of the Ministry of Foreign Affairs in Paris comes to 844.[14] This makes it one of the smallest of the French Ministries. Compared with the figures of 319 officers mentioned above, this number is high. It is certainly not the *contrôleurs civils* and *Administrateurs de la France d'Outre-Mer* which account for this difference. The Quai d'Orsay utilizes the services of officials detached from various other ministries: army, navy, air, inspectors of finance, professors (for the General Office of Cultural Relations), etc. Moreover, the middle and lower personnel, that is, administrative secretaries, office employees, stenographers, and messengers are used. Finally we should note that for historical problems, two historians, Pierre Renouvin and Maurice Baumont, professors at the Sorbonne, are advisers to the Minister. For legal problems, André Gros, Charles Rousseau, Paul Reuter and Charles Chaumont, professors of International Law, have a similar role. Another eminent professor of Law, and a specialist in Canon Law and religious sociology, Gabriel Le Bras, is adviser on religious problems which means primarily that he is liaison man between Paris and the Vatican when the latter is considering nominations to bishoprics.

The other two-thirds of the officers work in embassies, general consulates and consulates abroad where they remain at least two years, usually three years at a time. These centers include, of course, not

---

[14] The 1957 budget counts 941. This figure is exaggerated and includes diverse minor persons (chauffeurs, doormen, etc.).

only diplomats, but also military, naval, and air attachés dependent upon the ministries of the Army, Navy, and Air. The counsellors and commercial attachés depend in part on the Ministries of National Economy and of Commerce; the cultural attachés are in liaison with the Minister of National Education. There are, also, some financial attachés, press attachés, and labor attachés. All of them are subordinate to the Ambassador and report through him and the Quai d'Orsay to the various Ministries on which they depend.

A summary of the statistics of the *Annuaire Diplomatique* of 1954 (leaving out Germany, Austria, and the Saar which were at the time in a special situation) reveals that there were 72 military, naval, and air attachés. But their distribution is very uneven. The United States has, of course, the largest number—the area included extends to Panama: a brigadier general as military attaché, a vice-admiral as naval attaché, and a major general as air attaché aided by their five assistants. In Britain there are three military, naval, and air attachés and six assistants, but in Russia there are only two military attachés. The same attachés cover the Scandinavian countries and a like arrangement holds for those assigned to the Near East, Australia and New Zealand and for two groups of South American countries. Brazil has one military attaché for itself.

There are 46 commercial counsellors and 59 commercial attachés.

There are 32 cultural attachés. This rather low figure is compensated for in part by the existence abroad of numerous Institutes and French Lycées.

Finally, there are press attachés in Argentina (for South America), in the United States, Great Britain, in Sweden for Northern Europe, in Thailand for Southeast Asia, in Italy, and in Lebanon for the Near East, financial attachés in Italy, Argentina, Switzerland, Lebanon, and Great Britain and a single labor attaché in Great Britain.

These figures will help us to evaluate the nature and the tendencies of the contemporary French diplomatic corps. A certain number of myths have grown up about the traditional diplomat which, like all sentimental and impressionistic images, contain an inextricable mixture of truth and error. Marcel Proust created M. de Norpois who had the supreme distinction of a love of mystery about trifles, the superficial and brilliant mind which everyone outside the diplomatic corps readily associates with the diplomat. Roger Peyrefitte, in two successful novels, *Les Ambassades* and *La fin des Ambassades*, has described the diplomatic corps from which he had twice been expelled, with uncommon nastiness and an amusing but unfair irony. By collecting scandalous stories, even in the Archives at the Quai d'Orsay, Peyrefitte imposed the results of his research on the unfortunate French Embassy at Athens. He gave the impression, often with exact information drawn from many instances from many countries, that every French embassy was characterized by a mixture of futility, incompetence, personal quarrels, and more or less sordid moral conditions.

Now, if criticism can be made of the French diplomatic corps by impartial observers of its effectiveness, they are not in general those of Peyrefitte. France had some great ambassadors in the period between the two world wars, several of whom, like François-Poncet, Léon Noël, and Coulondre among others, have written their memoirs. Other diplomats have written their reflections on the profession following a practice several centuries old. Jules Cambon's *Le Diplomate* (1926), and Léon Noël's *Conseils à un jeune francais entrant dans la diplomatie* (1948) contain very precious observations on what is and what ought to be the career of a diplomat.[15]

We need not develop here the common features of all diplomatic services the world over, features linked with the evolution of the techniques of negotiations, such as the decline of the role of the ambassador in negotiations due to the rapid facilities for travel available to the Foreign Minister, decline of his role as a source of information because of the development of secret services, the growing importance of international economic problems, etc. It is more useful in a study of French diplomatic personnel to emphasize its characteristics.

The first of these is that the vast majority of the diplomats, properly so-called, are men with a general education. Their basic culture has to be very broad in order to enter the National School of Administration. The specialist in an economic, cultural, or other subject, or in a region like the Soviet Union or Japan, is the exception rather than the rule. The Quai d'Orsay tries to broaden their horizons rather than to use their particular competence. A young diplomat who knows Japanese has actually been sent to Tokyo for three years, then to the

---

[15] For a list of such works since the sixteenth century, cf. J. B. Duroselle, "L'évolution des formes de la diplomatie" in *Les fondements de la politique étrangère* (Paris, 1954), pp. 326–327.

Saar for three years, to Paris for one year and now is in Lebanon. One of his contemporaries who knows Russian has spent two years at Saarbrucken, two at the central administration and two years in Greece —where he has learned modern Greek. Only after this experience is he sent to Moscow. There are many such examples. Even more frequently one sees an ambassador form a team of younger collaborators and try to take it with him from one post to another rather than seeing a diplomat settle in one place and never move from it—if we exclude the Eastern, Far Eastern, and East European secretaries. This desire of the French diplomat to have a broad culture is not generally criticized in France as it is in the United States where according to the Hoover Report the advocates of extreme specialization are numerous.

Now this raises a problem. The United States can afford to maintain a group of broadly educated men because they have the direct or indirect help of technicians. Besides the various attachés at the American embassies extensive use is made of the Foreign Service Reserve Officers who are generally engaged by contract for four years: specialists in oil, agriculture, education, radio, atomic energy, etc. To carry out the various foreign aid programs—military, economic or technical—the United States maintains numerous teams of technicians and specialists abroad. The problem of coordinating the effort of all these specialists is the work of the team presided over by the ambassador. It is here that the need arises for the liberally educated man. France does not have a group like the Foreign Service Reserve Officers. It is not the financial aspect of the problem which raises difficulties—the United States has about 200 and France could get along with about 50—but rather the extremely sheltered character of the career which works against it.

It is here we believe that the principal weakness may be found. French diplomacy obstinately rejects outside help or keeps it at least to a minimum. Except for advisers on legal, historical, religious, and technical questions—never more than ten in all—it practically never seeks the help of outside specialists. But a legal adviser, however brilliant he may be, is not an authority on all legal problems. In a given case it is probable that there is a specialist who is more competent. Even more frequently the report requested by a Minister on a problem involving basic technical aspects is made by a liberally educated diplomat. The numerous studies made for the State Department by professors, engineers, and legal experts are not of course all used and often they simply occupy shelves in the Archives. Yet the system does permit seeing the problems in a more scholarly and more modern way and reduces the amount of off-hand impressionism inevitably found in studies of technical problems made by non-specialists.

In France, the diplomat coming from the Supplementary Group, is admitted only to the extent that he accepts the traditions of the service and the traditional exclusivism of the Quai d'Orsay. It will be interesting to follow the case of the *contrôleurs civils* and *Administrateurs de la France d'Outre-Mer* who can be induced to enter the regular diplomatic corps.

The present tendency shows no sign of transformation; the Service remains a closed caste ever prone to believe in its omniscience. However, there is unquestionably a change in the way the younger diplomats are viewing their work. In all countries diplomats are chided because they have to go to five or six cocktail parties every night where they always meet the same people—other diplomats and a certain portion of the local high society. This concept of the job, which has come down from the princely courts of other days, is undergoing a radical transformation. Today, French diplomats are, for the most part, serious-minded, hard-working men who love their profession and practice it with imagination and dedication. They realize that social influence is no longer confined to the salon set. They meet and associate with much greater profit with the elite of unions, industry, science, and the intellectual life. Recruitment through the National School of Administration, which opens the door to candidates of modest backgrounds, permits the outside observer to be more optimistic about this evolution which is of the highest importance. It refutes "Monsieur de Norpois" who may still be found, but in decreasing numbers, on all levels of the hierarchy. We can say that at present all the key posts at the Quai d'Orsay and abroad are held by hard-working, serious-minded men who exact as much from themselves as from their subordinates. This has not always been the case.

As a final observation on the French diplomatic corps we should note that it remains faithful to its tradition of brilliance and charm. French diplomatic texts are written with an eye to style as well as to clarity. The publication of numerous collections of diplomatic documents shows that this is not always the case elsewhere. Moreover, the

Service has a brilliant literary tradition. Charles de Chambrun published in 1946 a collection of literary texts written by French diplomats dating back to Commines.[16] Chateaubriand, Stendhal, Lamartine, Gobineau, and in our own time, Giraudoux, Paul Claudel, and Paul Morand have been diplomats. Alexis Léger, for many years Secretary General, is none other than the poet Saint John-Perse. Peyrefitte, the prodigal son of the Service, is one of the best known contemporary novelists. Jacques de Bourbon-Busset, for many years assistant director in the Schuman Cabinet, then Director of Cultural Relations and at present on leave, has just made a brilliant entry on the literary scene with the publication of several novels. Romain Gary, Consul General at Los Angeles, won the Prix Goncourt in 1957.

French ambassadors are obviously not all writers. They are, however, almost never recruited as in the United States from business circles, and rarely from among journalists. Those recruited from outside the regular service are sometimes generals (Catroux at Moscow), often from the Universities (Joxe, Massigli, François-Poncet, Henri Bonnet), high government officials, prefects (Cornut-Gentille), inspectors of finance (Alphand, Couve de Murville). Political leaders are called upon less frequently than before the war. However, Francisque Gay, founder of the MRP, has been ambassador to Canada; Palewski, a collaborator of General de Gaulle, is ambassador at Rome. Occasionally an outstanding personality of the learned world like Jacques Maritain, who was ambassador at the Vatican, has been called upon.

III. The Structure of the French Diplomatic Service

This section will be devoted to the framework within which the personnel we have just studied functions. Description of the framework will be combined with an attempt to evaluate the extent to which the framework has adapted itself to present needs both in the Central Administration, the "Department," as well as in foreign posts.

While the organization of the French diplomatic service has had to face problems common to other diplomatic services, it also has had organizational difficulties peculiar to it. Since 1945, France has in fact lost its privileged position in various regions: in 1945, Syria and Lebanon where it had been a mandatory power since 1920–1923; in

[16] *L'esprit de la diplomatie* (Paris, 1946), p. 461.

Indo-China where it had to recognize the complete independence of the Vietnam, Cambodia, and Laos in 1954. France has had to adapt itself gradually to these new situations and to transform the High Commissions in Germany, Austria, Syria, Lebanon, Tunisia, and Morocco into regular embassies; to transform the embassy at Saar-brucken into a delegation of the embassy of Bonn with the prospect of converting it into a Consulate General; to create normal diplomatic missions to Vietnam, Cambodia and Laos. In spite of the particular links which subsist between France and some of these countries, the course of events has necessitated important revisions. Indo-China, which had depended on the Ministry of Colonies before the war, has come under the jurisdiction of the Quai d'Orsay. As Tunisia and Mo-rocco were protectorates subject to the Quai d'Orsay, their independ-ence has involved a revision of the structure of the services. In some governments there were Secretaries of State for German and Austrian affairs, and ministers or Secretaries of State for relations with the as-sociated states. The services for German and Austrian Affairs have been almost completely liquidated. The services for relations with the Associated States were partially assimilated in 1957 into the normal services, but only in part. There is still a general office for Tunisian and Moroccan Affairs; it has a Secretary of State at its head. But it is by no means certain, in view of current political conditions, that this organization will remain stable.[17] In respect to those areas, it may be said that the Quai d'Orsay is going through a period of transition and of transformation.

The political authority at the head of the Central Administration is the Foreign Minister and one or two Secretaries of State, each helped by Ministerial Cabinets. The position of the Foreign Minister and of the Secretary of State and their Ministerial cabinets is closely linked to the stability or instability of the government. To overcome the effects of the instability of government on foreign affairs there has been a tendency to maintain the same Foreign Minister in several successive governments. Up to June, 1954, there had been great sta-bility, for with the exception of the brief transition ministry of Léon

[17] In the Mendès-France government (June, 1954–February, 1955) a special minister for Tunisian and Moroccan Affairs, independent of the *Quai d'Orsay*, was created. This was also the case for the Edgar Faure government. The governments of Mollet and Bourgès-Maunoury had only a Secretary of State.

Blum (December, 1946–February, 1947) there had been only two Foreign Ministers, and both belonged to the same party. Bidault of the MRP was at the head of the Quai d'Orsay from September, 1944, to July, 1948; Robert Schuman from July, 1948, until December, 1952; then Bidault returned from January, 1953, to June, 1954.

Subsequently there was a period of uncertainty. Mendès-France, President of the Council from June, 1954, to February, 1955, kept the Foreign Affairs post for himself. His successor at the Quai d'Orsay, Antoine Pinay, a pro-European Rightist, held the office until January, 1956. Then stability appeared to have returned to the Quai d'Orsay, for under two successive governments, Pineau and Maurice Faure have retained their positions until the events of May 1958.

The Ministerial cabinet (*cabinet ministériel*) named by the Foreign Minister and dissolved upon his departure, is a very interesting and original French institution. This Cabinet is much more than a special secretariat. It is a team of men chosen by the Foreign Minister for their competence, fidelity, and even their friendship, to help him daily with his work. Shortly after the Liberation it became the custom for a number of Ministers to have large Ministerial Cabinets which formed a supplementary administration. Communist Ministers in particular used them to keep business away from the permanent administration which, in large part, distrusted them. It was also a way of making the state pay for communist propagandists. Strict measures were taken to limit the number of members in these cabinets to less than ten persons in order to maintain order, give them some coherence, and for reasons of economy.

How is a ministerial cabinet recruited and how does it function, especially at the Quai d'Orsay? It is headed by a Director of the Cabinet who has an Assistant Director. The Director is the right hand man of the Foreign Minister, his confidant and daily adviser, his representative in many negotiations. He has, therefore, considerable influence and authority. It is almost a rule for a Minister to retain the same Director of the Cabinet whatever be the department he runs. The personal interests of the Director are linked to those of the Minister; he is the key man of the team. Under him there are several technical advisers who specialize in different branches of the Ministry's work. Then, there is the Head of the Cabinet, primarily a political figure, who looks out for the relations of the Ministry with the parliamentarians and has a Parliamentary attaché to help him. Finally, there are a few cabinet attachés or *chargés de mission* with various functions. Often they handle the vast correspondence of petitioners and voters. The cabinet has its own special secretariat.

There are, quite naturally, always some diplomats in the Foreign Minister's Cabinet. But other personalities who have had nothing to do with the Quai d'Orsay may be named. Members of the ministerial cabinets are drawn largely from the Council of State which is composed of men highly competent in administrative law. High officials, professors, even journalists, militant unionists, lawyers, etc., are also found there. If we take the Directors of Cabinets, for example, we note that Bidault always had as his Director, Falaize, a plenipotentiary minister. Léon Blum, likewise, always had Fouques-Duparc, later ambassador to Rome. Schuman, on the other hand, chose as his Director, Clappier from outside the service. But his Assistant Director, de Bourbon-Busset, was a diplomat. Mendès-France chose a plenipotentiary minister, Baudet, who had been ambassador at Belgrade, and as assistant Director and adviser on foreign affairs, Soutou. Pinay chose his Director, Yrissou, from outside the service and his Assistant Director, Laloy, from the service.

Though largely open to diplomats, the ministerial cabinets draw on personalities of diverse backgrounds. Even if it had only the task of deciding who would be received by the Minister or who would waste his time, the cabinet would have great responsibility. The tendency is more and more to choose as extraordinary negotiators not members of the Central Administration, but members of the Cabinet. Thus, under the ministry of Mendès-France, Soutou carried out important negotiations with Germany and more recently, members of ministerial cabinets, Laporte and Goëau-Brissonière important negotiations with Tunisia.

Below the Ministerial cabinets there is the permanent administration, the solidity and influence of which are linked to the stability which the ministerial cabinets, political organisms, do not enjoy. The only permanent service annexed to the cabinet of the Minister is the Service of Diplomatic Visas and Passports. All the rest is subordinate to the Secretary General.

We have already mentioned this high official who is practically the second highest in the French Civil Service after the vice-president of the Council of State. His role is fundamental. He is the stable element, the coordinator and planner—insofar as he has the time to make long range plans. Named by a decree of the Council of Ministers (like the directors general, directors, and ambassadors) he presides over all other nominations in the Department and in various posts. He is really the key man in French diplomacy; all the services depend directly or indirectly on him.

Under his immediate direction are a group responsible for various studies, another responsible for the coordination of atomic energy questions, and the important *Secretariat of Conferences*. This last group takes care of everything concerning France's relations with the United Nations and its special subdivisions, preparations for their meetings, and the study of the general problems raised by the participation of France in international organizations.

The general and special offices depend upon him indirectly. The organization of these at present is as follows:

1) There is first of all the *General Office of Political and Economic Affairs* (*Direction générale des Affaires politiques et économiques*) with two assistant General Directors—one for political affairs, the other for economic and financial matters. These essential organs will be discussed later.

2) The *General Office of Personnel and of General Administration* (*Direction générale du personnel et de l'administration générale*) deals with personnel, budget, technical matters, internal service, social works, inspection of diplomatic and consular posts, accounting, decoding and dispatch service, diplomatic pouch service, and translating service, and for the time being with the general administrative service for Cambodia, Laos, and Vietnam. Everything connected with these three countries is at present concentrated in the former German embassy on the *rue de Lille*.

3) In the *General Office of Cultural and Technical Affairs* (*Direction générale des affaires culturelles et technique*)—the technical affairs branch has only been united with the cultural affairs since the end of 1956. This General Office includes: a) the bureau on teaching (teaching of French abroad, exchange of teachers and students, scholarships, French archaeological missions); b) the Office of Cultural Exchange (books, films, documentary material, international congresses, reception of distinguished foreign visitors, relations with

UNESCO and the cultural committees of regional organizations, and authors' royalties); c) Office of Exchange in the arts; d) Office of International Technical Cooperation (technical assistance experts); e) an administrative and financial bureau; f) a Bureau for Cultural Affairs of the Associated States.

4) *The Office of Administrative and Social Affairs (Direction des Affaires administratives et sociales)*: chanceries, legal matters, French citizens abroad, consular affairs, vital statistics, and administrative and social agreements—especially relations with the Red Cross, International Postal Union, maritime and fishing, etc., status of foreigners, and administrative and social services for Laos, Cambodia, and Vietnam.

5) *General Office of Moroccan and Tunisian Affairs (Direction générale des affaires marocaines et tunisiennes)*.

6) *Office of Protocol (Direction du Protocole)*.

7) *Archives*.

8) *Legal Service (Service Juridique)*.

Before analyzing this distribution we must study more closely the General Office of Political and Economic Affairs and its two subdivisions. For political affairs the division of the services—as is natural—is primarily geographical. Its offices are as follows:

a) *Europe:* north; central; south; east including the Soviet Union; European organizations.

b) *Asia-Oceania:* India, Nepal, Pakistan, Ceylon, Afghanistan, Burma; China, Japan, Korea, Philippines, Malaya, Indonesia, Australia, New Zealand; Thailand and SEATO; Geneva agreements on Cambodia, Laos, and Vietnam.

c) *Africa-Middle East:* Iran, Arab countries as far West as Lybia, the Sudan, Egypt, British protectorates in Arabia.

d) *America*—North America: Canada, United States, Hawaii, Puerto Rico, Caribbean Commissions, Commission of the South Pacific; Latin America.

e) *Relations with Cambodia, Laos, Vietnam*.

f) *Office of Pacts* (NATO and the allied troops in France).

g) *Press and Information*.

As regards economic and financial affairs the division is geographical only in the office of bilateral agreements which is also subdivided into America, Africa-Middle East, Asia-Oceania. Western Europe and Eastern Europe have two separate bureaus. On the other hand, the

Office of Economic Cooperation, the Office of International Transportation and the Private Property Office are divided functionally.

This rather arid enumeration has been necessary for understanding the following comments.

All reformers of the Ministry of Foreign Affairs have to face the dilemma: geographical or functional subdivisions. The Hoover Report in the United States proposed a division of the State Department into exclusively regional units, each one to be concerned with the political, economic, social, administrative, and cultural problems of its region. Dean Acheson, although a member of the Task Force which had proposed this reform, did not dare carry it out to its logical limits. In fact, the geographical division is carried much farther in the United States than in France, for six Assistant Secretaries watch over European, Far Eastern, Near Eastern and African Affairs, Latin American Republics, and International Organizations, under the direct authority of the Secretary and Under Secretary. But, at the same time, they maintained the functional division with Assistant Secretaries for Economic and Social Affairs, Congressional Relations, Public Affairs.

In France, the division of the principal services has been exclusively functional and has almost always been so.[18] "The geographical division," says M. Outrey, "has the advantage of avoiding, or at least of reducing to a minimum difficulties or errors in assigning work, and permits centralizing and coordinating more effectively all decisions relating to a given country or to a given group of countries. The division by subject matter permits considering, according to the same rules, problems of the same kind and to disengage gradually the few general principles which could be usefully applied to problems of the same category." Geographical divisions within the political services [19] were sketched out by Talleyrand during the Directory which created a section for the North and another for the South (to which the United States was joined). The current four geographical subdivisions were created on June 14, 1918. The *ordonnance* of April 13, 1945, generalized the division by subject matter. This *ordonnance* created in particular the General Office of Economic, Financial and Technical

---

[18] Cf. the pamphlet of Amédé Outrey, "The French Administration of Foreign Affairs," Offprint of the *Revue française de Science politique* (1954), which carries the study up to 1945. For the periods 1945–1952, Dischler, *Der auswärtige Amt Frankreichs* (Hamburg, 1952), two mimeographed volumes.

[19] Outrey, *op. cit.*, p. 48.

Affairs and transformed the modest Social Service Department, created in 1919, into a large General Office for Cultural Affairs to which technical assistance services have been connected since 1956.

The Press Service also was created in 1919. While in the United States Public Relations have a place apart under a special Assistant Secretary, in France the Press Service is under the Assistant General Director of Political Affairs.

The French Office for the League of Nations, created in 1919, has become by the *ordonnance* of April 13, 1945,[20] the Secretariat of Conferences which is directly linked to the Secretary General.

There is no special office in France corresponding to that of the Assistant Secretary for Congressional Relations. This is because under the Fourth Republic its work was done by the Ministerial cabinet and because the Foreign Minister always is a Parliamentarian as is, with very rare exceptions, the Secretary of State.

In the geographical division itself we saw the anomalies involving Cambodia, Laos, and Vietnam on the one hand, and Morocco and Tunisia on the other. These anomalies will one day disappear as has the special office for German and Austrian affairs. In these cases France is faced with two degrees of integration.

1) For Cambodia, Laos, and Vietnam the business involved is divided among the normal offices but all the bureaus so involved are concentrated in a special building on the rue de Lille separate from the Quai d'Orsay.[21]

2) Though planned for the near future the integration has not yet taken place for Morocco and Tunisia. There is a special General Office for them likewise in the rue de Lille.

The foreign posts include 72 embassies and 7 legations. The diplomatic mission to Ghana will be transformed into an embassy and another will be created for Malaya which recently became independent.

As of 1957 there were 23 first class and 27 second class consulates general, 37 first class and 40 second class consulates or a total of 50 consulates general and 77 consulates. (A notable fact is that with the exception of the consular services of the embassies, there is only one consulate, at Cracow, in the countries of the Soviet bloc.) Like

---

[20] This ordonnance was completed by the Decree of July 17, 1945.

[21] At the time of this writing the reform, consisting of placing these three countries under the Office of Asia-Oceania, is taking place.

most countries France uses "consular agents," local personalities, some-
times foreigners who have been given some of the powers of a consul.
There are at present 447 of these but the figure varies somewhat.
France is a country with little emigration. Outside Tunisia and
Morocco there are only 300,000 Frenchmen residing abroad.[22]

French embassies retain their traditional structure in that they have
a very limited personnel. The largest is at Washington (with an annex
at New York) and has 17 diplomats, 8 attachés for the three armed
services, 8 commercial counsellors and attachés, two cultural attachés,
one press attaché and two decoders, or a total of 38 persons not counting the lesser personnel. The London Embassy has ten diplomats, nine
armed services attachés, one financial attaché, seven counsellors and
commercial attachés, two cultural attachés, one labor attaché, one
press attaché, two chancellors and two decoders or a total of 35 persons. For financial reasons France has not been able to create, like the
United States and the Soviet Union, big embassies involving several
hundreds or even more than a thousand officers and subalterns spread
over numerous specialties. It is true that in the case of Germany and
the Saar, France attempted to set up establishments of similar magnitude, because of exceptional political circumstances. These inflated
organisms are being rapidly reduced.

The study of the budget for Foreign Affairs (including Ordinary
Expenditures, Moroccan and Tunisian Affairs and the Relations with
Associated States) is very revealing for a knowledge of the evolution
of the system. Compared with the total French budget (roughly
4,870 billion francs in 1957 and 5,300 billion francs in 1958) Foreign
Affairs spends but a small fraction. Its expenditures for 1957 were
35,057 millions and 37,707 millions for 1958. That makes 0.719% of
the budget for 1957 and 0.705% of the budget for 1958.

A detailed analysis of the ordinary expenditures would show a
constantly increasing expenditure by the Central Administration and
the foreign services. The increases are not due to the creation of new
posts, but to the salary increases of the personnel.[23] For cultural relations which suffered important reductions for the years from 1950 to

[22] *Le Monde,* Sept. 28, 1957.
[23] Cf. Rapport de M. Felix Gaillard, Assemblée Nationale, session de 1954:
no. 9552; Projet de loi de finance de 1954; *id.* 1955; *id.* 1956; *id.* 1957 (Paris,
Imprimerie nationale); Budget vote de l'exercice 1954. Affaires étrangères: *id.*
1955; *id.* 1956, *id.* 1957 (Paris, Imprimerie nationale.)

1953, the increases in 1954–1956 meant in fact a return to normal order. However, in 1957 there was a slight decrease. The decreases coincide with a period of growing demands for French professors by foreign countries: India, Latin America, and, especially, Vietnam. The cuts make it difficult to meet the requests and obviously hurt French cultural expansion. Here is one of the most dramatic phenomena of France's position in the world: the gulf which exists between the possibilities of French cultural expansion connected with its educational system and its traditional prestige, and the financial limitations imposed by the imperfect adaptation of certain sectors of the economy to the new conditions of production. This proves once again that the administrative organization itself is closely linked to the prevailing political, social, and economic conditions.

IV. THE ADAPTATION OF FRENCH DIPLOMACY TO THE NEW WORLD CONDITIONS

After this account of the framework within which French diplomacy functions and how it is organized, it is proper to consider the problem on a higher level and see whether the French diplomatic system is an effective tool in the modern world.

It has undergone but slight transformation. The Quai d'Orsay had slightly more than 500 diplomats in 1939 and today has about 650. It has retained its functional rather than geographic organization and has not undergone any essential modification. The formation of its officers and their recruitment has undergone, through the Supplementary Group and the National School of Administration, a certain modification, but the influence of the National School of Administration will not be felt for another ten or twenty years. Some sixty officers, all young, and therefore in the lower ranks, have come from there, hence, less than 10%. Furthermore, many of them would have been normally received through the Major and Minor Examinations if these had been maintained. If there has been a transformation, it has been due to the characteristics of the wartime and postwar generations more than to a profound social evolution.

1. The "Programs"

French diplomacy can only be that of a medium-sized power. The characteristic of the diplomacy of a great power in the world of today

—and this applies to the United States and the Soviet Union—is that it involves not only diplomatic relations but especially various forms of interventions. This is the outstanding phenomenon which words and diplomatic forms fail to reveal but which is one of the keys to our times. Each of the two great powers apply over large sections of the world what Americans call a "Program" or "Doctrine."

What is a program but an intervention on the economic, technical, and military levels accepted by other states? It is the recognition of a real disequilibrium sanctioned by the fact that one of the partners has the means of helping the other which is in need. From 1945 to 1947 the United States helped numerous countries economically in an irregular, fragmentary, and haphazard way because it considered this as temporary relief to exhausted countries. On March 12, 1947, the Truman Doctrine introduced the principle of systematically organized and planned aid over a long period. The Marshall Plan, NATO, and Point IV enlarged the system which, for the last several years, has increasingly favored the Asiatic and African countries. The European Recovery Program and Military Aid Program indicate a profound revolution in traditional diplomacy. The Hoover Report of 1949 set forth a principle which has on the whole been observed; namely, that the State Department elaborated programs which were carried out by other agencies. The purpose of this was to preserve its traditional role in foreign relations associated with diplomacy. But there cannot be numerous and active Military Advisory Groups in a multitude of countries without these having a profound influence on diplomacy. The creation of Country Teams grouping representatives of missions which carry out the programs and diplomats under the direction of the ambassador gives the latter a new role. Even normal diplomacy resents this. How can the beneficiary country be other than exceptionally attentive to the reactions of the country which is helping it? And why should not the helping power use this enormous means of pressure for its own political interests? The less well known economic relations between the Soviet Union and its satellites, or China, seem to present comparable phenomena.

This raises the question of whether French diplomacy is condemned to remain traditional or whether it should try to carry out similar programs on a smaller scale. The notion of a program evokes in the mind the idea of wealth, power, and intellectual productivity. France has neither the wealth nor the power and to imagine that the enormous disproportion between it and the United States will decrease is for the present to conjure up an optimistic and academic hypothesis. France can envisage programs, however, if they are geographically limited: Tunisia and Morocco are open to such initiatives but the war in Algeria poisons her relations with these countries. Black Africa is at present a favorable terrain for aid programs. There, no doubt, they would be the means of assuring a more peaceful evolution of the region toward new links with France. But Black French Africa, which enjoys quite substantial aid, forms part of the Overseas Territories and does not depend on the Quai d'Orsay.

There is an area, however, where France is already at work with a program: cultural relations and technical assistance. But in her conception of cultural relations she seems to be too attached to old myths, defending the French language and French literary culture. In *Les Ambassades*, Roger Peyrefitte criticized with gusto the conception of the Foreign Ministry which required the French embassy in Greece to arrange for a lecture by an old academician who was completely unconscious of what might interest his audience. It is true that the trips of the *Comédie française* to New York and Moscow were great successes as were the showings of French paintings abroad. But these reach only a limited audience, only the artistically-minded. Such expositions in time give the foreigner a false picture of France, one of an art-loving, dilettante France somewhat frightened by the rough modern world in which she seems to be an anachronism. It is essential to turn the problem around, and instead of having a General Director of Cultural Relations and Technical Assistance to create a General Office of Technical Assistance in which cultural relations would be a branch.

Germany enjoyed dominant influence in Iran between 1933 and 1941. After its eclipse during the war, Germany recovered its place. At present hundreds of Iranian students go every year to German universities where, incidentally, they learn German. Was it by creating cultural institutions at great expense, or by sending writers with orders to speak only German that Germany acquired this influence? It was rather by winning markets and by giving technical assistance.

Is it preferable to send to Latin America a French novelist who speaks only in French of his works or those of other French novelists to a limited audience? Or a host of engineers who speak Spanish or Portuguese and will inspire by their very efficiency hundreds of young South Americans to come and study in France where, incidentally, they will learn French? Now France is a country of great intellectual activity. If the State, and big business with the encouragement of the State, organize technical assistance systematically, they will open up more than markets, for they will introduce French culture even though and especially if they deign to prefer the languages of the country, or even English. Technical assistance means not only engineers, but teachers, economists, sociologists, psychologists, doctors, demographers, biologists—even novelists and poets. The error of the French system is in encouraging only novelists and poets or, at any rate, in giving them a disproportionate place.

France can have a program of technical assistance, and in this area the disproportion with the United States would not be so great. In any case, in this noble undertaking in which competition is not imperialistic, it is quite able to rival all the great European countries. Such a program would not compete with the solid French cultural institutions which already exist in numerous countries. Nothing would support them better. But there must be a "Program."

2. Planning

The broad outlines of foreign policy are elaborated by responsible political leaders. The instability of the French system and the rapid evolution of international relations have created a climate in which political problems have to be met more or less on a day-to-day basis. Lest the cabinet be subjected to a dangerous interpellation, French foreign and domestic policy has a marked tendency to avoid facing bold solutions, to delay the inevitable, to hide realities behind words. In Indo-China in 1949 France should either have withdrawn or sent 500,000 men and loudly demanded American help. In fact, she stayed there with insufficient forces and knowingly rejected the idea of direct American intervention in order to avoid being squeezed out. When she finally did request aid, at the time of the siege of Dien Bien Phu in April, 1954, it was too late. Raymond Aron recently complained of this particular habit of many French politicians of failing to tell the public the truth in order not to frighten it. They prefer to let it learn the truth through the overwhelming disaster when it comes. "We shall be victorious because we are stronger" was posted on all the walls in early 1940. But France was not the stronger and the government knew it.

France is thus led to follow a policy imposed upon her by events. This clearly raises the problem of planning; that is, of assuring continuity through long term evaluations of the relations between means and ends. There used to be "planning." It was linked to the problem of slow communications and showed itself in the elaborate instructions to ambassadors which had been carefully drawn up at leisure in Versailles or Paris. The use of the telegraph between 1840 and 1870 dealt a mortal blow almost everywhere to such instructions which hardly exist any more except for the form. "Telegraphy," Albert Sorel wrote in 1883, "has upset all the former conditions of the old diplomacy. It suddenly strengthened, without preparation or transition, an element in the relations between states which up till then the art of chanceries had tried to banish: passion." [24]

Should we be content with this incoherence, or should something be done about it? The United States, whose world role is a recent phenomenon, has tried to meet it. Two organs were created in 1947: one on the political level and the other on the level of the State Department—the National Security Council and the Policy Planning Staff. The first, which includes among others the President, the Secretary of State, the Secretary of Defense, and the Chairman of the Joint Chiefs of Staff, lays out the broad outlines of policy. In France, as in all countries with parliamentary regimes, there is no need for such organs since all power emanates from the Council of Ministers which discusses the major foreign problems as a group. At the beginning of the century it was understood that this would be taken care of by the President of the Republic, the President of the Council, and the Foreign Minister. [25] But ministerial stability is lacking—the main problem of the French government.

But should France create a permanent planning commission on a modest scale? The American experiment, which has not worked too well, is not encouraging. Members of it, like George Kennan for example, have been used primarily as advisers on current problems. The

---

[24] "La diplomatie et le progrès" in *Nouveaux essais de critique et d'histoire,* p. 281.

[25] Caillaux, *Mémoires,* I., 221.

present Republican administration does not seem to attach much importance to it. This is not to say that the idea is not a good one. Indeed, in the light of recent events, it is a necessary organ. The Secretary General has to have a grasp of all the problems of French foreign policy and since he has a rather stable position, why not create around him a small, long-term planning commission composed of diplomats, technicians (financiers, economists, jurists, and sociologists), and specialists in international relations? Such a body, free from day-to-day responsibilities, but having access to all available information, would be in a position to draw up various long-range plans. The Secretary General could be in constant consultation with it. It would be one means of overcoming, if this were desired, the small-time "politics" which have characterized France since 1944, even in the days of the *"politique de grandeur."*

3. Coordination

Planning means having coherent views on the future, coordination, a coherent policy in the present. It is made increasingly necessary by the enormous expansion of the work of the modern state. The interconnection of diplomatic, military, and economic problems is growing. The problems which have to be met have become so complex that it requires groups of men, not just individuals, to study them. To be sure, unity of decision and responsibility remain, but the statesman can no longer make certain great decisions by intuition alone. There has to be considerable coordination.

In France, as in all democratic countries, this has to take place on two levels: agreement among the ministers and then with parliament. Nowadays the problems of foreign policy do not concern the Foreign Minister only. Numerous ministers are involved and they all feel a certain responsibility for the conduct of Foreign Affairs.[26] In 1913, besides the Ministry of Foreign Affairs, the Central Administration had only three bureaus which specialized in international problems: the Customs Office (under the Ministry of Finance) and two offices in charge of economic and industrial affairs in the Ministry of Commerce,

---

[26] For what follows I have used extensively the remarkable report of M. Dutheillet de Lamothe made for the *Fondation nationale des sciences politiques* (1955, mimeographed): "La participation des ministres autres que celui des Affaires étrangères à l'élaboration des décisions de politique extérieure."

Industry, and Postal Service. In 1938, there were fifteen. By January 1, 1954, this figure had risen to sixty-six specialized bureaus to which should be added diverse international activities of non-specialized bureaus. Without going into detail, we might note that forty-seven of these bureaus are under the economic ministries (finance, economic affairs, industry, commerce, agriculture, public works, civil aviation, merchant marine), seven under National Defense, seven under the social and cultural ministries (education, labor and social security, health and population), five under the ministries of the interior and justice.

While an Imperial Decree of 1810, which is still in force, requires the centralization of all relations with the foreigner in the hands of the Minister of Foreign Affairs, in practice this is far from the case. Coordination has become a vital necessity if only for the effectiveness of foreign policy. This coordination takes place first of all on the governmental level. The Council of Ministers is the ultimate case in point but it cannot settle all details. More and more it has become customary to have limited councils (meetings of only a few ministers) or interministerial committees, sometimes with fixed membership which bring together ministers and high officials.

Coordination is especially necessary on the administrative level and often operates in an informal or semi-official way. The Office of Economic Affairs at the Quai d'Orsay, for example, the Office of External Finances of the Ministry of Finance, the Office of External Economic Relations of the Ministry of National Economy are often managed by inspectors of finance, or the directors of these offices have inspectors of finance attached to them. These have a common background and know each other personally. But the need for official organs of coordination is more and more necessary since one notes, as Dutheillet de Lamothe says, "a very strong repugnance in the French administration to admit that the Foreign Ministry has a predominant role over the others and that it can arbitrate the most important questions." Such organs are gradually coming into being. The most important one at present is the General Secretariat of the Interministerial Committee on questions of European economic cooperation which was created in 1948. It prepares, in cooperation with the interested administrations, the French decisions concerning French participation in the Organization for European Economic Cooperation, concerning the economic problems raised by NATO, and the problems of the European Steel and Coal Community. There is also the Permanent General Secretariat for National Defense headed today by a Plenipotentiary Minister.

In brief, as Dutheillet de Lamothe concludes: a) the Ministry of Foreign Affairs no longer has a monopoly on information or even the initiative, but its role in these two areas still remains dominant. b) "Once a decision is taken it retains in most cases the essential responsibility for carrying it out." c) "On the other hand, it no longer plays its traditionally predominant role in all the intermediate stages when decisions are being formulated and, especially, during negotiations. It no longer has sufficient authority to settle by itself the divergent views which emerge from the several administrations and has to have recourse to political arbitration. However, the success or failure of negotiations depends on its initiative." Thus, the negotiations which led to the Coal-Steel pool were carried out almost entirely by Jean Monnet and the General Commissariat of the Plan, but they were supported by the effective action of the Minister of Foreign Affairs, Robert Schuman.

This relative decline in prestige of the Quai d'Orsay leads one to believe that the real leader of French foreign policy is no longer the Minister, but the Prime Minister, the supreme arbiter. This is so true that the periods of most active French foreign policy were the two short periods when the Prime Minister was also Foreign Minister; Léon Blum (December, 1946–January, 1947) and Mendès-France (June, 1954–February, 1955). Perhaps this will be the formula of the future. It should be noted, however, that a sensible effort is now being made to assure liaison between the Prime Minister and the Ministry of Foreign Affairs. This was achieved under the governments of Edgar Faure, Mollet and Bourgès-Maunoury by Berard (ambassador), E. Noël (assistant director of the cabinet of Mollet), and Jean Baelen (ambassador).

Cooperation with Parliament raises even more serious problems. Parliament has constantly increased its powers over foreign policy and the Constitution of 1946 institutionalized this growing encroachment. A vote of the National Assembly is now necessary for a declaration of war (Title II, art. 7), and for the ratification of most treaties (Title IV, art. 17). There are more and more foreign policy debates inciting the intervention of orators while the government tries, sometimes in vain, to get its policy approved.[27] When the Assembly is about to invest a Prime Minister, it does so in virtue of a declaration which often devotes a substantial section to foreign policy. The Foreign Affairs budget, on the other hand, is almost always approved without discussion. It is true that the sums involved are very small in comparison with the total budget. Finally, as Grosser points out, the number of interpellations on foreign affairs is very small and never gives rise to discussions.

There is no such effective organ of parliamentary control as the Senate Committee on Foreign Relations in the United States. The Commission of Foreign Affairs of the National Assembly plays only a limited role. Its membership, forty-four, is large. From thirty to thirty-five members, often well-known deputies, regularly attend its meetings. But a member can send a substitute,—a rule which weakens the coherence of a commission already too large. There is hardly any *esprit de corps*. Its secrets are poorly kept and the presence of Communists in it makes the government distrustful of it. The press often publishes detailed reports of its meetings. Moreover, the commissioners are not all qualified for the work. Tradition requires that the President of the Commission have access to the dispatches of the Quai d'Orsay. In fact this applies only to the dispatches received at the Quai d'Orsay not those sent. The President has no means of knowing whether all dispatches have been sent to him, for he has no office in the Ministry. He has the right to see them personally, but does not have the right to submit them to the other members of the Commission. There is no organic link between him and the Secretary General of the Quai d'Orsay, but there was one between himself and the cabinet of the Foreign Minister up to the time of the government of Mendès-France (from 1947 to 1954). Finally, the Commission hears hardly anyone except the Foreign Minister, practically never the high officials. There is nothing comparable to the detailed hearings in the United States. In short, the role of a Commission which does not represent the exact opinion of the Assembly and which is uninformed as regards numerous secrets, reduces it to a simple agency of control with very limited power.

[27] I follow closely the excellent report of M. A. Grosser made for the *Fondation nationale des Sciences politiques* (1955, mimeographed): "L'action du Parlement sur la politique étrangère."

The result is that in France control is exercised only by the Assembly as a whole in its debates on foreign policy. These are not favorable conditions because of the length of the debates, the numerous interventions, and the endless repetition of the same arguments. It is all a nerve-wracking and exhausting experience for the Foreign Minister. France unquestionably needs to modify its system. A commission limited in membership and sworn to secrecy which is in constant liaison with the Ministry and accustomed to frequent discussions with high officials would be considered authoritative and have a clear position at the time of the great debates. But is not the absence of such an organ linked with the weakness of the French governmental system?

CONCLUSION

The problems raised here have not escaped the attention of responsible authorities. The present Secretary General Joxe, has created a committee headed by a Minister Plenipotentiary, Lebel, to study them. He is giving great attention to the problem of adapting the Quai d'Orsay to the modern world. Although his solutions are not always the same as those outlined here, it may be said that there is now in the department a center of dynamic initiative with a will to reform, and a passionate desire to find the best possible way to give this elite body a maximum effectiveness. The Study Group would have plenty of work even if its task were limited to that of organizing on a logical basis, rather than an empirical one, the evolution of the careers of the officers—or to that of increasing through mechanization or a better administrative organization the "productivity" of the Ministry.

Lebel believes that with an additional annual credit of 100,000,000 francs—an insignificant sum compared to the total national budget of 5,300 billion francs in 1958—most of the technical problems can be solved. Unfortunately, since the Foreign Affairs budget has little electoral appeal, the deputies have hardly any inclination to make even a token gesture in its favor.

Two important reforms have already been practically agreed upon and will go into effect, if the funds needed to carry them out are voted, as seems most likely:

1) The creation of an Office of Documentation subject to the head of the Archives and not to the head of the News Service. It will have the task of preparing—as it does in the United States—background

material for diplomats on all subjects on which they need to have a certain general competence, such as atomic energy and oil.

2) The creation of a refresher program for diplomats at the Quai d'Orsay. Diplomats would come periodically for a few weeks or a few months to this center which is comparable to the State Department's Foreign Service Institute. Here they would receive an intensive training in foreign languages and take background courses in various subjects. The Study Group's conception of this program is perhaps somewhat limited since it does not envisage any of these courses as being given by men from outside the department. Nevertheless, it is a revolutionary undertaking despite its modest appearance; there is every reason to hope that this program will develop further.

In short, we must not view the present state of the French diplomatic service with the critical and disdainful attitude which too many superficial observers think it fashionable to adopt toward it. France has a remarkable instrument which a few wise reforms will suffice to improve considerably. It is on the level of politics, not in its execution, that French foreign policy is weak. In other words, and once more, the great weakness is in the French system of government not in its administrative organization.

Postscript:
  * The above text was written before the events which followed the upheaval of May, 1958. These events were the culmination of a fast developing evolution which, in four months, led France from the Fourth to the Fifth Republic. The latter, as we now add this note, is only beginning to function. We shall therefore simply draw attention to several points which, at this moment, seem to be significant.

  1) The establishment of a more stable regime cannot fail to have profound repercussions on French foreign policy. The return to power of General de Gaulle permits anticipating a more optimistic evolution of the means and ends of French policy. This means no doubt a return to a "policy of grandeur," but it will be a more liberal, a more supple, and a more durable one too. The weak and incoherent character of French action in international affairs, on which we have so much insisted, is likely to disappear in favor of a more normal influence.

  2) But there is no indication that the instrument of this policy, that is, the French diplomatic corps, will have to undergo profound changes. The structure of the bureaucracy, the recruitment of the personnel, the system of the ministerial cabinets will all continue as well as the notable traditions of that great corps of officials which constitutes the Quai d'Orsay. The personnel has not been changed; the general offices have retained the same heads. There has been absolutely no purge whatsoever. The diplomats, like all other Frenchmen, were completely free to vote "*non*" in the constitutional referendum, and to say so.

  3) There will be—in fact already has been—an essential change at the level of

the Foreign Minister himself. The new Constitution forbids being both a Minister and a member of the Assembly at the same time. Already since last June, a diplomat, M. Couve de Murville, former ambassador at Washington, then at Bonn, has held this position. Will the trend be to continue naming high officials to head the Foreign Office, or to name deputies or senators who will agree to give up their electoral mandates? We cannot tell as yet.

4) It is certain, however, that the existing structure can act with an increased efficiency in carrying out the country's policy. Continuity of policy is indeed necessary to assure continuity in action. The vote of the people shows that public opinion is profoundly conscious of this imperative necessity which holds true for democratic regimes just as much as it does for totalitarian ones.

III

New Actors and Changing Roles

Chapter 13

CANADIAN DIPLOMACY

Edgar McInnis

CANADA is a country that is relatively new to the field of formal diplomacy, but not to the realities of world politics. Few nations, at least in the New World, have had more reason to be conscious from their earliest beginnings of how inextricably their destinies are bound up with external conditions and external events. Canada has never been in the kind of circumstances that made it possible for the United States to turn its back on Europe for almost a century. On the contrary, the European balance of power and its international repercussions have been of direct concern to Canadians throughout their history. So too has the proximity of the United States, adding its constant reminders that our welfare and even our existence may be linked to the policies of other and stronger states. And there is our traditional connection with Great Britain, which has not only been a pivotal factor in our calculations, but which helped to educate us in the techniques of negotiation long before we achieved an independent position in world affairs.

Canada's progress to independence was by the path of gradual evolution, and one of the most prolonged aspects of that evolution was concerned with external relations. It was nearly sixty years after our national foundations were laid in the Confederation of 1867 before we gained full control of our own foreign affairs. When that was at last achieved, the next task was to decide how best to exercise the powers that had been won. Like other nations, we had to relate our policies to our interests and our position and our relative strength. We found ourselves in the position of a middle power, saddled with inescapable responsibilities because of our resources and potentialities, yet limited in our freedom of effective decision by our inferiority in strength to the great powers which had the determining voice when major issues were at stake. The fact that we stood in a very special relation to two of those powers, in a fashion that is hardly paralleled by any other country, was a further conditioning element of prime significance for the formation of Canadian policy. These are some of the initial factors that have shaped Canadian foreign policy during the past three decades, and not least in the years since the Second World War.

Now, when in the course of human events a dependency shakes off the rule of an outside authority—usually by revolutionary means—the full attributes of sovereignty are acquired in one fell swoop, and they are often pretty difficult for an embryo nation to digest. When the attributes of sovereignty are acquired piecemeal, as they were in Canada and most of the other Dominions, the first to be gained are naturally those that are closest to the immediate concerns of the inhabitants, and which they are most insistent on controlling for themselves. The right to elect, the right to legislate, and above all the right to tax—these are among the first claims of any movement aiming at self-government. And all these had been acquired, apart from a few purely nominal modifications, by the Canada of 1867. Representative government dated from 1791. Responsible government—that is, the dependence of the executive on the support of a majority in the legislature—dated from 1849. The British government, after certain unhappy experiences in Boston and elsewhere, gave up trying to tax the colonies in 1778. They said the attempt had been found "to occasion great uneasiness and disorders among his Majesty's faithful subjects." So Canada ceased paying taxes to George III almost two centuries ago. We even secured control of our own tariff system, including the right to levy customs duties on British goods, in 1859. Consequently, by the time of Confederation, domestic affairs were effectively under Canadian control.

There was already, however, a growing restiveness over Britain's control of Canada's foreign relations, and particularly relations with the United States. Next to our dealings with London, and not always second even to those, the most persistent external difficulties affecting

Canada were apt to originate in Washington. Trade relations and transportation arrangements, boundary controversies and border threats such as the Fenian raids, had all played their part in persuading the Canadian provinces to unite in the first place, and these problems did not disappear with Confederation. Not all Canadians were convinced that in such matters the British Foreign Office was a sincere and effective champion of Canadian interests. This was just one more area in which Britain had interests of her own, and they were by no means always identical with those of Canada.

What we first secured was a limited advance in substance under the existing forms. In 1857, when reciprocity was negotiated between Canada and the United States, the spokesman for Canada was the British official who held the post of Governor-General. In 1873, when a renewal of reciprocity was in question, along with fisheries and canals and the San Juan boundary, it was not the Governor-General but the Canadian Prime Minister, Sir John Macdonald, who upheld the Canadian viewpoint in the negotiations leading to the Treaty of Washington. He was not, however, an independent representative of Canada, but a member of the British commission, and his British colleagues were prompt to remind him of this fact when his stubbornness on behalf of Canada's claims threatened to balk the amicable agreement at which Britain was aiming. Not for the first or last time, a Canadian discovered that being in the middle can be a pretty uncomfortable place.

The years that followed saw Canada making further efforts to edge into the field of foreign relations. We established our own representative in London, calling him a High Commissioner to overcome the British horror at the thought that one part of the empire was trying to establish diplomatic relations with another part as though it were on the same footing as a foreign country. We got a voice in trade negotiations, and eventually carried on those negotiations through our own envoys, though it was the British ambassador who had to append the formal signature to the resulting agreement. We established direct relations of a limited and functional kind with the United States when the International Joint Commission was established in 1909. All this however fell far short of separate and independent representation abroad, or separate and independent negotiation of political agreements on behalf of Canada. As far as diplomacy was concerned, London was determined to maintain the unity of the empire and to retain the sole authority to speak for the empire as a whole. As late as the Imperial Conference of 1911, the British Liberal Prime Minister Asquith bluntly told the assembled Prime Ministers:

Authority cannot be shared in such grave matters as the conduct of foreign policy, the conclusion of treaties, the declaration and maintenance of peace, or the declaration of war and, indeed, all those relations with Foreign Powers, necessarily of the most delicate character, which are now in the hands of the imperial government.

What changed all that was, of course, the First World War. In that conflict, Canada and the other Dominions made contributions and sacrifices second only to those of the great powers. They did so of their own free will as voluntary partners in the struggle. They were unwilling at its close to be relegated once more to the position of dependencies, to be told that, while countries like Belgium and Portugal could take their places at the conference table as sovereign states, Canada and Australia and South Africa could speak only through the British representative. Although they formed part of a single British Empire delegation at the peace conference, they insisted successfully on appending their separate signatures to the peace treaties, on being admitted as full members of the League of Nations, and on gaining in the world organization a status of full equality with other sovereign states.

Other consequences followed swiftly. A rear guard effort to retain a united foreign policy for the whole empire had clearly broken down by 1923. Canada announced her refusal to be committed by British treaties in whose negotiation she had not shared, such as the treaty of Lausanne, and later the treaty of Locarno. She established her right to negotiate treaties on her own behalf in the Halibut Treaty with the United States in 1923, in spite of the claim of the British ambassador that he ought to sign the treaty, and the attempts in the United States Senate to make it apply to the whole British empire. With the recognition of her right to establish her own diplomatic posts in foreign countries, and the appointment of her own minister to Washington in 1927, Canada's control over foreign relations was virtually complete.

It is worth remarking in passing that in this protracted progress from dependency to autonomy, Canada received relatively little aid or comfort from her neighbor to the south. Americans were ready enough to see Canada break away from Britain—indeed, there were times when they grew pretty insistent about it—but this was almost always accompanied by the assumption that Canada would then recognize her manifest destiny and sue for admission into the American union. The idea of a fully independent nation on the northern border of the United States evoked a striking lack of enthusiasm. If Washington had to deal with Canada as a separate entity, it much preferred to conduct such dealings through London. Canadians were much too insistent on pressing their own point of view. The British government, in contrast, was more concerned to maintain friendly relations with the United States than to back up Canada in her periodic controversies with the republic. So it was very useful for the State Department to be able to tell London that, while the American government wanted only peace and friendship, these obstreperous Canadians were making it very difficult, and if they kept on there would certainly be trouble. And since the last thing that Britain wanted was trouble with the United States, her natural inclination was to tell Canadians to stop making nuisances of themselves and endangering Anglo-American relations which were really more important to Canada than those petty local objectives that they were pressing so irresponsibly. All of which was fine for Washington, if not quite so good for Ottawa, and there was real reluctance to see this useful lever nullified by the fragmentation of imperial unity in foreign affairs. It took the American government some time to adjust itself to the new situation—indeed, it was not until the administration of Franklin D. Roosevelt that the United States started treating Canada, not only as a good neighbor, but as an equal as well as a friend.

Here then was a new and major field at last opened to Canada—the final area of activity that completed her status as an independent self-governing state. Yet after all her insistence in gaining access, she showed herself pretty cautious about occupying it. In the period between the wars it seemed that Canada had been more concerned with formal status than with practical functions, more anxious to prevent others from making decisions for her than to implement positive policies of her own.

It is not a complete explanation to attribute this, as is sometimes done, to the negative temperament of Mr. Mackenzie King. There were at least two other factors that exerted a strong influence, and both of them were permanent elements in Canada's basic national interest.

One of them was the ever-present problem of national unity. Canada's biracial structure has more than once given rise to deep divisions that threatened to split the nation asunder. In the nineteenth century these were concerned with race and language and religion. In the twentieth century the most serious of them stemmed from questions of external policy. On the one side were strong sentiments of imperial loyalty; on the other were deep suspicions that the interests of Canada were being subordinated to those of England. One of the bitterest controversies arose over the introduction of conscription in 1917, and its echoes haunted Canadian politics for a full quarter-century.

In particular, it obsessed Mackenzie King. One of his fixed determinations was to avoid any repetition of this kind of crisis. The maintenance of national unity was a cardinal principle throughout his political career; and in his mind this meant avoiding any foreign entanglements that might once again divide the French and English sections of Canada. A divided nation, he burst out in a critical debate in 1939, could be of little help to any country, and least of all to itself. When war finally came, the Canadian government acted promptly and effectively, and it was able to do so because the old scars had largely been healed, and had been given the time that was needed to heal them by the policy, negative though it was, that had been followed in the years between the wars.

A second factor of vital importance to Canada was the maintenance of harmony between Britain and the United States, and here again the interwar years presented something of a dilemma. It was not that there was any serious antagonism between the two countries; it was rather that they followed divergent courses in world politics, and that Canada found these difficult to reconcile. While Britain remained an active factor in the balance of power, the United States withdrew into isolation. Canada was not prepared to follow the latter course. The security of western Europe was still one of her prime interests; the survival of the free world in the face of totalitarian aggression was vital to her own national freedom. Yet her leaders, rightly or wrongly, felt inhibited about active participation that might arouse criticism or suspicion in the United States, and tended to maintain an anxious aloofness toward the mounting crisis in Europe—an attitude particularly evident in the League of Nations, where Canada unexpectedly found herself the sole North American member, and where she presented an apprehensive opposition to the various efforts to put teeth in the League.

This attitude was reflected in the slowness with which Canada extended her representation abroad. We already had our High Commissioner in London. Our chief aim after that was to get our own representative in Washington. It was inevitable that this should be followed by the establishment of a mission in Paris. Our growing interest in the Pacific found expression in the thirties in the establishment of direct diplomatic relations with Japan. We were in no great hurry to go beyond this. It was only in 1939 that we accredited a minister to the joint posts of Brussels and the Hague; and when war broke out, there were only 33 foreign service officers under the Department of External Affairs.

The Second World War and its aftermath brought striking changes. Canada was very conscious that in the dark days after the fall of France, she stood next to Britain as the strongest member of the coalition that held the axis at bay until hostilities were successively forced on Russia and the United States. She was called on to make substantial contributions to the victory of the free nations. She was prepared to be called on for equally substantial contributions to postwar reconstruction and the maintenance of peace. There could be no stability or prosperity or security for Canada unless there was a stable and a prosperous and a peaceful world, and in our own interests we had to contribute positively and actively to creating the kind of world that was essential to the kind of Canada we wanted.

So the days of timorous and half-hearted participation were drastically ended. We reached out to establish direct and continuous contact with other members of the world community. In contrast to the handful of foreign missions in 1939, we now have 59 posts in 45 different countries, staffed by 356 foreign service officers. We are involved in nearly all important international organizations. We have not yet joined the Baghdad Pact or the Organization of American States, but there are not many other important exceptions. This rapid expansion and these widespread obligations represent, not only a serious financial burden, but even more a heavy demand on Canada's resources in qualified personnel, and I think we can take a justified pride in the high level of ability that we have succeeded in establishing in the service of External Affairs.

More significant, of course, is the evolution of Canadian foreign policy. We are now in world politics up to our necks. We have taken on commitments abroad that would have been unthinkable twenty years ago. Canada's place in world affairs has been determined by inescapable realities, and Canada has accepted these realities and translated them into positive policies.

This has been possible in the first instance because the inhibiting factors of the thirties have largely been overcome. Internally there was a notable subsidence of racial tension, particularly over issues in foreign affairs. With materialistic and atheistic communism emerging as the number one adversary, Catholic French Canada discovered that it too was a part of the free world, and that the security of its cherished culture and institutions depended on a wider unity than the solidarity of the Province of Quebec. Members of Parliament from Quebec overwhelmingly supported the accession of Canada to the North Atlantic Treaty and the participation of Canada in the operations in Korea. On the other side, the old type of attachment to the empire on the part of English-speaking Canadians has all but vanished. There is a deep sentimental attachment to Britain as a bulwark of the free world, but much less tendency to accept automatically the wisdom of British policies. This attitude is not completely dead, as we discovered in the Suez crisis, but it is certainly dying. What has happened is that both racial groups are acquiring the habits of national independence, and in the process are discovering that they are all Canadians, with a consequent narrowing of the gap that formerly separated them when there seemed to be a divided loyalty on the one side and a narrow parochialism on the other.

The second factor is the change in the attitude of the United States. The illusion of Fortress America has been abandoned; the acceptance of the responsibilities of power has been recognized as an unavoidable necessity. It is quite impossible to overemphasize the significance of this change for Canada. The power and the resources of the United States are the indispensable bulwarks of the free world. If these were withheld, as they were in the years between the wars, the strength of the free world would be utterly inadequate to resist the pressures against it. In such a case, Canada herself would be remote and largely isolated, torn between her vital stake in the freedom of western Europe and her inability to contribute decisively to its maintenance. It has been the readiness of the United States to step into the position of world leadership that has rescued Canada from this dilemma, as well as from the ancillary dilemma of having to choose between Britain and America. It still remains true that Britain and America do not always see eye to eye on every specific issue. It is even true that Canada, while welcoming American leadership, is sometimes critical of the precise way in which it is exercised. Yet the basic fact remains that the United States has identified her national objectives in foreign policy with those of the free world as a whole, and more particularly with those of the English-speaking democracies who are her closest associates.

In this changed situation, Canada had both the opportunity and the incentive to frame her own policies in accordance with her own national interests. This meant first of all answering the question: what kind of world do we need in order to build the kind of Canada we want? The answer in its broad outlines was not hard to find. We are an expanding nation, geographically remote from the risk of direct aggression yet vulnerable to changes and dislocations in world conditions. We need capital to develop our resources and markets as outlets for our national staples. We are the fourth trading nation in the world, and we depend on a continual expansion of trade to maintain and improve our standard of living. We need the free exchange of goods and capital for our economic well-being; we need a free and democratic world for our own political security. The spread of either totalitarianism or anarchy, the persistence of poverty in large areas, or the shocks and uncertainties resulting from political or economic irresponsibility on the part of other nations—all of these can jeopardize our welfare and even, in the last resort, our national survival.

Canada's interests are thus world wide. Our direct connections, political as well as economic, are predominantly with Britain and the United States; our indirect but none the less lively concern encompasses most of the globe. We know that we may be profoundly affected by the spread of communist power in Asia, or by the rise of anti-colonialism in Africa, or by political or economic chaos in the Middle

East, and that, so far as within us lies, we must give active support to policies that are calculated to prevent such adverse developments.

But, while our objectives may be universal, our power to implement them is distinctly limited. This is true of any nation, even the greatest, and the disparity increases as you go down the scale. The kind of world we want is not one that we can create single-handed. We must act with other like-minded friends, and particularly with friends who can provide the strength that we lack for the attainment of common ends.

The widest combination for this purpose is of course the United Nations. In this world forum the member states have a unique chance to assess both the practicality of a given line of policy and the range of support that can be rallied to it. Through the United Nations we can establish contacts with other countries with whom we have no special ties otherwise, and we can do this in a way that is often closer and more effective than is possible through the ordinary channels of diplomacy.

The United Nations is one of the foundation stones of Canadian foreign policy. I think our support is based on a pretty realistic view of what the United Nations is and what we can expect from it. We recognize and accept its limitations. We think it is foolish to demand from it achievements or actions that are beyond its resources—particularly when such demands come from countries that have neither the capacity nor the intention to contribute toward their realization. But we believe that within these limits the United Nations still has very real powers of constructive action, of a kind and scope that cannot be paralleled by any other instrument in the international sphere. I think our record shows a consistent effort on the part of Canada to remedy the defects and to strengthen the virtues of that body, and this from a reasoned conviction that our own national interests demand an effective world organization for their full realization.

There is another combination of a very different sort that holds a fundamental place in Canada's external relations. That is the Commonwealth of Nations. Perhaps combination is hardly the right word to describe this peculiar institution. It has no constitution. It has no central institutions. It has not even the kind of formal agreements between its members that have been adopted by the Organization of American States. Their foreign policies range all the way from the outward-going initiative of Australia to the insistent neutralism of India. Yet in spite of diversities and even disparities, this enduring anomaly somehow manages to hold together, linked by common institutions and common values and a shared historical development.

There is a deep and abiding attachment to the Commonwealth on the part of Canadians generally. A good deal of it is sentimental, based on a long standing connection with nations which sprang from a common stock and bore a long allegiance to a common mother country whose contributions to world literature and to world stability and to the great ideals of political freedom are things in which we can all take legitimate pride. Yet along with this go more tangible considerations. They are not the ordinary kind of specific interests that usually draw nations together. For example, the Commonwealth as such is not of major importance to Canada in a direct material sense. We are not part of the sterling area that is of such significance to most of the other members. Our trade with Britain is only second in importance to our trade with the United States, but trade with the rest of the Commonwealth is a very small part of our total external commerce. Similarly, in matters of defence, our primary concern is with areas in which other members, apart from Britain, play little or no part. But underneath all that is the fact that here is a group of nations which we can count on as friends, with whom we can talk frankly about matters of common concern, with whom we can differ in the confidence that for all our differences we still want the same kind of world—a world of freedom for nations and individuals, a world of freedom from fear and freedom from want.

This is the political aspect; and one of the most important things for Canada in the political aspect has been the emergence of the Asian members of the Commonwealth. There was never any assurance that India and Pakistan and Ceylon, once they were freely given their complete independence, would choose to retain their association with Britain and the older Dominions. The fact that they did so has given Canadians a tremendous new interest in the Commonwealth and a new and active stake in its continued development. Through it we have a direct connection with Asia, where the upsurge of nationalism and the results that may flow from it hold the most vital implications for the future of the free world. In the Asian members of the Commonwealth, and especially in India, lie the hopeful prospects that

Asia may be held for democracy against the lure of totalitarian communism. Those prospects are tremendously strengthened by their continued Commonwealth associations. Canadians, like Americans, are sometimes impatient about the over-refinements of Indian policy. But we are perhaps more aware than Americans of the gigantic problems that India has to face in the process of nation building, and of the possibility that without strong and skillful leadership India might by now have become at best another Indonesia, at worst another China. It has been a cardinal Canadian policy to retain India's friendship, and India's confidence in Canada's friendship for her, and I venture to say that we have been as successful in this as any country in the western world.

When however it comes to concrete and specific interests, there is one region above all that is of paramount concern to Canadians. That is of course the North Atlantic area. Our roots are here by virtue of geography and history. Its secure defence is our prime military objective. Our trade is overwhelmingly concentrated within the area. And embracing all these factors is our intimate and virtually inescapable connection with the two major pillars of the Atlantic community, Britain and the United States.

Now of course those are just the factors that cause our main problems and give rise to our chief dilemmas in foreign policy. If action is to be effective, at least on major issues, it has to be action in concert with our stronger associates who can provide the effective power. That does not mean that Canada has no policies of her own. On quite a number of questions her independent judgment leads her to conclusions that are different from those of her friends. We differed from the United States on certain Far Eastern questions, and from the United Kingdom on Suez. We were gravely perturbed about the re-armament of Germany and visibly unenthusiastic about including Greece and Turkey in NATO. The trouble is that a middle power can only push dissent so far. It does not by itself have the strength to implement an alternative that is unacceptable to its major partners. It can withdraw its participation if the prospective burdens seem unbearable or the probable consequences disastrous. But that does not mean that it can carry out its own policy instead—it may only mean that nobody does anything. And so a middle power like Canada periodically has to strike a balance between its dislike of a course of action on which its larger friends are determined, and its need to maintain unity with and among its friends even at the cost of acting against its better judgment.

We have lately found ourselves facing comparable dilemmas outside our main area of concern. In principle, Canada strongly prefers to avoid a dispersal of its limited resources. We think we can make our maximum contribution by concentrating on the North Atlantic area, with which we are most familiar and where we can act most effectively, and leaving the task of stabilizing other areas to other nations who are more directly concerned. But our own stake in stability is world wide, and·it is not always fair or even practical for us to press for action in these areas without being ready to act ourselves. This is particularly true when for one reason or another the great powers have to step out of the picture. When that happens, there are two countries that at once emerge into the front rank. They are India and Canada, and the respective roles they are best fitted to play are sometimes very different. So Canada has found herself being drawn into activities in various areas from which she would have much preferred to remain aloof. It happened in Indo-China; it has happened recently in the Middle East. And here again we get into the problem of balancing our obligations against our resources, and making our fullest contribution to the general cause of world peace without vitiating our participation in the defence of the particular area on which our immediate security depends.

From these various considerations it must be apparent that, in the really fundamental questions of foreign policy, Canada's decisions are pretty well determined by the inexorable logic of circumstances. The latitude for decisions on any given issue is very limited indeed. I think it is to the credit of the Canadian people that by and large they recognize and accept these limitations. It is not every nation that is realistic enough to reconcile itself to the inevitable, particularly in these days when a rampant emotional nationalism seems to have swept aside all sense of responsibility in all too many lands. In Canada there is virtually no disagreement on fundamentals. There may be arguments about methods—whether we should do less in the UN and more in NATO, whether we ought to give more support to Britain or show a more vigorous independence of the United States. But these are the details of application; when it comes to essential principles, it would be hard to raise even a minor dispute, let alone to work up the kind of Great Debate that seems to be such a perpetual diversion in the United States.

This must look like an enviable situation to those leaders in some other countries who have to conduct foreign policy in the midst of the turbulence of popular discussion and legislative recriminations. Of course our parliamentary type of constitution also helps a good deal. Responsibility for foreign policy rests in the first instance with the Minister and the Cabinet. They are of course responsible to the majority in the House of Commons, but the members of that majority do not lightly oppose their party leadership when they know that any serious split in party solidarity may bring the downfall of the government. And when they are aware that their constituents accept and endorse the government's foreign policy—and when, moreover, the opposition shares that awareness—parliamentary control over foreign policy is apt to be more tacit than positive. Paradoxically, this situation heightens the significance of any really serious criticism that may be aroused. An attack on foreign policy that the Administration in Washington would accept as a normal political hazard would shock the Cabinet in Ottawa out of its bootstraps and bring a prolonged and perturbed examination of the issue that provoked it.

As things stand, about the last thing one would expect in Canada is a major split over foreign policy. The public accepts the limitations imposed by the nature of our national interests and the limits of our national power. It is confident in general that within those confines the national interest is being served and upheld to the extent that our resources make possible. It seems that we have achieved a remarkable degree of national unity in a field where we once faced our greatest danger of national disruption, and that achievement is not one that we would willingly jeopardize by ill-judged adventures in the wake of impetuous associates.

Yet I come back at the end to one recurrent and all-important theme, and that is our dual association with Britain and the United States. The maintenance of harmony between them is one of our vital interests; the maintenance of the closest friendship with both of them is our daily concern. It is not to be expected that we should always see eye to eye on every single point. There are occasional irritations and occasional strains, sometimes of a serious nature. But in the last resort it is unthinkable that Britain and the United States should ever find themselves in opposing camps, and equally unthinkable that Canada should choose irrevocably between them. We may not always approve of British policies, but we know that, if Britain should go down, the whole of Europe would be lost, and the New World would stand desperate and at bay. Similarly, we may sometimes find American policy too impulsive for our tastes. We may feel a twinge of apprehension every time Mr. Dulles gets up to speak. But we know that the United States is the indispensable pillar of the free world, and that if the United States should become involved in a conflict in which its existence was at stake, we must rally to its side because our own survival would be equally in jeopardy. This is the solid foundation of friendship under all the passing irritations that always afflict neighbors from time to time. And surely it is not too much for a Canadian to suggest that the United States on its part has more than a little reason to value this good neighborhood on the part of Canada. There is not too much of that spirit abroad these days; and, if you look around you, you will find beyond question that Canada remains the most patient and the most understanding and the most reliable friend that the United States has in this turbulent and critical world.

Chapter 14

INDIAN DIPLOMACY

A. Appadorai

DEFINITION OF DIPLOMACY—SCOPE OF THE PAPER

IN contemporary writings the term 'diplomacy' has been used in various senses, foreign policy, negotiation, as well as the process and machinery by which negotiation is carried out.[1] It is well, therefore, to indicate the sense in which it is used in this essay. Diplomacy is used here to mean the process of making and executing foreign policy. In describing it thus, apart from the authority which the present writer has from an editor of this volume,[2] he merely follows Edmund Burke, who in 1796 described it as the conduct or management of international relations, and Sir Ernest Satow, who defined it as "the application of intelligence and tact to the conduct of official relations between the governments of independent States";[3] the conduct of official relations between governments should in a real sense cover the process of making policy and implementing it. Thus, the study of diplomacy is not, except incidentally, concerned with the foreign policy itself or its merits. But it is concerned with the process of making and implementing policy, including in the term "process" the agencies engaged and techniques employed in the process. Apart from these matters, this chapter will attempt some evaluation of the measure of

[1] H. Nicolson, *Diplomacy* (London, 1950), p. 13.
[2] "One of our objectives," wrote one of the editors, "is the study of the fundamental dilemmas which confront all liberal, democratic governments in the process of making and executing foreign policy in the changing theatre of world affairs. Your essay would be part of a symposium, *Diplomacy in a Changing World*."
[3] E. Satow, *A Guide to Diplomatic Practice* (London, 1922), I, 1.

success which has attended the implementation of policy and indicate what appears to the present writer as the central problems in Indian diplomacy.

Tradition

This essay is concerned with Indian diplomacy after India became independent in 1947. But the question may be raised whether India's background in the period before 1947 has any relevant contribution to make to understanding its contemporary diplomacy. On first consideration, a negative answer seems called for. Not until 1946–47 did Indian statesmen have to consider the problems of foreign policy for a united India for the first time. It was then that the first Indian foreign service had to be established. Moreover, such influence as recent history, especially since 1886, has had on India's relations with the outside world has been in the field of policy rather than in the realm of diplomacy. It is true that the existence of a separate External Affairs Department of the Government of India can be traced to 1937 when the Foreign and Political Department was divided into an External Affairs Department under the Governor-General in Council to deal with foreign affairs and a Political Department under the Crown Representative to deal with the Princes and their states. But the fact that the Viceroy was, also, the Member for External Affairs in the Executive Council and that, constitutionally, the Government of India was responsible to the British Secretary of State for India meant that India's foreign relations were governed by that requirement and that the British Foreign Office had the final say in the matter.

Tolerance

But the roots of the present lie deep in the past. It may be argued that the traditions of Indian thought through the centuries must have some influence on the men who make policy and on the mass of the people whose ideas must be taken into account by the leaders of a democratic state, though it would be impossible to say how and to what extent those traditions make their influence felt. If this is accepted, a word about those traditions may be relevant.

The vital thing to stress is the habit of tolerance developed by Indian philosophy and tradition. By tradition, the Indian outlook is pluralistic. Indian thought has never insisted upon the acceptance of one particular version of truth. Truth is one but wise men call it by various names. This tradition explains, for instance, the stress on non-alignment and peaceful negotiation which is the pivot of Indian diplomacy. It has made the Indian people react instinctively against the claim of communism to embody the sole truth; and likewise it has prevented them from regarding communism with as much disfavor as anti-communists do. The ideal of equalitarianism, the social content of communism, has some appeal for Indians but they do not at all want to realize this aim by communist methods, the basis of which is intolerance and violence. Again, the tolerant attitude inclines Indians to the belief that peaceful negotiation and conciliation have a much larger place than some other nations might be prepared to grant; those who believe in the virtues of peaceful negotiation would watch more than others for opportunities for negotiation and for improving the circumstances in which it can operate.

Means and Ends

A second stream of thought which has come down through the ages is that the means to be employed to achieve an end are as important as the end itself and both should be according to the moral law, an idea which in recent times has found its best expression in Mahatma Gandhi's writings.[4] A Tamil classic, the *Kural* puts the idea in the following terms:

Avoid at all times action, that is not in accordance with the moral law.

Success achieved without minding the prohibitions of the moral law brings grief in the wake of achievement.

To seek to further the welfare of the State by enriching it through fraud and falsehood is like storing water in an unburnt mud pot and hoping to preserve it.[5]

It should not be gathered from the above that Indian thinkers always equated private morality with public morality or that Indian rulers always conformed to ethical precepts. A well-known political

[4] D. G. Tendulkar, *Mahatma* (Bombay, 1954), p. 42; Mahatma Gandhi, *Young India, 1924–26* (Madras, 1927), pp. 264, 435; M. K. Gandhi, *Sarvodaya* (Ahmedabad, 1954), pp. 6–7

[5] *The Second Book of Kural: A Selection from the old Tamil Code for Princes, Statesmen and Men of Affairs,* translation and notes by C. Rajagopalachari (Madras, 1937), pp. 49–50. The *Kural* was written about the second century B.C. by Thiruvalluvar.

thinker of the fourth century B.C., Kautilya, for instance, in his *Arthasastra*,[6] did recommend the adoption of methods of statecraft according to circumstances and expressed the view that what produces unfavorable results is bad policy; a policy is to be judged by the results it produces. For him diplomacy was an art, not concerned with ideals but with achieving practical results for the state.[7] By and large, however, the unity of means and ends is a dominant note in Indian thought.

Reference may also be made to an aspect of Indian diplomacy which probably derives from Indian tradition, that is, the desire to get world opinion on the side of the country in the policy which it adopts. It is sufficient to cite in this connection the *Mahabharata*, the Hindu epic which (together with the *Ramayana*) is the most widely read by the common man in India. Sri Krishna, when he was requested by Yudhisthira to go as a special envoy to the court of the Kauravas, explained that even if he did not succeed in averting war, his mission would be useful in showing the world how they were right and the Kauravas were wrong.

Going thither I will remove the doubts of all men who are still undecided as to the wickedness of Duryodhana. Thither in the presence of all kings I will enumerate all those virtues of thine that are not to be met in all men, as also the vices of Duryodhana. . . . I will also recite the vices of Duryodhana before both the citizens and the inhabitants of the country, before both the young and old, of all the four orders that will be collected there. And as thou askest for peace no one will charge thee as sinful, while all the Chiefs of the earth will censure the Kurus and Dhritarastra. . . .[8]

---

[6] Kautilya, *Arthasastra*, translation by R. Shama Sastry (Bangalore, 1915), Bk. VII. Kautilya, the author, was the Chancellor of Chandragupta Maurya 323–299 B.C. The book provides among other things a record of ideas of government and politics of that period in India.

[7] "When any one of these is on the point of rising against a weak king, the latter should avert the invasion by making a treaty of peace, or by taking recourse to the battle of intrigue (*mantrayuddha*), or by a treacherous fight in the battlefield. He may seduce the enemy's men either by conciliation or by giving gifts, and should prevent the treacherous proceedings of his own men either by sowing the seeds of dissension among them or by punishing them." *Ibid.*, Bk. XII, Ch. I.

[8] *The Mahabharata*, translated into English Prose by Pratapachandra Roy (Calcutta, 1890), p. 239. This great Epic dates from the centuries just preceding the Christian era, while the event it celebrates is placed by scholars in the twelfth century B. C. The authorship is uncertain but sometimes attributed to Vyasa, an Indian saint.

In attempting to secure the acceptance of Indian objectives, such as the abolition of racial discrimination and colonialism, India pays special attention to world opinion. Anyone who knows how much India relies on the support of world public opinion for achieving her ends will realize the significance of the quotation for understanding modern trends.

Making Foreign Policy: Major Influences and Structural Organization

Making foreign policy decisions in India is essentially the responsibility of the Cabinet as a whole. India has a parliamentary executive more or less similar to the executive of the United Kingdom, with the difference that Indians have an elective persident as the head of the state instead of a monarch. This means that vital policy decisions of the Government are taken by the Cabinet, whose members are chosen from the party which commands a majority in Parliament. It means, too, that since the Cabinet can continue in office only so long as it continues to have the confidence of Parliament, the decisions it takes and their implementation must be such as are acceptable to Parliament. The initiative and the primary responsibility in making foreign policy decisions for the consideration of the Cabinet (as in all governments) rest with the Minister in charge of External Affairs, Jawaharlal Nehru, who is also Prime Minister. When the Cabinet has taken decisions, the Ministry of External Affairs implements the decisions under the direction of the Minister. Parliament when it meets (normally three sessions that add up to about seven months in a year) devotes a number of days to hearing a statement on foreign policy by Nehru and to discussing it before approving the policy.

This bare statement of the formal position must be supplemented by some indication of the influences which bear on the decision of the Cabinet and in particular on the Minister of External Affairs as well as of the Parliament. Here the most important single factor is the personality and the background of Nehru; the second, an awareness by the Cabinet and the Parliament of the needs of India and the temper of the people who are affected by the policies of the Government; and the third, the organization of the Ministry. A word about each one of these will be useful.

Nehru's Personality

There is no question that in the shaping of foreign policy the predominant role has been Nehru's. His personality, his foreign contacts, the leading part he took in securing independence for the country, his contacts with the masses, and his prestige as the political successor of Mahatma Gandhi designated by the Mahatma [9] himself are important in understanding this role. In pre-independence days, Nehru guided the Congress resolutions which did much to set the framework of India's present foreign policy. The combination of leading posts in the Party and in the Government which have fallen to him made him India's authoritative spokesman in the international forum. The fact that since independence the Congress Party has had an overwhelming majority in parliament, and consequently has had no effective opposition, willing and able to provide an alternative Government, is also a factor in enhancing Nehru's prestige. But this does not mean that Nehru decides just as he likes. He has his advisors within and outside the Cabinet; it is well known, for instance, that the late Sir Girja Shankar Bajpai, who formed the foreign service of independent India, was one to whom Nehru listened; it is, also, generally known that Nehru frequently consults Dr. S. Radhakrishnan and V. K. Krishna Menon. Similarly, Nehru must inevitably pay some heed to the advice of the Foreign Affairs Sub-Committee of the Cabinet which includes three senior Ministers of Cabinet rank. At the Secretariat level, the Secretary-General is the principal official advisor to the Prime Minister on matters relating to foreign policy. Senior officials of the Ministry accompany the Prime Minister on diplomatic trips abroad; the Ministry, particularly the historical division, prepares data papers on the subjects under discussion. The combined effect of all these on policy making cannot, of course, be precisely gauged, but in any proper assessment of influences shaping foreign policy, it cannot be ignored. With all these the secret of Nehru's influence will be missed if we do not emphasize the fact that he knows the pulse of the people, their hopes, their fears, their needs (indicated briefly in the next paragraph). He knows their pulse because in addition to listening to the speeches of representatives

[9] Speech to the All-India Congress Committee, January 15, 1942, at Wardha. See D. G. Tendulkar, *Mahatma*, Vol. VII, 52.

in party meetings and Parliament, he explains his ideas at innumerable meetings throughout the country and watches the reactions of people. The democratic basis of the formulation of his policy is a real factor.

The Needs of India

The second influence is the domestic situation which the Prime Minister, Cabinet, and Parliament face. Apart from the influence of the traditions, domestic, economic, and political aims, for instance, account for the eagerness with which India espouses the need for regional peace, the avoidance of world conflict, and stresses peaceful negotiation. The Indian Government is determined to advance the economic development of the people to provide at least better employment opportunities and tolerable living standards. It recognizes that an infant democracy can be built up only in a relatively untroubled atmosphere and with the full co-operation of more advanced countries—which would be impossible if a regional or world conflict broke out.

The Organization of the Ministry of External Affairs

Third, the organization of the Ministry of External Affairs: [10] that the way of organization of the Ministry may influence the formulation of policy cannot be denied. Whether the Ministry is able to take independent decisions or has to be guided by another government Ministry (say Finance), before it can take vital decisions, whether there is adequate coordination with other Ministries which are also concerned (for example, Commerce) with international relations and integration within the Ministry itself, whether there is a free flow of information and opinion between the Ministry and its officers abroad, whether there is sufficient expert knowledge at the Ministry to deal adequately with the complex issues of modern international relations—these are all relevant to the proper formulation of policy.

At the head of the Ministry is the Prime Minister who holds the portfolio of External Affairs. Associated with him are a Deputy Minister and one or two Parliamentary Secretaries. The senior permanent official is the Secretary-General who assists the Minister of External Affairs and advises him on matters of high policy. "Next come two

---

[10] For details, see the very informative article on the organization of consular and diplomatic services by H. Dayal, formerly Joint Secretary, Ministry of External Affairs in *India Quarterly*, XII (1956), 268–282.

officers of the rank of Secretary to the Government of India designated respectively Foreign Secretary and Commonwealth Secretary, between whom is divided the supervision of various divisions of the Ministry." There are eleven such divisions, some territorial (East Asia and North-east, Frontier, Pakistan, etc.), some functional (Administration, External Publicity). The territorial divisions handle all political matters relating to the geographical areas with which they deal, while the functional divisions concern themselves with particular functions allotted to them, matters that may concern all or most of the divisions. For example, the Administrative Division handles all matters concerning recruitment, training, appointment, leave, transfers, and the procurement of funds, the External Publicity Division is responsible for the handling of all matters relating to Indian publicity abroad, and so on.

India's diplomatic missions, consulates, and other establishments abroad are under the control of the Ministry. In February 1956 there were seventy-eight such establishments, including embassies, high commissions, legations, special missions, commissions, consulates general and consulates, and minor establishments. Several diplomatic missions have specialist officers such as commercial secretaries and military attachés, but it is an established principle that they are all subject to the general orders and disciplinary control of the head of the mission and are required to keep him informed of their activities. While on routine matters relating to their particular fields, these specialist officers report directly to the Ministries specially concerned with those subjects, on all matters having an important bearing on foreign policy the channel of communication is through the head of the mission to the Ministry of External Affairs. This procedure, according to a competent observer, helps to preserve the existing structure of departmental responsibility and, on the other, co-ordination over the wider field of foreign policy.

The staff required to fill the various posts both at headquarters and in the various establishments under the control of the Ministry number some 1,800; nearly 200 of these are what may be called of the senior level (posts of the diplomatic rank and certain consular posts) and are drawn from the Indian Foreign Service (A) and the rest from the Indian Foreign Service (B). In the first years after India became independent, candidates for the Foreign Service were recruited through interviews. These were carried on partly by a Special Selection Board set up by the Ministry and partly by the Public Service Commission. The recruits came from many fields: from the existing all-India services such as Indian Civil Service, the Audit and Accounts Service, from public life, business, and the professions, and from emergency commissioned officers who had served in the armed forces during the war. Since 1947 the system of annual competitive examinations open to candidates between the ages of 21 and 24 and holding a university degree has been in operation. Until August 1, 1956, subordinate posts, concerned with administrative tasks less important than the senior posts referred to above, posts in ministerial and stenographer grades etc., were filled from the Central Secretariat Services or *ad hoc*. In 1956, however, a junior (B) branch of the Indian Foreign Service was constituted to include these subordinate posts, provision being also made for a limited number of promotions from the "B" branch to the Indian Foreign Service proper.

It may be added that posts at the headquarters and posts abroad are not kept in watertight compartments. There is a reasonable flow of officers from posts at headquarters to the field and vice versa.

The training of the Indian Foreign Service probationers, in operation since August 3, 1956, comprises (a) a six months course (largely academic) at a training school in such subjects as the constitution and administration of India, Indian history, Asian history, economic theory with special reference to planning in India, and Hindi; (b) district training in the states for four months; (c) secretariat training in the Ministry of External Affairs for nearly six months; (d) training in a residential university abroad covering the study of diplomatic and world history, international law, economics and a foreign language; (e) departmental training in external commerce and trade in an Indian mission abroad for one month; (f) attendance at the British Foreign Office course for Foreign Service officers of Commonwealth countries for one and one-half months, and finally, (g) posting in a mission abroad. In this last period he is expected to attain proficiency in the language of the area to which he has been posted and to familiarize himself as far as possible with the customs, history, literature, and social problems of the people. The training has been evolved with a view to giving future foreign service officers sufficient theoretical and practical knowledge of the problems of India and its history, knowledge of the academic basis of diplomacy, adequate acquaintance with a foreign language other than English, and familiarity with the social customs as well as with the habits of thought of the people or a region.

This outline of the organization of the Ministry of External Affairs and the Foreign Service may be concluded by referring to the problems raised at the beginning of the section. As India was able to start, so to speak, with a clean slate, a more or less integrated service to handle diplomatic, commercial, and consular work has been developed, though there is reason to think that adequate integration has not yet been achieved in the policy-making structure at headquarters.[11] The Ministry is also providing itself more and more with expert assistance for its work through its Historical Division and the newly created legal officers, though it will take time for the development of these sections. The Ministry has inadequate assistance in the economic aspects of its work;[12] but perhaps the deficiency is in part made good by the assistance of other Ministries which have economic advisers attached to them. On the question of free flow of information between headquarters and the officers abroad, no published information is available. But there is reason to think that the regular fortnightly reports received by the Ministry from its missions abroad as well as other correspondence, the visits of heads of missions to Delhi individually and in groups, and the occasional regional conferences of heads of missions to discuss with the Prime Minister their special problems do help to provide that exchange of information so vital to policy making.

BROAD TECHNIQUES OF INDIAN DIPLOMACY

In assessing Indian diplomatic techniques, it will be useful to recall the broad aims which she has been seeking to achieve through her diplomatic efforts. Those aims, first stated by Jawaharlal Nehru on September 26, 1946, have basically remained the aims of our policy ever since: promotion of international peace and security, friendliness with all nations, more particularly with neighboring countries in Asia,

[11] The rules of the business of the Government of India assign foreign affairs to the Ministry of External Affairs but place commercial matters within the exclusive jurisdiction of the Ministry of Commerce and Industry and place economic matters partly under that Ministry and partly under the Ministry of Finance (Dayal, *op. cit.*); inter-ministerial conferences help to achieve such co-ordination as is possible.

[12] Dayal, *op. cit.*

co-operation with the United Nations, freedom for dependent peoples and opposition to racial discrimination. In this original context it was unnecessary for Jawaharlal Nehru specifically to mention that the promotion of the legitimate interests of India, more particularly the security of India and securing international co-operation in India's economic development, has naturally been an important objective of India's foreign policy.

It is natural, however, that in a decade of historic international developments which witnessed the emergence of several new nations in Asia and Africa, the rise of the Soviet Union to parity with the United States in atomic strength, the domination of Eastern Europe by the Soviet Union, and the emergence of China as a communist state, a minor shift of emphasis should have taken place on one or other of the principles outlined above, one or two might have been added, and the fuller implications of some of them made clearer to the statesmen in charge of affairs. For instance, in regard to colonialism, it would perhaps not be far from the truth to say that there has been a growing realization in Indian policy that while she should stand unequivocally for the liquidation of colonialism and for a clear international responsibility for the welfare and progress of dependent peoples towards self-government, India must also take note of the complexities introduced by a multi-racial plural society such as that of Malaya, or the presence of a large number of European settlers among native peoples as in Algeria. There has been a fuller understanding of the complexities involved in the application of the technique of the plebiscite as a way of eliciting the desires of peoples, whether in Kashmir or in other states of India. International co-operation has been coupled with active co-existence as applied to societies with different ways of life, democratic or communist. That in the long run, if not in the short, the efficacy of foreign policy is dependent largely on a country's capacity to solve its own domestic problems is being more fully realized. Above all, the present writer feels that there has been an emphasis on the positive aspects of our foreign policy, that India should take every opportunity to promote by diplomatic effort the objective of reducing international tensions and enlarging the area of peace, and welcome opportunities, as in Korea and Indochina, when all the parties involved in a dispute invite her to do so, to place her services at their disposal for the promotion of harmony and peace.

Non-alignment

It will be noticed that non-alignment with the Western or the communist bloc, often considered to be the keynote of Indian policy, has not been included in the account of India's aim. The non-alignment so described is not an *end* of policy; it is rather a *means* to achieve the basic aims of policy. The *raison d'être* of non-alignment is perhaps best stated in Nehru's own words:

By aligning ourselves with any one power, you surrender your opinion, give up the policy you would normally pursue because somebody else wants you to pursue another policy. I do not think that it would be a right policy to adopt. If we did align ourselves we would only fall between two stools. We will neither be following the policy based on our ideals inherited from our past or the one indicated by our present nor will we be able easily to adapt ourselves to the new policy consequent on such alignment.[13]

Elsewhere, he has added that, keeping self-respect apart, "purely from the point of view of opportunism, if you like, a straightforward honest policy, an independent policy is best."

I think that not only in the long run, but also in the short run, independence of opinion and independence of action will count. . . . We want the help of other countries, we are going to have it and we are going to get it too in a large measure—I am not aware of this having been denied to us to any large extent. Even in accepting economic help, or in getting political help, it is not a wise policy to put all your eggs in one basket, nor should one get help at the cost of one's self-respect. Then you are not respected by any party; you may get some petty benefits, but ultimately even these may be denied you.[14]

Peaceful Negotiation

India's main diplomatic technique, the emphasis on peaceful negotiation, is linked with non-alignment. Of course, reliance on peaceful negotiation is not by any means India's monopoly; every nation resorts to peaceful negotiation to get disputes settled or to get solutions to international problems satisfactory from the point of view of its own interests. In a cold-war atmosphere, however, in which many nations

[13] *Jawaharlal Nehru's Speeches, 1949–1953* (Delhi, 1954), pp. 192–193.
[14] *Independence and After: A collection of the more important speeches of Jawaharlal Nehru from September 1946 to May 1949* (Delhi, 1949), pp. 216–217.

are, so to say, tied together by military alliances, a non-aligned nation is in an advantageous position to explore more fully than others the possibilities of negotiations, as will appear later in analyzing India's diplomatic technique in regard to Korea and Vietnam. The advantage in not being a party in the cold-war disputes is that friendly contacts are maintained with both parties and these enable the non-aligned states to watch for opportunities to get the cold-war parties together to talk over issues. The gain here is not necessarily that the right or ideal solutions are always found, but that non-alignment helps "to establish an attitude and approach that makes these solutions possible."[15] "It is not our intention," said the Leader of the Indian Delegation to the General Assembly,

to be a part of . . . a third bloc, or to tell the world how to establish peace. In our circumstances, in the light of our history and in the great traditions of the man who made our national independence possible, we think it is always necessary to talk to one's opponent and to seek the basis of reconciliation and negotiation. Even after conflict, negotiation becomes necessary.[16]

And in such negotiation, the essence of India's approach has been that if the result is to be stable, an attempt must be made to see that neither of the parties engaged in the conflict suffers a significant loss. That was Gandhi's technique in trying to solve India's domestic tensions as well as to secure freedom for India. It is best explained in the following summary of a statement by Dr. Rajendra Prasad recalling Gandhi's services to India:

Rajendra Prasad spoke of Gandhiji's leadership of the first satyagraha adopted in India at Champaran in Bihar to redress the grievances of peasants working in indigo plantations. Dr. Prasad recalled that the Mahatma had said early in the campaign that neither the planters nor the cultivators should suffer in any solution that was reached and that came true.[17]

Gandhiji's technique is in fact a modern application of the principle stated in the *Mahabharata*. When Sri Krishna was about to proceed with negotiations for a settlement between the Pandawas and the

[15] Leader of the Indian Delegation at the 533rd meeting of the General Assembly, October 4, 1955.
[16] *Idem.*
[17] *The Hindu*, October 23, 1956.

Kurus, he summarized the object of his mission in the following words: "Yes, I will go to King Dhritarashtra, desirous of accomplishing what is consistent with righteousness, what may be beneficial to us and what also is for the good of the Kurus." [18]

The technique assumes that in meetings arranged for negotiations concerning vital international questions it is good not to "exclude those who differ." [19] In the context of conflict [20] it is all the more necessary to be aware of and to utilize what little common ground there is as a starting point for a move towards reconciliation. Quoting from Abraham Lincoln, the leader of the Indian delegation explained the viewpoint of his country in the following words:

There are no great principles which are not flexible. Principles in Politics are not like points in geometry, without dimensions. Principles must enable people to meet and reconcile their differences. It is no derogation of principle if the principal divergent points of view can honestly be reconciled within it.

This approach to negotiation is illustrated by India's tireless efforts to have Peking admitted into the United Nations, her unwillingness to vote on the resolution naming China an aggressor, her warning to the Western powers not to cross the 38th parallel, and her efforts to achieve a negotiated settlement on Indo-China and on Suez.

On the fundamental aspect of such negotiation, whether it should be "open" or "private"—an important question ever since Wilson included in his Fourteen Points the dictum of "open covenants of peace openly arrived at"—Indian opinion, it seems to the present writer, has yet to be crystallized, because India is still a relative new-comer to diplomacy. Indian practice, however, shows a judicious mixture of both. In a democratic state, it is necessary to gain popular support for the major lines of the country's approach towards international problems. In the cases of India's membership in the Commonwealth, Kashmir, Suez, and Indochina, the broad issues were explained to the people in Parliament and public forums before a decision was finally taken on India's position. It is also inevitable that the details of India's

[18] *The Mahabharata,* translated by Pratapachandra Roy (Calcutta, 1890), p. 256.
[19] 448th Plenary meeting of the General Assembly, September 28, 1953, para 89, p. 199.
[20] *Ibid.,* p. 196.

stand should be settled in private negotiation with the parties concerned.

Outlining his views on "open diplomacy," Nehru said on March 22, 1949:

> I sometimes think that it would be a good thing for the world if all the Foreign Ministers remained silent for some time. I think more trouble is being caused in foreign affairs by the speeches that the Foreign Ministers or their representatives deliver in their own respective Assemblies or in the United Nations. They talk about open diplomacy and I suppose in theory most of us believe in it. Certainly, I have believed in it for a long time and I cannot say that I have lost that belief entirely. Open diplomacy is good enough, but when that open diplomacy takes the form of very open conflicts and accusations and strong language hurled at one another, then the effect, I suppose, is not to promote peace.[21]

And it is known that such work for reconciliation of opposing points of view as India did in connection with Korea, Indochina, and Suez was done by the late Sir Benegal Rau and Krishna Menon in private discussions with representatives of the countries concerned.

On October 4, 1955, the leader of the Indian delegation to the General Assembly categorically affirmed the conviction of the Government of India that private discussions on important matters are very valuable:

> Both last year, and the year before, my delegation drew the attention of the Assembly to Article 28, paragraph 2, of the Charter, and suggested that the Foreign Ministers of the countries which were members of the Security Council should seek to carry out the provisions of that article in private discussions. We felt that the diplomatic approach, the Conference approach, might produce some results, but we regret that during the year that has elapsed since the last session no such meeting has taken place.[22]

Apart from non-alignment and peaceful negotiation, other significant aspects of Indian diplomacy are (a) reliance for effective results on world public opinion; (b) personal contacts with heads of governments and foreign ministers; (c) seeking closer support of Asian and African countries for the realization of its aims.

[21] *Independence and After*, pp. 245–246.
[22] General Assembly, 533rd plenary meeting, October 4, 1955, para 46, p. 235.

Appeal to World Public Opinion

The power of a nation, its ability to bring about a change in the policy and conduct of another nation, depends on a number of factors: armaments, economic strength, national character, alliances, and ideas. The prevailing view has been that only the voice of nations having armaments and economic strength count or should count in changing policy. But India appears—though the appearance is not the whole story—to rely almost entirely on the power of ideas to influence the policy of states in a desired direction. The reliance upon ideas to influence the policy of other states is expressed in the Prime Minister's speeches on international issues in Parliament (notably, for instance, Nehru's strong criticism of Britain's attack on Egypt as "naked aggression") and elsewhere on public platforms, press communiques jointly with visiting statesmen particularly on the principles of peace known as the *Panchshila*, the speeches of India's accredited representatives in the United Nations and on public platforms, and the activities of India's External Publicity Services. (Of these the last does not seem to be in the Prime Minister's judgment an important agency for popularizing India's own position in world affairs.)[23]

"Is that reliance adequate?" the critic asks, because military and economic power held in reserve has, throughout history, been the main influence in international relations. How can ideas, without physical force to back them, have appreciable effect? The criticism is not, historically, without justification, but, on the one hand, it underrates the influence of ideas as such, and on the other, it fails to take adequate note of the changed circumstances in which diplomacy has to operate in the contemporary world.

[23] In a frank speech before the Indian Parliament Nehru said: "The Honorable Members may think that we should try to flood foreign countries with facts and figures in the nature of propaganda. I do not think that it is desirable for us to do so or that we can, in fact, do so. I do not think our approach should be the pure publicity or the advertisement approach. We cannot do it because the way to do this would be to spend far vaster sums than we can ever afford. But my main reason for not desiring to do so is . . . that approach tends inevitably to become a tendentious approach, and while it may, perhaps create an impression now and then, the value of it lessens progressively when people realize that it is excessive propaganda of a particular type. I would much rather place the facts before the public here in India or outside . . . and allow other people to judge." Nehru, *Independence and After*, p. 224.

To take the first point, the more one thinks of historical changes, the more one is inclined to say that the influence of ideas has perhaps been greater than most people think, though the influence may have been effective only in the long run. Who, for instance, can underestimate the importance of the ideas of liberty, equality, and fraternity advanced by the French Revolution, not only in the age of the French Revolution but in subsequent ages, not only in France but throughout the world? It is India's view that in the "one world" of today ideas, such as anti-colonialism and racial equality, properly developed and conveyed, do exercise an important influence in shaping world opinion towards the desired end.

Furthermore, there is the point that the circumstances of diplomacy have changed. There is no doubt that India's non-military approach to international issues stems clearly from a realization of the horrors of atomic warfare. If the victor and the victim of a total war in this atomic age are to suffer equally, it may be asked, what is the sense in a military approach? No doubt the issue is simplified for purposes of this argument, but in evaluating Indian diplomacy, due note must be taken of the background from which the importance of ideas and of cultivating world public opinion has to be judged. It is now possible through the developed means of communication to appeal to world opinion directly in a manner which could not be thought of in the days of the old diplomacy; let the public of the world be convinced of the justice of a cause, and in democratic states, at any rate, their informed opinion will have some, sometimes an appreciable, effect on the policies of their governments. When Britain attempted a military solution in Egypt, there was an enlightened minority in Britain which was against the policy adopted by the government of the day. This critical opinion was a helpful factor in the government's later change of policy, when it bowed to public opinion of the world as expressed in the United Nations (which itself was influenced by the courageous policy of the United States).

Personal Contacts

Diplomatic theory, especially as expounded by one of the masters of the art, Nicolson, holds that the tendency of democratic countries to allow their politicians to take a personal part in negotiation is a "dangerous innovation in diplomatic practice."

Clearly there are moments when it is essential that the Prime Minister or the Foreign Minister should attend important Conferences. Yet repeated personal visits on the part of the Foreign Secretary of one country to the Foreign Secretary of the other should not be encouraged. Such visits arouse public expectation, lead to misunderstandings, and create confusion.[24]

It is difficult to disagree with this sound judgment of Nicolson, for if expectations raised by personal visits are not realized in reasonable time, misunderstandings and confusion are likely to ensue. This is perhaps substantiated by one known fact from Indian experience: Nehru's visit to the President of the United States in 1949 did raise expectations which were not fully realized; the misunderstandings between the United States and India for some years might in part be due to this. As against this we must point out that Nehru has himself used personal contacts with heads of governments and foreign ministers as a major technique of his diplomacy. It is unnecessary to add that these contacts have been facilitated by the quick means of transport developed during the past twenty years. Since he assumed office as Prime Minister, he himself has had personal discussions on a variety of international issues with the leading statesmen of the United States, Britain, the Soviet Union, France, West Germany, Yugoslavia, China, Japan, Indonesia, Burma, Ceylon, Pakistan, Egypt, and a host of other countries, visiting them in their own country or receiving them in India. The Minister without Portfolio (V. K. Krishna Menon) has also visited a number of capitals for talks with leading statesmen. There is no doubt that such personal discussions have, in the very large majority of cases, resulted in the setting out of agreements satisfactory from India's own viewpoint and interests, especially in the direction of enlarging the area of collective peace in which she is vitally interested. Speaking in the Indian Parliament six years ago, Nehru confessed that "as I grow older, I learn more and more to value men; what a man *is* rather than what he thinks"; and to know men, obviously, personal contact is most valuable. In another context, he expressed strongly his personal belief in the utility of personal contacts with statesmen:

Personal contacts and exchange of views resulted in our reaching a helpful, reasonable, and realistic appreciation of developments in the Soviet

[24] Harold Nicolson, *Diplomacy* (London, 1950), p. 100,

Union. These developments were regarded as 'significant' and were welcomed. It was recognized that the improvement in the relations between U.S.S.R. and the other Great Powers should help to remove the fear of war and further peace. . . . There was the recognition that a peaceful settlement of the Formosa area was imperative to stability and to removing the dangers of conflict which would frustrate the hopes of peace. (Report to Parliament on his one-month visit, June 3–July 21, 1956, to London, Bonn, Paris, and other places.)

The broad conclusion seems to emerge from India's experience that personal contacts at the highest level may be a valuable means for a newly independent state to understand the men in charge of affairs in leading states and the political climate in which they operate. These contacts help to get useful information and to put across an attitude or approach to international issues (as distinct from the details of agreements) which could not be done perhaps equally effectively, without such personal contacts.

Closer Co-operation with Asian and African Countries

The convening of the Asian Conference on Indonesia in New Delhi (1949) to consider the situation arising out of the Second Dutch "Political Action," participation in the Colombo Conference (1954), and co-sponsorship of the Bandung Conference (1955) may be cited as evidence of India's desire to work with the Asian and African countries in support of its diplomatic efforts.[25] Even in the brief account required here, three points concerning this policy call for mention. First, in view of the fact that before 1947 the views of Asian and African countries did not count for much in diplomatic circles, independent India had an understandable desire to state the viewpoint of those Asian countries with such common problems as underdevelopment of industry and the legacy of issues deriving from a colonial rather than a national economy, and to seek their support for furthering policies for the good of all. Second, the co-operation envisaged does not involve any military commitments for the countries concerned. In other words, there is no attempt to form a bloc against other countries. Third, as repeatedly expressed at the Bandung Conference, that Con-

---

[25] A. Appadorai, *The Bandung Conference* (New Delhi, 1955), gives an assessment of that Conference.

ference was merely an endeavor on the part of a certain group of countries to ensure that their problems and their approach to world problems might be better understood both by the members of the group and by others. The Bandung Conference was not cast in the mould of agitation. The principles of world co-operation accepted by its twenty-nine participants were based upon the Charter of the United Nations, as may be seen from the repeated references in those principles to the phrase "in conformity with the Charter of the United Nations."

Reference may also be made in this context to the Asian-African Group in the Assembly, in which India has taken an active part along with Afghanistan, Burma, Egypt, Indonesia, Iran, Iraq, Lebanon, Pakistan, the Philippines, Saudi Arabia, Syria, and Yemen. The group first appeared as a political fact in 1950; Sir Benegal Rau had much to do with its formation in the years when the Korean issue was hotly debated in the Assembly. The objectives of the group include taking counsel together in Assembly matters which concern them vitally. It has taken concerted action, though not always unanimously, on such questions as opposition to the United Nations forces crossing the 38th Parallel, the question of the treatment of people of Indian origin in South Africa, the freedom of dependent peoples in Tunisia, Morocco, and Algeria; the Palestine issue. As it is neither necessary nor possible to assess here the work of the group as a whole, it may suffice to cite the opinion of one competent observer [26] that the group served in a certain mediatory or moderating capacity in the Korean situation (largely due to the influence of India in the group) and that "to the extent that the Arab-Asian bloc has successfully identified itself with the conscience of mankind, one can only rejoice that the claims of colonial or racial minorities have not gone unsponsored, or unheard —objectives in which India is vitally interested."

Two Case Studies

To appreciate the techniques followed in Indian diplomacy, an analysis of two situations in which they were employed will be useful —Vietnam and Korea.

[26] Sherman S. Haydew, "The Arab-Asian Bloc," *Middle Eastern Affairs;* V, pp. 152–153.

Vietnam

As the diplomatic efforts made by India to resolve the tensions in connection with Vietnam best illustrate her techniques of diplomacy, bringing out their merits and limitations, the case of Vietnam will first be discussed.

India saw with sympathy the challenge of the Vietnam Independence League (the Viet Minh), established in May, 1941, to French Colonialism. On August 19, 1945, after the Japanese surrender to the Allies, the Viet Minh proclaimed the Democratic Republic of Vietnam with Ho Chi-minh as President. The latter appointed Bao Dai, under the name Vinh Thuy, as Supreme Counsellor of State. Sixteen months of negotiations with the French convinced Ho Chi-minh that the French would not release their hold on Vietnam. Thus, fighting started in December, 1946, and only ended with the signing of a cease-fire agreement in Geneva in 1954. The French contrived to wean away Bao Dai from Ho Chi-minh's side and conceded territorial unity and independence to him in March, 1949, as a counterpoise to Ho Chi-minh. Thereafter, both Ho Chi-minh and Bao Dai claimed to represent the Government of Vietnam.

In this situation, India desired (i) the independence of the Indo-chinese territories—Vietnam, Cambodia and Laos, and (ii) peace in the area, as vital to her own interests. But how was she to implement these aims of her policy?

The whole basis of Indian diplomacy required that the desired aim should be achieved without military intervention. Such intervention would bring not peace but an enlargement of the area of hostilities, which she was eager to avoid. In the Indian view it was also essential that a solution of the Indochinese problem should not include partition. From her own experiences India knew only too well the disastrous consequences of partition.

India's approach to the solution of the problem may now be briefly reviewed. Negatively, one technique involved India's non-recognition of the Democratic Republic of Vietnam (which had been recognized by the People's Republic of China on January 19, 1950, and by the Soviet Union on January 30, 1950, among other states) or of the Republic of Vietnam (which had been recognized by the United States and the United Kingdom on February 7, 1950). The recognition of either of the two was out of the question as, without a nation-wide election, it could not be clear which of the two had the confidence of the people; recognition of both would only delay unity.[27]

But the more important question was, how could she be positively helpful? The war between the Viet-minh and the French which had begun in December, 1946, was continuing; repeated Viet-minh offensives and their successes in the territory around Dien Bien Phu led in 1953 to the growth of a feeling in the West that perhaps the military stalemate could be solved only by a large-scale modern war with the economic and military assistance of the United States. The joint Franco-American statement of March 30, 1953, made it clear: (a) that the total defeat of Communism in Indochina was the aim of France, that is, there would be no negotiation and no compromise; and (b) that military plans for achieving this were being jointly drawn up by France and the United States. Towards the close of the year, however, large sections of opinion in France veered round to the view that France should not and could not face the consequences of a large-scale military adventure. The Berlin Conference of January, 1954, significantly called for a conference to meet in Geneva (April 26) for discussion of two important Asian questions—Korea and Indochina. On February 22, 1954, India made a public appeal (through her Prime Minister in Parliament) for a cease-fire "without any party

[27] It must be pointed out that in the case of Germany, West Germany has been recognized by India but not East Germany—a legacy inherited from British days.

Subsequent to the German surrender in May, 1945, a Four Power Control Council was established in Berlin with power to legislate on matters affecting Germany as a whole, including Greater Berlin. Under the Control Council was the Four Power Allied Kommandatura responsible for the administration of Berlin. The Indian Military Mission, like other Missions, was accredited to the Control Council.

In June, 1948, the Soviet Union withdrew from the Control Council and the Kommandatura, which thenceforward functioned as Three-Power bodies. In September, 1949, Military Government was terminated in the Western Zones of occupation, and the Control Council was replaced by a Three-Power Allied High Commission. The Indian Military Mission, which had continued to be accredited to the Control Council in spite of the Soviet withdrawal, was now automatically accredited afresh to the Allied High Commission.

An Instrument of Revision of the Occupation Statute promulgated in March, 1951, by the Allied High Commission authorized the Federal Republic to establish diplomatic relations with other countries. Having terminated the state of war with Germany in January, 1951, India which was represented with the Allied High Commission, entered into diplomatic relations with the Federal Republic.

giving up its own position or whatever it might consider its rights." Her hope was that the cessation of hostilities might provide just the right atmosphere for negotiation at the conference which was meeting at Berlin two months later. It is noteworthy that the Canadian Prime Minister, then on a visit to Delhi, publicly welcomed the suggestion.

The public appeal did not immediately have the desired effect. "United action" in defence of the free world by the United States, Britain, and France was considered in March and April, especially in view of the deteriorating military situation. Britain, however, was unwilling to risk responsibility for a major conflict. Sir Winston Churchill said: "The Government are not prepared to give any undertaking about U.K. military action in Indochina in advance of the results of Geneva. We have not entered into any new political or military commitments." Whether there was any rift between Britain and the United States on the desirability and possibility of a major war on the Vietnam issue is not known, nor is the information necessary for understanding the lines of Indian diplomacy. What is significant is that the British attitude as indicated above helped India to persevere in her efforts to bring about a cease-fire and avoid a major conflict. On April 24, Nehru put forward a six-point plan for the solution of the crisis: promotion of an atmosphere of peace and negotiation and dissipation of suspicion and of the atmosphere of threats; cease-fire through constituting a cease-fire group of the actual belligerents and giving priority to cease-fire on the Geneva Conference agenda; a clear commitment by the Government of France to the independence of the Indochinese states; direct negotiations between the parties immediately and principally concerned; non-intervention—a solemn agreement between the United States, the Soviet Union, the United Kingdom, and China to deny aid (direct or indirect) for the purposes of war; and, finally, keeping the United Nations informed of the progress of the Conference.

The next important development in Indian diplomacy on Indochina was an effort to get the support of the Asian nations gathered at Colombo (April 28–May 2, 1954) for the specific suggestions contained in the Prime Minister's six-point plan. It is significant that the Conference, on India's suggestion, gave priority to Indochina on its agenda and adopted the Nehru plan as a basis for discussion. The joint statement issued at the end of that Conference on May 2, 1954, endorsed with verbal modifications most of Nehru's points. On non-intervention, to which Pakistan (obviously because of her interest in the Kashmir Problem) took objection, the communique simply stated that "the success of such direct negotiations would be greatly helped by agreement on the part of all the parties concerned, particularly China, the United Kingdom, the United States and the U.S.S.R. to prevent recurrence of resumption of hostilities." [28] On April 29, while the Geneva Conference was on, Sir Anthony Eden addressed a communication to the three Commonwealth Governments, India, Pakistan, and Ceylon, assuring them that Britain would not be a party to any agreement at Geneva in conflict with the legitimate aims of the Asian countries and asked the Prime Ministers if they would be ready to participate in a guarantee to secure the freedom of Indochina. Mr. Nehru replied on May 5, that India would be willing to be associated with, or to participate in, a guarantee of the type suggested, if any acceptable decision were reached and if India were invited by both sides.

It is not necessary to go into the later details of this story: the fall of Dien Bien Phu (May 7); Mr. Krishna Menon's informal discussions at Geneva with the Foreign Ministers gathered there, for India had not been invited to the Conference—Nehru said in the Indian Parliament on May 15, "if and when necessity arises, we expressed our viewpoint privately . . ."; [29] the cabinet crises in France and the rise of Mendès-France to power (he stated in the French Parliament that he would resign if he did not secure a cease-fire in Indochina by July 20); and the signing of the Geneva Agreement on July 20. By unanimous agreement India served as Chairman of the International Armistice and Supervisory Commissions of which Poland and Canada were the other members.

That the Vietnam issue still continues unsettled, in spite of the truce, marks a limit of the success of India's diplomatic efforts to have peace in the area. India and the other nations concerned did not fully appreciate the political implications of the fact that the Geneva Agree-

[28] Mr. Nehru later described this as an important improvement on his earlier wording which was negative. This was positive he said.

[29] Mendès-France speaking in the French National Assembly on July 22, 1954, acknowledged "the contribution which it [the Indian Government] has made to the success of the Conference."

ment was not recognized and not signed by South Vietnam any more than by the United States itself.[30] Even where and when these implications were understood, the states involved were unable to change the situation.

In any event the Saigon Administration, supported substantially by the United States, was naturally unwilling to help a political settlement so long as two basic facts are present: the Viet Minh has jurisdiction over a larger population than the Saigon Administration, and there is a feeling that Ho Chi-minh has partial support also in South Vietnam.[31] The story of Vietnam since 1954 is striking testimony to the validity of the thesis that peaceful settlement of disputes in any part of the world must await an ending of the cold war between the powerful states whose actions seem to determine the nature of the peace of the world.

Korea

The techniques of Indian diplomacy which we discussed in the case of Vietnam had been earlier applied in the case of Korea in much the same way. India had recognized neither North nor South Korea, for, as Nehru argued, this division between North and South Korea could not last. It was artificial and the less the division was confirmed, the better.[32] When the war between North and South Korea started on June 25, 1950, India had voted in the Security Council for the resolution describing North Korea as aggressor as it was perfectly clear from the evidence[33] that North Korea had "indulged in a full-scale and well-laid-out invasion"; but later, India was more concerned with the localization of the war than with the logical consequences of having declared North Korea the aggressor. Indeed, India herself did not think it possible to send her armed forces to join the United Nations forces against North Korea. The significance of this, in the context of Indian diplomacy, seems to the present writer as follows:

---

[30] Robert Gullian in *Le Monde,* May 21, 1955.

[31] The present writer who visited the area some months ago can testify to the existence of such a feeling; the fact however, that 1,000,000 people fled from Viet-Minh areas to the South indicates that South Vietnam may still have supporters in North Vietnam.

[32] Speech in Indian Parliament, August 3, 1950.

[33] Including the experience which India had as Chairman of the United Nations Temporary Commission on Korea.

One of the over-all aims of India's policy was to help to maintain world peace and reduce international tensions, and further, in implementing this aim, it was always useful to ensure that (1) neither party in a conflict should suffer so much as to leave lasting bitterness behind; and (2) the root causes of conflict should be solved in order that peace, and not merely a truce, should be achieved. The efforts that India made in helping to resolve the Korean crisis were therefore directed to securing a negotiated settlement of the issue. The possibility of such a settlement depended, India felt, on the inclusion of Peking in the United Nations, for it was clear to India that with the walk-out of the Soviet Union from the Security Council and the non-inclusion of Peking, the United Nations had ceased to be what it was originally intended to be: it would "inevitably drift towards being an agent for war or preparations for war." On July 13, 1950, Nehru addressed a communication to Marshall Stalin and Dean Acheson for representation of the Five Big Powers in the Security Council to facilitate the negotiation of a settlement in Korea. As Nehru later told Parliament, his emphasis was on "its urgency" rather than "the rights and wrongs of the matter." India was not deterred in her peace efforts by the unfavorable reception given to the appeal by the United States: Acheson, considering the issue as a question of principle, perhaps rightly, replied that "policy in regard to recognition of China should not be dictated by an unlawful aggression." The Indian comment on this attitude was well expressed at the time by C. Rajagopalachari, Minister without Portfolio:

Aggression has to be checked. I am for that. But what then? Are you going to garrison Korea for all time and keep off the enemy at the point of the bayonet? No: it is impossible. Therefore, something should be done in order to relieve the tension. . . . Independently of checking aggression, let us get all the nations together around a common table and decide.

When it appeared difficult to get the big powers together for peaceful discussion of the issues, India attempted to pool the help the smaller nations could give in resolving the conflict. She herself refrained from voting in favor of American and other resolutions condemning communist China in order to help get the parties together if and when possible. Sir Benegal Rau informally made a proposal on August 14, 1950, that a Committee of the six non-permanent members of the Security Council—then India, Yugoslavia, Norway, Egypt, Cuba, and Ecuador—should study all resolutions or proposals that have been or may be proposed for a peaceful and just settlement in Korea; though favorably received by the Western Powers, the proposal was not finally moved.

Indian diplomacy in the Korean crisis was perhaps at its best in relation to the crossing of the 38th Parallel by the United Nations troops. It will be remembered that in August-September 1950, when North Korea had suffered a military reverse, the question arose whether the United Nations forces should stop at the 38th Parallel in pursuit of North Korea's troops. India pleaded that the North Koreans had been adequately defeated for the time being and had been prevented from achieving their original aim of unifying all Korea by military means and that at the hour of United Nations success moderation should be shown and resort should be had to peaceful means for achieving the unification of Korea. India also warned that the crossing of the 38th Parallel by UN forces might have the unfortunate effect of bringing China into the war. On December 6, 1950, Nehru said in Parliament:

We consulted our Ambassador in Peking and our representatives in other countries about how the various Governments were viewing the scene. We had perhaps a rather special responsibility in regard to China, because we were one of the very few countries represented there. . . . The Chinese Government clearly indicated that if the 38th Parallel was crossed, they would consider it a grave danger to their own security and that they would not tolerate it.

The warning was disregarded; an Indian resolution proposing the appointment of a subcommittee to take into consideration all resolutions, proposals, and suggestions concerning the Korean question in order that it might recommend to the committee a resolution on the subject commanding the largest measure of agreement was defeated and an eight-power resolution virtually authorizing United Nations troops to enter any part of Korea and create conditions for the unification of Korea was passed (October 7). On October 9, the United Nations forces crossed the 38th Parallel and Chinese volunteers joined the forces of North Korea. It is clear from available evidence that Britain was not wholeheartedly behind the UN resolution. In the evening of the ninth, writes K. M. Panikkar, "the Prime Minister transmitted to me a message from Ernest Bevin to be communicated personally to Chou En-lai. It was friendly in tone and contained vague assurances." [34]

Consistent with India's stand that it was not desirable that a military solution to the problem of the unification of Korea be sought by either party, India also appealed to Mao Tse-tung to halt the "volunteers" when it appeared that the Chinese volunteer forces were driving the United Nations forces beyond the 38th Parallel. The appeal was ignored by Peking just as the West had ignored an earlier appeal by India not to cross the 38th Parallel.

The further story of the achievement of a truce in Korea need not be dealt with at length. It is significant that the Indian approach to the problem, not to press a political solution by military means, was, in its essentials, finally accepted by the parties, but only after much blood had been shed.

When the militarist approach had resulted in a stalemate, the Security Council, on November 8, 1950, accepted a United Kingdom resolution calling upon the representatives of the People's Republic of China to appear before the Security Council. On November 30, President Truman hinted that the atom bomb might be used in Korea. Then followed Attlee's visit to Washington; apparently Attlee read more in Truman's statement than Truman perhaps meant.[35] Nevertheless, the visit was certainly worthwhile as it helped Attlee to apprise the President of the fear widespread in several commonwealth countries that United States policy was inclining more and more toward a military solution of the Korean problem. It is significant, too, that there had been communications between Nehru and Attlee prior to the latter's discussions with Truman. Nehru said in Parliament on December 6:

We welcomed the decision of the Prime Minister of England to go the United States to meet President Truman and wished him Godspeed in his endeavors to prevent war and to find a peaceful way out of this tangle. We found that there was a good deal in common between the British Prime

[34] K. M. Panikkar, *In Two Chinas* (London, 1955).

[35] This is clear from a statement issued from the White House, three hours after Truman had given the hint about the possible use of the atom bomb at a press conference: "Consideration of the use of any weapon is always implicit in the very possession of that weapon"—all that apparently Truman had meant to say.

Minister's views of the present situation and ours. We let him have our own viewpoint in detail in case he needed it during the discussions.

On December 12, 1950, the thirteen nation Arab-Asian Group, with the support of the United States and the United Kingdom, submitted a draft resolution requesting the President of the General Assembly to constitute a group of three persons, including himself (the Iranian representative), to determine the basis on which a satisfactory cease-fire in Korea could be arranged and to make recommendations to the General Assembly as early as possible. Though the Soviet Union opposed it, it was adopted by the Assembly and a commission of three was formed of Iran, India, and Canada. The group made some suggestions for cease-fire in Korea, but, as Peking considered the resolution, under which the group had been constituted, illegal, null and void until Peking China was seated in the United Nations, the representative of India had to report the failure of the group to the first committee. In doing so he emphasized the need for continuing the efforts for a negotiated settlement. Norway took up the suggestion and successfully sponsored a resolution that the President of the Assembly should communicate to the Government of China the four principles of the supplementary report of the group for its comments. The principles were: an immediate cease-fire, negotiation and withdrawal of all foreign troops from Korea; holding of elections and the setting up of a body consisting of the United Kingdom, the United States, the Soviet Union, and China to discuss all Far-Eastern problems including Taiwan. Peking stuck to its earlier position that cease-fire should follow and not precede negotiations, but agreeing that a negotiated settlement of the Korean crisis was desirable and possible put forward a counter proposal. India sought clarification of the counter proposal from Peking and placed it before the Assembly. India and the other members of the Arab-Asian Group then acted on a Canadian suggestion and introduced a proposal suggesting a conference of the United Kingdom, the United States, France, the Soviet Union, China, Egypt, and India for discussion on Korea. This was not adopted. Instead the United States sponsored a resolution declaring China an aggressor. This resolution, though not co-sponsored by Britain and Canada, was adopted. India voted against the resolution. The military stalemate continued. Opinion even in the United States and the Western countries gradually veered round to the view that a large-scale war to defeat China was undesirable and this resulted in the historic decision of Truman on April 10, 1951, to dismiss MacArthur from the post of Commander of the United Nations forces. Dean Acheson on June 2, and Jacob Malik on June 23, virtually expressed their readiness for cease-fire negotiations which commenced on July 8, 1951.

AN ASSESSMENT

Are we, finally, in a position to assess the success which has attended India's diplomatic efforts to achieve the aims of her policy? Only history can, of course, measure the success which has attended the foreign policy of any country during a particular period. In any case the last ten-year period is too brief for taking stock of a dynamic situation. One or two points, however, may be made. First, no one is more conscious than India's Prime Minister that in this big world of richer and more powerful states the influence that India can exert cannot be very great. Nehru said in Parliament: "I do not pretend to say that India, as she is, can make a vital difference to world affairs. So long as we have not solved most of our own problems, our voice cannot carry the weight that it normally will and should." [36] Secondly, such success as any country sees in the fulfillment of her aims is due to the co-operation of several like-minded states and a multiplicity of other factors, among which her effort is just a single part. Viewed in this background, perhaps it may be said that world public opinion, as judged by the United Nations resolutions, has come to realize almost unanimously that colonialism and racialism are clearly undesirable; we see before us a growing realization of the necessity of the renunciation of force except in self-defence, and the urgency of defining the two most difficult terms in international law, namely, self-defence and aggression; the area of peace has clearly been enlarged; there is a growing realization of the necessity of international action in developing underdeveloped countries, as evidenced by the recent setting up of the International Finance Corporation and the continuing interest in the establishment of the SUNFED; there is increasing participation of the Asian States in international affairs and a growing sensitiveness of the Western States to their views and interests. Perhaps, also, India can have legitimate satisfaction in seeing that now she is more and

[36] Speech in the Parliament, March 17, 1950. *Jawaharlal Nehru's Speeches 1949–53* (The Publications Division, Government of India), p. 144.

more trusted in international councils, as may be seen in the invitation to her by the parties concerned to take up the Chairmanship of the Neutral Repatriation Commission in Korea and of the International Armistice and Supervisory Commission in Vietnam, Cambodia, and Laos.

So far as securing international co-operation in India's economic development is concerned, Nehru's hope that foreign economic aid would not be denied to her on account of India's independence policy would also appear to have been justified, for the record [37] of external assistance authorized and utilized for the years 1951–56 shows that in these years a sum of 297.59 crores of rupees was authorized, of which 203.38 crores of rupees were utilized; further, the external assistance negotiated during 1956–57 was more than 300 crores of rupees [38]—fair evidence to substantiate the point made above.

While India's efforts in some directions of her foreign policy are bearing fruit, Korea, Vietnam, Palestine, and Formosa remind us that there are still many trouble spots in Asia and elsewhere; disarmament and the banning of hydrogen bomb explosions is still to be agreed upon; the Peking Government has not yet been admitted to the United Nations; there is still much to be done in the field of establishing international responsibility for hastening the development of dependent peoples to self-government; racialism is still alive, more particularly in Africa; and we are still far away from an assurance of world peace. The mere enumeration of these—and there are many other unsolved problems—only shows that problems of international affairs have a way of creating new ones, even in the course of partially solving an old one, and need continued vigilance and effort for their satisfactory solution.

Nearer home, Indo-Pakistani tensions remain unsolved and Goa still remains a problem. The unanimous passage of a Security Council resolution (January 24, 1957) on Kashmir (the Soviet Union abstaining) reminded India that while in the wider international arena, her non-alignment policy had succeeded in winning confidence in her impartiality, she had few friends on a question vital to her interests

---

[37] *The Second Five Year Plan*, p. 103; *Five Year Plan Progress Report for 1953–54*, p. 25, and the *Five Year Plan Progress Report for 1954–55*, p. 18.

[38] See the revised estimates in the *White Paper on the Budget*, 1957–58, pp. 10–11.

and felt completely isolated. This led to criticism in Parliament.[39] A question was raised as to whether the Prime Minister was alive to India's own special interests. He was also asked urgently to consider whether India, without giving up the principles of her foreign policy, could not "so conduct it as to gain friends in those circles where we have none at the present time." The critic, H. N. Kunzru, agreed that the non-alignment policy was in India's best interest as was the policy of promoting world peace. But he urged one modification of India's diplomacy; this was the pursuit of India's foreign policy in its essentials consistent with gaining the friendship of other countries which was necessary to enable India to strengthen herself and to raise the standard of living of the masses. "We change our manner a little— perhaps if we remain silent on some occasions instead of expressing our opinion on all points always, it may be that this will be more in the interests of India than what we call frankness at the present time." [40]

It is significant that V. K. Krishna Menon speaking for the Government agreed with the view expressed by Kunzru that "even though we may have strong views it is not always necessary to express them."

The issue raised by Kunzru in his criticism and in his suggestion is a fundamental one: for a non-aligned country like India, anxious (in her own long-term interests as well as the interests of the world in general) to contribute to the avoidance of a world conflagration and to the preservation of world peace and to the ending of colonialism and racial discrimination, it would appear necessary to express its opinion on many international issues—sometimes in praise, sometimes in condemnation. Examples include India's criticism of United States policies with regard to China, Japan, SEATO, and hydrogen bomb tests, of British policy with regard to Suez, of the Netherlands with regard to Indonesia, of France with regard to Tunisia, Morocco, and Algeria, of the Soviet Union with regard to Hungary. These powerful countries, thinking in terms of their own views of their vital interests, and proud of their standing in the world, are annoyed with India; but the issue really is, are they taking their position on Goa or Kashmir because they are annoyed with India, or because they consider such stands as vital to their interests? In other words, if India moderates

[39] *Parliamentary Debates,* Rajya Sabha, March 27, 1957.
[40] *Ibid.*

her criticism or speaks less often on such questions, would such action lead to a change of policy on the part of the countries concerned? The Government spokesman in Parliament denied that "we have been left friendless," and added that "we are not to expect from other sovereign nations that because they are friendly to us, they would necessarily accept our view of things." [41]

The present writer would hardly venture to express an opinion on the general issue raised. But a word may be said on Kashmir. If the hypothesis that the unfriendly attitude of the major countries of the world on Kashmir was due to the annoyance felt by them on account of vociferous Indian criticism of their policy is uncertain and if, as is true, India without a single dissenting voice at home, considers her case in Kashmir just, has there been something wrong in the diplomatic handling of the question by India during the past nine years? An able and dispassionate critic [42] has written:

It was a mistake for the Government of India to take the Kashmir issue to the Security Council under Articles 34 and 35 of Chapter 6 of the Charter which is entitled "Pacific Settlement of Disputes" instead of under Chapter 7 which is specifically concerned with Acts of Aggression. Again, India needlessly placed herself at a tactical disadvantage by later adopting the term "plebiscite" which does not occur in the earlier communications. Lord Mountbatten's letter of 27 October 1947 accepting Kashmir's accession to India said that "as soon as law and order have been restored in Kashmir and her soil cleared of the invaders, the question of the State's accession should be settled by a reference to the people." The later intrusion of the term "plebiscite," although conditional, has enabled India's critics to fasten on the plebiscite while forgetting the conditions.

In our anxiety to reach a settlement we have undoubtedly made certain tactical mistakes which our critics have quite naturally attempted to turn to their advantage. We have, for instance, in the protracted process of negotiation allowed ourselves to be persuaded to sidestep certain preliminary hurdles which action has later quite unjustifiably been interpreted as acceptance by us of these preliminary points.

Since January 24, 1957, however, India's case has been more ably handled, and, as a result, there is a better understanding of India's

---

[41] He added: "we have publicly and privately accepted the motives of the United States in regard to whatever policies it adopts in relation to us."

[42] Frank Moraes, *The Times of India*, April 16, 1957.

case as is evidenced by the Jarring Report published on May 1, 1957, and world reactions to it. The Swedish diplomat was impressed by "the changing political, economic and strategic factors surrounding the whole of the Kashmir question together with the changing pattern of power relations in West and South Asia." He added that "the implementation of international agreements, which had not been achieved fairly speedily, may become progressively more difficult because the situation with which they were to cope has tended to change"—a reasoning more appreciative of India's point of view than had been visible in the earlier years.

The foregoing analysis points to certain problems in diplomacy for a non-aligned country like India. First, even though a non-aligned country is following an independent policy, criticisms are sometimes heard from both sides that in fact she belongs to the other bloc.[43] These criticisms may neutralize one another. Nevertheless, ways and means may have to be explored to see that such criticisms are inhibited. Second, further study should be directed to ascertaining whether limiting India's criticisms of other powers' attitudes on international issues is likely to help in gaining their sympathy for India's interests. Finally, the sanction for the implementation of India's views is essentially moral. India is not able or willing to adopt a military approach. How far is such a sanction effective? The best illustration one can think of in this connection is the divergence between the Soviet Union's adherence to *Panch Shila* and her action in Hungary, and it is known that India felt there was a divergence between the two. There can be no final answer to the question. It will, however, be useful to indicate the view of the present Government of India on the subject.[44] It relies on such effects as the promotion of toleration and neighborliness can produce, and believes that in any case the military approach, historically, has not fared better:

[43] Meany's reported remarks that he felt "stronger than ever that (Nehru) is an agent of the Soviet Union, and I hope to see him and tell him so to his face," cited in the *New Republic*, December 31, 1956, p. 8. See also China's reply to the Indian note on Tibet to China on October 30, 1950: "with regard to the viewpoint of the Government of India on what it regards as deplorable, the Central People's Government cannot but consider it as having been affected by foreign influences hostile to China in Tibet and expresses its deep regret."

[44] The Leader of the Indian Delegation in General Assembly, 533rd meeting October 4, 1955. *U. N. General Assembly Tenth Session Plenary Meeting*, October 4, 1955, *Official Records*, p. 244.

We have found that the promotion of neighbourliness, agreements on non-aggression and mutual respect are ways of promoting co-operation. It may be asked: is your system likely to succeed? Can you rely on it? With great respect, we are entitled to ask: have the other systems succeeded? Can anybody turn round to us and say that the doctrine of the balance of power is more likely to help us, or to succeed—that doctrine which is the legacy of Metternich, of Castlereagh and of Talleyrand, which wrecked the principle of universalism and culminated in the war of 1914, and which to this day is making its incursions into international affairs? I am reminded of the statement of a great Frenchman, Rousseau, who said that the strongest is never strong enough to be always master unless he transfers strength into right and obedience into duty.

Chapter 15

GERMAN DIPLOMACY

Herbert Krüger

I

IN politics the imponderables are certainly as important as those factors that can be physically observed or assessed by measurable standards. Therefore, the first part of this essay will be devoted to the underlying imponderables of the foreign policy pursued by the German Federal Republic since 1945.

The first imponderable to be considered is the intellectual, spiritual basis of German foreign policy. This consideration goes beyond the guidance provided in the text of the constitution [1] and the practice of the Government, to include the attitude of the people, especially their habitual reactions to questions of foreign policy. Germans do not have

[1] Cf. Articles 24–26 of the *Grundgesetz* (Basic Law) of May 5th, 1949:

Art. 24. (1) The Federation may, by legislation, transfer sovereign powers to international institutions. (2) In order to preserve peace, the Federation may join a system of mutual collective security; in doing so it will consent to those limitations of its sovereign powers which will bring about and secure a peaceful and lasting order in Europe and among the nations of the world. (3) For the settlement of international disputes, the Federation will join a general, comprehensive, obligatory system of international arbitration.

Art. 25. The general rules of international law shall form part of federal law. They shall take precedence over the laws and create rights and duties directly for the inhabitants of the federal territory.

Art. 26. (1) Activities tending to disturb or undertaken with the intention of disturbing the peaceful relations between nations, and especially preparing for aggressive war, shall be unconstitutional. They shall be made subject to punishment. (2) Weapons designed for war-to be convinced that a defeat today, joined with the collapse of society's structure, undermines even a people's view of the world. A lost war, above all, a lost total war, compels a sweeping change in one's thinking. Indeed, that is one of the very few advantages that the vanquished enjoys over the victor, for the latter obviously likes to believe that his victory derives from the excellence of his ideology. After 1945 Germans felt little inclination to worry about a fresh concept of foreign policy. As a sharp break from the recent past it was assumed that in the future the German people would be able to dispense with a foreign policy as well as with building up even modest military strength.[2] But paradoxically the Germans were pushed into the sphere of armaments and foreign policy by the very powers who earlier had opposed German militarism and German foreign policy. Within a few years the victors looked on these matters differently and they sought to use German forces and policy again upon the chess board of international politics.

It is difficult to ascertain anything definite about the spiritual basis of German political life and its foreign policy, all the more because there is a pervasive and welcome German reaction against the holding of ideological principles, and the reaction prevails in social problems, as well. Thus, it is perhaps necessary to proceed more schematically and to inquire into the conceptions that Germans have as regards the *aims* and, then, the *means*, of their foreign policy.

1) There is no comprehensive survey of the foreign policy aims of Imperial Germany,[3] the Weimar Republic, and the National

---

fare may be manufactured, transported or marketed only with the permission of the Federal Government. Details shall be regulated by a federal law.

Article 3 of the Convention on Relations between the Three Powers and the Federal Republic of Germany:

Art. 3. (1) The Federal Republic agrees to conduct its policy in accordance with the principles set forth in the Charter of the United Nations and with the aims defined in the Statute of the Council of Europe. (2) The Federal Republic affirms its intention to associate itself fully with the community of free nations through membership in international organizations contributing to the common aims of the free world. . . .

[2] This assumption is the basis of the efforts to achieve a "neutralization" of Germany as propounded by the so-called "Nauheim Circle."

[3] A very one-sided account by George W. F. Hallgarten, *Imperialismus vor 1914—Die soziologischen Grundlagen der Aussenpolitik europäischer Grossmächte vor dem ersten Weltkrieg*, two vols, (Munich, 1951).

Socialist dictatorship. Thus, it is not possible to illustrate or illuminate the contemporary position by means of comparison, quite apart from the fact that everybody condemns the aims and methods of National Socialist policy.

a) If, therefore, without regard to historical background, the most general question possible is asked of Germany's foreign policy, namely what place it wishes to enjoy among the powers of the world, we shall be able to establish an entirely realistic viewpoint: Where the war's victors may succumb to illusions, or hold on to venerable opinions, Germany is, perhaps, the only European state in which it is clearly and soberly recognized that Europe's role as a great world-political factor is near its end, that the vocation to make history has shifted from Europe to the east and west, and that therefore a fundamental re-adjustment to the new situation has become a matter of survival. Nothing from her past will mislead Germany into abandoning or, indeed, postponing this readjustment of thought. She is burdened with no colonies, she has no powerful economic positions in foreign lands or continents to defend, and, above all, is not in the fatal position of wanting to maintain unilaterally established military strongpoints, for she possesses no such places. External circumstances, therefore, permit Germany above all to understand anew the significance that in our day a European state can have for a world which is no longer centered upon Europe, for which, perhaps, Europe is on the point of becoming merely peripheral. And nobody in Germany doubts that there is no longer any question of the categories as well as the policies that went with those classifications.

b) Herein lies the actually puzzling nature of European integration, the next point relevant to the Federal Republic's concept of foreign policy. Today, everybody in Western Europe is a supporter of European integration in some form, even if, like England, he is averse from taking part in an actual union. If this integration is justified by the necessity of winning Europe away from its old-fashioned nationalistic conceptions to modern continental ideas, then, quite naturally, the question arises what is involved. It is doubtful whether this question can be simply answered, as this would presume the existence of a European concept of world policy, the beginnings of which are, perhaps, just becoming visible. For the present, many interpretations are possible. At times, for example, the view is expressed that European integration can be used in an attempt to rebuild the declining world position of the West. But as this position can no longer be maintained, the attempt is made to gain strength by attracting forces that are not considered to be dangerous.[4] But, apart from the question whether this sort of thing really reflects the temper of a *new* Europe, the time for such action is too late, as a new power would prefer to enter a scheme that is healthy rather than one that is in need of rehabilitation.

Anyway, apart from this, it is not entirely clear what European integration really aims at. In itself, of course, such "integration" is desirable. For, just as the ideas of the French Revolution dissolved the structure of society without reuniting the disintegrated forces into a new order, in the same way the old European order founded on the principle of national states disintegrated in 1919 without, in the meantime, organizing Europe into a new unity.[5] There is a fear that the mentality of 1919 still predominates and particularly affects the order of things in the territory lying between the Baltic and the Balkans. Instead of being sceptical as regards this state of affairs,[6] there is also the hope of being able to overcome this confusion with a possibly intensified conception of the isolated national state, although this idea, as a result of the dislodging of Germans, is no longer valid and hence unrealizable by the interested parties themselves.

If European integration is primarily considered as a problem of the fundamental modernizing of European thinking, especially in connection with its concepts of foreign policy, then Germany must be especially careful that this integration does not lead her again to a universal way of thought based upon the past,[7] since she is least burdened with the ballast of the past in the form of colonies, recollections of world-wide power, etc.

c) The third question is whether Germany can stand aloof or

---

[4] Herein lies the dilemma that these very states who think of Germany in this respect have to face. On the one hand the attraction of a third party for the sake of reinforcement is only sensible if this party brings with it a measure of strength, on the other hand it is important that it should not be strong because therein, it is thought, lies a danger.

[5] Woodrow Wilson deserves mention as being the only person to have seen this problem, and to have sought a solution by means of the League of Nations.

[6] A notable exception in this respect is made by Gr. Burdeau, *Traité de Science Politique* (Paris, 1949); H. A. Smith, "Modern Weapons and Modern War," in *Yearbook of World Affairs*, Vol IX (1955), 222 ff. is critical of the function of a *cordon sanitaire* composed of small, isolated, adjacent national states.

[7] In this connection the Suez crisis should be considered a warning.

whether she must join one of the two camps into which both world and European politics is split. The former possibility implies international *"neutralization."* It is of no particular consequence how many Germans support this idea. In all probability such a neutralization would not be tolerated by those very powers from which German neutralists seek escape by this means. In principle neutralization is a stratagem by means of which third powers, unable or unwilling to utilize a certain factor in their sphere of influence, prevent it from being utilized by someone else. To achieve such an aim care must be taken that the factor in question will not fall to the exclusive share of either one of the two parties. This can be guaranteed only when the factor in question is relatively unimportant and its military significance drastically minimized, as, for example, in the case of the Alpine passes in Switzerland. But such is not the case with Germany. Here, the parties may be satisfied only by preventing one party from coming into possession of the whole, and by having both parties subordinate, interpenetrate (or whatever we care to call this state of affairs), one half only.

The settlement of the problem of neutralization also solves the second alternative—orientation towards either "East" or "West," for it would run counter to the German policy of the two world forces outlined above, if one of them permitted that the part subordinated to it would turn to the other side. Hence the orientation of German foreign policy is functionally dependent upon the state of relations between the two world powers. Thus from the purely doctrinaire point of view, with no consideration of practical compromises, the complete freedom of orientation would be possible for Germany only when every tension and every anxiety between the two world powers had been extirpated, or every contention had lost its military or political significance.

In connection with this it must be mentioned that since 1945 the Soviet Union has set up in Eastern Europe a military forefield, and so caused serious fears in Germany. No one in Germany denies the right of the Soviet Union to make absolutely sure that the events of 1941 are not repeated. But whether in the face of the development of nuclear arms the extension of the frontier to the Oder-Neisse line (that point at which the North German-Baltic low-land is narrowest, and therefore most easily blocked) is any longer of decisive significance, whether it is worthwhile maintaining the psychological shock action—that is a question which grows in magnitude almost without the asking.

d) In addition to all this there is a fourth set of problems which certainly does not come last in order of importance—*reunification.* The fact that, without Germans wishing it, this has become a problem of international politics needs no substantiation after what has been said above.[8] Reunification is so much a common aim of both parts of Germany, that they fervently reproach each other for not pressing for it sufficiently. But also the third powers, orientated towards East or West, keenly profess their support for the reunification of both parts of Germany. The naive observer will think it incomprehensible that an idea which apparently has the support of all should not be realized. The impediments lie in the modalities of reunification, and here also the difficulties rest on the already mentioned power-political considerations. Such power politics need not be aggressive. It may be conceived as entirely defensive in so far as it is a matter of dividing power between possible rivals, so that the nation in question might find favorable means of escaping an entanglement.

From this point of view the problem of international *disarmament* takes on a particular significance for Germany. Like all peoples of the world Germans long wholeheartedly for the amelioration and removal of the threat that, in the form of atomic weapons, hovers over the existence the freedom of all, whether directly concerned or not. But the German peoples have a further cause to desire the attainment of a disarmament agreement: it is only the feeling of security that can remove from the above-mentioned power-political considerations which today hinder the unification.

2) Just as there is no definite pattern of aims pursued by the foreign policy so there is no systematic description of its ways and means. The problem whether particular methods and means can or cannot be specifically applied to certain peoples, has, indeed, scarcely been examined. It is even less clear upon what causes such a combination

---

[8] It should not be overlooked that the relations between the Federal Republic of Germany and the German Democratic Republic are not based upon international law but, *sui generis,* upon political law. Cf. Herbert Krüger "Bundesrepublik Deutschland und Deutsche Demokratische Republik," Hamburg 1956 (pub. in hectograph by the Forschungsstelle für Völkerrecht und ausländisches öffentliches Recht der Universität Hamburg, No. 26).

might be based, whether, for example, such causes should be searched for in the mentality, the constitution, or the external political circumstances of a nation. Is there, for example, in respect of the means a typical "democratic" or typical "totalitarian" foreign policy? Or is it possible to distinguish between the political conception of an agrarian people and that of a commercial nation? For all these questions there are, as yet, no known answers. Hence the present writer may perhaps be permitted a somewhat unsystematic examination of certain points arising from them.

a) Although today the resort to force is forbidden by Art. 2^{VI} of the Charter of the United Nations we are not thereby in a position where it is no longer necessary to reflect upon this theme. The international lawyer must at least consider what is to be looked upon as force, whether only *vis directa* or also *vis compulsiva*, etc., so that it may be established whether a particular action can be considered as force or not. Historians and sociologists will have to consider whether force, quite apart from the juridical prohibition, has not developed to such a degree that it has outlived itself as a means. For the employment of force only makes sense, if at all, when the user can so control it that it produces the desired results and, indeed, no more than that. It appears that the use of nuclear force involves uncontrollable power, and hence this force threatens to part all company with the purpose it is meant to achieve. Is it possible, speaking concretely, to attribute any sense to the employment of force when the application of nuclear power will destroy not merely the enemy but pose the danger of destroying the whole of mankind indeed, extinguish it together with all other life.

If this assertion is correct then a chapter in the history of human relationships which, at the latest, began in the stone age, will be closed, If, from the technical point of view, the stone axe could still be recognized as a means of regulating social conditions, then the nuclear weapon cannot even in this respect make a claim. Today one must examine radically the technique and instruments used by men for establishing their mutual influence. It is also a matter of supplanting primitive tools and methods with more refined, less wasteful, and more productive ones. In this respect, within the sphere of mutual relationships, it is finally a matter of displacing force with argument.

German foreign policy has special cause to give consideration to this development, for it has been specially associated with *Realpolitik* [9] in the sense of power politics or *Machtpolitik*. In the eyes of a popular, not to say vulgar history, Bismarck's policy has become the prototype of this force. However necessary and useful it may be to examine these matters thoroughly, the fact remains that German foreign policy must deal with such interpretations. If sociology teaches us that in order to dissociate and remove itself from a "negative social ideal," every human group must have a "scapegoat," still one cannot recommend such an attempt or even allow oneself to slip into it. Moreover, these are contingencies that the military mind often overlooks. A foreign policy which is inspired not by statesmen but by military thinking will unavoidably not only smell of power politics but also of militarism. [10]

If German foreign policy is examined from this point of view, it can be established that it has accommodated itself thereto. Yet the domestic opponents of the present German Government have reproached this foreign policy with being a "policy of strength." Their criticism is not convincing because it is not obvious what factors contribute to such a strength.

b) Today, power has become a doubtful instrument of foreign policy. Behind the concept of "collective security" there is a thought that even small and medium powers can make a contribution towards the preservation of world peace if so organized that the aggressor finds himself opposed by an overwhelming majority of defenders. This concept either irrevocably or from the start, does not divide the participants of this arrangement into right or wrong. Moreover, it assumes the absolute tactical mobility of the various participants so that a comprehensive coalition of all the others can be formed against every conceivable aggressor. Both assumptions are today no longer practicable. The division of the world into "East" and "West" signifies a similar *a priori* moral valuation. Thus for the West everything in the East is from the start irredeemably bad, whereas the East has the same opinion concerning the West. [11] And the moral values are no less firm

---

[9] The conception *Realpolitik* is here used as the antithesis of *Idealpolitik* in the sense of ideological politics. Cf. A. L. v. Rochau *Grundsätze der Realpolitik: angewendet auf die staatlichen Zustände Deutschlands* (n. Asg., Stuttgart, 1859).

[10] Cf. Gerhard Ritter *Der Schlieffenplan* (Munich, 1956).

[11] A symptom of this is the idea of "intimidation." It supposes as obvious that transgressors are only to be found extra-murally!

than the political attitude. If then the "Concert of Europe" was conceived as a permanent rotation of a constellation in relation to the demands of a specific situation, we now have two worlds standing opposite each other in firmly cemented blocks. Vacillation, as happened with Yugoslavia, has become the rare exception.

"Collective security," as a concept, has, in this way, lost its workability. Thus the less strong or minor powers have been deprived of the possibility of achieving anything positive on behalf of world peace. Collective security is therefore of no value except as a preparation towards an initial self-defense which must serve until really effective formations can take over protective measures. This dependence upon giants, who can provide adequate protection, prevents the lesser states from adhering to an isolationism that some may think desirable. As the possibility of different orientation no longer exists, the only alternative left is to choose one of the two big blocs into which the world has divided itself.

c) Therefore, since today power and force are of only relative value to the lesser states, they are called upon to emphasize other factors in the relationship between one state and another. This is not merely a matter of replacing wrongdoing with the bestowal of benefits. It rather implies creating and offering a more civilized manner of human coexistence. Here particularly, it seems to me, lie Europe's opportunities with her age-old historical and social experience. At the moment, however, it does not look as if Europe were inclined to exploit this particular opportunity. Rather do we see everywhere a picture of complacent adherence to old conceptions which partly owe their existence to the fact that National Socialism or Communism has attacked them or is still attacking them.

There is, for example, surely considerable genuine enthusiasm for European integration. But would it be possible to conceive earnestly of the integrated Europe as one bounded by the Pyrenees and the Elbe? This question is asked in order to show that a pregnant answer requires the rejection of the barren notion that Europe is best off with her middle and eastern parts excluded,[12] but also that obviously such

[12] Cf., for example, the report of Paul Sethe on how, after 1945, the Western European powers prevented the restoration of a unified German state under one Government. See *Zwischen Bonn und Moskau* (2nd ed., Frankfurt, 1956), pp. 12ff.

abandonment would not necessarily be generally accepted. The same picture is shown in the life of the state: the abandonment of *étatisme* and individualism involves a failure to provide a model for those peoples who are in search of a new order, though, indeed, the desire for a new orientation is scarcely noticeable. The same could be said of the social and economic spheres. On the surface there appears to be left but one ideal, the "raising of the standard of living." Whether such an ideal is specifically European, or whether thereby Europe is offering the world a new watch-word no one wants to assert.

In the terrible and bloody revolutionary wars of the sixteenth and seventeenth centuries Europe learned that it is not possible to convert all men to one religion or *Weltanschauung*, and that therefore there is but one alternative: to induce people, with their religious and other differences, to live together in peace. Whereas the young world powers, the United States and the Soviet Union, tend to abandon a "policy of idealism" for a "policy of realism," which may make possible a state of peaceful coexistence, Europe, as regards political questions, seems to be inclined to treat the political questions ideologically. Obviously a Europe with an "ideologizing" foreign policy has nothing to offer to a "de-ideologizing" world. All the more, then, Germany, which in the framework of Nazism has passed beyond the frenzy of an ideology, regards foreign political problems and methods as free from all missionary or propaganda elements, and thus leads foreign policy back to that solid realistic basis which is so obvious to matter-of-fact traders in the form of *do ut des.* Such a *Realpolitik* has nothing in common with cynicism, with power politics or indeed with Machiavellianism as has occasionally been assumed. A good trader will have nothing to do with, for example, pressure or breach of contract as only a brief success, if any, is thereby achieved.

It is, however, doubtful whether the term "Realism" is adequate to characterize what is demanded by Germany's foreign political situation as regards the renewal of methods. Perhaps the idea that in foreign policy we should not put greater weight on persuasion may seem fantastic. All too often the observer is faced with the paradox that the period in which we live is exceedingly proud of its rationalism and intellectualism, but that it tends to overcome its social and international differences with means which, if compared with its rationalism and intellectualism, seem to belong to remote antiquity. The submission of international relations to law—a solution that has been regarded as a veritable panacea—can effect only the extirpation of force or of ideologies if the law is not exclusively used to stabilize forcibly the established positions of power by proclaiming them legally and morally unassailable. Law as a genuine argument remains especially discredited as long as the point of view is maintained that even under threat or compulsion ratified international agreements can make a claim to inviolability.[13]

The placing of foreign relations on a basis of economics and law is important but not the final phase in replacing force with agreement. In order to introduce further inquiry we are not asserting this point. At this point we only stress the necessity of an extensive research into the methods of foreign policy. One can hardly exclude the spiritual force from a survey concerning those methods, provided, of course, that the competence and the will exist to bring about a spiritual re-building which, indeed, could be of interest to other nations also. Here the prospects for Germany's future are greater than the prospects afforded by efforts devoted to economic prosperity.

II

In the external history of a nation the fact that a certain event has not taken place is, occasionally at least, as important as the fact that an event has taken place. This applies to Germany, for her external position is overshadowed by the fact that it has not been possible for Germany to terminate the Second World War by a formal peace treaty.[14] We need not examine the reasons that have prevented the conclusion of such a treaty. Nor shall we discuss whether this failure is to Germany's advantage or disadvantage. It is only the consequence of this strange situation that is to be emphasized; there was no alternative for Germany but to try, in the absence of a peace treaty, to establish peaceful and ordered relations with those states with whom she had been at war. As their alliance opposing Germany had in the meantime disintegrated it became necessary to restore peaceful relations in isolated undertakings.

[13] Cf. Herbert Krüger "Der Grundsatz der Effektivität oder: Über die besondere Wirklichkeitsnähe des Völkerrechts," in *Festschrift für Spiropoulos* (Bonn, 1957), pp. 265–284.

[14] Cf. V. Scheuner "Der fehlende Friede," in *Festschrift für H. Kraus* (Kitzingen, 1954), pp. 190ff.

After the three principal victors had occupied Germany and divided it into occupation zones, the setting up of a normal relationship based upon international law in the place of the *occupatio bellica* became imperative.

Only so was Germany able to enter the field of foreign relations on her initiative and responsibility instead of leaving it to the exclusive care of the occupying powers. How the Federal Republic rebuilt its Foreign Office and diplomatic relations will be described in detail below.

Fortunately the story of the new German foreign policy, inaugurated by the Federal Republic, records no dramatic events. Moreover scarcely anything has happened—if one disregards the resumption of diplomatic relations with the Soviet Union [15]—that could be included in a specifically German history of foreign policy. The entry into the organizations of the so-called Western World [16] is no more than a union with what already existed, even if, as with the Brussels Treaty, a fundamental reconstruction was made to accommodate Germany's taking part. As regards the European Coal and Steel Community (the Schuman Plan) the matter was not quite the same. From the political point of view it was an attempt mutually to remove by means of a common surveillance all anxiety concerning military eventualities that might be connected with a heavy-industrial power. Yet, in spite of German enthusiasm, this does not belong to the specifically German annals of foreign policy, but rather to European history.

One case of strange duplicity in our foreign policy is peculiarly German. The German Democratic Republic, which comprises middle Germany, is in fact not subject to international law; indeed, the Federal Republic challenges its legitimacy as a state, and, indeed, the former maintains diplomatic relations only with the so-called Peoples' Democracies. If we take the German Peoples' Democracy, a creation hard to define, and consider its foreign policy through comparing it with that of the Federal Republic it would be a mistake to speak of synchronization. Of the two it seems that the former has subscribed to

[15] An agreement to resume diplomatic relations was reached in Moscow on September 13th, 1955.

[16] The Federal Republic joined the Council of Europe as an associate member in July 1950, as a full member in May 1951. Its adhesion to the Brussels Treaty on October 23, 1954, became effective on May 6, 1955; to NATO on May 6, 1955.

a kind of Hegelian dialectic insofar as it has set up an "Eastern" antithesis for every "Western" thesis of the Federal Republic.[17] It is difficult to comprehend the sense of this dialectic: above all it can hardly be expected that a German "synthesis" can evolve from a dialectic of this kind.

III

With the collapse and the total occupation of the German Reich in the spring of 1945 which resulted in the dissolution of the Foreign Office, all diplomatic and consular relations with foreign states, including those that had remained neutral, ceased. For the foreign service the unconditional surrender of Germany was disastrous. Thereby German diplomacy has lost the basis upon which its principles rested. In the history of modern times such a thing had never occurred. On the other hand, various forms of German representation had been maintained in neutral countries after the German defeat in 1918. But relations were also rapidly resumed with those countries with which the Reich had been at war. Six months after the signing of the Versailles treaty there were, for example, German chargés d'affaires in London and Paris and, a few months later, ambassadors.[18] Moreover, diplomatic property was returned to the Reich.

1) *Development up to the Occupation Statute*

In the spring of 1945, after the occupation of Germany, the situation was, as has already been pointed out, quite different. According to the terms of the Berlin Declaration of June 5, 1945, the occupation powers assumed supreme sovereignty in Germany,[19] which was then completely cut off from the outer world. Germany possessed no diplomatic status. Officials of the German foreign service were almost without

---

[17] The foundation of the Federal Republic in May 1949 was followed by that of the German Democratic Republic in October 1949.

The Paris Treaties occasioned the Warsaw Treaty of May 14, 1955. The sovereignty of the Federal Republic, the end-result of the Bonn and Paris Treaties, occasioned the treaty of sovereignty between the Soviet Union and the German Democratic Republic, concluded on September 20, 1955.

[18] Krekeler, "Deutschlands Vertretung im Ausland," in *Politische Bildung* (1952, No. 26/27), p. 150.

[19] Official Gazette of the Control Council for Germany, app. 1.

exception interned until the end of 1946 or the beginning of 1947. With an eye to possible peace negotiations, the so-called "German Bureau for Peace Affairs" was brought into being at Stuttgart on April 15, 1947 with the approval of the American General Clay. This Bureau, in which a number of former officials of the Foreign Office were employed, devoted itself to problems connected with public international law, public law, and private international law, and also with questions of frontiers (East, North, and West), reparations, international economic cooperation, etc.[20] In this manner there was created the small beginnings of a foreign service.

Over the years, the increasing commercial relations between the Western Zones of Germany and foreign states made it most desirable to establish commercial representation abroad. At first such a request received the sanction of only the American and British occupation powers. For the time being the French Government did not accede to this plan on the ground that these commercial missions would also engage in political activities. However, it could not permanently deny the necessity for such representations.

2) *The Foreign Service under the Occupation Statute*

When on September 21, 1949, the Occupation Statute came into force,[21] the Western Allies extended the Federal Republic some freedom in acting under international law. It is true, the Governments of France, the United States, and the United Kingdom, then represented by High Commissioners, expressly reserved the right to deal with all international agreements to which Germany, or whoever acted on her behalf, was party. It was only with the Petersburg Agreement[22] of November 24, 1949 (No. 4), that the Federal Republic was permitted gradually to reopen consular and commercial relations with "such countries with whom relations of this type appear to be advantageous." On December 15, 1949, the ECA agreement was made between the Federal Republic and the United States of America. Soon the Federal Republic entered into OEEC, and was accepted into the Council of

---

[20] *Deutschland-Jahrbuch 1949* (Essen, 1949), p. 112; *Die Neue Zeitung*, August 22, 1949.

[21] *Official Gazette of the Allied High Commission for Germany*, September 23, 1949, pp. 2 and 13 (2c).

[22] *Bundesanzeiger*, I, No. 28 (November 26, 1949).

Europe as an associate member. In June, 1950, she took part in the discussions connected with the Schuman Plan.

By now it was urgently necessary to create a center where the organizational prerequisites for the creation of a German consular service should be, so to speak, built up from scratch. Already in the late autumn of 1949 the so-called Organization Bureau was brought into existence under the direction of Staatsrat Haas of Bremen.[23] In order to preserve contact with the High Commissioners a liaison office was opened in Bonn, the director of which was the former Ministerial-direktor Blankenhorn, appointed by the Federal Chancellor. Some months later, on January 26, 1950, the three Western High Commissioners urged Chancellor Adenauer to establish consular representations in London, Paris, and Washington. Thereupon Consul-General Schlange-Schöningen, originally destined for Washington, was sent to London, Hausenstein to Paris, and Krekeler to Washington. None of these three came from the Foreign Service. Schlange-Schöningen was the director of the bizonal food office in Frankfurt, a. M., Hausenstein was a Professor of Fine Arts, and Krekeler came from industry.

The Office for Foreign Affairs (*Dienststelle für Auswärtige Angelegenheiten*) was made the central office in Bonn, and consisted of three groups—the Organization Office, the Liaison Office, and the Consular Department (Departments I, II, and III). This office was directly responsible to Chancellor Adenauer. At the end of May, 1950, Theodor Kordt was appointed director of the Consular Department. The coordination of the groups was left to the former Ministerial-direktor Blankenhorn and the Office of Foreign Affairs was entrusted to the newly appointed Undersecretary of the Chancellery, Hallstein.[24] As long as no legal department existed, questions of international law were dealt with by the Consular Department. But independently of this the well-known lawyer, Professor Erich Kaufmann, advised the government on matters of international law.

In the course of 1950 as many as eleven states agreed to the suggestion made by the Federal Republic as regards the establishment of consular representations, Australia, Belgium, Canada, Denmark,

[23] *Aussenpolitik* (1950, No. 4), 250ff.
[24] *Aussenpolitik* (1950, No. 4), 252.

Greece, Italy, Luxemburg, the Netherlands, Switzerland, South Africa and Turkey.[25]

3) *The Building Up after the Revision of the Occupational Statute*

It was the Korean war which changed the whole political picture in the world, and out of the tension of East and West effected a change in the relationship of the Federal Republic towards the Western occupation powers. On September 19, 1950, at the New York Foreign Ministers' Conference, as a result of events in Korea, the question of German rearmament was debated. It became evident that in the event of Germany's rearming an amelioration of the occupation regime would be necessary. In a communique (September 19, 1950) the Foreign Ministers of France, the United Kingdom, and the United States declared that the Federal Republic was to be empowered to set up a Ministry of Foreign Affairs, and to establish diplomatic relations with foreign states "wherever this might seem expedient." Thereupon the organization of German diplomatic representations in twenty-five states was planned as well as the establishment of thirteen Consulates General and four Consulates.[26] A delay in the implementing of the resolutions taken at the New York Foreign Ministers' Conference was caused by the question of the Federal Republic acknowledging pre-war debts as well as post-war debts incurred for economic assistance. This acknowledgement had been a condition demanded by the Western Allies prior to a revision of the Occupation Statute.[27] It was only half a year later, in March 1951, six years after the end of hostilities, that there was created the legal basis upon which the revival of normal foreign relations of the Federal Republic could be based. No. 2 c of the revised Occupation Statute now read as follows:

(c) foreign affairs, including international agreements made by or on behalf of Germany, but the powers reserved in this field will be exercised so as to permit the Federal Republic to conduct relations with foreign countries to the full extent compatible with the requirements of security, other

[25] *Archiv der Gegenwart* (1950), pp. 2564f.
[26] *Europa-Archiv* (1950), pp. 3408f.
[27] *Archiv der Gegenwart* (1951), p. 2846; *Notes et études* (1951), No. 1456, p. 3.

reserved powers, and obligations of the Occupying Powers relating to Germany.[28]

In clause 11,[29] concerning the competence of the Federal Republic in the field of foreign affairs, the Federal Republic was expressly empowered to set up a Foreign Ministry (Art. 1). The establishment of diplomatic and consular relations as well as provision for commercial representations required, in principle, the acquiescence of the Allied High Commission. But in the case of those states with which the Federal Republic had been empowered to maintain consular officials before the coming into force of the revised Occupation Statute, this consent was not required. Diplomatic relations with France, the United Kingdom, and the United States were exempted from the above rulings. For them the Federal Republic needed the permission of the High Commissioners for the establishment of a diplomatic representation (Art. 3, I, and II). In those countries the Federal Republic was able to maintain only the official agents (*agents officiels*) (Art. 4). The diplomatic and consular representations set up within the Federal Republic were, according to Article 5, Resolution 11, now normally recognized and legalized by the Federal Republic. Moreover, the Federal Republic and the governments of the *Länder* had at all times to inform the Allied High Commission about every international transaction. The latter could intervene in such transactions insofar as they affected their own particular spheres (Art. 6). On October 23, 1951, the Allied High Commission waived its right of veto in the trade agreements concluded by the Federal Republic with the exception of those with states of the Eastern bloc. The Federal Republic had thus won almost complete freedom of negotiation in commercial affairs.

Indeed the Basic Law of the Federal Republic created the constitutional foundation upon which a future foreign service could be erected: according to Article 59 of the Constitution, the Federal Republic is represented in international law by the President of the Republic, who, also, in the name of the Federation, concludes agreements with foreign states. He accredits and receives heads of diplomatic missions. The maintenance of relations with foreign states shall be the affair of the Federation (Art. 32[I]). Yet, before the conclusion

---

[28] *Official Gazette of the Allied High Commission for Germany,* March 6, 1951, p. 792.

[29] *Ibid.,* March 6, 1951, pp. 795ff.

of a treaty affecting the special conditions of a *Land*, the *Land* must be consulted in advance (Art. 32^{II}). Insofar as the *Länder* are competent to legislate, they may, with the approval of the Federal Government, conclude treaties with foreign states (Art. 32^{III}). The Federal Republic's foreign policy is determined by the Federal President together with the Federal Chancellor, who is responsible for the guiding principles of policy (Art. 59 and 65). The decrees and ordinances of the Federal President require the countersignature of the Federal Chancellor or that of the competent Federal Minister (Art. 58). Legislation, in connection with foreign affairs, is exclusively in the hands of the Federation. The Foreign Service is numbered among those departments that shall be conducted by a direct federal administration with its own lower level administrative offices (Art. 87^I).

On March 15, 1951, President Heuss appointed Adenauer, the Federal Chancellor, to be Foreign Minister. Foreign Minister Adenauer declared that the Federal Republic would take as its model the organizational build-up of the former Foreign Office, and that the name "Foreign Office" (*Auswärtiges Amt*) would be retained. In addition to a personnel department, responsible for the selection of officials with relevant qualifications, questions concerning political, consular, and legal matters were shared by two other departments. Among other things it was incumbent upon one of these to prepare for the peace settlement and affairs appertaining to international organizations as well as the maintenance of relations with the Allied High Commissioners. The other department was to impart guidance to the work of foreign missions in political, consular, and legal affairs. The commercial department was responsible for all questions concerning foreign politico-commercial interests. The cultural department was given the task of rebuilding the myriad cultural connections with foreign countries as well as with German scientific institutes, churches, schools and hospitals. The protocol department concerned with questions of ceremony [30] deserves to be mentioned also.

On March 15, 1951, the Consuls-General in Paris, London and Washington were created chargés d'affaires whereby they received diplomatic status.[31] In 1953, they were given the personal rank of ambassador without changing the status of their missions.[32]

---

[30] Hallstein, "Das Auswärtige Amt," in *Aussenpolitik* (1951), p. 456.
[31] *Ibid.*, p. 453.
[32] *Archiv der Gegenwart* (1953), p. 4054 A.

Thus, after two years of rebuilding, the Federal Republic had thirty-eight diplomatic and consular representations in twenty-six countries. In Europe there were embassies in Athens, Belgrade, Brussels, The Hague, Copenhagen, and Rome: and there were legations at Bern, Dublin, Luxemburg, Oslo and Stockholm. In Paris and London there were diplomatic representations, and Consulates-General at Amsterdam, Basle, Milan, Marseilles, Istanbul, and Zürich. On the continent of America there were embassies at Buenos Aires, Ottawa, Rio de Janeiro, Santiago; legations at Bogota, Caracas, Lima, and Montevideo; a diplomatic representation at Washington; consulates-general in Chicago, New York, San Francisco, São Paulo; consulates at Atlanta, Los Angeles, New Orleans, and Montreal. In Africa, a legation in Pretoria-Johannesburg; in Asia, ambassadors at Karachi, New Delhi, Djakarta, and Tokio, and a consulate-general at Bombay.[33]

In addition, the Federal Republic maintains representatives or observers at international organizations.

It is hardly necessary to mention that the work of building up a foreign ministry involves considerable difficulties. No beginning could have been more radical. The changes and developments of the post-war period had come about in other countries gradually and almost unnoticed. The German representations found themselves in these new conditions without having experienced the transition. Apart from traditional form and custom the duties of the foreign representations had to be tempered to the specific aims of the government.

A further difficulty, not to be underrated, was the fact that at the time it was not possible to find independent accommodation for the ministry. Before the erection of the new building in Koblenzer Strasse the Foreign Ministry was dispersed in thirteen different buildings.[34]

The problem of replacement was a particularly difficult one because there was as yet no center for the training of recruits. In 1950, the directorship of training was undertaken by Pfeiffer, then Consul-General. At Speyer candidates were given short courses of six months. Prominent men were invited there to give courses or single lectures on politics, industry, international law, and geography. Moreover, the candidates had to pass tests in languages and take the examination for

---

[33] Krekeler, "Deutschlands Vertretung im Ausland," *Politische Bildung* (1952, No. 26/27), p. 167.

[34] *Bulletin der Bundesregierung* (1953), p. 7.

the diplomatic-consular service. These short courses were planned for the immediate use of functionaries.[35]

4) *The Declaration of Sovereignty*

With the implementation of the Paris conventions and the ending of the occupation regime on May 5, 1955, the Federal Republic became an equal partner in the concert of nations. On the same day, the Allied High Commission was dissolved; [36] according to Article 1, paragraph 2 of the new general agreement,[37] the Federal Republic received the full power of a sovereign state over her internal and foreign affairs. With this the diplomatic representations in the countries of the three former occupying powers became embassies (Paris and London on May 26, 1955, Washington on May 6, 1955).[38] On May 5, 1955, the British Ambassador, Sir Frederick Hoyer-Millar, as well as the French Ambassador, André François Poncet, and on May 14, 1955, the American Ambassador, James Conant, handed their letters of credence to President Heuss.[39]

IV

1) *The Foreign Service Today: Organization*

Since 1955, the control of the Foreign Office has been in the hands of Heinrich von Brentano. The office of Undersecretary of State is held by Professor Hallstein.

A personal advisory committee is directly responsible to the Federal Foreign Secretary, the function of which, as its name implies, is to deal with the Minister's immediate affairs.

a) THE HEAD OFFICE

The organization of the present-day Foreign Office essentially resembles that of pre-war days. Thus, the protocol, personnel administration, law, and cultural departments have, as regards their set-up and functions, scarcely changed. Yet, on the other hand, on account of the considerable widening of the spheres of activity, the former politi-

---

[35] *Aussenpolitik* (1950, No. 4), 251.

[36] *Official Gazette of the Allied High Commission for Germany* (1955), p. 3272.

[37] *Bundesgesetzblatt* (1955), II, 305.

[38] *Auswärtiges Amt: Vertretungen der Bundesrepublik Deutschland im Ausland* (September 9, 1956), pp. 41, 63, 66.

[39] *Europa-Archiv* (1955), p. 7937.

cal department has been separated into two, the political and the regional state departments.

The regional department is split into two subdivisions—East and West. The newly formed commercial policy department is also subdivided. On the whole, the present division of the central office is less rigid than it was before World War II.

Within the sphere of the *political division* fall the consideration of all problems connected with general foreign policy as well as all questions affecting re-unification. Furthermore it is the competent departmental authority for the offices in Berlin and Saarbrücken, for the Saar affairs and the cooperation between inter-state and super-state organizations. The latter two include the Council of Europe, the Schuman Plan, the United Nations with its special organizations, the peaceful exploitation of atomic power, the European technical unions. In addition, questions of defense, disarmament, and European political integration come within the competence of the division. The committee within the division, dealing with German affairs, observes the development of internal political matters, and maintains relations with the Bundestag and the Bundesrat, especially with the foreign committees, with the plenipotentiaries of the *Länder*, the churches, industrial combines, trade unions, etc.; at the same time, it is a cabinet department. The committee for German affairs permanently briefs the Foreign Minister and the Undersecretary of State as well as the German foreign representations concerning developments in internal politics. Moreover, foreign representations within the Federal Republic are informed about questions concerning domestic political problems. The committee has contact with foreign parliaments and parliamentarians, and observes the activities of international bodies.

To the political department also belongs the so-called Conference Secretariat, which primarily deals with constitutional problems arising from the activities of German delegations taking part in negotiations concerning European unity. At the same time it administers the allocations made available for these purposes.[40]

The regional department is, as has been said, split into two large subdivisions—East and West. These are again arranged into groups of countries. The department also includes the Information section

[40] Kraske-Nöldeke, *Handbuch des Auswärtigen Dienstes* (Tübingen, 1957), pp. 4ff.

which, in conjunction with the Press section, supplies the German foreign representations with brochures, news of general interest concerning other representations, press information, etc.

The subdivision "West" has the following nine sections: Scandinavia —Great Britain and the Commonwealth, Iceland—France, Benelux, Italy, Switzerland—Portugal, Spain, Tangiers, Vatican City—Greece, Jugoslavia, Austria, Turkey—U.S.A., Canada—Middle and South America—Africa south of the Sahara. The subdivision East is split up into seven sections: German eastern problems, geographical service—USSR, Eastern "Lektorat"—Albania, Bulgaria, Poland, Roumania, Czechoslovakia, Hungary—China (Peoples' Republic and Formosa), Mongolian Peoples' Republic, North Korea, North Vietnam, Hongkong, Macao—Near East—Middle East, Southeast Asia—East Asia, Australia, New Zealand.

The two above-mentioned divisions naturally form the nucleus of the Foreign Ministry. It is here that all questions of high policy are handled. Officials of these divisions must be exactly informed of conditions in the countries with which they deal. Close cooperation between the two departments is indispensable.

The *commercial policy division* is, together with the political division and the regional division, the most important in the Ministry. It is well-known that in international relations economic questions frequently play more decisive roles than political ones. This division is the counterpart to the foreign division of the Ministry for Internal Economic Affairs. It will not be necessary to stress that the experts of the commercial policy division must have a thorough knowledge of the economic affairs of those countries that come under their aegis.

A particularly important part is taken by this division in the negotiation, conclusion, and supervision of commercial treaties. The leadership of trade delegations is often in the hands of officials from the commercial policy division of the Foreign Ministry. The division is split into two: a subdivision for commercial policy in general and one for commercial policy towards foreign states. The former deals with fundamental questions as well as with inter-state and super-state economic relations. In addition, it is responsible for the economic affairs of the foreign missions, the furtherance of foreign trade, the elaboration of trade agreements as well as questions appertaining to communications. The second subdivision, built up regionally, has the following sections: North and West Europe—Sterling Area—Mediterranean countries—East-West trade, embargo policy—North and Central America—South America—Near and Middle East, Africa (not including sterling countries and colonies)—Far East—the economics of rearmament.

The delegate for Franco-German relations and the representative for commercial treaty negotiations are attached to the commercial policy department.

The *law department* consists of the usual sections: international law and treaties, public and administrative law, law concerning legations and consular matters, law of transportation, law of officials, criminal law, the law of taxation, customs rights, private international, and civil law, law concerning social affairs and social policy, German property abroad and German prisoners, as well as questions connected with a peace settlement.

The functions of the *cultural department* include the encouragement and extension of cultural relations with foreign states. In these are included church matters, German hospitals, school and university affairs, youth problems, sport, science, art, films, broadcasting, books, etc.

The *personnel and administrative department* is subdivided into two: one for personnel matters; the other for all questions connected with administration such as the budget and finances, official premises, and salaries. The administrative department is, also, responsible for the office's postal services, ciphering, telephones, languages, archives and library.

Before the outbreak of World War II the library contained some 200,000 volumes. Of these, all but 60,000 were lost. In the meantime the stock has increased to about 110,000 volumes.[41] Appropriate to the work of the office the library consists primarily of relevant bibliographical material in the fields of jurisprudence, especially international law, political law, international civil law, commercial law as well as social sciences, politics and geography, in addition to periodicals, gazettes, rulings, legal codes, etc.

In the archives are kept the files referring to foreign representations. The so-called historical section prepares surveys and expert opinions

[41] *Deutschland im Wiederaufbau; Tätigkeitsbericht der Bundesregierung* (1956), p. 82.

on political precedents and historical interrelations based on their files.[42]

During August and October 1956, the bulk of files of the years 1867–1913 and 1936–1945 (some 100 tons) were brought back from England. The remaining files (some 200 tons) are to be returned by December 31, 1958.[43]

The Minister, or Undersecretary, has at his direct disposal the Legal Adviser as well as the Press liaison officer's Bureau which has taken the place of the former Press section.

The head office has, moreover, at its special service an ambassador and a minister as well as another minister acting as chief of protocol.[44]

b) THE FOREIGN REPRESENTATIONS

The present extension of the German diplomatic and consular representations abroad must, as far as the present political situation allows, be considered as final. The Federal Republic is not represented in countries of the Eastern Bloc with the exception of an embassy in the Soviet Union maintained since March 12, 1956: nor is she represented in either of the Chinas (Peoples' Republic and Formosa). In Finland there is only a trade mission.

In the year 1956 the Foreign Office had at its disposal 47 embassies and 21 legations. To these must be added representatives of the Federal Republic acting as permanent observers, that is, an ambassador at the United Nations in New York, an ambassador in Paris, accredited to the North Atlantic Treaty Organization, a minister in Strassburg at the Council of Europe and a representative at OEEC.[45]

Whereas in former years the majority of diplomatic representations were legations, the aim today is to convert the legations into embassies. This trend began shortly after World War I. Today the practical significance is small, and is limited to the sphere of ceremony.

Since World War I the increase of duties has changed the structure of diplomatic representations. Formerly the head of a mission had at his disposal, in addition to a few officials, a military and a naval

---

[42] Kraske-Nöldeke, *op. cit.*, p. 4.

[43] *Deutschland im Wiederaufbau: Tätigkeitsbericht der Bundesregierung* (1956), pp. 82, 83.

[44] Kraske-Nöldeke, *op. cit.*, p. 6.

[45] *Auswärtiges Amt: Vertretungen der Bundesrepublik Deutschland im Ausland*, September 1, 1956, pp. 3ff.

attaché, but nowadays a fairly large representation has a whole staff of experts. Such, for instance, are advisers in economics, cultural, press and social affairs. Larger representations even have financial and agricultural specialists. Service attachés, moreover, have undergone a course of training at the Foreign Office.[46]

Every German diplomatic mission is also entrusted with consular tasks and has a consular sphere of jurisdiction.

The consular service is carried out by 31 Consulates-General, 62 Consulates and 142 Honorary Consulates.[47] The latter will probably be considerably increased. In the mid-thirties the German Reich had about 400 such consulates, and before World War I about 600. Consulates-General and Consulates are coordinated offices standing in no relation to one another, whereas the Honorary, Commercial Consulates are subject to officers of the regular service.

The diplomatic and consular representations are outwardly a unity. The policy adopted towards the host country is determined by that diplomatic representation upon whom liaison with the host government devolves. On the other hand, the regular consulates are directly under the Foreign Office. Even if consulates report directly to the Foreign Office they are, nevertheless, bound to inform the head of the diplomatic mission on all matters within their jurisdictional area that may be of importance to him. The latter, on his part, informs the consular officer about important occurrences.[48] The Honorary Consuls, on the other hand, do not report straight to the Foreign Office but to the diplomatic or consular representations under whose authority they act. Honorary Consuls need not, like other honorary officials, be German, although the appointment of Germans is the rule in normal times. The special circumstances which followed World War II resulted in appointing more foreigners as Commercial Consuls.

Privileges and other rights enjoyed by consular officials abroad depend less on general usage based on international law (as is the custom with diplomatic officials) than on treaties. These contain the special rights conceded to consular officials, especially the so-called

---

[46] *Deutschland im Wiederaufbau: Tätigkeitsbericht der Bundesregierung für das Jahr 1956*, p. 82.

[47] *Auswärtiges Amt: Vertretungen der Bundesrepublik Deutschland im Ausland*, September 1, 1956, pp. 3ff.

[48] *Kraske-Nöldeke, Op. Cit.*, pp. 8f., 52.

most favoured nation clause, that is, consular representations enjoy all rights which are conceded to consuls of other states.

The allocations for the Foreign Service for the budgetary year 1957/58 amounted to DM 242,967,000 an increase of DM 2,585,700 against the fiscal period 1956/57.[49]

[49] *Bundesgesetzblatt,* 1957, II, p. 515.

Chapter 16

A NEW ARENA OF DIPLOMACY:

THE MIDDLE EAST

John C. Campbell

THE "Eastern Question" may perhaps be called the classic field for the exercise of diplomacy. For well over a century the great powers of Europe had to find means of regulating their relations and balancing their interests in the Near and Middle East, an area of primary strategic importance occupied by a declining Ottoman Empire and a weak Persia. The so-called "Concert of Europe" had long assumed a special relationship with the Ottoman Empire, partly based on long established claims or treaty rights of the European powers to intervene in a country outside the civilized "Christian world," to protect their nationals or even the Sultan's Christian subjects. Its most useful purpose, however, was to enable the European powers to keep watch on one another, to prevent any one of them from obtaining undue advantage over the others by war or by pressure on Turkey. For the essence of the Eastern Question was the clash between the southward expansion of Russian power and the efforts of the Western powers, especially Great Britain, to block it because it threatened the routes of Empire. Those efforts rested on a combination of force and diplomacy.

Diplomacy was an instrument of national policy determined largely by considerations of strategy and the balance of power, often more effective than the resort to force. Those wars which were fought during the eighteenth and nineteenth centuries were what today would be called "limited," both in aims and in scope, and they took place against a background of continuing diplomacy. Palmerston, Disraeli, and Salisbury held Russian power in check and away from the crucial Straits by a combination of sea power, support of the principle of the integrity of the Ottoman Empire, and cooperation with other states such as Austria-Hungary which had a similar interest in containing Russian expansion. The Congress of Berlin in 1878 was a triumph for British diplomacy not because Disraeli brought home "peace with honour" but because he succeeded in isolating the Russians and depriving them of the fruits of their military victory over Turkey. The "integrity" of the Ottoman Empire, moreover, was a flexible concept. As the Balkan states broke free in the north, the British strengthened their position in the south by taking control of Cyprus and of Suez. Sometimes it was necessary to compromise directly with the Russians, as in the entente of 1907 covering Persia, Afghanistan, and Tibet, but Russian gains in each case were matched by British gains, all at the expense of the Middle Eastern peoples. The diplomacy of settlement by partition was always in the background, if the diplomacy of shoring up weak partners and of building "positions of strength" should fail.

The two world wars, in which Germany bid for world supremacy, changed the picture temporarily by bringing Russia and the Western powers together, but the remarkable fact is that on both occasions the old pattern so quickly reasserted itself once the danger from Germany was removed. The First World War had even brought a British promise to let Russia control the Straits, a reversal of historic policy, but it ended with an Allied fleet in occupation of them. Other new factors were the Russian Revolution, the breakup of the Ottoman Empire and the emergence of a new, nationalist, self-assertive Turkey, and the carving up and division of the Arab areas between Britain and France. Despite these great changes, the continuity of the Eastern Question and the similarity of the problems of diplomacy to those long established by history and tradition were quite evident. For all its repudiation of Russian imperialism and appeals to the "toilers of the East," Soviet aims in the Near and Middle East bore a close resemblance to those of the Czars. Although military weakness in the interwar period ruled out a direct challenge to the West and turned Soviet diplomacy into the construction of treaty systems intended to ensure "friendly" policies on the part of the immediately neighboring states, there remained the fundamental conflict between Russia's land-based empire, now dedicated to world revolution, and the Western system based on sea power and a complex of allied states, protectorates, mandates, and colonial possessions.

Britain's position after the First World War was strong, in that the major part of the Arab world with its great oil resources was in British hands, but it was not as impregnable as it seemed. For if Soviet Russia could not win the Middle Eastern peoples to communism, neither could Britain and France win them to permanent acceptance of Western tutelage. Western diplomacy faced a greater challenge to its diplomacy in handling the rise of nationalism from India to Morocco than it did in its relations with the Soviet Union in that region.

With Turkey the efforts were largely successful, once the Western powers were reconciled to accepting Turkey's full sovereignty, its "friendly association" with Moscow and its control of the Straits (limited by the Lausanne Convention and then by that of Montreux). In the end, Turkey became the ally of Britain and France in 1939, though on terms enabling her to avoid being drawn into conflict with the Soviet Union. Iran, on the other hand, stuck to its traditional neutrality, so distrustful of both Russia and Britain that it offered a promising field for German penetration. The Western powers had an even more difficult problem in the case of the Arab lands where they attempted to combine the inevitable transition to independence with treaties and other arrangements that would ensure that the area could be held in case of war. This process was but half complete when Hitler launched the Second World War.

Allied diplomacy was not able to bring Turkey into the war on the Western side despite intensive efforts to do so in 1943 and 1944, but nevertheless Turkey's neutrality was of great help in keeping the Germans out of the Middle East and preventing any "liberation" by the Russians. Moreover, while the Allied war effort never received the full cooperation of the Arabs, their dependence on the West for supplies and the force at the disposition of the Allies were sufficient to keep the area safe and its oil, bases, and communications available for Allied use. In Iran there was the added factor of the presence of Soviet forces, along with those of Britain and the United States, and of Soviet policies which were being directed against the West rather than against the Germans; the cold war was on in Iran long before the war with Hitler was over in Europe.

The Eastern Question, as the war ended, looked much as it had in the past. Britain was the dominant power in the Middle East and was directing her diplomatic efforts to remaining in that position. But now the Russian challenge was more formidable than ever before. Stalin, with his armies in occupation of all Eastern Europe, undertook a campaign in which diplomatic demands on his Western partners were combined with intimidation and pressures on the peoples of Greece, Turkey, and Iran in an attempt to strike for high stakes when the moment was ripe, counting on the postwar confusion in those states and the war-weariness of the Western powers.

Britain had not resisted Mustafa Kemal when he stood at the Straits in 1922, but had later settled for an international regime regulating their use in both peace and war. Would she resist Stalin when he demanded virtual control of the Straits in 1945? Would she allow Soviet troops to remain indefinitely in northern Iran, despite treaty commitments to withdraw? The British Government was prepared to play its historic role. Ernest Bevin was in the tradition of Lord Palmerston when he indignantly denounced Soviet demands in the Mediterranean as "a thrust across the throat of the British Empire." But the British Empire was not what it had been, nor was England herself the same. British diplomacy could not hope to repeat its successes of the past because it no longer had the same military and economic strength behind it. And if the basic character of the Eastern Question had not changed, many of the conditions under which the game was played had changed, including the nature of diplomacy itself. These changes will bear brief examination.

II

One new fact is the concentration of power in two states, the Soviet Union and the United States, and the consequent tendency of all other states to be drawn into the orbit of one or the other. Not only has the "Concert of Europe" disappeared, but the European powers no longer play the leading role in world affairs. This fact was not immediately evident, especially in the Middle East where Great Britain had so long been the dominant outside power. Yet the handwriting was on the wall by 1947, when the British turned over their responsibilities in Greece and Turkey to the United States and made the decision to give up the Palestine mandate as a hopeless job; and it was, above all,

American rather than British diplomacy which stiffened the Turks in their resistance to Soviet demands on the Straits and induced Stalin to withdraw from northern Iran.

Another new fact is the sudden appearance on the world stage of a great number of newly independent nations. In the Middle East alone Syria, Lebanon, and Transjordan joined Yemen, Egypt, Saudi Arabia, and Iraq as independent Arab states. Libya, Sudan, Tunisia, and Morocco came along later. The result was enormously to complicate the task of Western diplomacy and Western strategy in holding off Russia. There was still a vacuum of power in the area, as there had been for many years past, but the West could not fill that vacuum by arrangements to prop up the sovereignty of a single state like the declining Ottoman Empire nor could it exercise the power it had had under the mandate system to maintain necessary military positions and to control the decisions of Arab governments. The problem of finding a basis for relations with nationalist Turkey, which had proved so difficult after the First World War, was now multiplied manifold throughout the whole region.

The triumph of nationalism in the Middle East placed a terrific burden on Western diplomacy. First, the means had to be more subtle and more diverse. The persuasion of the diplomats and of the Foreign Office and State Department had to replace the authority of the High Commissioners and the Colonial Office. Second, the "Balkanization" of the Arab world placed Western decisions at the mercy of the instability and local conflicts of the new states, whose cooperation was necessary if the West was to hold the Russians at bay. In the nineteenth century the British were always up against the danger of being deceived or played off against another power by the Sublime Porte, but it was now a matter of taking that risk with over a dozen small nations glorying in the exercise of their newly won independence. Their own immediate problems, their differences among themselves, and their heritage of resentment against the West all helped to create openings for Soviet diplomacy and to complicate the task of the West.

British diplomacy at the close of the war had tried, by encouraging the formation of the Arab League, to establish some kind of working relationship with Arab nationalism that would make it possible to keep Britain's position more or less intact so far as defense of the area against Russia was concerned. Unfortunately from that viewpoint, the

League came to serve Egyptian rather than British diplomacy, and the prime aim of the former was to get the British out of Egypt, including the great base at Suez. The Arab League has shown no great effectiveness as an alliance or as an organization for security, but the West has been able to take little comfort from that fact. Its weakness has merely accentuated the complexities of the problems confronting Western diplomacy, while on those occasions when it has shown some strength and solidity the purpose has generally been to oppose Western "imperialism" or to intensify the campaign against Israel.

Certain other new elements in the picture have served to magnify these difficulties. One has been the atomic stalemate between the United States and the Soviet Union which makes each extremely wary of provoking a nuclear war which might mean national extinction. The fact of mutual deterrence between the "super-powers" gives the smaller states in the middle a freedom of diplomatic maneuver they did not have before. Nuclear power, moreover, because it cannot be used except in the last resort, is not easily translated into diplomatic gains. The disparity in military strength between Great Britain, now possessed of an arsenal of nuclear weapons, and Egypt is greater than it ever was, but the British are unable to deal with Egypt as in the days of Curzon and Cromer, or even those of Churchill and Sir Miles Lampson. The power of the West cannot be easily turned to advantage or used to coerce Middle Eastern nations, first because they know it will not be used against them, and second, because it is balanced by the power of the Soviet bloc.

The existence of the United Nations has had the same effect of strengthening the hand of the small states. In so far as the great powers choose to act through the United Nations—and they do in considerable degree because they are concerned with world opinion—they are bound by the existing rules which give every member one vote in the General Assembly, where the newly independent countries of the Middle East, Asia, and Africa can muster a formidable bloc of votes. The Arab states alone can outvote the British Commonwealth and the United States. Not only do the principles of the Charter, such as the renunciation of the use or threat of force, give a small state like Egypt in a dispute with stronger powers an immunity to coercion even when its own conduct has been most provocative, as the crisis of 1956 well illustrated; the procedures of the United Nations can also prevent the practical working out of problems, as we saw in the way Egypt dealt with the U. N. Emergency Force and the plan for a U. N. administration in Gaza.

These things are not said in disparagement of the United Nations, which it is in the interest of all to strengthen as a means of settling disputes and keeping the peace, but merely to point out the limitations which its existence and its processes place on the exercise of diplomacy. If the purpose of a state's diplomacy is to induce the consent of other states to certain propositions and actions, the United Nations provides opportunities and channels of communication which did not exist before. But it also provides for the veto in the Security Council and the two-thirds majority in the General Assembly. The Arab-Asian bloc under those rules becomes a more potent force in world affairs than it would otherwise be, and every Middle Eastern state gains an additional bit of bargaining power in its relations with the West.

III

We know that the Bolshevik leadership since 1917 has used diplomacy as an instrument of conquest, that Soviet diplomats are in fact agents of a conspiracy that reaches to all corners of the world, and that the agreements they make with non-Soviet states are but tactical moves in a grand strategy. They play the game of diplomacy simultaneously on two levels, that of official relations between sovereign states and that of the underground conspiracy. They will stress one aspect at one time or another, according to the tactics of the moment. Partly because the communist parties in the Middle East have been so singularly unsuccessful in attracting public support or in gaining political power, the Soviets in the last decade have found it more profitable to put the emphasis on official diplomacy, and their propaganda has been aimed less at winning converts to communism than at supporting the political or diplomatic tactic of the day.

Since Stalin's abortive attempt to break into the Middle East in 1945–1947 by the methods of threat, occupation, revolution, and civil war, Soviet policy has concentrated on other methods: the disruption of Western-sponsored alliances, the creation of trouble and fomentation of disputes, the assertion of the right to be heard on Middle Eastern questions, all aimed at the extrusion of Western influence from the region. These goals could best be pursued openly, in full view, not by conspiracy and revolution. Picking up the Leninist theme of the solidarity of the colonial peoples with the proletariat of the West and with the workers' state, Soviet Russia, Stalin's successors put on the mantle of Gandhi, Atatürk, and Zaghlul Pasha. They became the great defenders and advocates of Middle Eastern nationalism. Thus, they have sought to base their diplomacy on a historical force which has already proved its potency in sweeping Western control and Western influence out of large areas of the Middle East and Asia. It is a strategy which has many points in its favor: one is the fact that historically the West has been present in the area while Russia has not (save for parts of Turkey and Iran), and the force of nationalism is directed principally against the West; another is the irresponsibility with which the Soviets can act, for they profit from trouble, not from stability, from the exacerbation of disputes, not from their settlement.

The Soviet leaders have shown their grasp of the conditions and the limitations under which great powers must conduct their diplomacy in the Middle East today. Experts in stifling the sovereignty of states which come within their power, they have taken on the role of stout defenders of the sovereignty of Middle Eastern states in all their disputes with the West, whether the issue be military bases, "unequal" treaties, conditions for Western aid, or international control of the Suez Canal. Sensing the weakness of the Baghdad Pact, they attempt to undermine it by encouraging every local objection to it, rather than by trying to break it up by direct assault. They have made themselves patrons and partners of new leaders of the type of Abdel Nasser who are set on asserting themselves against the West and against Israel, but cannot do so without support from somewhere else. The question of Israel, which the Soviet Union helped to create by voting for the partition of Palestine in 1947, is made to order for this kind of diplomacy. Since 1954 the Soviet Union has given the Arab cause strong support, but without completely committing itself or placing its own vital decisions in the hands of irresponsible Arab rulers. The Soviet leaders do not propose to help the Arabs destroy Israel; they merely want to keep the issue alive while it serves the purpose of helping to eliminate the influence of Western powers from the Arab world.

All the other instruments of Soviet policy have been brought into play and coordinated with the diplomatic effort. Deliveries of arms and special trade deals are used to win the confidence of Middle Eastern governments worried about the military balance with their neighbors and markets for their major exports. Ceaseless propaganda preaches the common interests of the Soviet and Middle Eastern peoples and the sins of the common enemy. Reciprocal visits of all kinds of delegations, participation in trade fairs, the provision of experts and advisers for the armed forces, for engineering projects, and for agriculture—all these methods serve to extend Soviet influence. The very quantity of friendly contacts, moreover, tends to open the doors of public office and influence to communists and pro-Soviet elements on the local scene and to facilitate the covert operations which are a permanent instrument of Soviet policy.

IV

Western diplomacy, by contrast, operates under serious handicaps. Most obvious are those responsibilities to their own peoples which are a part of the democratic form of government: constitutional procedures, a due regard for public opinion, and a greater degree of consistency in policy and attachment to principle than is required of a totalitarian dictatorship. Because of those basic differences probably no democratic state could be expected to act with the speed, flexibility, and canny exploitation of opportunity which the Soviet Union has shown in the Middle East in the past few years. The Western democracies, moreover, have had special obstacles to surmount in dealing with that area, none the less difficult for being obstacles of their own creation. The heritage of "imperialism" and "colonialism," whatever might be the objective judgment of history on the period of Western domination, has made it next to impossible for Great Britain and France to establish relations of confidence with nations they formerly ruled. The British Government has been caught between its natural reluctance to give up positions and bases on which British security and prestige have so long depended—an attitude which always had behind it the "die-hard" elements of the Tory party and on some central issues, like Iran in 1951 or Suez in 1956, a much larger segment of party and public—and its need to find some new basis of understanding with Middle Eastern nationalism.

The United States, while not so tarred with the brush of imperialism (despite the efforts of Soviet propaganda), is not immune from the effects of the record of the past. The best example is the question of Palestine. A mixture of humanitarianism and domestic politics led the President of the United States to play a leading part in the decisions leading to the establishment of the State of Israel. Once that was done in the way it was done, a problem had been created that was beyond the capacity of Western diplomacy to solve. The Arab-Israel conflict goes so deep that the Western powers cannot satisfy either side and cannot find an acceptable middle ground. For the United States Government the difficulties inherent in the situation on the spot are compounded by the pressures on the domestic scene. The Eisenhower Administration is less influenced by such pressures than its predecessor, but it was made sharply aware, by the obvious mood of Congress when sanctions against Israel were under consideration early in 1957, of the limitations on its conduct of diplomacy.

Difficult as the task of Western diplomacy in the Middle East is, it need not be hopeless. There are, it would seem, two lines available to it in meeting the Soviet challenge. One is that of negotiation with the Soviet Union to achieve a settlement or at least an agreed balance which would remove some of the dangers of the situation and safeguard essential Western interests. The other is that of the continued use of all feasible means in relations with the Middle Eastern nations to check Soviet advances and maintain a position of strength.

The Soviet Government has served notice on the West that it is vitally concerned with the affairs of the Middle East and does not accept exclusion from the councils of the powers dealing with them: for example, in its denunciation of the Tripartite Declaration on Palestine, its policy statement of April 1956, and its proposals of February 1957 for four-power agreement on certain principles for settling the Middle East crisis. It has insisted that the Western powers handle critical situations not among themselves but in concert with the Soviet Union or through the United Nations, where the Soviet Union is represented and has the veto power. The Kremlin's diplomatic intervention in the crisis of November 1956, threatening Britain and France with rocket warfare and proposing joint military moves by the Soviet Union and the United States to "stop the aggressors," was a dramatic and ominous declaration of intention to play a leading part, if not the leading part, in the area.

The claim would appear to be justified. As the heir of Czarist Russia the Soviet Union is obviously directly concerned with what goes on in the Middle East if only by virtue of geographic proximity. It must be considered a "Middle Eastern power" if the criterion is the extent of its influence; it surely has a better claim to that status than France. Should the West recognize that fact and establish a new "concert of powers," including the Soviet Union, to deal with the Eastern Question as the "Concert of Europe" did in the past, by periodic consultation, negotiation, and settlement? Should the Middle East be added to the agenda of the periodic "Big Four" conferences that meet to negotiate on Germany and European security?

If one could assume a Soviet desire to negotiate for the purpose of stabilizing the situation and achieving settlements, the answer would be "yes." Everything we know about the nature of Soviet diplomacy, however, and everything that it has thus far done in the Middle East leads to the conclusion that it seeks not stabilization and settlement but continued conflict and confusion from which it can derive advantage.. So long as the Middle East remains part of the free world, outside the zone of direct Soviet control, the West has no need for new Yalta declarations (the U. N. Charter serves that purpose) or for bargains which attempt to fix spheres of influence or to prevent further Soviet advances by giving some kind of recognition to those already made. Soviet policy is dynamic, not static. To Moscow, negotiated bargains are useful to consolidate positions which are then used as bases for undermining the settlement reached and striking out for new gains. The diplomacy of settlement by partition, useful at times during the nineteenth century, offers nothing but more trouble now.

To be aware of these dangers is not to rule out all negotiations with the Soviet Union on the Middle East. It is impossible to ignore the fact that the Soviets, by gaining a foothold in Iraq and the United Arab Republic have acquired substantial bargaining power. There may be certain limited problems, such as the control of arms deliveries to Israel and its Arab neighbors, on which it would be wise to negotiate with the Soviets, provided that concessions in substance are not exchanged for mere promises and Soviet violations can be met by counter-actions resulting in no net disadvantage to the West. The machinery of the United Nations is also there to be used. If the Western nations do not make use of it to mobilize wide support for what they wish to do, they will find it being used by others to embarrass and to thwart them. They need not fear confronting and negotiating with Soviet representatives in the United Nations, so long as their own approach and their own propositions are soundly based on realities in the Middle East itself. It is safer to build on freedom than to try to save it through a bargain with its enemies. And only solid building can give the West the bargaining power to negotiate successfully.

The main task of the West, then, is to develop a diplomacy capable of helping the nations of the Middle East to build and consolidate their freedom and independence without disastrous conflict among themselves or dangerous flirtation with the Soviets; a diplomacy which can establish common interests with the Middle Eastern states so that a solid political basis exists for the necessary military and other arrangements necessary to Western security; a diplomacy that makes full use of the new techniques of propaganda, economic aid, technical cooperation, and cultural relations in a coordinated strategy; a diplomacy that unites the West in support of its irreducible common interests, while strengthening those ties which despite all antagonisms have continued to link the West with the Middle East. It is a formidable assignment, easier to prescribe than to execute.

Chapter 17

SMALL STATE DIPLOMACY

Annette Baker Fox

COUNSELLING the prince of a small state in sixteenth-century Italy Machiavelli wrote that since conflict according to law, the method of men, was not always sufficient, the ruler sometimes needed recourse to the method of the beasts. Thus the prince "must imitate the fox and the lion, for the lion cannot protect himself from traps and the fox cannot defend himself from wolves. One must therefore be a fox to recognize traps, and a lion to frighten wolves. Those that wish to be only lions do not understand this." [1] Like much other advice offered by the Florentine political thinker this counsel still seems valid for those with little armed might.

The small state with which this paper is concerned is a state lacking the military power to carry out a policy by force against a large state for any protracted period.[2] Such a definition excludes a number of countries which are not traditionally regarded as great powers but which for one reason or another have escaped most of the consequences of smallness. Close association with other states acting collectively, for example, Canada's and Australia's membership in the British Commonwealth of Nations, may remove such states from the category of "small" because they are unlikely to have to stand alone. Other states excluded are those difficult to subdue because they are inaccessibly distant from the centers of power or because of the vast area they cover. India and China may thus be eliminated. The patterns of diplo-

[1] *The Prince* (Modern Library edition), p. 64.

[2] See Klaus Knorr, *The War Potential of Nations* (Princeton University Press, 1956) for the importance in a prolonged struggle of the sheer quantity of military manpower and material relative to such qualitative elements as physical stamina and generalship. This point is particularly developed on pp. 29–31.

macy to be described will refer to the practices of the traditional small states of Europe (Scandinavia, the Low Countries, and the Balkans, among others), the Latin American states, Turkey, Iran, and Thailand, and the newer sovereignties of the Middle East, North Africa, and most of the Far East (Burma, Ceylon, Viet Nam, South Korea, the Philippines, and Indonesia).

In a conflict these states could not long stand up to a great power if they had to depend only upon the use of violence. But there are other sources of influence and other instruments of power than armed might. The tools of statecraft include the economic: compliance can sometimes be bought. They include also the ideological: propaganda can occasionally affect the decisions in another state. They include the legal: where international law has been broadened to protect particular rights of all states it does so regardless of their size. They include the organizational: combinations of states may cooperate successfully to further their common interests. For the small state the art of diplomacy is the government's strong arm. Far more than states with large military potential, the small states must be able to protect themselves by adroit diplomatic use of favorable opportunities for advancing their interest.

The small state has one important advantage over the great power: its interests are local and limited.[3] Thus all attention can be focused upon a single objective, whereas the large state, with varied and extensive interests, must balance these and give only a relatively fleeting glance towards a particular small power. With favorable conditions canny governments of various small states have successfully utilized negotiating techniques in order to resist the pressures of the great powers. Their performance helps to explain the paradox that while power in world politics has become increasingly concentrated in a very few great states, not only has the number of small states multiplied but they have also shown remarkable vitality.

II

There are small states and small states. There are also periods of time during which, and particular circumstances under which, a small state can enjoy a greater scope in its diplomacy than otherwise.

[3] For the tiny minority with colonial possessions, their interests are more than local but are still not world-embracing as in the case of the great powers.

There are secular changes in the political status of small powers on the world scene. The concept of the small state as puppet dates from before the First World War, when the several great states of Europe were able to enhance their power with respect to their rivals by controlling the actions of key small states. The First World War began in a quarrel over the small state of Serbia. The diplomatic maneuvers which lined up the small states with the great were carried on by small elites, even within the great powers, and the techniques of violence which they had at their disposal in case diplomacy failed were puny in scope compared with those available today. The inter-state game was played almost exclusively in the capitals of Europe, although the scramble for colonies and protectorates in Africa and the Far East was related to the contest. This period was, nevertheless, one of striving towards legal solutions for international conflict and towards a wider scope for international law—developments favoring the states with little military potential. Although during World War I neutrality ceased to be as respectable as it had been in the nineteenth century, some of the unambitious small states had some success in maintaining their neutrality even during this protracted and extensive great power conflict.

Following the war several new small states, formerly parts of larger legal entities, came into existence. Far from satisfying the cry for national self-determination this process encouraged in some areas further expression of parochialism, xenophobia, and irredentism. So weakened by division and the destruction of war the small states had few counters to use in their diplomacy and exhibited great confusion over their goals. Fortunately the great powers, their potential oppressors, were equally divided. Again, however, in the years after 1919 the League of Nations helped to provide for the more stable small states a legal and moral status not earlier available. Some of the small states of Europe took leading roles in League deliberations,[4] and the European states were joined in world politics by the small states of Latin America, whose prestige was enhanced by membership in this international organization for regulating conflicts.

With the world-wide depression and the growing power of the

[4] An interesting illustration may be found in Erik Lönnroth, "Sweden: The Diplomacy of Undén," *The Diplomats*, Gordon A. Craig and Felix Gilbert, eds. (Princeton University Press, 1953), pp. 86–99.

Fascist countries which scoffed at the law, security through legal protection and collective action once more became a vain hope.[5] In some of the small states there appeared increasingly vocal extremist groups, groups which had more in common with the countries then threatening the peace than with their own compatriots. Confusion within these countries became worse confounded. Some East European leaders, seeing Hitler's violations of international agreements rewarded rather than punished, believed they could follow suit and thus revise unfavorable treaties. Others, in observing the helpless behavior of the Western democracies, decided that they must at least compromise, even if they did not cooperate, with Nazi Germany, in order to save themselves. Among the small states of Western Europe the fear of becoming involved in another great power conflict, this time through membership in the organization to which they had earlier looked for protection, caused their withdrawal from plans for collective action against an aggressor. Thus, on July 23, 1938, Belgium, Holland, Luxemburg, Norway, Sweden, Denmark, and Finland issued a declaration in which, without reverting to traditional neutrality, they counted themselves out of any further punitive action by the League of Nations against a law-breaker. The failure of sanctions against Italy roused fright and disillusionment; Munich dealt the *coup de grâce* to their expectation of safety through a combination of the peace-loving. These small would-be neutrals then sought to sit very quietly in the corner, hoping no one would notice them. When the deluge came, some went down like nine-pins; others escaped, for reasons to be discussed later. Many of the unhappy states of Eastern Europe, however, became the prototypes of the satellite state so familiar since the war, some of them before being physically conquered by outsiders.

The tremendous upheaval of World War II brought changes of great significance to the small states. The colonial revolution now surged all over the globe, carried on by former subject peoples who had found their voices and were ready to use them without restraint. This development would have occurred quite independently of the equally important and more readily recognized conflict between the free world

---

[5] The reflection of this change in the career of a diplomat of one small power may be seen in Paul Zinner, "Czechoslovakia: The Diplomacy of Benes," *The Diplomats, op. cit.,* pp. 100–122.

and the Soviet Union. Nevertheless, the simultaneous unfolding of the two series of events has related them closely.

The alignment of forces around two poles, represented by the superpowers, Russia and the United States, had disastrous consequences for some small states in the Soviet orbit. Meanwhile it offered some additional bargaining strength to others outside either orbit.[6] For the small states in the North Atlantic group the coalition techniques and distribution of weapons were exceptionally reassuring guarantees that within this circle no war could be planned against any member by another. When in 1956 a certain tendency toward depolarization became evident, the small states, which had felt the pressure of the larger Western powers, began to act more independently, and even one of Russia's satellites appeared to have a certain but limited initiative. The "puppets" seemed to be pulling their own leading strings.

These developments have taken place concurrently with two other post-war changes in the source of influence and the method of exercising power. First, nuclear weapons, threatening the destruction of all civilized life if not life itself, once appeared to distinguish the superpowers more sharply from the other states. Paradoxically, their very potency has, up to now, inhibited the great powers from pushing their quarrels too far, while the hydrogen bomb is unadapted to exercising control over the small states. The governments of some of these states can therefore dare to pursue their own policies without expectation that these will bring on the ultimate conflict.

Secondly, the creation and functioning of an almost universal international organization, the United Nations, has offered to the small states, particularly non-European states, unprecedented scope and opportunity for exercising their diplomacy. As a consequence of the assumption of state equality which is implicit in the general international organization, the small states as a category have a relatively large representation in United Nations activities. Since the great powers, which possess the special veto privilege in the Security Council, have been unable to agree on many issues, these have been aired in the General Assembly. Here the small state's vote weighs the same as that of a big state, and here the formation of voting blocs of

[6] One need only mention in passing the unprecedented availability to the underdeveloped countries of foreign economic assistance.

small powers has increased their influence. Moreover, the vastly increased network of communications has contributed to a changed perspective among the political leaders of great powers. Particular small states are no longer merely names in a history book or atlas but have become the homes of real and not easily manipulated people. The greatly increased popular control over foreign policy in some of the large states puts further into the past the time when their governments could treat certain small states as pawns on the international chess board. Now the threatened small state can reach public opinion in the constitutional democracies.

III

This brings us to the actors. What kinds of small states came into the international spotlight in the 1950's? There are some small states which are scarcely "considered" at all by the great power governments, since they are outside the arena of world politics. There are others at the very focus of great power rivalry. The remainder lie somewhere along the continuum of power between those of no concern to any great power and those of crucial concern to more than one, at least momentarily. Toward the weak end of the continuum are the small states so far inside the orbit of one of the great powers that their position is seldom actively disputed. The small state in which one and only one great power is greatly interested is in a precarious position. The small state with which two or more great powers are concerned would superficially appear to be in even greater danger, but the very danger provides the opportunity for its diplomacy. Over and over again small power diplomats have demonstrated their ability favorably to modify the expectations of those pressing them when there are great power competitors to be considered by those making the demand.

Even among the small states inside the orbit of a great power there is a vast difference. For example, the Latin American countries behind the protecting wall provided by the inter-American version of the Monroe Doctrine vary greatly from the satellite states introduced to the world by Hitler and more completely developed by Stalin. The United States is always concerned about Central and South America, if not continually attentive. Yet these areas are at the periphery of European great power interest when they are considered at all. Freedom of diplomatic action is enjoyed by all Latin American states, whose chief limitations are economic weakness and the certainty that they could not adopt a communist form of government.[7] For the fully co-ordinated satellite state there can be no diplomacy in the usual sense of the word. As with domestic affairs, the satellite government's moves are all dictated from Moscow and no bargaining can take place with any other state except as a mouthpiece for the Soviet Union.[8]

An equally novel kind of actor among the small states since World War II is the former dependency. In most of this group the majority of the inhabitants is colored. While the power of the satellite was diminishing to zero, that of states until recently colonies was rapidly rising, making difficulties not only for the great powers but also for some of the older small powers, especially in Europe.

Just as they differ in their internal political, economic, and social characteristics, so the satellite and former dependency differ markedly from the older small states of Western Europe in the circumstances conditioning their freedom of diplomatic action and in the goals sought. In both the satellite and ex-colony there have been revolutionary class tensions making any government's hold precarious. There has been no constitutional consensus, for bitter national, racial,

[7] The Guatemala incident of 1954 illustrates this limitation, which has not applied to other kinds of dictatorships.

[8] The process by which such a state becomes a satellite and the way in which it may free itself, though germane to an account of small power diplomacy, are more properly the subject of a study of revolution, counter-revolution and the *coup d'état*. The external condition—a re-balancing of the great powers with respect to each other—is only a part of the story. A summary of the process of becoming a satellite can be found in Cyril Black, "People's Democracies of Eastern Europe," *European Political Systems*, Taylor Cole ed. (New York, 1953), pp. 188–265. Illuminating first-hand accounts for particular states are Stephen D. Kertesz, *Diplomacy in a Whirlpool: Hungary between Nazi Germany and Soviet Russia* (Notre Dame, 1953) and Ivo Duchacek, "The Strategy of Communist Infiltration: Czechoslovakia, 1944–48," *World Politics*, April, 1950, pp. 345–372, and "The February Coup in Czechoslovakia," *ibidem*, July, 1950, pp. 511–532. A detailed account of the Yugoslav break with the Soviet Union may be found in Robert Lee Wolff, *The Balkans in Our Time* (Cambridge, Mass., 1956), pp. 352–429. Contrasting accounts of the experience of Czechoslovakia, Hungary, Rumania, Bulgaria, Albania, Poland, the Baltic states, East Germany, and Yugoslavia, in addition to two which never became satellites, Austria and Finland, may be found in Stephen D. Kertesz, ed., *The Fate of East Central Europe* (Notre Dame, 1956.)

ideological, and religious as well as economic hatreds divide one group from another.[9] Their governments have often lacked the diplomatic skill which comes from long experience on the international scene and which in turn invokes additional respect from the representatives of great powers.

With important variations, economic distress and low standards of living mark these countries. Pressing economic and social reforms have taken second place to nationalist agitation. The ex-colonies are far less developed economically than the states of Eastern Europe, although even these are not so industrialized as Western Europe. In addition, the ex-colonies are racially distinct and have non-European cultures. Thus their perspectives differ from older small states. Yet the perspectives in the satellites have also been different from Western European attitudes, because like the colonial countries their leaders have tended to look abroad for their salvation, although they have not excoriated the givers of aid as have some colonial leaders. Having so small a stake in the present distribution of power, politically interested and active people in these two kinds of state often appear much more desperate and irrational than those of Western Europe.[10]

The small states of Western Europe met the ultimate test of power during World War II. Some, like the Low Countries, Norway, and Denmark, were engulfed by the war despite their efforts to remain out, but all survived and are again among the strongest of the small states in their relations with the great powers. Two states on Russia's western frontier also belong in this category, Finland and Turkey, for they escaped the plight of all those lying between the two.

IV

Unlike the comparatively satisfied small countries of Europe and Latin America (since the Good Neighbor Policy), many political leaders in Russia's satellites and the newly-independent states of Africa and Asia are intent on throwing off the continuing restraints of some larger power, rather than merely standing ready to resist their ex-

[9] Even Czechoslovakia from the late 1930's onward began to exhibit these characteristics, and the Nazis' treatment of Czechs and Slovaks over seven years made far easier the Russian task of Sovietization than the Western democracies realized at the time. Cf. Ivo Duchacek, "Czechoslovakia," in *The Fate of East Central Europe*, pp. 179–218, esp. 179–197.

[10] Other reasons for their erratic behavior will appear below.

tension.[11] In Poland the struggle for an independent foreign and domestic policy which came to a head in 1956 was confined by the legitimate government to a conflict capable of compromise, a loosening of ties with the Soviet Union. The leadership continued to be communist and membership in the Warsaw Pact was still accepted. In Hungary, on the other hand, the rebellion aimed at the complete overthrow of the regime which had been imposed by the Soviets, and, unlike the Polish revolt, this one was ruthlessly quelled. Moroccan and Tunisian leaders, having obtained legal independence of France, have given moral support to the Algerian rebels, who are seeking the same status for an area the French regard as part of the metropolitan country. In Egypt, where complete independence had already been secured, the Nasser government sought to extend Egypt's control over an international waterway running through Egyptian territory.

Within the ex-colonies there is an additional aim, to attain the degree of respect of the older states which has long been enjoyed by others. For example, the Indonesians have not been content with independence for themselves but have sought to wrest Irian in New Guinea from their former mother country. Such states press to eliminate every remnant of empire, whether to attach it to themselves or to detach it in some way from the colonial powers. In the latter pursuit the former dependencies have been vociferous leaders within the United Nations whenever non-self-governing territories are discussed.

Leaders of the small states creating problems today are thus demanding an expansion in the scope of their decision-making. In the colonial world this means alterations in governmental status, or increases in territory, or the abolition of economic, judicial, and military concessions, or a re-distribution of the world's wealth. The rebellious groups within the satellite world look toward the restoration of their sovereign rights to choose their own form of government, police themselves, control their own economies, get rid of foreign troops, and conduct their own diplomacy. Like leaders in the ex-colonies the rebels in the satellites want to choose their own diplomatic friends and trade with whom they please. So impotent are the satellites generally that there is no current evidence of another objective often found among

[11] The leadership referred to here is often without government authority in satellites.

the leaders in the colonial world. This is a desire among some politicians not only to direct the course of their own countries without outside interference but also to influence affairs beyond their boundaries, as does Nasser in the Arab world. This tendency is also discernible in the ex-satellite of Yugoslavia.

Delineation of these several objectives is easier than establishing priorities among them. Another distinctive feature of the colonial countries and of the states on their way to becoming satellites has been the mixture and confusion of goals, some of which seem incompatible. Thus the demand for aid in industrialization, which the underdeveloped crave as a means of increasing their power, runs counter to the claim to no external interference in financial and administrative affairs which must go with such aid to make it effective.

For the small states of Western Europe in their time of crisis the situation was far different. For them there was one supreme objective upon which to concentrate: survival, which meant for their diplomats no belligerency and no military occupation. If occupation was unavoidable, the next aim was to resume their former exercise of sovereignty as soon as possible. This simplicity of objectives made their task less formidable than that of some Eastern European governments at the same time. Yet the fact that some of the western states were overrun by the Germans in spite of the use of diplomatic techniques employed by the successful neutrals underlines the limiting conditions under which a small state can resist the pressures of a great power.

V

The achievement of some small European states in World War II in maintaining their neutrality, although subjected to tremendous pressures from both sides to participate, with belligerents on their doorstep and, in some cases, surrounded by one power, suggests what might be possible for other small states placed in an equally precarious situation.[12] Within the boundaries set by the general balance of power

---

[12] Some of the ensuing observations are elaborated upon in my study, *The Power of Small States: Diplomacy in World War II,* to be published by the University of Chicago Press in September, 1959. This book deals with five small would-be neutrals on the periphery of the European theater. It makes a detailed and comparative analysis of these countries' diplomacy, crisis by crisis, in terms of the demands made on them, the expectations of the participants, the techniques employed, and the political consequences. The states so examined are Sweden,

between opposing great states there was often some choice for the small state's diplomats. The choice in fact depended upon the balance. A number of factors can be isolated which, in various combinations, increased the small state's power to hold its own course during the war. At any given moment the small state's good fortune was in proportion to the number of great powers with differing demands which were interested in its actions and able to express their interest by practical means.[13] Turkey was so situated at the outbreak of the war, when negotiations for a tripartite alliance with Britain and France had advanced sufficiently so that the Turks could hold the Russians at arms' length when confronted with demands for, *inter alia*, joint control of the Turkish Straits. Meanwhile, the Germans, faced with the prospect of a Turkey allied with Britain and France, felt obliged to ask of Turkey only that it remain non-belligerent, and thus set a course for their relations which lasted not greatly modified throughout the war.

The closer the balance of military strength between the opposing sides in the area of the small state at the time of heavy pressure from one side, the better the chance for successful resistance. Only Finland among those whose independence was threatened late in 1944 by victorious Russia was able to survive without this condition. The proximity of friendly Sweden, a small state, but a strong small state, may not have been decisive, by itself, but it did mean the Finns received some outside economic and diplomatic support.

Despite the need for balance, it was advantageous—almost essential —for the small state to be located away from the most direct line of contact between the contending great powers. Except for the special

---

Norway, Finland, Spain, and Turkey. In the Royal Institute of International Affairs, *Survey of International Affairs, 1939–1946: The War and the Neutrals* (Oxford University Press, London, 1956) may be found a chronicle of the wartime experience of the European states remaining neutral—Portugal, Eire, Switzerland, Spain, Sweden, and Turkey—and the British economic warfare involving them.

[13] Fatal for the future European satellites of the Soviet Union was the free hand secured in this region by the Russians, who had the only military forces there when the war drew to a close. For all practical purposes the British and Americans abandoned any responsibility in the area in order to obtain greater latitude of action elsewhere. Cf. Philip E. Mosely, "Hopes and Failures: American Policy toward East Central Europe, 1941–47," in *The Fate of East Central Europe*, pp. 51–74.

case of Switzerland, the successful neutrals in the European theater all lay on the periphery of the continent, and thus had a better chance to stay out than, for example, the Low Countries, which were situated in between Hitler and the Western Allies. The small state was the more likely to slide past the critical time of pressure, if the leaders of the encroaching great powers had to be concerned with a great number of interests. Spain under Hitler's pressure for transit to Gibraltar was fortunate in that the Germans were increasingly concerned about the Eastern Mediterranean. Furthermore, if the side making a demand was not unified in pressing a particular policy, the small state had greater opportunities for resistance. In this way Sweden could put off total embargoes on certain strategic goods going to Germany until Hitler's retaliatory power was weak. As in the case of Spain, the British and Americans could not agree on how hard the Allies should press these neutrals to stop the shipment to Germany of particular kinds of material for the Nazis' war industry. If the unacceptable demands came from a power whose government was under a moral inhibition not to use force providing there was a feasible alternative, the small state was more likely to escape a violent reaction to its refusal. Thus was Eire saved from British occupation despite the harm the Germans were enabled to inflict on Britain as a result of the strictly neutral policy of the Irish.

These conditions involving freedom to choose one policy rather than another are for the most part imposed from outside the small state. There are other conditions equally difficult to alter which are imposed from within. Thus, the more impressive the physical barriers to invasion existing on the small state's borders, the more formidable its ability to resist appeared to a would-be invader—and the more desirable an easier alternative route to the invader's goal. The classic example is Switzerland, but Spain derived much protection from the Pyrenees and Turkey from the Transcaucasian ranges. If the small state controlled one or more scarce commodities of strategic value to the great powers its bargaining position was measurably improved. Turkey had its chrome, Sweden its iron ore, Spain and Portugal their wolfram. These raw materials were so important to the German armament industry that the Nazis were careful not to interrupt their flow by hostile actions, while at the same time the small states involved could obtain concessions from the Allies in return for stemming the flow.

The greater the resources within the small state for maintaining its economy without foreign trade the less vulnerable it was to outside economic pressure. Norway and Sweden improved their economic position by large-scale stockpiling prior to hostilities. Thus they were far less vulnerable to British economic warfare measures than in World War I.

Another unalterable condition was the age of the small state. How long had it existed as an entity with which great power diplomats had to deal respectfully? A number of the small European countries have long diplomatic traditions and several of them, for example, Spain, Sweden, and Turkey, seem still to dwell in the aura of former greatness. In World War II great power negotiators tended to treat diplomats from such countries as if they expected them to be more resourceful bargainers than those without a long history of participation in European politics. One of a number of factors explaining why Germany did not occupy Hungary until March of 1944 was a similar history of diplomatic practice by Hungarians.[14] The importance of the factor of custom may be seen where it was absent: consider the cavalier British treatment of Norway which developed into a willingness to embark on what would have been an invasion of Norwegian territory and the disdainful Russian treatment of Finland in 1939 ending in the rash attack upon the Finns. These two small states still presented the image of the inexperienced newcomer. The longer the diplomatic tradition of the small state in world affairs, the greater the caution with which the opposing sides pressed their demands. (This did not protect Holland and Belgium from Hitler, but it did moderate the pressures put upon them by the British to bend their neutrality toward the Allies prior to the Blitzkrieg.) Similarly the very ancient tradition of Switzerland as a neutral helped to inhibit the great powers from deciding to impair its venerable status.

[14] Cf. a memorandum containing a Nazi proposal for the absorption of Hungary dating from this period which stated:

"In spite of the extraordinary geopolitical and economic importance of Hungary for the Reich, German foreign policy has made no serious attempt during recent years to gain an influence on developments in Hungary . . .

"Those Hungarians who look back, in the field of foreign policy, to a centuries-old tradition as a great power, incline fundamentally towards a conspiratorial policy. The complete lack of German attempts at influence has inevitably trained them to follow that policy of playing off one power against another which has now attained an intolerable character. . . ." Kertesz, *Diplomacy in a Whirlpool*, p. 237.

Given some of these conditions favoring successful resistance to great power pressure during war-time, there were other advantageous factors which were much more easily manipulated by the government of a threatened small state. Very important during such a period of danger were the ability and willingness of the small state to employ force to the limit in order to resist invasion, and of course, it was important that the great powers perceive the ability and willingness. The determination and military preparedness of Switzerland and Sweden were important ingredients in their escape from invasion. The lack of pre-war defense measures in Norway and Finland made them look like easy prey. The Finns' resourceful and stubborn, last-ditch resistance later earned them much of the freedom which they continue to enjoy though twice defeated. The two-months' Norwegian struggle against the Germans, far more prolonged than any other Blitzkrieg struggle, has suggested what might have been accomplished with adequate preparation in this touch-and-go operation.

At the same time that self-defense was stressed by the successful neutral, a conciliatory approach to particular demands was desirable. The Spaniards provided the Germans with fair words and such favors as the uninhibited circulation in Spain of their propaganda and intelligence agents and, on occasion, the use of Spanish territorial waters for refueling German naval vessels. Thus they kept alive the Germans' hope of Spanish aid in an attack on Gibraltar until disillusionment set in too late for effective counter-action. Where the great power's dominance was unquestionable, concessions were useful so long as the main bulwarks of the small state's integrity were not yielded. Among these was the right of military transit.

When Finland was forced to grant the Russians transit to a military base obtained in the treaty that concluded the Winter War, the Finns attempted to balance this concession by granting a similar privilege to the Germans (passage northward to the border of occupied Norway) in return for arms with which to resist further Russian advances. This was the beginning of the end of the Finnish chance to stay neutral. Important steps in the encirclement of Hungary were marked by permission granted to German troops to pass through, first to Rumania, in October of 1940, a privilege which included the stationing of German military personnel in Hungary, and then in April of 1941 to Yugoslavia, thus enabling the Germans to conquer that neighbor.

Sweden alone among the successful neutrals granted a belligerent the right of transit, but this privilege was so circumscribed in use and duration and the circumstances so special to the case that the Swedes avoided the disastrous consequences likely to have befallen any other small state. Having resisted very strong German pressure to permit transit of military men and material during the active phase of the Norwegian resistance, the Swedes conceded this right on a limited basis on June 19, 1940. The formal war in Norway had ended, the Germans were victorious on the continent, and the Swedes were momentarily expecting a fate like that of their Scandinavian neighbors. The Swedes withdrew the privilege in the summer of 1943, when the Germans began to be in difficulties elsewhere. The Swedish Government also permitted one division of armed German soldiers to pass from Norway to Finland immediately after the German attack upon Russia. This relieved their friends in Norway of unwanted troops while reinforcing their friends in Finland in resisting the Russian attack. One reason the Swedes dared to permit military transit was their control over iron ore supplies which the Germans regarded as indispensable to the prosecution of the war.

Equal to the vital question of transit privileges as a most dangerous concession was the use of the small state's territory for a military base. Spain and Turkey could not be persuaded by any kind of subterfuge to become belligerents so that their countries might in reality serve as springboards. The Turks' reluctance was reinforced by the fear that such a move, so strongly urged by Churchill, would serve the Russians as an excuse to enter Turkey.

The sovereign rights to make alliances, to declare war, and to enjoy exclusive jurisdiction over internal security against enemies of the state were jealously guarded by the successful neutrals. Finland, forced to war but free at the war's end, also resisted very strongly any encroachment on these rights. In spite of the presence of German troops in the far north, the Finns refused to break off relations with the United States and until the bitter end to conclude a written pact with Germany.[15] Finland's censorship was self-imposed, as in the successful neutral countries.

---

[15] Although the Germans finally wrested an agreement of no separate peace from the Finnish president, the Finns declared it no longer valid when the office changed hands. The president resigned after the Finns secured part of the military

It was essential for the small state that the people maintain political unity in the face of subversive efforts, loyally support the government, and preserve their self-control and their single-minded devotion to the state even when under terrible strain. These very difficult tasks were notably performed by the Finns in their two David and Goliath struggles with the Russians, 1939–40 and 1941–44. Even though this tiny state had to fight twice, its fate differed markedly from Russia's neighbors further south, which did not exhibit Finland's internal political stability and national solidarity. Civic solidarity and self-imposed discipline greatly aided the Swiss, who had to deal with very serious efforts at subversion. Whether or not a state was a democracy or a dictatorship did not appear to affect its success as a neutral in World War II; Sweden, Switzerland, and Eire were democracies, while Spain, Portugal, and Turkey were dictatorships. Where leadership was conspicuously strong, the absence of social cohesion appeared to be less important.

Related to internal unity as a condition for success was the ability to endure deprivation of other values for the sake of the main goal. Cherished democratic liberties had to be curtailed in Sweden and Switzerland. The conflicts over different political questions, such as minorities, had to be suppressed. Irredentism had no place in the small state's diplomacy, especially when the more important objective of survival was at stake. The revisionist aims of some of the states of East Central Europe made them particularly vulnerable to pressures from either the Germans or the Russians or both.[16]

The cry for Gibraltar was a useful propaganda technique in Spanish dealings with the British, but Franco could not be induced to receive it at the hands of the Germans. None of the small states which survived and stayed in the free world could be lured by promises of favored treatment at the peace table, especially in questions of territorial readjustment.

Of the greatest advantage to the small state were good relations with neighboring small and middle-sized states. Not only did this

aid which was the price of the pact. Cf. John H. Wuorinen, ed., *Finland and World War II, 1939–1944* (New York, 1948), pp. 173–176, and *The Memoirs of Marshal Mannerheim*, tr. Eric Lewenhaupt (London, 1953), pp. 481–483.

[16] The dangers of such aims are illuminated by a map showing "The Territorial Evolution of Hungary from 1910 to 1952," in Kertesz, *Diplomacy in a Whirlpool*, pp. 102–103.

decrease the small state's vulnerability, but on occasion provided non-military support. Finland was a close friend of the other Northern states and Turkey and Spain had buried conflict with their closest historical rivals, Greece and France, respectively.[17] On the other hand, chauvinism and hostility marked the relations between the Eastern European states, which greatly weakened their chance to escape satellite status. Hungary was in the most unenviable position at the close of the war, having no active supporters anywhere.[18]

The small state profited when it could draw upon the services of negotiators with long experience and flexibility as well as nerve and the ability to dissimulate. These characteristics were necessary in order to play a very complicated and closely calculated game of diplomacy particularly suited to the small state. The players had to have available superior political and military intelligence regarding the great powers and had to recognize accurately their dispositions, as the Turks understood the Russian intentions in 1943–44. The game consisted in being able to balance the demands of opposing sides while obtaining concessions from each. For example, even during the height of Hitler's power the Swedes and Spaniards escaped violent retribution for trading with the West while they continued to receive supplies sent from Germany to check any growth in their dependence upon Germany's enemies. Until the last year of the war they were able to maintain a similar posture with the West. Although Sweden was otherwise completely cut off except by air from the West, the Swedes were able to maintain the "Gothenburg traffic" with the acquiescence of each side, for both recognized advantages in not pushing too far their power over Swedish overseas trade.[19] In this way Sweden avoided

[17] Turko-Greek hostility was only revived fifteen years later when the Greeks raised the Cyprus issue. During the Greek struggle with the Axis the Turks provided relief at some danger to themselves even though they did not give military aid (which they were under no legal obligation to do).

[18] See Kertesz, *op. cit.*, pp. 86 and 101ff., for the disadvantages flowing from such isolation.

[19] Under this system the British agreed to a limited number of Swedish ships sailing to and from Gothenburg, on condition that the ships carry British navicerts, follow British-recommended routes, and not submit to German contraband control, and that Sweden accept the British rationing of its imports. For the most part the Germans permitted safe conduct for ships sailing between this city and non-Allied ports. W. N. Medlicott, *The Economic Blockade*, Vol. I (London, 1952), 629–630; Francis La Ruche, *La Neutralité de la Suède* (Paris, 1953), pp. 127–130.

the fatal situation in which the small state's economy and living conditions depend almost entirely on one side, the first step towards satellite status. Switzerland's economic relations with Germany and the Allies followed a pattern rather similar to that of Sweden. The balancing techniques employed by such states were not without their disadvantages—each belligerent occasionally punished the small neutral with economic weapons—but the costs were small compared to the gains. Since the dominance of a particular great power in the region of the small state was likely to change momentarily, the small power diplomats had to be ready to make a shift with lightning rapidity towards the side of increasing power while not appearing to the losing side to have withdrawn any favors of substance. The Spaniards did so over night with the Allied landing at Casablanca.

The success of the small state's diplomacy during wartime, whether belligerent or not, depended upon the ability to procrastinate until the timeliness of a particular demand had disappeared and the attention of the great powers was diverted elsewhere. Finland, long at the point of military defeat, staved off until September, 1944, the conclusion of an armistice. Then the Germans were too involved elsewhere to retaliate close to the concentration of population, while the Soviet interest in more vital centers of power kept Russian troops from occupying Finland. This was an important reason why Finland did not become a satellite. An unwanted decision could sometimes be deferred by holding out the possibility of making the desired concession—at a price—and then setting the rate so high that the great power was unwilling to pay. The Spaniards and the Turks negotiated over a lengthy and critical period with the Germans and British, respectively, on the terms under which they would enter the war but they never had to make good on their proposals.

Small state diplomats sometimes sought to distract a demanding great power by calling attention to the costliness of the desired concession in terms of the belligerent's other interests. Or they would try to minimize the value of such a concession to the great power's war effort. They frequently worked on the fears of the importunate government that a concession would bring costly retaliation from the enemy. All these arguments were used by Norway and Sweden in early 1940 when the British and French threatened an incursion into

Norwegian territorial waters to stop German iron ore traffic. The Allies temporarily turned to other means for accomplishing their purpose.

At other times small power negotiators found it useful to trade off less critical concessions to avoid yielding more vital points. In June, 1941, the Turks concluded a general pact of friendship with the Germans, who had reached their border, instead of granting the military transit for which the Germans were pressing; then the Germans turned eastward to Russia, leaving Turkey on the sidelines. It has been said of Franco that his strength lay in "knowing how to wait."

The successful neutrals were able to draw on the interest of each belligerent in maintaining some countries outside the war in order to collect information about, and to facilitate communication with, the enemy. Switzerland, above all, was a valued "window" for both Germans and Allies, but like Geneva the capitals of the other neutrals were also very useful listening posts.

Secrecy in negotiations and no public declarations of a proposed policy were universally sought by the successful small power diplomats. It was desirable to appear "uncertain" or "vacillating" so long as the small state seemed to keep its place on the list of possible adherents. The Germans treated the Turks cautiously because they had no assurance but only a hope that they might win Turkey over to the Tripartite Pact. The small state could occasionally escape responsibility for leaning in one direction if the impression were blurred by acts of some officials, leading business groups, or the press. However, the successful government could never be faced with a *fait accompli* by one official or unofficial agent in serious conflict with the basic official policy.

The successful small state diplomats were adept at exploiting divisions within the demanding side, playing off one opinion group against another. On more than one occasion the Spanish reduced the weight of the oil sanction against them by manipulating the differences between the British and Americans and among the Americans themselves.

The outer limits to small state diplomacy during war were set by the military power of the belligerents. Within them the small state diplomats were often seriously circumscribed by the great powers' economic pressure, the method characteristically employed by the belligerents to influence neutrals. While a small state's diplomacy could make an invasion look too expensive for the belligerent's objective, this judgment would usually intensify economic warfare conducted on and through the neutral. Eventually all the small neutrals had to yield to the Allied demands to stop selling strategic materials to the enemy.

The small states' diplomacy proved unsuccessful in other ways. Blocs of the militarily weak crumpled at the time of crisis for which they were designed. At the crucial point each of the small states had to fall back upon its own resources; none of the small and half-hearted groupings added up to significant power compared to a great state. Most of the small states were afraid to be allied to a great power, seeking their security instead by avoidance of alignments. The Turks did not share this dread, but their alliance with Britain and France proved no support when these great powers reached the nadir of their strength. The tripartite association did, however, give the Germans and Russians pause earlier, when they were making demands on Turkey in the fall of 1939. The leaders of the small states universally regarded a long war as more disastrous than a short war, especially because it meant for them a Russian victory. Thus, they made numerous attempts at mediation, all of which proved conspicuous or inconspicuous failures to influence any side.

The ultimate weapon available to the small state involved in a great power tug-of-war was the possibility of fighting on the enemy's side, but this was a dangerous threat. Retaliation for such a policy would come, if it came at all, from the opposing great power, and its direct force would be upon the small state rather than the enemy. Without openly proclaiming such an intention, the Spaniards were able to extract profit from the Allied expectation that they were wavering towards joining the Axis. They lost little from daring to permit the impression to continue, while simultaneously safeguarding themselves from the Fascists.

Most of the factors described above as favoring success in small power diplomacy were not peculiarly useful to small states; they would also have helped the governments of powers with greater military potential. Larger states, however, were less dependent upon these conditions and did not have to calculate so closely how far and how much to concede without incurring violence or losing their autonomy.

In all the successful small state diplomacy the strength of one great power was borrowed to eke out the limited power of the small state in dealing with another great power. While the small state was unfortunate in being, if only momentarily, a point of conflict between great powers, it also reaped an advantage from not being entirely within the domain of one. Spain at the Straits of Gibraltar and Turkey at the Turkish Straits were a constant concern to the contending parties in World War II, and they could not have defended their positions alone, but both were spared participation in the war. These states were neither puppets nor pawns. They were rather like small sailboats, which used the more powerful elements to drive them obliquely along their course, tacking when necessary and constantly trimming their sails to gain the greatest advantage from the wind but never pressing too close to it nor venturing into the open sea.

To say that under certain circumstances there were techniques and choices available to certain small states to preserve their integrity is not to say that such means were open to particular well-intentioned public servants. It was not enough for an individual to be wise if he could not influence his government's conduct. In some of the Eastern European states the odds were against the efforts of such patriots, partly because of conditions within their own countries. Not all their disasters were inflicted from outside.

VI

The conditions and techniques for successful small state resistance to great power pressure applied especially to a time of war. The choice available depended upon the small states' influencing the expectations of the great powers, so as to promote the small state's goal—to be let alone. This is therefore a different situation from that faced by leaders in a satellite or a colonial state seeking to enlarge their share in decision-making when no global war is being fought. That such leaders in the satellites are not usually in control of their government is another difference. Revolutionary tension is equally marked in the ex-colonies although manifested differently. For example, leaders like Nasser act as though their unsteady regimes could be made more secure by foreign ventures. Unlike Franco, when he remained unconvinced that entering the war would unify the Spanish people, they do not all recognize that external conflict may end in domestic disintegration rather than a more stabilized regime.

Between the war-time neutrals and the small states presenting problems since World War II there is a difference in perspectives but there is a similarity also. The ex-dependencies' fear of white western colonialism and relative insensitivity to the threat of Communist Russia may be compared to the general attitude among the small states of Europe during World War II although the devil's identity has been reversed. Most of the latter were at one period ready to accept, if reluctantly, a German victory which looked likely anyway, but they were almost universally terrified of the expansion of Russian imperialism. Thus they were nearly as far away from the perspectives of the Western powers at the time as is the colonial world today.

In spite of the differences between the World War II period and the present, the general condition of great power rivalry continues. So do the general categories of great power measures for seeking influence over the small: violence (including intimidation); economic pressure (both lure and deprivation); propaganda (favorable to the emanating state and to the small state, unfavorable to the foe); diplomacy (including action in the United Nations); and subversion (whereby the small state becomes a satellite through the rule of some of its own citizens dominated by an external power). That this competition for uncommitted small states has been waged between two poles rather than being the three-cornered contest of World War II is not so significant a difference as may at first appear. During World War II, for most of the small states and on most occasions, the contest for control was between only two of the great powers. (Turkey was the outstanding exception, in 1939 and 1943–44.)

The condition—great power rivalry—for small power diplomatic maneuvering is present for the newly-independent countries, especially key small states like Egypt, although for the satellites, by their very nature, it scarcely exists. For the ex-satellite, Yugoslavia, however, the competition between East and West has proved very useful in maintaining Yugoslav independence and promoting economic advance, especially because the country is located in an area where the balance of military power between the two worlds is close.

None of the ex-colonies could fulfill the condition of relative economic autonomy, because they are all underdeveloped. The only way they could make themselves less vulnerable to outside economic pressure would be to give up their precious industrial aspirations and return to completely peasant economies. Since this seems out of the question, they are susceptible to various kinds of economic persuasion. However, this very pressure fills the coffers of the currently strategic small states, who are favored above those of less political concern just as some World War II neutrals secured more economic aid than certain small allies of the great powers.[20] A few small states possess the strategic resource of oil, which greatly increases their bargaining power. The difference this makes for an otherwise very weak state was amply illustrated by Mossadegh's defiance of the British desires during the Iranian oil nationalization crisis.

The plight of the satellites is made more difficult because they lie directly between Russia and the West and because one of the ways in which they became satellites was their integration with the Russian economy. They, like the other small states, may still profit from the fact that Russia as well as the Western great powers has many intricate interests which must be balanced and because even in the Soviet Union and within the Soviet sphere there have emerged sharp divisions. Furthermore, they have one advantage not enjoyed by the ex-colonies: they are countries with a longer diplomatic history (though for some only since World War I). Further, they share the same culture with the West and have representatives in large numbers among the second-generation foreign born in the United States. There are far more Poles and Hungarians living in America than there are Indonesians or Egyptians. But for the satellites, the existence of the United Nations does not greatly add to the strength of those wanting to free themselves from Russian domination, as it most startlingly does for those in what was the colonial world who are striving to prove their independence of the colonial powers. One need only observe the difference in treatment within the United Nations of the Egyptian and Hungarian crises in the fall of 1956.

Taking the Egyptian and Hungarian cases, which arose almost simultaneously, let us see how small power diplomacy operates in the United Nations. The existence of the General Assembly, whose au-

[20] In the post-war years the Latin American states have felt economically the lack of concern for their position compared to some states in more controversial areas.

thority rests on a "decent respect to the opinions of mankind," worked very much in favor of protecting the small state of Egypt against Britain and France, where this decent respect, working through public opinion, acted as a brake on governmental policy. The same organization was no protection to the people of the small state of Hungary, whose opponent was a very different kind of great power. The voting in the General Assembly on the two issues showed that small members do not act similarly in conflicts which they view differently, especially those involving colonialism and the cold war. While the small states of Europe, Latin America, the Middle East, and Asia indicated their solidarity in condemning violence as perpetrated by Britain and France and one small state against another small country outside Europe, they were by no means united in condemning the at least equally shocking use of force against a European small state perpetrated by communist Russia. Thus, Indonesia and Ceylon, to name two of the ex-colonies not voting for the condemnation of Russia and the demand that Soviet troops be withdrawn from Hungary, explained that they opposed outside (United Nations) interference with the "internal" regime of Hungary. But among those outspoken in favor of the resolution were such small states as Denmark, the Philippines, Greece, and Argentina.

Although the Afro-Asian bloc was not united in its action on the Hungary dispute in the General Assembly, on other occasions this informal grouping of small states has found the United Nations a useful megaphone for expressing views on what they regard as remnants of colonialism, verbally flailing members governing dependencies (except the Soviet Union). Thus they hope to modify the attitudes of other states when relevant questions arise, such as the future status of Algeria. Through the United Nations programs for aid to underdeveloped countries the small states of Asia and Africa can hope also to have a voice in some re-distribution of the world's wealth and the spread of skills associated with greater power. Now that the United Nations numbers over eighty states, many of them newly-created, the possibility exists that where a two-thirds vote is required the Afro-Asian bloc plus the Soviet bloc can outbalance the United States and the rest of the free world, including Latin America.[21] However, this

[21] Such a vote is necessary for "important questions" such as recommendations regarding international peace and security, the election of non-permanent Security

fact has not gone unnoticed by the great as well as the small, and the growing disinclination of the leading states of Western Europe to work through the United Nations is a reaction against some small members' use of their power in the Assembly. The attitude of the British and French indicates that there are clear limits to the exploitation of this new strength accruing to the small states outside Western Europe.

The techniques available to the new kinds of small states in the cold-war era differ somewhat from those open to the small states during World War II, but again there are continuing advantages to some measures, such as promoting good relations with neighboring small states. (Nasser's vulnerability in the Suez crisis was the enmity of Israel.) Yet today certain kinds of small states are among those doing the demanding instead of resisting demands from the great powers, a situation which brings different diplomatic techniques to the fore. It is hard to practice the arts of procrastination while taking the initiative. Efforts to rally a group of small states into a military bloc are still likely to be as ineffective as earlier. They usually multiply feebleness, even if they occasionally impress a desperate great power. Attempts at mediation between the great are equally unlikely to have effect; the "bridge" is used to tread upon.

Yet, having taken a step which might have brought a violent reaction from a great power, the small power diplomats can continue to employ such techniques as distraction, the exorbitant price for settlement, trade in insignificant concessions, and the exploiting of divisions among their opponents.

Like Spain in World War II, the small states causing conflict in the post-war era cannot hope to gain their economic objectives without some dependence upon help from the great powers, and the question is again raised, how to obtain such aid without losing political independence? Like the would-be neutrals of World War II, the post-war small states which were not sucked into that conflict continue for the most part to be wary of any attachment to a great power constellation. They do not follow the lead of the Benelux countries, Norway, and Denmark, for fear that they could not maintain their freedom in this way. The balancing of demands and concessions be-

Council members, and the admission of new members to the United Nations, in accordance with Article 18 of the United Nations Charter.

tween the great power blocs, so exquisitely performed during World War II by the successful neutrals, is still necessary today, but the dangers to the small state of exploiting its weakness seem greater. The process of becoming a satellite is now well-known: a combination of economic entanglement, entrance of foreign troops, and subversion of the legal government. The penalty—loss of independence—is universally feared.

The great problem posed by the post-war types of small states in world politics is an internal weakness, that is, the far greater readiness towards self-destruction in the struggle against foreign influence. The ultimate weapon which the small state has available against one great power—joining the other side—may be pressed against the small state itself. The controversial small power today is unlike the small non-belligerents of World War II, who were never the threat against either side that the belligerents perceived them to be. The problem small state of the 1950's can, by choosing suicidal measures, commit helpless great powers to a greater extent than these more powerful states could involve a small state with a determinedly independent policy.

A basic question in small power diplomacy is whether or not there is sufficient self-control and strength of leadership to carry out a rational policy. The answer is in doubt in the frequently mob-ruled countries now in the forefront of world politics, but it will determine in large part whether a particular small state is in a powder keg, a whirlpool, or the still center of the storm.

IV

The United Nations

Chapter 18

THE ROLE OF THE

UNITED NATIONS

Dag Hammarskjöld

RECENT events have, I believe, cast a clearer light upon the role of the United Nations in these times. The Charter, read as a whole, does not endow the United Nations with any of the attributes of a super-state or of a body active outside the framework of decisions of member governments. The United Nations is, rather, an instrument for negotiation among, and to some extent for, governments. It is also an instrument added to the time-honored means of diplomacy for concerting action by governments in support of the goals of the Charter. This is the role the organization has played, sometimes successfully, sometimes with disappointing setbacks, throughout its life.

From time to time complaints are heard about the limitations upon the organization's power. It has even been suggested that, unless these limitations are corrected, the usefulness of the United Nations is so questionable that the main effort of the governments in the search for peace should be concentrated in other directions.

This view does less than justice to the contributions of the United Nations in its short life. Especially, it fails to take into account that the real limitations upon action by the organization do not derive from the provisions of the Charter. They result from facts of international life in our age which are not likely to be by-passed by a different approach or surmounted by attempts at merely constitutional reform.

To turn aside from the United Nations now because it cannot be transformed into a world authority enforcing the law upon the nations would be to erase all the steady, though slow and painful, advances that have been made and to close the door to hopes for the future of world society, toward which present efforts and experiences should be at least a modest stepping stone.

We should, rather, recognize the United Nations for what it is—an admittedly imperfect but indispensable instrument of nations in working for a peaceful evolution toward a more just and secure world order. The dynamic forces at work in this stage of human history have made world organization necessary. The balance of these forces has also set the limits within which the power of world organization can develop at each step and beyond which progress, when the balance of forces so permits, will be possible only by processes of organic growth in the system of custom and law prevailing in the society of nations.

These processes of adjustment take time. Systems of alliance, maintained side by side with the United Nations in recognition of the prevailing balance of forces, may serve a useful purpose during the period through which we are passing. However, most of us agree that such systems of alliance, like other traditional means of diplomacy and defence of the national interests, are limited in their value as safeguards of the present and future security and welfare of our countries. Nations and groups of nations will never again be able to live and to arrogate judgment unto themselves in international affairs in ways which once were a matter of course.

The greatest need today is to blunt the edges of conflict among the nations, not to sharpen them. If properly used, the United Nations can serve a diplomacy of reconciliation better than other instruments available to the member states. All the varied interests and aspirations of the world meet in its precincts upon the common ground of the Charter. Conflicts may persist for long periods without an agreed solution, and groups of states may actively defend special and regional interests. Nevertheless, and in spite of temporary developments in the opposite direction under the influence of acute tension, the tendency in the United Nations is to wear away, or break down, differences, thus helping toward solutions which approach the common interest and application of the principles of the Charter.

With its increase in membership, the United Nations more fully mirrors the realities of the present world situation than ever before, although necessarily the picture given in the debates and votes in the United Nations can be truly evaluated only after a careful analysis. The United Nations reflects, but is in no sense a cause of, the renaissance of Asia. The awakening of Africa and the other great changes that are under way in the balance of power and relationships of the peoples are likewise part of the dynamics of history itself. As always, they bring with them many grave problems of adjustment. These all too easily may become the occasion for arousing passion, fear and hatred, and lead in turn to violent upheavals and to the ultimate disaster of war in this atomic age.

The functions of debate and vote are an essential part of the processes by which the United Nations can assist the governments in avoiding these dangers and in guiding the development in constructive and peaceful directions. But if it is accepted that the primary value of the United Nations is to serve as an instrument for negotiation among governments and for concerting action by governments in support of the goals of the Charter, it is also necessary, I believe, to use the legislative procedures of the United Nations consistently in ways which will promote these ends. In an organization of sovereign states, voting victories are likely to be illusory unless they are steps in the direction of winning lasting consent to a peaceful and just settlement of the questions at issue.

Full weight should also be given to the fact that the processes of adjustment and negotiation which the institutions of the United Nations make available to the member governments embrace much more than the public proceedings of its Councils and Assembly. In the diplomacy of world organization the quiet work of preparing the ground, of accommodation of interest and viewpoint, of conciliation and mediation, all that goes into the winning of consent to agreed solutions and common programs, this forms a basis upon which the United Nations can become an increasingly influential and effective force to aid the governments in pursuit of the goals of the Charter.

Indeed, I think the experiences of the past thirteen years have demonstrated that there is need to redress the balance between the public and private procedures of the United Nations if we are to make better progress in peace-making. By private procedures I mean the methods of classical diplomacy as applied within the new framework provided by the Charter and the institutions of the world organization. There has always been this practice of private—or quiet—diplomacy in the United Nations, and there has been a marked increase in its use within the past year or two. But the need for it is not sufficiently understood. The best results of negotiation between two parties cannot be achieved in international life, any more than in our private worlds, in the full glare of publicity with current public debate of all moves, unavoidable misunderstandings, inescapable freezing of position due to considerations of prestige, and the temptation to utilize public opinion as an element integrated in the negotiation itself.

"Open agreements" represent the response to a sound demand. How and to what extent they should be "openly arrived at," on the other hand, is a principle which requires serious consideration in the light of the very aims which the public procedures are intended to serve.

Considered simply as the only meeting place on the common ground of the Charter of the ambassadors of 82 member countries, the United Nations provides a unique opportunity for the continuous exercise of classical diplomacy for peace-making without any formal procedures. We can register efforts to give such diplomacy the support of firmer procedures. Such procedures may help and they represent a further elaboration of classical diplomacy as exercised within the United Nations. They are, however, to be regarded as particular cases, the bulk of the private diplomacy at the United Nations being wholly informal.

For example, two constructive and highly useful committees established by the General Assembly in the past three years are very small committees which meet entirely in private. Both of them happen to be advisory committees to the Secretary-General, but a similar pattern could be usefully followed even if this were not the case.

One is the Advisory Committee on Atomic Energy—that is, its peaceful uses. On this committee of seven, outstanding nuclear scientists sit as governmental representatives of the three major atomic powers, the United Kingdom, the United States of America and the Union of Soviet Socialist Republics. It has contributed a great deal to paving the way for agreements and action by governments which have helped to break down the barriers of the cold war so far as peaceful uses of atomic energy are concerned.

The other Assembly committee is the Advisory Committee on the

United Nations Emergency Force, which has done much to bring quiet to the armistice line between Egypt and Israel. This is a committee exclusively of smaller member states, most of whom have provided contingents serving with the United Nations Force. Its work is an example of the practical value in the United Nations of a formal instrument of private diplomacy in carrying forward action once the main policy lines have been laid down by a decision of the General Assembly. That decision, in turn, was made by the General Assembly in the public proceedings of parliamentary diplomacy only after the informal procedures of private classical diplomacy had done their work. Thus, this case is also an example of a kind of three-stage operation which is natural in the United Nations and which is capable of yielding constructive results for peace-making not to be achieved by other means: private diplomacy preceding public debate and then employed again to follow through.

A third example is the experiment in private negotiation of the Suez Canal issue in which the Security Council engaged in early October 1956 before the invasion of Egypt. This experiment brought together the Foreign Ministers of the member nations of the Council in private session instead of the usual public session. It led to informal meetings of the Foreign Ministers of France, the United Kingdom and Egypt in my office which resulted in unanimous agreement on six principles for the peaceful settlement of the Suez Canal question. These principles established the basis for the further private diplomatic steps toward such a settlement.

Such private diplomacy, within the framework of the Security Council, can be usefully employed on other issues and, if so employed, could contribute in new directions to the importance of the role the Charter intended the Council to play in the task of peace-making.

Public debates must continue to be a primary function of the Assembly and Councils of the United Nations. Unlike the Assembly and the Councils, however, the Office of the Secretary-General, by its very nature under the Charter, must practice private diplomacy on almost all occasions until results are reached. In recent years the Secretary-General has increasingly been used for operations of a purely diplomatic type, either on behalf of the United Nations as such, or for one government in relation to another on a good offices basis. He is in a position of trust *vis-à-vis* all the member governments. He speaks for no government. It should go without saying that in the course of a negotiation, or a mission of good offices, he must respect fully the laws of diplomatic discretion. He can never give away what must be considered the property of the government with whom he is working. Nor could he pass public judgment upon its policies without wrecking the use of his office for the diplomatic purposes for which experience shows that it is much needed. When a mission has resulted in a formal agreement between the parties, the agreement is made public, but it is not for him to evaluate it in public.

There are, I believe, promising and practical opportunities for improving the practices and strengthening the institutions of the United Nations in this area of multilateral diplomacy. I hope this evolution of emphasis and practice, which has occurred particularly during the last two years, will be pursued and broadened in the future. This seems to be a more urgent task than to attempt formal constitutional changes, the consideration of which the Committee of the whole Assembly, charged with studying the problem of time and place for a Charter review conference, at all events unanimously wished to postpone until a later stage.

Chapter 19

DIPLOMACY AT THE

UNITED NATIONS*

Sir Pierson Dixon

Meaning of Diplomacy

The United Nations being an association of sovereign countries in which the members are pledged under a Charter to work for certain common ends, there can, or should be, no place for the exercise of diplomacy in the classical sense—the conduct of business between states on a basis of national interest. The conception at the root of this world organisation is that the members, far from using it as a place to further their national interests, should subordinate those interests to the attainment of certain ends assumed to be in the common interests of all—peace with justice, development of friendly relations among peoples, and the promotion of the social and economic advancement of peoples. In theory the members should all be outbidding each other for these ends, but the practice has fallen short of the theory and it is in fact true to say that, at present, diplomacy in the classical sense is commonly practised at the United Nations.

In another sense diplomacy can be defined as the practice of solving international disputes by peaceful rather than warlike means, that is by the methods of negotiation and conciliation. Diplomacy in this sense is a proper international activity at the United Nations and indeed an activity basic to the purposes laid down in the Charter. Although much genuine effort is devoted to utilizing the great po-

* The author's account reflects the situation in the spring of 1958.

373

tential of the United Nations for negotiation and concilation, and the results have been encouraging, the other practice—utilization of the United Nations for national interests—has been followed by many member states, to the detriment of the practice of negotiation and conciliation and of the operation of the organization as a whole.

Nature of the Organisation

The complexities of the international activity pursued at the United Nations derive from the nature of the organization itself. The United Nations is a free association of sovereign countries. Containing as it does 82 members it now comes near to representing the totality of the countries of the world, with their many diverse traditions, institutions and interests. It is not a coalition or an alliance with specific and binding conditions. This of course is how it differs fundamentally from an international organization such as the North Atlantic Alliance where certain nations have joined together for well-defined common objectives and where decisions can be made and are taken in the common interest. If the United Nations functioned with theoretical perfection and all its members conducted their international affairs through the United Nations and subordinated their national interests to the requirements of the U. N. Charter, there would be no need for such regional organizations. But this postulates an ideal, friction-free world, and the framers of the Charter themselves recognized, in Articles 51 and 52, the justification of such collective security arrangements in present conditions.

In practice the United Nations has not developed as we and the United States, who conceived the project, planned and hoped. The plan and hope was that it would provide an international forum in which all members would co-operate for the common ends which I have already mentioned. Difficulties have arisen from a number of factors, in the forefront of which must be placed the way the Soviet Union has treated the United Nations as a place for the promotion of its purely national interests. Then there has been the distortion of the aims of the Charter in favor of anti-colonialism and ultra-nationalism, which has complicated the task of the so-called colonial powers in making the contribution which they wish to make to the purposes of the Charter. And finally, there has developed a double-standard of behavior as applied to different parts of the world.

For all these complications the United Nations has made and is making an essential contribution to international peace and stability; but in order to understand how it really works and how diplomatic activity is conducted at the United Nations, it is essential to realize how much the task of international diplomacy is complicated by the factors I have listed, which I will now examine in greater detail.

Misuse of the United Nations

It is not my purpose to overstress the past and present difficulties which divide the communist and the free worlds. On the contrary, we must be forward-looking and seek to clear away the road-blocks of the past. But we must look forward with our eyes open. Our difficulties with the Soviet Union, as reflected at the United Nations, have arisen from the fact that a major member has blocked so many serious efforts to deal with world problems and latterly has even exploited the organization as a vehicle for its own national ambitions. This has caused the democratic world to consume much time and effort in circumventing and countering these tactics. This has been a major task for our diplomacy and has complicated our efforts to move towards the objectives which the founders of the United Nations had in mind.

Perhaps the greatest damage to the effectiveness of the organization has resulted from the behavior of the Soviet Union in the Security Council, where they have the veto. The Security Council was intended to be an executive arm with major responsibility for peace and security. The Security Council has been gravely handicapped in this role by the misuse of the veto power by the Soviet Union in order to frustrate some move genuinely designed to preserve peace and security, or to promote some particular national aim of its own.

In the wider forum provided by the General Assembly during its annual three months session much time has been wasted and useful initiatives have come to nothing owing to the propagandist use to which these meetings have been turned. The Soviet line has been to play on the fear of war, using the slogan of peaceful co-existence, and representing themselves as the true apostles of peace and progress and the Western Powers as aggressive trouble-makers and imperialists. Opportunities have not been lost to intensify this propaganda effort by capitalizing their remarkable advances in science and by alternating peace propaganda with intimidation.

In the United Nations our task is not only to counter this kind of propaganda but, in spite of it, to create and maintain conditions favorable to conciliation and agreement. This requires considerable effort and unremitting patience.

One of the principal targets of Soviet diplomacy are the so-called uncommitted countries, and, however superficial the Soviet propaganda line about peaceful co-existence may appear, it must be admitted that it has some appeal and wins some support among these countries. The desire of such countries for peace is understandable, but experience teaches that peace is something that has to be striven for; it is not something that can be bought by a paper agreement or by a slogan. Yet it is slogans that are often offered from the platforms of the United Nations.

Colonialism

Besides posing as the apostles of peace, the Soviet propagandists also represent themselves as the great anti-colonialists and supporters of nationalistic movements. The object is to play on the emotions of the emergent countries of Asia and Africa and to fan prejudices which do not in fact correspond to the realities of the modern world. The countries of America and Europe are profoundly sympathetic to the historical movements in Asia and Africa which have resulted in independence for so many peoples. Yet Soviet propaganda seeks to represent Great Britain as a would-be colonizing power and the United States as the imperialists of today. The facts are that the United States is contributing to the progress of underdeveloped countries in a significant and disinterested way, and Britain for the past century and more has been leading the dependent parts of her Empire to independence. The Soviet Union on the other hand has acquired and consolidated an imperial hold over people of non-Russian race, both in Central Asia and in Eastern Europe.

When the Russians make propaganda on these lines it is of course necessary to answer them in the United Nations. The resulting clash of views clearly does not help to ease world tensions but has the opposite effect. It would be a good thing if there could be an end to name-calling in the United Nations—an appeal which we have more than once made in the past but unfortunately without durable effect.

As things are, diplomatic activity at the United Nations has to proceed against the unproductive background of the cold war.

The Double Standard

I must now mention the controversy which came up on both sides of the Atlantic as a result of the steps which the General Assembly took to deal with the crises in Suez and Hungary in the autumn of 1956.

The General Assembly at that time passed a series of resolutions calling upon British and French forces to withdraw from Egypt and Soviet forces to withdraw from Hungary. The British and French Governments, whose action of course followed the Israeli attack on Egypt, felt able to comply with the Assembly's resolutions in view of the formation of the United Nations Emergency Force to preserve peace in the area. In the case of Hungary, the Assembly did not judge it worthwhile even to propose such an international force in view of the uncompromising attitude of the Soviet Union. The Assembly called on the Soviet Union to withdraw its forces from Hungary and the Soviet Union rested on defiance of the Assembly's request. Attempts to secure compliance have been unavailing. A number of people both in the United Kingdom and other countries considered that the United Nations was applying a double standard in the two cases and that this represented a grave weakening of its moral strength. This view was held by people who supported the Anglo-French intervention in Egypt and by some who opposed it.

The answer which was made was that the General Assembly had in fact acted just as promptly and decisively in the case of Hungary as in the case of Egypt. Indeed, the tone of the Assembly's resolutions on Hungary, including as they did a specific condemnation of the Soviet action as a violation of the Charter, showed clearly that the Assembly recognized a vast difference between the two interventions. The General Assembly, so runs the argument, cannot be blamed if one member state defied its wishes while two others complied, since its possesses no means of enforcing those wishes. This argument is, of course, valid so far as it goes. It amounts to admitting that a double standard was in fact applied, while claiming that this was not because the Assembly had a double standard of truth, but because it was powerless to bring about a different result. The result is to weaken the reputation for even-handed justice which a world organization evidently should enjoy.

It is sometimes contended that it is illogical that the smallest member states should have the same vote as the greatest and that this imbalance should be corrected by the introduction into the United Nations of a system of weighted vote. I am inclined to think that it would be impracticable to introduce such an innovation. The real remedy lies in the development of a greater sense of responsibility in the United Nations as it is at present constituted. That sense of responsibility, so far as the more powerful nations of the West are concerned, certainly comprises a great respect for the sovereign voice of each independent nation and a recognition of the fine contribution which many of the smaller and less experienced countries of the world are making. In many cases this contribution is out of all proportion to their size or power. It is, in my view, salutary for world peace and international harmony that the voices of the smaller nations should be heard with effect as they can be in a world organization where the smallest nation has the same vote as the greatest. In return it is desirable that there should be full recognition for the great contribution which the more advanced and more powerful countries can make towards keeping the peace and promoting the economic advancement of peoples.

The tradition of private diplomacy between individual states was a tradition of mutual respect. This was not merely because its practitioners believed in mutual respect as a virtue in itself; they also found that it helped them to bring their business to a successful result. When diplomacy becomes public, this respect is harder to achieve. If every time a diplomat shakes hands with his rival or opponent a photograph of the event appears in the next day's paper with a political implication, then he may decide that it is safer not to shake hands. If an impolite speech wins bigger headlines than a polite speech, there is obviously a temptation to make it. But it is still true that mutual respect is a valuable adjunct to diplomacy. It is indeed essential in the give and take of multilateral diplomacy in a universal organization, which by its very nature is designed to further, not the interests of individual countries, but the common interests of all.

How the United Nations Can Help

I thought it necessary to paint in this realistic background in order to help indicate how international relations are conducted in the United Nations as it actually operates at present. Enough has been said to show that widely conflicting interests, as in international relations generally, are active in the United Nations, and that diplomacy is therefore hard put to it to develop the United Nations as a working center for harmonizing the actions of nations and a place where we can make a contribution to peace with justice and the development of friendly relations among peoples.

Within its existing limitations the United Nations is, however, a most valuable institution. It would, I think, be generally admitted that, if it had not been in existence during the past twelve years, the international situation would be graver today. Equally there is, I believe, a general and strongly-held conviction—certainly in my country—that the modern world needs an international organization of this universal character for the purposes of preserving peace and resolving differences between nations.

I will now briefly examine the ways in which in my view the United Nations can contribute in a practical way.

I should perhaps make it clear in parenthesis that I am not in the present context dealing with the important and successful work which the United Nations does in the economic, social and legal fields, though we should not forget that, for the newer and poorer countries of the world to be more prosperous and more contented, and for the United Nations to keep pace with the ideals and aspirations of the twentieth century, is in itself a contribution to world stability and thus to world peace.

Within the political field it has three main functions:

Threats to the Peace

1. Dealing with threats to the peace and breaches of the peace, that is preventing war breaking out and dealing with it if it does.

As I have shown, the United Nations at present is gravely handicapped in this, its most important function. It is true that it was able to halt aggression in Korea; but this was only because by a tactical miscalculation the Soviet Delegation was absent from the Security Council and therefore not able to impose its veto when the important decision was taken. Still, much can be done by bringing the force of public opinion to bear. The United Nations failed to keep the peace between Israel and Egypt, or to stop the Soviet invasion and suppression of liberty in Hungary. But the alarm and distress caused by both these events was widespread and widely voiced in the United Nations. The advertisement of world opinion in this way may be a valuable deterrent for the future. The establishment of the United Nations Emergency Force in the Gaza Strip between Egypt and Israel has proved a valuable and practical contribution to the reduction of the tensions surrounding the Palestine question.

Conciliation

2. The United Nations' second main function is to act as a center of conciliation.

This of course overlaps with the first function: the surest way to prevent a breach of peace is to deal with and resolve the cause of the dispute. The Security Council has been able to make its contribution, particularly in regard to Palestine problems; though it has not, of course, been able, despite strenuous efforts, to make advance towards turning the armistice into a peace. Our diplomacy here consists in patient work, often behind the scenes and not in open Council, in ironing out those differences and dealing with those incidents between Israel and her Arab neighbors which can so easily flare up into war. In this and other cases there has been a genuine common effort by Western and non-communist powers as a whole, with the invaluable help of the Secretary-General of the United Nations.

The United Nations is also of course potentially a center of conciliation between the communist and non-communist worlds.

It is indeed the obvious center for such conciliation simply because communist and non-communist representatives sit side by side in the various United Nations bodies and are in constant contact in the halls of the United Nations building. There are thus regular means of contact and discussion. In the past the Soviet diplomatic offensive has not been conducive to fruitful discussion but, on the contrary, has forced the non-communist countries to defend themselves and struggle for the initiative in this propaganda battle not of their choosing. Nonetheless, the possible openings arising from the mere fact that the Soviet bloc is represented at the United Nations provide possibilities which our diplomacy should constantly bear in mind.

The United Nations can be very helpful in providing a suitable forum, particularly for progress on disarmament. On the other hand it is a mistaken idea that the United Nations is being "by-passed" if some important international problem is dealt with in some other way. All channels for resolving international difficulties should be considered open, and sometimes one medium is more appropriate in the circumstances than another; sometimes a combination of United Nations action with direct inter-state diplomacy is the method most likely to lead to agreement.

Open Debate and Private Diplomacy

I now turn to less clear-cut issues where strains are liable to arise for friendships within the free world when a matter is raised in the United Nations.

I have here particularly in mind so-called colonial questions which arouse a lot of feeling and where even our closest friends appear sometimes to overlook the great changes that are taking place in what used to be the Colonial Empires. This complicates the task of the so-called Colonial Powers in continuing the process of leading dependent peoples to independence.

The difficulties arise largely from the simple fact that they are raised in the United Nations. The United Nations proceedings are public and its decisions are taken by voting. This has value when some broad issue of international concern is being debated. But when it is a specific issue affecting the vital interests of a major power, this open procedure can prove awkward. A problem which might be solved by the old-fashioned methods of private, non-publicized diplomacy, often becomes intractable when debated in the United Nations. A relatively minor problem becomes magnified out of proportion to its true importance, owing to the clash of differing views in debate at the United Nations. But private diplomacy is not only unfashionable: it has come to be regarded as positively immoral. This is perhaps because private diplomacy smells of secret diplomacy, and secret diplomacy in the popular mind is plotting behind people's backs. Yet "open covenants *privately* arrived at" is often the best method of agreement. Covenants are often not arrived at at all if they have to be reached through the medium of public debate. The moral for diplomacy at the United Nations is more restraint in advocating the treatment of thorny questions in public debate and greater use of the many alternative media available in the flexible organization of the United Nations.

Nonetheless private diplomacy is quietly and regularly pursued at the United Nations as well as diplomacy by public debate. My experience is that a preliminary phase of such behind-the-scenes preparation for the public debate in Council, Committee or Plenary, is normally the best way of reaching a good result. The helpful role of the Secretary-General in this kind of activity is of very great value. But the view of the majority of the United Nations seems to be that freedom of public discussion must be untrammelled and that every matter is debatable at the United Nations if a member government wishes to bring it up.

My own view is that the United Nations should be rather more selective in its choice of matters to discuss. It should in my opinion consider carefully whether discussion of a particular problem brought before it by a member nation is going to be helpful to the finding of a peaceful solution or whether discussion is against the terms of the Charter itself and is just going to give one group of member nations a chance to make propaganda against another group. It would be foolish not to recognize that discussion of some problems at the United Nations may actually hinder the interests of peace and stability in the area concerned.

An incidental result of indiscriminate discussion at the United Nations is that a strain is placed on relationships between friends, since differing positions have to be advertised publicly on questions which would otherwise never have been raised in public at all.

These differences are accentuated by the procedure in the United Nations—unavoidable in public debate—of expressing an opinion by a vote. A vote can be for, or against, or an abstention. If, for example, the United Kingdom votes for and the United States against, this advertises a serious difference. If one votes for or against and the other abstains, it is clear to the world that some difference exists.

I do not, however, take a negative line about public discussion at the United Nations. Quite the contrary. In a world in which public opinion strongly influences the shaping of policy by governments, discussion at the United Nations can be an immensely influential force even if it produces no immediate definite decisions. If this force of public opinion is used selectively as I have suggested, it can be extremely valuable in bringing the pressure of world public opinion to bear when it is needed.

3. This is indeed the third main function of the United Nations. Until the international situation improves to the extent of the major countries working together and the United Nations being given executive powers for collective security, I believe that more emphasis should be laid than at present on this third function of the United Nations as a world forum and clearing house for ideas, a place where countries are influenced by the opinions of other countries and by world opinion, a center where foreign representatives can meet, talk quietly and get to know each other. The General Assembly was conceived by the founders as having that function, while the Security Council was to be primarily the organ concerning itself with matters of peace and security. There is a real danger in attributing to the General Assembly executive attributes which properly belong to the Security Council. The world, with its hundred separate nations, is not a unity, but a diversity. It is diverse by race, creed and national interest. The United Nations, being an association of sovereign nations, cannot do more than reflect the sum total of international relations as they actually exist. At present there are cleavages of varying depths between the nations, and these cleavages inevitably are reflected in the United Nations. It would be a self-delusion to postulate a unity that does not exist and to entrust to the United Nations as it stands the powers of a world executive. Our goal is that degree of world unity which will ensure co-operation instead of rivalry. We shall further it by recognizing the United Nations as it is, with its present limitations. By understanding its immense potentialities we shall reduce the differences that divide the nations of the world today.

How to Make the United Nations More Effective

How then can we make the United Nations more effective? Not, I believe, by trying to turn it into a world executive, or by trying to ascribe to the General Assembly the powers of decision and execution which belong to the Security Council. The real remedy lies in the hands of member states, particularly the more powerful ones. But, in the absence of an improvement in international relations, the United Nations will, I think, make its best contribution by running its affairs in accordance with the structure laid down at San Francisco in 1945, which provides for a flexible balance between the major organs of the United Nations.

Above all, I believe that we need to develop certain techniques to respond to the unsettled state of international relationships and the peculiar conditions of an 82 nation open forum; and I offer in conclusion some reflections on the methods of diplomacy most likely to be successful for the purposes of the United Nations.

In any worthwhile diplomatic activity there are three stages:

(1) appraisal of the facts of the case;

(2) determination of the best course to pursue;

(3) a conclusion which is as widely acceptable as possible not only to governments but also to world opinion.

(1) Requires a good hard look, a cold appraisal divorced from cant or emotion;

(2) requires cool and skilful judgment taking a long view and often involving the steering of a difficult course between various conflicting interests;

(3) requires thorough consultation with other countries, ranging from the closest friends and allies, through the range of neutrally minded countries, and extending to those actively opposed. It is also necessary to sound and prepare opinion through the media of public discussion, and to frame the case with due recognition of the fact that it will come under the searchlight of world public opinion at the United Nations.

It often occurs at the United Nations that these processes, essential for a good result, are either ignored or become bedevilled by emotion or propaganda. The would-be cure is then worse than the disease. I have already spoken of the way in which Soviet diplomacy plays on emotions like the fear of war and ultra-nationalism. When the emotions rule, the true purposes of the United Nations are liable to be lost sight of, and international diplomacy becomes diplomacy by slogan. The actions of nations cannot be harmonized by pleas for peace at any price or denunciations of "Imperialism." The result is rather to increase international tension and embitter, not improve, relations between peoples.

As I see it, the basic function of the rather special kind of diplomacy which operates in a universal organization whose proceedings take place in public, is to arrange that the problems which come within its purview are dealt with by the methods most likely to conciliate the diverse interests involved and most conducive to agreement; diplomacy by patience and planning and not diplomacy by slogan, diplomacy based on a genuine regard for the Charter as a whole and not diplomacy that picks and chooses according to the tactical advantage of the moment.

If we can work out a generally accepted diplomatic approach on these lines at the United Nations we may hope to develop peaceful methods of resolving disputes and promote understanding between peoples at a moment in world history when it has never been so important to find an alternative to agitation and strife.

Chapter 20

UNESCO: CENTER OF

CULTURAL DIPLOMACY*

Walter H. C. Laves

I

THE decision to include within the framework of this volume a paper on Unesco's role is a recognition of the significance of cultural relations as a new dimension in contemporary diplomacy. And the fact that we are discussing this subject at a time when Unesco has functioned for more than a decade means that we need not engage in mere speculation but have at our disposal a considerable record of experience.

The emergence of a center for cultural diplomacy and the particular form it took in Unesco were the result of a long evolution closely related to the history of international diplomacy. Diplomacy concerns itself with all those aspects of a nation's welfare that call for the conduct of foreign relations. Some aspects are matters of such general international concern that they require for effective treatment a multilateral rather than a bilateral approach. And, as the web of multilateral relations and activities grows and the international concern becomes more evident, there is need for systematizing and internationalizing the diplomatic efforts. Gradually the worldwide concern calls for a worldwide viewpoint. It becomes vital to have an interna-

* This essay was originally presented as a lecture at the University of Notre Dame. In revising it the author took account of developments up to the end of 1957.

tional center from which various national needs can be reviewed, analyzed, and served in a manner beyond the capacities of individual nations or of bilateral diplomacy. This stage had been reached by the twentieth century in respect to many matters of education, science, and culture because of their importance to the welfare of nation states. Several factors pressed steadily toward this stage.

The search for knowledge and for opportunities for creative expression have generally resisted the imposition of barriers. They have also resisted restrictions and particularly those that stem from political power. The great advances of knowledge in Western civilization were encouraged by the widening of the world in which men carried on their intellectual activities. The trend of intellectual development has been toward ever expanding horizons, the deliberate reduction of barriers, and the increase in intellectual contact across boundaries.

The need for international institutions and other instruments to facilitate greater exchange and cooperative relations has become increasingly apparent during the last seventy-five years and especially during the twentieth century. One answer was the creation of nongovernmental international organizations. The Congress of Historical Sciences, the International Council of Scientific Unions and the International Academic Union are important illustrations. A further step was taken under the League of Nations by creating an International Institute of Intellectual Cooperation. Some governments meantime showed interest in organized intellectual cooperation through cultural relations programs such as those of Germany, France, the United Kingdom, and, after the mid-thirties of this century, the United States. These, however, were in large part concerned with providing cultural or intellectual support for national foreign policies.

The movement toward creating a United Nations agency as a center of cultural diplomacy was given special emphasis by two factors. One was the great disparity in the educational and scientific development of countries as well as the variety in their cultural development. Effective cooperation in international affairs promised to become more difficult if disparities were not reduced and varieties better understood. Of particular importance was the educational and scientific development of countries whose economic growth has been retarded and whose people were expressing their rising aspiration in all areas of human development, especially education. (A later response to the needs and demands of these countries was the United Nations Expanded Technical Assistance Program.)

The other factor leading to the creation of a United Nations agency dealing with educational, scientific and cultural matters was widespread recognition that the prospects for peace in the contemporary world are limited by lack of informed world public opinion. Once a universal United Nations was created it was of paramount importance that people understand better the elements of effective cooperation in a world community. Here emerged Unesco's function to promote international understanding as one means of contributing to peace and security. Through its various activities in education, science, and culture it was to provide necessary support for the United Nations system. Thus, the creation of Unesco was the most recent and in many ways inevitable next step in the cooperative relations of men and of nations in the pursuit of knowledge, the advancement of culture, and in the promotion of international understanding.

II

A closer look at Unesco reveals that it is something new in the framework of international politics and diplomacy. No comparable international organization in terms of purpose, of structure or of membership has existed before in the area of education, science, and culture.

Novelty of Purpose. The purpose of Unesco as set forth in its constitution represents an ambitious and optimistic attempt to fill a major gap in the scope of international organization. It stated in broad terms the task to be performed and spelled out some of the methods to be employed. It is useful to quote here the full text of the clause dealing with the purpose of the constitution.

The text of Article I, Section 1 reads:

The purpose of the Organization is to contribute to peace and security by promoting collaboration among the nations through education, science and culture in order to further universal respect for justice, for the rule of law and for the human rights and fundamental freedoms which are affirmed for the peoples of the world, without distinction of race, sex, language or religion, by the Charter of the United Nations."

Section 2 then outlines how this purpose will be carried out:

(a) Collaborate in the work of advancing the mutual knowledge and understanding of peoples, through all means of mass communication and to that end recommend such international agreements as may be necessary to promote the free flow of ideas by word and image;

(b) Give fresh impulse to popular education and to the spread of culture; by collaborating with Members, at their request, in the development of educational activities;

by instituting collaboration among the nations to advance the ideal of equality of educational opportunity without regard to race, sex or any distinctions, economic or social;

by suggesting educational methods best suited to prepare the children of the world for the responsibilities of freedom;

(c) Maintain, increase and diffuse knowledge;

by assuring the conservation and protection of the world's inheritance of books, works of art and monuments of history and science, and recommending to the nations concerned the necessary international conventions;

by encouraging cooperation among the nations in all branches of intellectual activity, including the international exchange of persons active in the fields of education, science and culture and the exchange of publications, objects of artistic and scientific interest and other materials of information;

by initiating methods of international cooperation calculated to give the people of all countries access to the printed and published material produced by any of them.

There have been, recurrently, discussions as to whether the single purpose stated in the constitution should be used as the single criterion in program selection and as to how directly an activity must be related to furthering peace and security if it is to be considered appropriate within the constitutional language. This discussion soon tended to revolve around the issue whether Unesco activities should, in fact, always try to make a direct contribution to peace and security. Should they always seek to influence the immediate prospects for peace or should they seek sometimes merely to improve the climate in which the peace might more likely be attained in the future?

Unesco has not resolved this issue in terms of a formulated doctrine but it has in practice. Its preoccupation has been almost exclusively with the advancement of knowledge, the promotion of human welfare, and the furtherance of international understanding. All these activities have long-term goals and are intended much more as indirect than as direct contributions to peace and security.

Two things that are novel in Unesco's purpose should be noted here. First is the fact that the promotion of education, science, and culture and their use in the advancement of human welfare have been formally recognized as subjects of international politics. Because international politics is the process by which the needs of nations are asserted and sometimes obtained the creation of Unesco provides formal recognition that the promotion of education, science and culture constitutes a significant end of member state national policy. For the first time there is an international agency through which to express national educational, scientific, and cultural needs and through which to satisfy these needs.

A second novelty in Unesco's purpose is the fact that member states have subscribed to the objective of attaining greater international understanding and that they look to an international organization as a means again of expressing and of satisfying this objective of national policy. The implied intention to use an international agency to assist in preparing national public opinion to give support to governmental efforts toward peaceful international relations was potentially one of the most important postwar steps to make a viable community of peace-loving nations.

Novelty of Structure. Unesco represents something new also in its organization and structure. It is intergovernmental in that its membership is limited to sovereign states and in that all its activities must be authorized by the governments of member states. Unesco has a strong non-governmental flavor as well. It relies heavily upon the co-operation of international non-governmental organizations and has deliberately fostered the creation and development of many of them especially in professional and scholarly fields. These organizations are made up of private individuals and affiliated private national groups. Through direct relations with Unesco in a consultative or contractual capacity these non-governmental organizations provide important channels of communication between private professional interests and Unesco headquarters. This raises interestingly the issue of the degree of the exclusiveness of governments as the conveyers of the will or demands of people in that part of the process of international politics with which Unesco is concerned.

Under Unesco's constitution member states are expected to create

National Commissions or Cooperating Bodies which also provide significant channels of communication from the people of member states to the organization. Even when these communications are tightly controlled by government, the Commissions or Cooperating Bodies identify special groups of supporters for Unesco within member states. Where the commission idea has been more fully developed, as in the United States, it has led to citizen involvement in the determination of national policy toward Unesco and to participation of fairly large numbers of specialists in education, science, and culture in governmental delegations to Unesco conferences and in a great variety of technical meetings. Through such participation citizens have had a direct influence on policy matters, and the organization has attracted interest and direct support of a considerable number of citizens and citizen groups. It has served effectively to bring people with common professional interests together across national lines and has contributed in a small degree to the cohesion of this important segment of the world community.

The Novelty of Unesco's Membership. In a third respect Unesco represents something new. This is the breadth of its membership. Largely because of the rapid increase of the number of states during the postwar period, Unesco has within its membership not only an extraordinary variety of cultures but also a variety of nations that include every level of educational and scientific development. As a result, Unesco has had to undertake a very formidable and unprecedented task in fashioning a program that embraced the broad sweep of education, science, and culture of this heterogeneous group of states. The demands made upon Unesco by member states are extraordinarily varied, and the process of reaching an agreement upon program and policies is inevitably complex. All the basic differences between the Western and non-Western worlds, between democratic and other societies, and between the industrialized and less economically developed countries are brought into sharp relief as the organization seeks to promote strengthening of educational, scientific, and cultural resources on a worldwide basis. Unlike its predecessor, the International Institute of Intellectual Cooperation, under the League of Nations, which was largely Western and touched only a few countries, Unesco is an agency serving the full gamut of peoples that inhabit the earth.

Unesco has been compelled, by virtue of the novelty of its purpose, structure, and membership to devote much time during its first ten years to the exploration of techniques for reaching policy decisions as well as for carrying out programs designed to serve its member states. Internationally appointed expert and advisory committees as well as seminars and the international Secretariat have played significant roles in this respect.

Center for International Policy. Experience has shown that Unesco provides a new element in international diplomacy. This is the international approach to problems for which purely national approaches are inadequate. Sometimes, Unesco was able to provide coordination that individual national action could not secure. Sometimes, an international viewpoint was required in preference to a national one in dealing with a problem of transnational concern. Sometimes, Unesco action was able to overcome national prejudice or resistance based on fear of foreign domination as in the case of technical assistance to economically underdeveloped countries. Sometimes, its primary contribution has been in providing an international forum in which a national need could be expressed and in finding appropriate means of providing assistance. This is illustrated in the work to preserve monuments, develop fundamental education, and to encourage the creation of national clearing houses of information on education. Unesco has sometimes provided international standards to which nations were led to aspire or which peoples of member states could use as leverage to achieve domestic reform.

Unesco has thus been an instrument for the formulation of international policy. For this purpose an international institution is required which can mobilize worldwide talents motivated by a greater than national loyalty and able to see national demands in the perspective of worldwide needs.

Unesco has to a high degree become such a world institution for the development of international policy. When the General Conference of government delegates develops policies, it acts as something more than a collection of independent sovereign voices. It develops a will of its own that is more than the sum of the wills of its national parts, even though these set ultimate limits within which it operates. The process of developing a collective will may lead to readjustment of individual national wills under influence of discussion and joint deliberation.

The Executive·Board is elected by the General Conference to represent its will between sessions. Its relatively small membership is intended to represent the total will of the General Conference and not solely that of the states from which its individual members come. The Director General, appointed by the General Conference, is the principal administrative officer of the organization and is in charge of an internationally recruited secretariat. Members of the Secretariat, though remaining nationals of their own countries, take an oath of allegiance to the organization and may not take orders from individual member states on matters related to the organization's work. Through the hands of this staff passes all the correspondence of seventy or more member states; they receive statements of national needs; they compile statistics and prepare reports on the status of member states in the realm of Unesco's concern; they serve the Director General, Executive Board and the General Conference with all secretarial and related conference and documentation services. They bring together the expert groups needed in accordance with program requirements, directing them, briefing them, and helping them with drafting and reports. The staff is responsible for the issuance of all Unesco's official documents and numerous publications.

An important aspect of Unesco's international work are the numerous (forty or more annually) meetings of experts and specialists, internationally selected, that meet to carry forward through study, discussion, and recommendation many of Unesco's program activities. Seminars are a special variety of such meetings. Many of Unesco's programs have developed in detail out of a General Conference resolution, a work plan developed by the secretariat and approved by the Executive Board and then examined in detail and put into a formal recommendation by a body of experts. This was especially well illustrated in the development of the European Center for Nuclear Research.

Unesco missions requested by member states and Unesco technical assistance experts under the United Nations Expanded Technical Assistance Program are internationally recruited, instructed by the organization and responsible to it for their work. They are not agents of their national states and their recommendations are intended as the best expert advice available from world sources. Finally, the nongovernmental organizations which work with Unesco are only those of international character and their advice and their services are set in an international perspective.

In all these ways Unesco provides the world setting from which to view the educational, scientific, and cultural problems with which member states want it to deal. Through these and other ways Unesco therefore provides the basis for the formulation as well as the administration of international policy to international programs. Except as requested by member states (as in the case of educational missions and technical assistance activities) Unesco's jurisdiction of course stops at national boundaries. What happens in member states depends upon member state action, but insofar as it is an outgrowth of an internationally conceived policy or program the significance of Unesco's part becomes greater, a primary objective in having international policies at all has already been achieved.

III

Only gradually has Unesco's program taken clear shape as member states individually and collectively determined their own needs and demands upon the new organization and through experience found the practical role which Unesco could play in this phase of international politics.

To the casual reader Unesco often appears to have done a little of everything and to have accomplished nothing in particular. Though this view is widely held it is far from the fact and arises largely out of ignorance.

Many factors in Unesco's history have contributed to much of the ignorance that prevails regarding its work. Its constitutional objectives were loosely and perhaps optimistically stated. The efforts of member states to write the program at successive sessions of the General Conference have often tended to be without precise focus and have reflected the broad and different interests and frequently their uncertainty. Resolutions authorizing the Director General to carry on certain activities often have been too broadly worded and too numerous for the organization's resources. It has taken nearly the whole decade for the organization to shake down to a program pattern which is clear and understandable. It has taken that long for member states to identify clearly their own needs and to determine the kinds of services Unesco can provide that will produce tangible results and benefits.

A further cause of ignorance about Unesco is the fact that it has no direct means of communication with the public in member states. It has no world mass communication network and its publication funds are meager. The people of member states are informed most sporadically and incompletely about the work of the organization. Few of Unesco program activities seem newsworthy. In the United States, for example, it is a rarity to see even a mention of Unesco in any but a handful of daily papers and even in these the coverage is slight and irregular. Governments of member states do not appear to have means for, or to be concerned with, the problem of reporting to their people about Unesco's activities.

The most important cause of ignorance about Unesco's work is to be found in the methods by which it functions. These include study and analysis by the Secretariat of the needs of member states and of possible ways of meeting them and program possibilities; correspondence by the Secretariat with member states; arranging meetings of experts; publishing reports for the use of governments or of experts and specialists; sending missions of experts at the request of member states. None of these activities is spectacular and few are noticeable to individual citizens. Most are designed for the purpose of making definitive action possible by the member states themselves. Combating illiteracy is a task of each member state because education is a matter exclusively within national jurisdiction. Improving the quality of educational statistics calls for technical aid but the job to be done is a national one. Advancing knowledge through the development of universities, of research facilities, and secondary school systems can be encouraged by the Unesco reports, conferences, resolutions, and advice, but the actual work is done by member states. But Unesco has carried on many activities to make this national action possible.

If one could travel on a magic carpet or look with the benefit of world television at the world of activities and programs thus sparked or begun by Unesco, or which have been undertaken because of its encouragement, or which are carried on with its advice, the picture would be impressive to anyone. And if one would simply list all that has been accomplished during the first ten years of Unesco the record would be surprising to most citizens of member states.

For example, there is in effect for the first time in modern history a Universal Copyright Convention to protect international authors and their property. Unesco brought about the drafting of this Convention. It also brought about the drafting of a convention for the reduction of barriers to the flow of educational, scientific, and cultural materials and achieved significant reductions in postal rates on such matters. The European Center for Nuclear Research is in process of being built near Geneva, Switzerland, as a result of discussions at the Unesco General Conference of 1950 and subsequent concerted efforts by the secretariat in Paris. Unesco assisted in promoting the initial planning for the International Geophysical Year. In Mexico and Egypt there are in daily operation centers for the training of teachers in the techniques of fundamental education. Each serves the countries of the region. A third center is in process of development in Thailand. In most libraries of the world today and in educational institutions there are available Unesco volumes setting forth nearly all fellowship and foreign study opportunities in member states of Unesco. The first public library in India functions today at Delhi as a result of a Unesco experimental project and advice. Major international research projects on living in arid zones, in humid tropical zones, and at high altitudes, are presently under way as a result of Unesco's initiative. A research center in Calcutta is conducting studies on the impact of industrialization upon the social life of underdeveloped countries. The first cooperative effort to write a Cultural and Scientific History of Mankind is well along on its schedule of preparation with the aid of leading scholars from many countries. This is a Unesco project. An international commission of distinguished citizens representing eighteen countries is currently at work developing proposals to increase understanding between the peoples of the Western and non-Western worlds. This is one of the most important problems of our time. In the United States this work is being furthered by a major effort of the United States National Commission for Unesco beginning with its National Conference in San Francisco on this subject late in 1957. Similar special efforts are expected in other countries.

International professional organizations in economics, social, and political science, comparative law, the arts, and natural sciences owe their origin to Unesco initiative. In nearly every economically underdeveloped country desiring help one can find today one or more members of a Unesco educational or scientific mission to advise on educational or research programs. Throughout this group of countries one easily finds evidence of reforms instituted in primary and secondary school systems as a result of advice secured through experts or publications of Unesco. Unesco has sponsored the preparation of a series of popular statements based on scientific studies of the racial issue. In Montevideo, Cairo, New Delhi and Jakharta there are Unesco Science Cooperation Offices for the purpose of speeding the flow of natural and social science knowledge and material to the less developed countries and to encourage exchanges among them. A project is under way to preserve at least a photographic record of historic monuments in Egypt now threatened by plans to flood large areas in connection with the Aswan Dam. Many professional bibliographies have been prepared and special efforts made to promote more effective international exchanges in the field of bibliography and documentation.

One cannot here enumerate all that Unesco is doing or all that it has done in response to the wishes of its member states and to facilitate their efforts.[1] Perhaps, however, it would be useful to summarize the kinds of things done in the principal areas of Unesco's work.

Its efforts toward the advancement of knowledge have been designed to increase communications among scholars, teachers, specialists of many kinds. It has improved existing channels as well as opened new ones through organizations, publications, travel grants, etc. Science cooperation offices as well as publications, seminars, and grants have particularly attempted to link the less developed countries with the technologically more advanced ones. Agreements of considerable importance have been developed relating to copyright, postal, and freight rates, and custom duties on educational, scientific, and cultural materials. Special efforts have been made to develop world standards for educational, cultural and scientific activities.[2]

Unesco's program relating to the promotion of human welfare generally has dealt with a variety of subjects: the creation of a European center for nuclear research; developing cooperative international research on living in arid zones, and at high altitudes; encouragement of research in marine science; and on the social effects of technological change. Unesco has provided the primary initiative and leadership in the development of fundamental education and related programs for economically underdeveloped countries. It has aided many member states through educational missions in the development or reform of

---

[1] A detailed study of many program activities will be found in Walter H. C. Laves and Charles A. Thomson, *Unesco: Program, Progress and Prospects* (Bloomington, Indiana, 1957).

[2] For details see *ibid.*, Chapters 5, 6.

educational systems at primary and secondary levels, the training of teachers and the development of systems of free and compulsory education.

Least directly productive have been Unesco's efforts toward increasing international understanding. In one sense everything Unesco does probably contributes to some kind of national understanding by increasing knowledge about other people. Specific efforts intended to contribute to international understanding have included activities to increase international educational exchanges, including students, scholars, artists, and labor leaders. Teachers and school administrators have been brought together to consider ways of improving the teaching of geography, history, languages, etc. Special conferences, round table seminars have been arranged for philosophers of various countries. Efforts have been made to disseminate knowledge about the music and art of different countries. The history of the scientific and cultural development of mankind is a major step aiming to provide a more satisfactory educational base for international understanding. Research has been encouraged on problems of social tensions that effect international peace. Considerable emphasis has been placed on educational programs relating to knowledge about human rights.[3]

IV

Significance of Unesco as a Cultural Center

How significant is Unesco as a center of cultural diplomacy? What is its place today and what are the prospects for its future role? Answers to these questions must of necessity be brief and somewhat speculative because of the relatively short time Unesco has existed and because the international scene is changing so rapidly. Nevertheless, some things already seem fairly clear.

1. The existence of Unesco is evidence of the importance which member states attach to the development of educational, scientific, and cultural resources in the promotion of human welfare. This implicitly is, also, evidence of the place of educational, scientific, and cultural leaders in the political power structure of member states. Though this varies greatly among member states it is incontestable that the attention given by governments to the creation of Unesco reflects important

[3] See *ibid.*, Chapters 10, 11, 12.

pressures within member countries for greater governmental attention to the development of education, science, and culture.

2. The existence of Unesco likewise indicates that the character of many of the problems related to the development of educational, scientific, and cultural resources is such as to require concerted international efforts and the development of international rather than merely national policies.

3. The record of Unesco and its extensive achievements already provide evidence of the vitality of the concerns mentioned in the two preceding paragraphs and of the practicability of Unesco's role as a center of cultural diplomacy.

4. Unesco's activities have been most effective in relation to technical and professional problems involved in the promotion of education, science, and culture. It has been least successful in efforts intended to make a direct or immediate contribution to peace and security.

5. Unesco has been an important agency through which especially the economically underdeveloped countries could express their needs and secure a considerable amount of very tangible aid. But even the most developed countries have been able through Unesco to achieve important ends of their national policy, including technical and professional objectives and the giving of encouragement to the more rapid development of economically underdeveloped countries whose status affects the prospect for world peace and security and also affect the welfare of all other countries.

6. Unesco has served to introduce new states, formerly colonial territories, to participation in world affairs, and has permitted many of them to acquire prestige even in the absence of economic and military power. Japan was able to participate in important international activities through Unesco before its admission to the United Nations. Germany is still receiving this benefit.

7. It is difficult to document any direct relationship between a nation's participation in Unesco and its status among nations or its influence in other areas of international negotiation. However, I suspect that national participation in programs and activities in the area of Unesco's concern redounds to the credit of member states and serves to provide evidence of common interest which strengthens the prospects of collaboration in other areas. Thus I suspect that more deliberate effort by the United States to participate actively in Unesco work

could do much to overcome the inevitable reaction of fear and suspicion on the part of many countries to our overwhelming economic and military power. It would also be more effective in many respects than some phases of our bilateral cultural relations and activities. It would give tangible evidence, moreover, of our actual commitment to the United Nations system.

V

Unesco and Contemporary International Politics

The as yet unanswered question is whether Unesco can play a significant role in areas of acute political tension such as underlie the cold war. So far the doctrine has prevailed that Unesco should contribute to peace by very indirect means such as are involved in longer range cultural exchanges. The absence of the Soviet Union until 1954 and the inadequate representation of continental China served to keep Unesco largely out of the cold war area. But the intensity of the crisis that embraces all aspects of international relations today combined with the sense of terror that new arms, possessed by both sides, have instilled in all peace-loving people raise the question whether an effort should not be made to mobilize Unesco more directly in the search for peace.

Governments might well consider using Unesco much more intensely in three ways that could significantly contribute to the achievement of greater prospects for peace.

The *first* is to seek by every possible means to involve more and more people of the Soviet controlled and the non-Soviet worlds in cooperative educational scientific and cultural undertakings. The exchange of ideas and experiences, the common effort to seek more effective solutions to common problems and the sharing of ideas can only be useful and may lead to pressures by citizens upon governments to cooperate more effectively in the search for peace. At the very least such efforts would help reduce somewhat the area of ignorance and of blind prejudice. But to be useful in the rapidly deteriorating current situation efforts of this kind must be extensive, carefully planned and much more intensively administered than is now the case with the ordinary Unesco program.

A *second* way in which Unesco could be utilized to make a much greater contribution to peace is through larger scale projects of educational and scientific development in depressed geographic areas like the Middle East, Asia, Africa and Latin America. Unesco's experience with fundamental education programs and its science cooperation offices and with the United Nations Expanded Program of Technical Assistance show how great a contribution can be made to help newly developing countries. So far, however, these efforts have been much too limited and have lacked the kind of coordinated area planning that is obviously required if the great energies and enthusiasms of the new nationalisms are to be channeled into solid programs of economic and political development. The kind of effort I have in mind should, of course, be under United Nations auspices and the work of Unesco would be complemented by that of the World Health Organization, the International Labor Organization, the Food and Agriculture Organization and other United Nations agencies.

A *third* way is that of promoting citizen education in all countries about world affairs and foreign policy. A major factor underlying the poverty revealed in governmental leadership throughout the free world today is the heavy drag of uninformed citizens. On economic, military and political aspects of world affairs, citizen thinking is still so focused upon the nation that governments, even where they are imaginative and constructive, have difficulty in winning public support for programs designed to provide world or regional solutions for world or regional problems. At the same time there are ineffective pressures from public opinion upon conservative governments, demanding imaginative action to deal with the kinds of problems that threaten the peace today. The vague concept of promoting international understanding through Unesco, which has prevailed so far, needs an injection of hard reality by promoting citizen understanding, for example, of the fact that high protective tariffs, the absence of a permanent United Nations peace force or the lack of sufficient economic development funds for new states are all basic obstacles to peace. This kind of understanding, followed by effective citizen political action is a necessary foundation for achieving governmental action appropriate to the needs of modern international relations.

It is not possible in this paper to go beyond pointing out this potential next step in the development of Unesco. I would not see such a development as an improper use for a world center for cultural diplomacy. Quite the contrary, I see it as a necessary development reflecting realization that without substantial and more rapid progress in these three ways there is unlikely to be much of a future for education, science and culture development anywhere. A modern war would bring disaster to most of our educational, scientific and cultural objectives. And to insure a peace meantime in which free people can enjoy the fruits of education, science, and cultural development would seem to be a primary objective of international cultural diplomacy.

If member states will see Unesco in this broader perspective and give to the development of its potential a more important place in national foreign policies the organization may yet come to live up to the high expectations of its founders. It will then also begin to play its proper role in the United Nations system.

INDEX